# The Red EMPIRES

# The Red EMPIRES

## a tale of love divided

**PATRICK LESCOT**

Translated by Steven Rendall

John Wiley & Sons, Ltd

Published in the UK by John Wiley & Sons, Ltd, The Atrium, Southern Gate
Chichester, West Sussex, PO19 8SQ, England

Phone   (+44) 1243  779777

Email (for orders and customer service enquires): cs-books@wiley.co.uk
Visit our Home Page on www.wiley.co.uk or www.wiley.com

*Other Wiley Editorial Offices*

John Wiley & Sons, Inc. 111 River Street, Hoboken, NJ 07030, USA

Jossey-Bass, 989 Market Street, San Francisco, CA 94103-1741, USA

Wiley-VCH Verlag GmbH, Pappellaee 3, D-69469 Weinheim, Germany

John Wiley & Sons Australia, Ltd, 33 Park Road, Milton, Queensland, 4064, Australia

John Wiley & Sons (Asia) Pte Ltd, 2 Clementi Loop #02-01, Jin Xing Distripark, Singapore 129809

John Wiley & Sons Canada Ltd, 22 Worcester Road, Etobicoke, Ontario, Canada, M9W 1L1

Wiley also publishes its books in a variety of electronic formats. Some content that appears
in print may not be available in electronic books.

*British Library Cataloguing in Publication Data*

A catalogue record for this book is available from the British Library

ISBN 0-470-09029-4

Typeset by Mathematical Composition Setters Ltd, Salisbury, Wiltshire.
Printed and bound in Great Britain by T.J. International Ltd, Padstow, Cornwall.
This book is printed on acid-free paper responsibly manufactured from sustainable forestry
in which at least two trees are planted for each one used for paper production.

*To Lisa*

*To the memory of Nadia, Zhang Bao, Li Lisan, and all the anonymous people who disappeared into the Gulag and Laogai, who saw with their own eyes how the sky fell on the earth.*

# CONTENTS

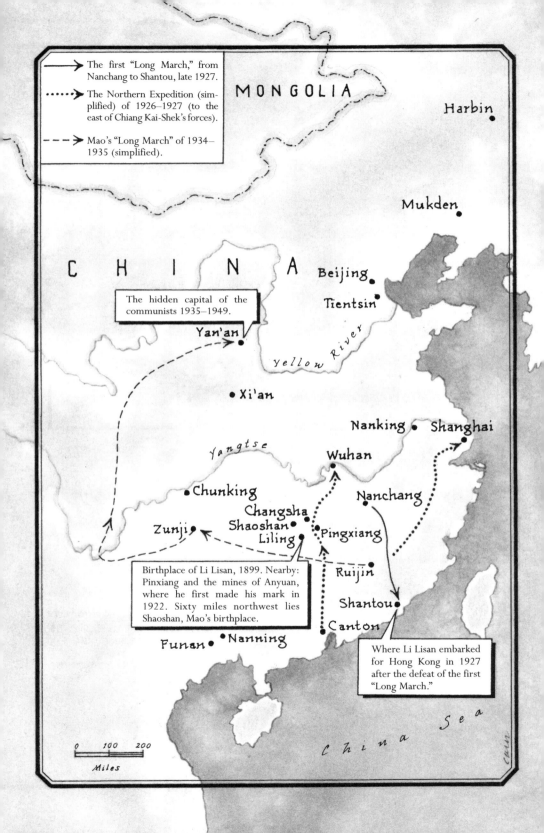

The first "Long March," from Nanchang to Shantou, late 1927.

The Northern Expedition (simplified) of 1926–1927 (to the east of Chiang Kai-Shek's forces).

Mao's "Long March" of 1934–1935 (simplified).

MONGOLIA

Harbin

Mukden

C H I N A

Beijing

Tientsin

The hidden capital of the communists 1935–1949.

Yan'an

Yellow River

Xi'an

Nanking    Shanghai

Yangtse

Wuhan

Chunking

Nanchang

Changsha

Zunji    Shaoshan    Pingxiang
         Liling

Birthplace of Li Lisan, 1899. Nearby: Pinxiang and the mines of Anyuan, where he first made his mark in 1922. Sixty miles northwest lies Shaoshan, Mao's birthplace.

Ruijin

Shantou

Canton

Funan    Nanning

Where Li Lisan embarked for Hong Kong in 1927 after the defeat of the first "Long March."

China Sea

0    100    200
Miles

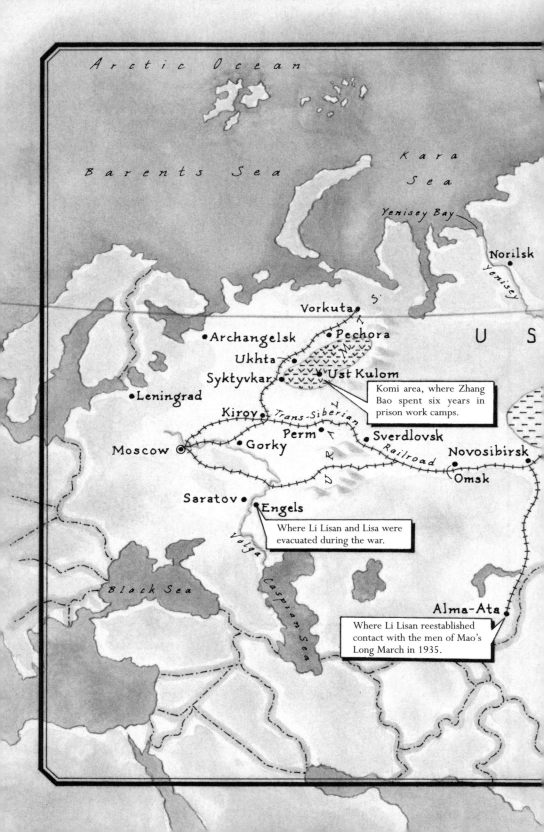

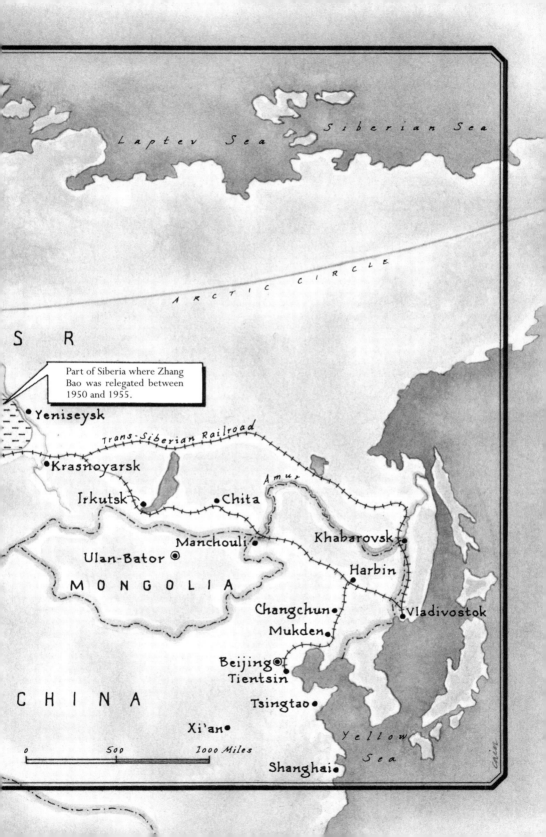

Part of Siberia where Zhang
Bao was relegated between
1950 and 1955.

*Laptev Sea*

*Siberian Sea*

*ARCTIC CIRCLE*

S   R

• Yeniseysk

*Trans-Siberian Railroad*

• Krasnoyarsk

*Amur*

Irkutsk • • Chita

Manchouli • Khabarovsk •

Ulan-Bator ◉

MONGOLIA

Harbin •

Changchun •

Vladivostok •

Mukden •

Beijing ◉

Tientsin •

CHINA

Tsingtao •

Xi'an •

Yellow

0          500          1000 Miles

Sea

Shanghai •

# The Red EMPIRES

# CHAPTER

# I

Leaning on the ship's rail, Li Lisan watched the docks of Shanghai's port slowly fading into the distance. In forty days, if all went well, he would reach Marseilles. The gray forms of the skyscrapers along the Bund, lining the boulevard that ran along the river, echoed back to him the bellowing of the steamer's horn.

The mid-October air had lost some of its dampness and carried acrid marine odors mixed with the indefinable smells of the city he could still see from the afterdeck. He suddenly realized that there was now no going back. Couldn't he get off the boat when it stopped at Hong Kong, Saigon, Singapore, Colombo, or Djibouti? Out of the question. No, he was really on his way to France. The steamer's forward movement and the muffled vibration of its propellers had the same inexorable momentum as a die rolling on a green felt table.

He could hear the exclamations of his companions in the

passageway below. Altogether, there were about forty of them making the voyage; like him, they came mainly from Hunan province, and they all belonged to the Movement for Studies in France. When Li had learned that the French government was offering educated young Chinese an opportunity to study and work in France, he'd jumped at it. The guns had finally fallen silent in Europe, France was in ruins, and there was no lack of work there, people said.

Ever since May, everyone on the campus had been talking about going to France: in order to understand why China had failed, they had to understand the West's success. They had to go there to see it at first hand, to experience its schools, its factories, its dreams.

All the more so because these Westerners, who were so fond of empires that they had brought China to its knees, now proclaimed the advent of a new order under the twofold sign of peace and justice. The thousands of Chinese coolies who'd come back from the battlefields of Verdun and the plains of the Somme had sworn it was true: the carnage over there had been terrible and the weapons terrifying. Some of them also claimed that in Europe people took a keen interest in what was happening in Russia. There, as in China, the emperor had abdicated and civil war was raging.

France—*Faguo,* as it was called in Chinese—"the country of the Law." He recalled its almost harmonious contours on the map: a small land bathing its feet in a sea, poking its nose into an unknown ocean, toward America. A strange country, a people whose frenzy had made all its neighbors tremble. It had revolted, killed its king, and then given itself an emperor before ending up with a republic, under the hostile but admiring eyes of the West: wasn't France the reservoir of ideals, scientific discoveries, novels, monuments, plays, songs, and paintings? France itself was so convinced of it that the republic had built an empire reaching into Asia, to the very doorstep of China.

In the streets of the French concession in Shanghai, they'd all bought postcards, black-and-white photos of the cobblestone streets of Paris. As they boarded the steamer, the joyful, noisy students—at twenty, Li was one of the oldest—passed around, laughing raucously, a photo of a famous actress in a black negligee. A great success.

"*Bonjour, mademoiselle,*" they said, giggling between the two words, and then joking about the school's French teacher. The candidates for the work-study trip, the *ban-du,* had spent the past few months in the hills of Beijing, learning the language of Molière. This training was obligatory, and they liked to repeat to each other the formula "the language of Molière," imitating the slightly haughty phrasing and expression of the French official.

Everyone agreed that it was too bad that Mao Tse-tung had stayed behind on the dock. A compatriot from Hunan, a schoolteacher who was looking for work in the library of the University of Beijing, he had accompanied them as far as Shanghai, but only China interested him.

Not liking farewells, Li had slipped away. Off by himself, his eyes riveted on the ship's wake, he was imagining the face of the woman to whom his father had married him three years earlier. The long, exhausting ceremony that followed the arrival of the red-draped palanquin in which his fiancée, hardly sixteen years old, had taken her seat. She was as frightened as he was, but more disciplined. Months later, their hearts were still not bound together. Siao Yang couldn't understand Li's passion for the books and strange magazines that claimed to be inventing a new China. And then their son was born. Li's father, the master of his household, had ordered that a feast be held.

The marriage was all his doing, his final attempt to tame his wild son. At fourteen, Li had already run away to join, after walking for two days and a night, a prorepublican revolutionary army that had ended up in Hunan. An impulsive act. The adolescent threw out his chest and lied about his age, but the recruiting sergeant immediately recognized a schoolboy. Instead of a rifle, Li was given a brush, ink, and hundreds of sums to do in a corner of the office, burying his dreams of glory hour after hour.

Two days later, the general came into the room. Wang Tsian was one of the superior officers and warlords who had joined the cause of the founder of the republic, Sun Yat-sen. He was looking for someone who liked to play *go,* Li's favorite game.

Putting his pieces one by one on the *go-ban,* the old soldier asked Li where he came from.

"From Liling."

"I'm also from Hunan. And I'm very familiar with Liling. What's your father's name?"

They played the game all the way to the end. The general won without too much difficulty. He congratulated his young opponent and then, looking him straight in the eye, said firmly: "And now, son, you're going to get your things, take off your uniform, and go home. You don't belong here; you should be in school and with your parents."

"But . . ."

"I knew your father well. He's a friend of mine. Moreover, young man, you must know that China needs educated people. Come back and see me when you've got your diploma."

"But . . ."

"I gave you an order. Get going."

Back in Liling, Li barely avoided getting a hiding from his father. But he had to spend a month shut up in his room, carefully copying poetry. His mother brought him his meals and said not a word.

The following year, he was sent to a boarding school in Changsha, the capital of Hunan. A hotbed of revolution and, in the summer, a real southern furnace. Education there was intense but agitated. There were lots of ideas churning about in Changsha at that time. Everyone was reading the speeches of Prince Bakunin, the Russian apostle of anarchism, on God and the state or on the Paris Commune, retranslated into Chinese from a Japanese translation. Li had devoured an abridged version of Rousseau's *Social Contract,* rendered into classical Chinese, a language accessible only to educated people. There were many other discussions of Western thought, which were feverishly being passed around and discussed all night long in the dormitories.

There were many clubs, fleeting fraternities in the shadows or the half-light, secret societies that lasted a single spring, in which people fervently debated, waving their long sleeves, the state of the country and the fate of its people. Changsha went on alert when warlords' troops approached the gates of the old medieval city on another campaign of rapine and terror.

THREE SHORT BLASTS OF THE SHIP'S HORN TORE LI AWAY FROM HIS reverie. He shivered. The air now tasted of the ocean. The boat began to rock slightly. A flock of junks passed under the stem. They were leaving the river and heading out into the China Sea. Going down toward the third-class dormitories, Li wondered whether he really had sea legs.

On the rough cobblestones of Moscow, the cart loaded with suitcases and sacks creaked and groaned. Six years old, trotting alongside her mother, Elisabeth Kishkin was all eyes, turning her head around to look in all directions, fascinated by the spectacle of the city.

"Lisa, look where you're going!" her mother said to her, breathlessly. Still a good half hour to push this cart before they got to her cousin's home. Ever since they'd left the train station, she'd been looking hard at all the Muscovites she met: pale and emaciated, even anemic, but they had food.

Back on the banks of the Volga, where she'd come from, there were tens of thousands of living skeletons, dragging themselves along with bewildered or feverish eyes, hoping for unlikely help coming from the river. In this month of October, in the year 1920, famine was beginning to torment the Volga. In August, at Tambov, the peasants had risen up against the Bolsheviks and demanded that a constituent assembly be held.

The train trip to Moscow had been exhausting. Four days and four nights rolling across a Russia ravaged by civil war, interrupted by endless stops in the middle of nowhere, surrounded by soldiers on alert, crowding together on the locomotive's running boards and around the machine guns that had been set up on floors of the cars. Near Tambov, General Antonov's peasant army had just wiped out a whole Red Army division.

In the freight cars, suitcases and packages paralyzed passengers fleeing famine, crushed by fatigue, and dreaming about Moscow, the new capital. An old woman from the southern Volga had told them that a starving family in a neighboring village had eaten their son, who had died of typhus. Back there, people were suspected of digging up the dead. They had to leave.

Lisa had listened without really understanding what they were talking about. But the trip had continued, and she liked watching the countryside pass by as she looked out the open door. Rocked by the monotonous rhythm of the train, she'd fallen asleep, curled up on her mother's knees.

★    ★

IN THE STREETS OF MOSCOW, HER MOTHER, PRASKOVIA KISHKIN, WAS WOR-
ried about being stopped by the militia. With her name, she feared the worst:
"Kishkin, isn't that the name of an aristocrat, a former aristocrat, I mean?"

Fortunately, she was dressed like a "citizen," not a "former aristocrat,"
and her hands had become callused since the death of her husband. They'd
had to work hard on the property after the Chekists* came to arrest
Pavel. That was two years ago already.

The cold was bitter that October morning, but the militia weren't out
early. Praskovia caught her breath, flexed her muscles, and starting pushing the cart again. Her head down, she thought about Pavel's eyes when
he'd taken her in his arms for the last time. It was a Sunday at the end of
the summer of 1918. Behind him, the Chekists were getting impatient.
Bolsheviks from the soviet of poor peasants, who'd come from the nearby
village. Calmly, Pavel, wearing a white shirt and holding his coat over his
right arm, had gotten into the horse carriage that was waiting for him. The
men of the new police force, with their gray-blue pointed hats on which
a red star had been sewn, their rifles slung across their horses, had surrounded him. The convoy headed toward Turki, twenty-five kilometers
away, and Pavel knew what would happen to him. The arrest of the czar a
year earlier had deeply affected him. He'd dreamed of an enlightened
Russia, traded with Germany, imported modern agricultural machinery
to use on his property. He'd opened the first school in the village and two
of his daughters, Lisa's elder sisters, had taught in it.

He hadn't been afraid of the Reds at the beginning, in 1917. After all,
during the first attempt to overthrow the czar, in 1905, it was the peasants who had defended the property.

"Kishkin? A noble, sure. But he's not a usurer for the tenant farmers,
and you can always work it out with him to repay your debt. And besides,
it's the only school around here. . . ."

Then the bands of rogues, set free from serfdom forty-five years
before, had left to roam elsewhere in search of fires, pillage, and land.

The property was only two thousand acres—nothing compared to

---

*Members of the Cheka, or Vecheka, an early Soviet secret police agency and
another forerunner of the KGB. —Trans.

the neighbor's property, which was more than twelve thousand acres in size—and hardly enough to attract notice at the czar's court.

Pavel had become alarmed only when he heard about the coup d'état in Saint Petersburg. It was then that he realized that Lenin and his Bolsheviks were fanatics. They'd dissolved the constituent assembly at bayonet point as soon as they'd realized that they were in the minority. Pavel would have liked to have the czar and a parliament. Misfortune had befallen Holy Russia, and between war and famine, the carnage was stealing away its children by the millions.

The carriage was going down the road and Pavel knew he was going to his death. A Kishkin doesn't surrender. Seated behind the driver, he had slowly put his hand into his pocket and taken out the cyanide pill he'd been carrying with him for weeks. After taking a last look at the sunbathed Russian countryside and a last whiff of the smell of his native land, he died amid the oaths of his terrified escorts.

AT THE AGE OF FOUR, LISA HAD NOT REALLY UNDERSTOOD THE story of her father's disappearance. And then she'd gotten used to it. Very soon, the important thing had become finding something to eat. The soup in her bowl had gotten thinner and thinner. Soon, they didn't have enough bread, and they had to wait all day to get their soup. One day, Mama had packed their bags and they'd gotten into a cab to go to the train station. They were going to live in the city. The Volga was doomed, but maybe they'd come back someday, Mama said.

So Lisa was trotting along in Moscow, dreaming with delight of the last onion she'd eaten the day before in the train, along with the last bit of bread. She suddenly stopped, frozen in her tracks, wide-eyed. As she looked on, a noisy carriage on four wheels was going along all by itself, without horses to pull it, and making an infernal racket. A black Ford, which made a funny noise with its pear-shaped horn as it passed a dilapidated carriage before disappearing around the corner.

Moscow was certainly full of surprises!

"Lisa! Keep moving!" her mother, already several steps ahead of her, shouted.

# 2

The din in the mill at Le Creusot was deafening. A stone's throw away, the tall furnaces poured out in a regular cadence their incandescent streams of molten steel amid a shower of sparks. Li was working hard, running from one ladle to another, carrying an iron bar that he thrust into the cast-iron pipes to puncture the air bubbles in the last batch of steel. Léon Berthier, a maintenance worker, was watching the curl of steel peeling off his lathe, while keeping an ironic eye on this bustling young Chinaman. Hard to say how old he was, this big fellow with an energetic face, a horsey jaw, and a craggy face. A newcomer, a young guy who'd recently arrived. Another one.

For the past two years, Le Creusot had almost 3,000 of these Chinese. Cheap laborers who'd stayed in France after the war, the remainder of the 140,000 coolies who'd been brought in to deal with a labor shortage. Chinamen in the mill! Berthier said to himself. Now I've seen everything. The bosses would bring in anybody from anywhere, so long as it's profitable.

This one was different, however. The foreman said he was one of about a hundred student-workers who had come to Le Creusot over the past few months. Young people from over there who were supposed to be studying while they worked, in theory. And that intrigued Berthier, who'd left the public school early to begin a long apprenticeship in using a file and a caliper.

Full of goodwill, but rather clumsy in his work, Berthier said to himself as he watched Li. They don't know how to do much, these guys from the colonies.

"He's a Chinamen," the foreman had assured him. "A Chinaman from China, not a Chinaman from the colonies, from Tonkin or somewhere." So far as he could tell, they all looked the same.

Berthier had a curious mind, and he remembered reading the *Petit Illustré,* in which China and the Chinese were sometimes mentioned— he'd read about missionaries being killed and the customs of this strange people, whose men wore a long braid and a big straw hat and pulled rickshaws, and whose women bound their feet to be beautiful. He looked at his watch and decided that at the break, while eating his snack, he'd get acquainted with this foreigner.

In the meantime, he carefully rolled a cigarette. The tobacco was really much better than the tobacco handed out in the trenches. He remembered the rumor that was going around at that time: "Soldiers' tobacco comes from China." In his company, when they wanted a smoke, the men said, "Pass me the Chinese."

It was already three years ago that he and his comrades in the trenches had separated, but Berthier hadn't stopped using that word, *comrades.* After he got back to Le Creusot, the break was the time when he ate his snack and read *L'Humanité.**

On this day in March 1921, the news promised to be still more exciting. The Russia of the soviets had finally won out over the White forces, after three years of civil war. "A gigantic blow struck against capitalists all over the world!" the paper had been trumpeting for days.

Socialism now had a country, and Léon Berthier was a socialist, like his father, even before the famous month of August 1914. Called up, he'd

---

*The daily newspaper published by the French Communist Party. —Trans.

survived the terrible butchery that had destroyed his confidence in the human race. One day in 1917, he'd learned in his trench that to the east of Europe, some of the czar's soldiers had refused to fight the Germans and laid down their arms. The Russians had made a revolution, over there in Saint Petersburg, and even a *worker's revolution,* people said.

After the armistice, Léon, who'd come back with his sleep full of nightmares, had started reading a great deal. He knew by heart Henri Barbusse's *Le Feu,* and he could recite whole passages of Karl Marx's *Communist Manifesto.*

That evening there was a union meeting. There were going to be conflicts again with the CGT people,* who were in the majority. At any rate, it wouldn't last long. Berthier had been resolutely in the minority ever since he got his card in the brand-new French Communist Party, just after the meeting in Tours a few months earlier.

At the break, he called to Li.

"Hey, you, Chinaman! Come see."

Li didn't hear him, but he felt a hand put firmly on his shoulder.

"You speak French?"

Surprised, Li stared at the face wearing a vaguely ironic smile.

"Yes, I speak a little French," he stuttered.

"Well, then, come eat your snack on my bench."

The tone was imperious, and Li followed Berthier to his corner behind the machine. It was the first time a Frenchman had approached him in this way, and he was going to have to discuss things in the language of Molière.

Berthier unfolded the bit of newspaper in which his wife carefully wrapped his snack and an apple every morning. Li, famished, took out his piece of bread and his slice of fatback. With his jackknife, Berthier cut the apple in two and offered Li half of it.

Embarrassed, Li repeated, *"Non, merci, non, merci,"* with a tense laugh.

"Don't be so formal. Don't you like apples?" Berthier said, putting the apple half in Li's hand.

---

*Members of the Comité Générale du Travail, the largest French national labor union.

Li loved apples. After taking a bite, the Frenchman went on, "Well, so you're Chinese, are you?"

"Yes, that's right, I'm Chinese."

"How old are you?"

"Twenty-two."

"So what's it like, in your country?"

Li forced himself to speak about China in French, saying that war, famine, and foreign invasions were the fate of the Middle Kingdom.

"So it's a mess," Berthier summed up, philosophically.

Li dared to mention Paris, which was more familiar to Berthier, who had gone there on furlough during the war. The Eiffel Tower was "quite a heap of iron," which had left both Berthier and Li rather in awe.

Li also talked to him about Montargis, in the Loiret region.

"What the hell were you doing in Montargis?"

"I was in school. They taught us a little French down there, before going to work in the provinces. We were supposed to study and work. In reality, we slave away, that's all."

But there was no break without reading the newspaper, and Berthier unfolded his as he did every day. Then he heard Li's rather nasal voice saying over his shoulder: "Ah, *L'Humanité* . . . That's good. I read it every day. Well, at least I try. It's hard . . ."

Léon Berthier almost choked on the last mouthful of his snack.

"What?"

"Will you lend it to me, when you've finished?"

Berthier slowly turned around and stared at his neighbor, whose almond-shaped eyes were looking at him in a slightly mischievous way.

"What? You read *L'Humanité?*"

Li concentrated and, pointing to the paper's subtitle, said as clearly as he could, "Workers of the world, unite . . ."

Berthier recovered and chortled as if to himself. "Well, I'll be damned! A Chinese communist!"

Up to that point, he'd known Germans, Russians, Italians, and a few Englishmen who were ready to line up behind Moscow.

He laughed out loud, and gave Li a nudge. "I like you, Chinaman!"

★     ★

THE FOREMAN BLEW THE WHISTLE, SIGNALING THE END OF THE break. Going back to his machinery, Berthier decided that he'd talk about this with his comrades that evening. If the Chinese got involved, the revolution was soon going to become really worldwide. He also thought that after all, he didn't know anything about China, and there were lots of them over there, according to the *Petit Illustré*. At least 500 million . . .

BACK IN THE DORMITORY THAT HAD BEEN SET UP BY THE MUNICIpality for the Chinese work-study contingent, Li announced that he'd made a friend, a *French* friend! He recounted the scene to his somewhat jealous comrades. Over the meal eaten together—noodles cooked on hot plates found somewhere—the conversation was lively on the only subject that could keep them awake for hours, despite their exhaustion: how could China be saved?

The recent news from China was as bad as ever. The Japanese were showing a ferocious appetite for territory; the French and the English were holding on to their concessions in Shanghai, Hankow, Tientsin, and elsewhere; the Americans were proclaiming virtuous anticolonial principles that flattered Chinese nationalism. But back there, the generals of the old Manchu army, when they didn't think they were Napoléon, were fighting among themselves over the throne, which had been vacant since 1911 and the failed advent of the republic.

In the dormitory, Li had a favorite subject: social revolution. In February 1921, he'd gone up to Paris to establish the Chinese section of the Young Socialists, together with Chou En-lai, a guy from Jiangsu; Cai Hesen, who was also from Hunan; and Chen Yi, a fellow from Sichuan.

Li had gained self-confidence. Since he'd been in France, it seemed to him, his ideas had become clearer. In Montargis, he'd devoured the *Chinese Workers' Review* and the Paris publications in his language. All of them saw a new idea flourishing: communism, or *gongchangdjouyi*. Proudhon, Bakunin, and Élisée Reclus were demolished in the name of scientific socialism. Marx, Moscow, and Lenin showed the way for China. The

French teacher in Montargis was certain that the Russia of the soviets was the glorious offspring of the French Revolution. The Chinese sat up late into the night, drawing up plans for taking the Europeans' revolutionary holy grail back to China.

When Cai Hesen married the beautiful Xiang Jingyu, one of the three women in the group, the laughing couple laid their hands on Marx's *Das Kapital* as they made their wedding vows before their joyful friends.

Li spoke well, and his comrades liked the passion with which he deciphered the turbulence of the time, the millions of dead freshly buried on France's battlefields, the incomparable Russian Revolution, the incredible popular and intellectual agitation of this Europe in mourning, the communist parties that were springing up like mushrooms and that promised a brilliant future, at the price of "justified violence."

China's future was European. After all, wasn't it all about imperialists, the exploiters, the proletarians, and war criminals back there as well? The regime had to be brought down, ill-gotten gains given up, and universal prosperity constructed.

Marxism had no recognized borders, and therefore it was Chinese. Less than the subtleties of scientific socialism or the coherence of its doctrine, it was the call to action that Li liked. The meetings with Chou En-lai in Paris, the secret rendezvous in the thirteenth arrondissement, near the rue de Broca, where one had to play the conspirator under the discreet and watchful eyes of the French police. There, comrades had established the Chinese Students' Mutual Aid Society, a secret fraternity that was learning the art of propaganda.

It was a matter of survival, since the Movement for Studies in France was collapsing, and its showcase, the Society of Franco-Chinese Studies, was going bankrupt. A few months after the arrival of the first sixteen hundred candidates, there remained not a penny to pay the costs of study and housing. Only a few hundred student-workers had found jobs in French factories. The others were living like bums, in the hope that they would receive help from their families or a postal money order that would allow them to take the boat back to Shanghai.

★      ★

As he went to sleep, Li remembered the steamer's arrival in Marseilles, on Christmas Eve 1919, accompanied by the gusts of the mistral, after a six-week voyage around the world and persistent seasickness. He smiled as he thought about his first night, in a hotel off the Canebière. A sleepless night spent cursing Western beds, using his two big pillows as blankets. It was only the next morning that the maid showed him how to open up a bed here.

Since he'd first told this story, as darkness fell someone in the dormitory always called out, "Hey, Li Lisan! *Kai tchuang ba!* Open up your bed. . . ." He liked hearing the laughter echo through the room before he fell into a sleep full of avenging dragons and rivers of molten steel.

During the summer of 1921, the Chinese ambassador in Paris, Mr. Cheng Lou, announced that there would not be a single penny for those bums with radical leanings. From now on, only students who had already earned their diplomas in China could apply for a scholarship in France. Only those who came from the Franco-Chinese university in Beijing or from the Catholic Aurore University in Shanghai, where Jesuits educated the cream of the new literate class.

In Lyons, the Franco-Chinese Institute opened in rooms at the Saint-Irénée fortress. It was to receive these new students, who came from wealthy families. The institute was the idea of the mathematician Paul Painlevé, who had come back from a visit to China and declared, in a formula that was more categorical than geometrical, "The twentieth century will be China's century."

In a café in the thirteenth arrondissement, near the rue Godefroy, where Chou En-lai lived, it was decided that the time for action had come. Li had just left Le Creusot in order to devote himself entirely to the struggle. Cai Hesen, the eldest, was thirty-one, and reproached him for wasting his time in a factory rather than studying revolutionary theory. To this wonk, Li replied that by working at Le Creusot he was gaining an invaluable knowledge of the world of the workers, of their combat methods and organization. China, he said, was in great need of the latter. Chou En-lai, at twenty-three, was scraping along by writing freelance pieces for

*Yi Shibao,* a newspaper in Tientsin, the great maritime port up by Beijing. The three men agreed that something dramatic had to be done. The student-workers' situation was catastrophic. The luckiest of them were surviving by washing dishes in restaurants. Others were starving to death, driven to commit suicide.

Before more than four hundred student-workers who had gathered in the Young Socialists' hall, Li had given a speech whose indignation was infectious: "We came to study and work, and we are hardly able to live! Now they want to deny us access to the Franco-Chinese Institute in Lyons, the only place where we could really learn something!"

That day, Li made his first call to action. He told the student-workers that they had to march on Lyons and occupy the institute's offices. Li the orator was born. The idea aroused the wild desire of those who had nothing left to lose, and perhaps a ticket home to win.

More reserved, Chou En-lai considered the fact that the preceding year, he had already spent a hundred days in a Chinese prison before sailing to France. The French police were not known for their indolence, and the student-workers would need courage in Lyons. If things went badly, he would escape to Berlin. But it was obvious that this Li Lisan fellow had courage to burn.

On Wednesday morning, September 21, 1921, near the train station, the shopkeepers in Lyons saw a group of about a hundred young Chinese, some of them in their Sunday clothes, others in rags. They came from Paris, Montargis, La Garenne-Colombes, Fontainebleau, and Le Creusot, and they were walking resolutely toward the banks of the Rhône. They resembled in no way the dignified merchants from China, who, wearing their traditional garb, occasionally visited the European silk capital.

The little group divided up in order to converge on the Saint-Irénée fortress. Li Lisan was in the vanguard, while Chou En-lai brought up the rear, posted along with others in the area to distribute pamphlets in French explaining their demands.

The demonstrators poured into the institute around ten in the morning, put up their banners claiming the right to study, and got ready to occupy the place. They sent a delegation to present their demands to the institute's authorities, who immediately called the police.

Édouard Herriot, the mayor of Lyons, was soon informed. Telephone calls were made between Lyons and Paris. His Excellency, Ambassador Cheng, considered the incident a lamentable but also unhoped-for opportunity to get rid of these starving troublemakers once and for all, and he declared that it was France's duty to expel them. The ambassador saw no objection to police intervention.

The police in their black capes took up positions in front of the institute. Inside, the director was being held until the protesters had received an official response, while the 104 student-workers camped out in the halls and classrooms. There were constant meetings in which speeches were made one after another, relieving the students' anxiety as they waited nervously in a cloud of cigarette smoke.

Li was making new friends and hanging out with Chen Yi. Twenty-one years old and robust, this young man from Sichuan had worked at Michelin and then at Le Creusot, and he was planning to find a military academy to attend when he got back to China.

The wait lasted less than twenty-four hours. Shortly before dawn, exhausted, sleeping on the floor, the young Chinese were awakened all at once by the noise of the police bounding up the stairs to roust them out. Heavy blows with rolled-up capes began to rain down on them, batons were swung by the bellowing policemen, beating the Chinese to make them run. After making a symbolic resistance, the student-workers sheepishly climbed one after another into the police vans waiting for them in the street.

The 104 student-workers were taken to the nearby barracks, currently unoccupied, which served as their temporary prison. The next day, Édouard Herriot took the train to Paris in order to discuss with the foreign minister what the press called "the Lyons incident." On the agenda for the conversations with Ambassador Cheng was the expulsion of the troublemakers. Let them go make a revolution in their own country. "But who will pay?" the mayor wondered.

Three weeks later, on October 14, 1921, the little group, defeated and wounded, embarked in Marseilles, heads held high and proud despite the humiliation. The preceding day, at dawn, the Lyons police had put them in special train cars bound for the south. Passing between two rows of policemen, the cohort boarded an old tub belonging to the Messageries Maritimes, which was going back to Shanghai and Yokohama.

Seated amidships, Li silently stared for a long time at the coast of France as it faded away into the sunset. The ship would soon be at sea; around him, his companions said not a word.

Those feverish days had bound these young men together. Cloistered in the Lyons barracks, they had considered the fate that awaited them. Chen Yi was there at Li's side. At sea, they would kill time by playing chess. Chou En-lai had escaped the roundup. From Berlin, he had cabled article after article to the Chinese newspapers. After the Lyons incident, the gazettes in Shanghai and Tientsin referred to the "expulsion of the Hundred and Four."

The shores of France had disappeared in the haze of the setting sun. Two years, almost, in the country of the Law and Enlightenment. Li thought about Berthier, his snacks and his revolutionary theories. About the French frenzy. In France, Li Lisan had ended up with a few lessons, a lighter bag, and a holy fire in his belly that would never leave him.

# 3

Lisa Kishkin was walking proudly alongside her brother Vladimir in Basmannaya Street, which they took every evening as they came home from school. On her white blouse, her Pioneer's red scarf, carefully rolled up, contrasted splendidly with the blue of her skirt. On this autumn evening in 1926, the weather in Moscow had miraculously remained good. The previous year, Lisa had finally been allowed to wear the much-desired uniform that some of her friends and classmates had already been wearing for months.

At eleven, Lisa had blushed with pleasure when the monitor of the Komsomols and Pioneers of the neighborhood *raikom* told her at school that finally, despite her class origins, she had been admitted to the ranks of the Pioneers. There was still this problem with Papa, the notation "landed property owner" that she had to put on all the forms, under the rubric "Parents' Class Origin." Lisa envied her classmates who could put down "proletarian," and who were the pets of the comrade secretary of the Komsomols, though one sometimes wondered why. Every time they had to fill out a form—and that was frequently—there was whispering among the girls on the benches. Out of thirty-six pupils, four were daughters of landed property owners and eight were daughters of proletarians. The rest were lumped together as "petit bourgeois." One of the proletarians had been named, of course, as the class leader. On the playground, the invisible line separating the well-born girls from the others tended to fade away. But Lisa remembered her classmate Maya, who'd told her in a hissing voice that if she, Lisa, was not admitted to the Pioneers, it was because she was an "exploiter's daughter"! To which Lisa had replied that her father had been dead for a long time and that her mother was a worker in the clothing industry.

Praskovia Kishkin's aristocratic hands had always known how to work with a needle and a sewing machine. She easily found work in the Red Flag clothing workshop. With 130 rubles a month, and especially the ration tickets, she was able to provide one meal a day for her two children: a *kasha,* a bouillon in which, on good days, there was a bit of fat.

NOW THAT SHE COULD SHOW OFF HER UNIFORM, IT SEEMED TO Lisa that people in the street looked at her differently.

"We'll see if you become a good communist Pioneer," the monitor had told her. "If you prove worthy of our confidence, you'll soon be able to become a Komsomol."

Lisa secretly hoped the uniform would dissuade those horrible *bezprizorniki*—the threatening bands of homeless orphans and down-and-outs that hung around near the Kazan train station—from yelling their usual gibes at her as she passed by. Her mother had told her she mustn't answer them, they were a bad lot. Most of them also came from the Volga region, having escaped from villages where hunger had killed their parents at the time of the great famine. In large groups, they'd taken over trains and made their way to Moscow. They were not afraid of anyone, and between police roundups they survived in the capital's streets and cellars by begging or attacking passersby.

Lisa knew them well. She saw them especially in the winter, when she and her mother were walking home at nightfall along Kazan station's railroad tracks. The *bezprizorniki* were often there, in front of the hole in the fence through which they sneaked in order to steal logs and lumps of coal that fell from the tenders of the locomotives. They had to get as many as they could as quickly as possible, bent down in the snow or on all fours, bare-handed, silent; the railroad militia patrols came by frequently. If they were caught, things could go very badly for them: *theft of property belonging to the socialist state.* Fortunately, the militiamen who caught them confiscated the coal and let them go. Coal and wood, in any case, were too expensive or unfindable. Every winter night, there was an army of silent shadows around the tracks, taking off toward the fence at the slightest alert. The locomotive drivers knew this so well that they threw a couple of shovelfuls of coal along the rails after the train had started up.

So Lisa and her elder brother Vladimir, who had joined them in Moscow, didn't shiver before the stove every night in their single room, 130 square feet they had been sharing for the past six years in the collective apartment in Red Gates Street, in the northern part of the city. They had to take turns doing their homework on the minuscule table, and Lisa sometimes got impatient when Vladimir was laboring over his geometry.

Six families, eighteen people, occupied the eleven hundred square feet of the apartment, which had belonged to some old notary who'd fled abroad after the Bolshevik victory. Moscow was inaugurating the "proletarian communitarian way of life." The plumbing worked, a rare advantage in the city. In the courtyards of countless neighboring apartment buildings, people lined up in the open air in front of the faucet. The one kitchen in the apartment had six gas burners, one for each family, around which six housewives bustled every evening. That was where the shouts that impressed Lisa and the other children sometimes came from. But at Number 37, they were lucky, and they knew it: the head of the apartment was a party member, and what he wanted most of all was peace and quiet after work. The only person with whom one had to hold one's tongue was the *dvornik,* the concierge, one of the three thousand registered GPU* informers in Moscow that year.

---

*Acronym for the State Political Administration, a political police agency that was the predecessor of the KGB. —Trans.

As soon as she'd arrived in Moscow, Lisa had learned to stand in line. Three times a week, the children left the neighborhood school to go to the soup kitchen distribution center operated by the American Rescue Administration, a charitable organization of the United States government. Famine was knocking at the gates of Moscow, and in the United States, the anemic faces of Russian children had moved public opinion. Lisa still remembered with delight the cocoa sprinkled on the dish of steaming rice or the *baboui,* beans in sauce, and the piece of white bread, which could not be found anywhere else. In the cafeteria set up for schoolchildren, the kids licked their bowls to get the last taste. On some days, clothes were also handed out. Lisa was finally able to get a pair of shoes, so that in the winter she could take off her drenched felt boots before going into the classroom. The shoes were too big, but they were good for two years of growth.

Later on, life got better. Lights appeared in shop windows in the evening, under the Lubiansky arcades, on the Tverskaia, or along the Kuznetsky Most. They found grocery stores open late, and some even sold soap. It was the NEP.* After the millions of deaths in the civil war, the victorious Bolsheviks were letting the people breathe a little. Lenin had died two years earlier, and the battle to succeed him, ferocious but muffled, had begun at the top level of the country. Trotsky wanted his permanent revolution, but he had already lost his post as war commissar a year earlier. With him, the adversaries of the New Economic Policy were sidelined. The fatal swing of the pendulum was slowly coming. In the halls of the Kremlin, taciturn and watchful, Stalin was making allies of his future victims.

For the time being, at the end of 1926, the peasants were authorized to do a little trading with the city, where markets had reappeared. In the morning, milk was put on the doorstep in exchange for bread, and artisans took up their tools in the courtyards of Moscow's apartment houses; foreigners took a chance on a little business. Hundreds of new prostitutes had appeared on the sidewalks along Tverskoi Boulevard and on Trubenaya Square. Between dives and gambling joints, a few nouveaux riches, whether *nepmen* (people involved in the NEP) or gangsters, were frolick-

---

*New Economic Policy, a program introduced by Lenin in 1920. —Trans.

ing in cellars to music played by starving musicians. They were easily identified: they were the only ones getting into the taxis that had first appeared in Moscow earlier that year, or into prewar tramway cars. The drivers of horse cabs, their noses red with cold and vodka, fought to control their animals as the taxis passed by, and cursed modernity.

Several months earlier, shelters had to be reopened for some of the 200,000 homeless people who haunted the capital's streets after dark. Moscow had hardly more than 2 million residents, but already more than 120,000 unemployed and tens of thousands of peasants had arrived looking for seasonal work in order to survive. The police and the workers' militias hunted down these intruders. When they were forcibly sent back to their provinces by whole trainloads, fights often broke out near the stations. Here and there, strikes were begun to protest the hiring of country bumpkins at low wages, or the rapidly increasing production quotas.

In class, schoolchildren obediently recited the poems of Mayakovski, whose verses were used in advertising, which had recently been authorized again. The official poet asked Muscovites to consume unlikely merchandise at the GUM or Mosselprom department stores, which were supposed soon to rival the great stores in Paris. Lisa and Vladimir knew many of his verses by heart, the ones about the radiant future as well as his pretty rhyming jingles painted on the walls of the big buildings, hung up on kiosks, molded into cookies, or printed on candy wrappers.

Two by two, Moscow's children visited the first exhibits on the revolution, everyday life and work, or the life of the peoples of the Soviet Union and listened solemnly to the teacher's explanations about the "terrible czarist oppression" and "proletarian heroism, the builder of a new world." Delighted, the children left singing the currently fashionable ballads at the top of their voices as they walked through the streets: "Proudly We March into Battle," "Along the Road," and "The Hero Chapaiev Is Marching through the Urals." In the evening, near the Bolshoi, the Moscow Art Theater was always full. Students lay in wait near the entrance for a worker who wanted to sell his seat, bought for a few kopecks at his factory, at an advantageous price. Between the clenched jaws of the triumphant *Proletkoult,* Konstantin Sergeyevich Stanislavsky, the father of modern stage direction, was putting on Alexander Ostrovsky's *Burning Heart,* after

Mikhail Bulgakov's *The Days of the Turbin Family*. The story of two brothers who had not seen the same revolution was certainly a great hit. Even Stalin had gone to see it, hidden from view at the back of a discreet loge, surrounded by dozens of fake theatergoers and real policemen.

Like almost all the schoolchildren in Moscow, Lisa had joined in the cascades of childish laughter that washed over the Moscow Circus when Vitali Lazarenko, Constantine Tanti, or the Alperov brothers came on. The country's three great clowns made fun of kulaks, aristocrats, and even commissars and bureaucrats.

More than anything, Lisa dreamed of someday going to the movie house, the Goskino, the privilege of grown-ups and the holy precinct of the new Russian art. There Vladimir had seen Eisenstein's *The Strike*, which had just come out. He'd told her about the magical moment when the lights are put out: the curtain rises, then the beam of light, the projector's brush on the screen, the incredible imaginary voyage that begins. Petrified on the benches, the rows of Komsomols had spent the hour openmouthed before the screen. The miracle was repeated in *Forward, Soviets!* a long and severe exercise in propaganda by Dziga Vertov.

On Sundays, Lisa and Vladimir liked to go with their mother to the Smolensk market, where a colorful crowd bustled around the thousands of vendors lined up in concentric circles, standing immobile for hours in the muddy snow, each selling, trading, sacrificing in silence their last precious objects, bits of iron, or clothes, under the worried or resigned gaze of the Tatar merchants, who were sitting behind displays of vegetables laid out on makeshift tables. Filled with wonder, the children found there unfamiliar objects: watches, clocks, paintings, trinkets, and jewels.

When the New Economic Policy began, their mother had left the factory and begun working as a seamstress out of her own home. Her earnings were not much greater, but she was more at peace. Soon, Lisa had gotten her first shoes in her own size.

VLADIMIR, WHO WAS WALKING NEXT TO LISA, SUDDENLY SAID, "When we get home we must tell Mama to take down the icon over the bed. The comrade secretary said you can't be a Komsomol and have reactionary religious objects at home. They might even come to inspect our apartment."

Lisa remained silent for a moment. She would never have thought of that. But at sixteen, Vladimir, who had been wearing his Komsomol uniform for a few weeks, was following all these political matters very closely. He surely knew what he was talking about.

"I hope Mama will be willing to take it down, because she really cares about it, you know," Lisa replied, wondering if Vladimir was counting on hanging up in its place the fashionable portrait of Lenin next to Stalin. She remembered her mother's grim, pained face last year, when Vladimir had begged her to stop taking his sister to church. Otherwise she would never be admitted to the Pioneers, and he would never become a Komsomol. Worse yet, as "children of enemies of the people," they would be forced to stop going to school, forbidden to attend the university, and have difficulty finding work. Praskovia held her tongue, knowing that what they said was only prudent. The Reds had already arrested many Christians.

Lisa smiled for a moment when she thought, blushing a bit, about the young priest's handsome, blond face, with its nascent beard, who officiated in the only church open in the neighborhood where her mother sometimes took her. He was a "red pope," a supporter of Krastnitsky the schismatic, who told the faithful in a soft voice that Our Lord was "on the side of the working class, with the Bolsheviks and against the exploiters." Praskovia fumed in silence and finally stopped going there, even at Easter. Under the cathedral of Christ the Savior, the Bolsheviks were piling up sticks of dynamite while waiting to blow it up. Krastnitsky had taken up his quarters there in defiance of Tikhon, the patriarch of all Russia, who had condemned Lenin, the Antichrist.

Lisa loved the young priest's sermons. She listened to them dreamily, without being able to take her eyes off his soft blue eyes. Some day, she secretly told herself, she would marry a priest.

# 4

In Shanghai, on this April morning in 1927, the pale sky was rent, here and there, by strangely shaped clouds rolling in off the Pacific. The docks were oddly calm and silent as the junk approached them over the greasy water and tied up. Li Lisan checked his pistol, a well-oiled old Mauser that had been picked up in some trench in France or Russia. Looking out of the cabin, he immediately spotted a man who was nervously walking up and down the landing stage. When he saw Li, the man came straight toward him, his hand plunged in his pocket.

*"Tongdje ma?"* he asked in a low voice, his worried eyes looking right into Li's.

*"Tongdje,"* Li replied, extricating his long body from the junk's narrow cabin.

"Comrade." Since the beginning of the accursed year 1927, that was the simplest and the most dangerous password there was. But this time Wang, the courier sent to wait for him, was really there. The communications had worked for once.

Without a word, the man, one of the heads of the communist long-shoremen's union in Shanghai, led Li to a limousine. Two other men came out of nowhere and silently got into the car, one in front, one in back, next to Li, while the driver, wearing a uniform, started the engine and quickly drove off.

"It's because of the roadblocks," Wang said. "You're a rich antique dealer in Nanking Street, I'm your accountant, and he's your secretary."

The passengers greeted each other with a silent nod.

"If there are problems, we get out and open fire. We each have a grenade. You get down in the car, and we'll get away as best we can. My orders are to prevent you from being captured, at any cost," he added, scrutinizing the street they were going down.

Between his two guardian angels, Li gave a nervous jerk when he looked at his long robe of black silk, the rings on his fingers, the false hooked fingernail—the faded finery of a mandarin's son that the owner of the junk, one of the most reliable couriers on the river, had made him put on before they arrived in Shanghai. Despite Li's protests, the old Yangtze mariner, who had seen it all before, said to him firmly: "Disguise yourself! There's a price on your head, and everyone knows it. Don't make trouble. And watch out for yourself, in Shanghai! The news is not good. In February, I saw heads cut off by sabers rolling in the streets. Lots of heads, you hear?"

The old man had gotten annoyed as he held the tiller that evening. He talked while he was maneuvering between the boats coming down toward Shanghai, slipping in the dark over the immense lapping of the river, a trembling oil lamp hung on the end of the boom. Many junks had left from Hankow, some even from Chungking, at the foot of Tibet, more than six hundred miles upstream. Their pilots, the lords of the Yangtze, were able to cross the rapids in the Three Gorges without breaking up their junks on the rocks that stuck up like crocodile's teeth in the water of the long river. Like all Chinese, Li knew about the peculiar wisdom of the Yangtze mariners. In Chinese legends, they were smugglers of both goods and men, but they were also messengers bringing good and bad news, working alone, skillfully arched over the river, their eyes peeled and their hands glued to their tillers.

Li knew why the old mariner was angry. In February, along with his comrades in the leadership of the Communist Party who'd set up shop in Hankow—three hundred miles upstream—he'd voted in favor of beginning a second uprising in Shanghai. This second attempt had been just as big a failure as the first one, which had taken place four months earlier. The *Beifa,* or Northern Expedition, the republican conquest of China that had begun in the south, in Canton, was at that time in full swing. One after the other, warlords were yielding to the republican cannons and their Soviet crews. In a campaign of scarcely eight months, the young leader of the Kuomintang, Chiang Kai-shek, had arrived within sight of Shanghai at the head of his troops. On February 18, the southern army's advance unit had taken up positions in Soutiang, less than twenty miles to the south of the city. The next day, five hundred delegates from the Shanghai General Labor Union had called for a general strike in support of the *Beifa* and against the cruelty of Sun Zhuanfeng, the local warlord who held the city.

The old mariner cursed the young: "A week later, in the streets of Shanghai, the Russians were cutting off Chinese people's heads with their sabers!" he cried, spitting over the side of the boat. The youths had been excited, and refused to believe the old adage about a wounded tiger—in this case Sun, the satrap.

The White Russians! Li had a deep hatred for them. The sworn enemies of the Reds, mercenaries of the counterrevolution, they had become foremen in Shanghai's textile mills, strayed Cossacks prized by Japanese employers, or else machine gunners who were brave and prepared to die, so long as they could do so while killing Reds and drunk on vodka. Sun had given them his armored train, and the international concession had willingly made use of their services.

The old mariner told Li about the heads of eleven striking workers from Commercial Printing that had been exhibited beside their bodies, on the sidewalk along the road to Baoshan. And still other heads, placed in cages at intersections.

"No, not just White Russians. Chinese sabers, too, Sun's men," the old man added, spitting in the river again.

Li, who knew all that, remained silent. He'd read all the reports on the defeat back in Hankow. Everything had happened so fast, in this Year of the Hare. Hardly a month after the bloody repression of the February revolt, during the uprising in March the common people of Shanghai took over a few police stations and administrative buildings, and almost gained power. The toughest opponents were the White Russians, with their armored train.

The Chinese Communist Party had done a good job. Li had been sent to Shanghai from Hankow to assess the situation and transmit the latest directives. When his junk arrived in port, his most recent information dated from his stop in Nanking, three days earlier.

In Hankow, the leaders were only wondering what revolution they should be devoting their efforts to now. The press ironically commented that the Chinese Communists saw a big difference between their Nationalist republican allies in the Kuomintang and the Soviets, whom they were so eager to see flourish. And Shanghai wasn't China. The victory of the insurrection was a magnificent surprise, of course, but the future looked like it would be no more stable than sand along the river at low tide.

As the car moved toward the French concession, Wang brought Li up to date on the events of the preceding day. He was shocked; the news was, almost without exception, absolutely catastrophic. Martial law was going to be proclaimed in Shanghai at any moment. The preceding day, April 12, 1927, at precisely four in the morning, when the signal was given by one of the gunboats anchored in the port, the attack had begun.

"There were at least two thousand of them. The tigers, the goons of the association for Mutual Progress, the killers under the command of Du, the head of the Green Society, the most powerful of the Shanghai tongs."

"Du Yuesheng?" Li asked, going pale.

"Yes. All our information points to him. His lieutenants led the charge. We killed several of them, but they took us by surprise. The fighting isn't over. Our men are still holding out at the Workers' Club. Not for long. We've lost contact with them, they're surrounded. The soldiers,

Chiang Kai-shek's, are tightening the noose. They're covering Du's men's rear and then cleaning up.

"Are there dead? Prisoners?"

"Lots," Wang said, his eyes riveted on the vehicle's window.

Li took a deep breath. It was worse than he'd imagined. His neighbor suddenly nudged him, and the other passengers froze. The car slowed and stopped in front of an army roadblock. His rifle pointed at the vehicle, a soldier with a severe look on his face beneath a helmet bearing the sun of the Kuomintang's army started barking orders.

"Get out. You're Mr. Li, the antique merchant in Nanking Street. Here are your papers," Wang whispered, slipping a set of documents into Li's sleeve. "Be calm and talk down to them."

Li climbed out of the car and stood before the soldier, who was impressed by the limousine, the driver, and Wang's bow as he opened the door for Li.

"My accountant and my two employees," Li said, pointing to the passengers with a slightly haughty air.

With a gruff gesture, the soldier signaled to them to move on. Crossing the barrier, Li noticed the machine-gun battery set up on sandbags. The car turned into the narrow streets of the concession; Wang, no longer able to control himself, asked in a low voice: "Hey, Li Lisan, is it really you?"

Li didn't have time to reply. The car suddenly pulled up in front of a two-story brick building that stood at the intersection of two streets.

"It's here," the driver said. "Hurry up, the owner of the hotel is waiting for you. You'll move to another hideout tomorrow. The comrades will come to inform you. I'm bringing them."

Three hours later, the first comrades came to report. The disaster was total. The Workers' Club had fallen. The best, most determined units of Shanghai's clandestine fighters, postmen and employees of Commercial Printing, had for the most part been wiped out.

Shanghai was in turmoil. Guilds, provincial associations, militias, political parties, and smaller groups were meeting continuously.

In the concessions, the French consul general, Naggiar, along with his colleagues Barton, from Great Britain, Cunningham, from the United States, and Yada, from Japan, were exchanging views.

"The Chinese are killing each other again, it seems . . ."

"Ever since that business in May 1925, two years ago, nothing has been the way it was before."

"This Mr. Du, then, what side is he on now? He's cutting down the Reds, and he used to march alongside them. People say he's interested only in opium and brothels."

"You're forgetting charity work. Mr. Du is a friend of the poor in Shanghai. That's why he's in competition with the Reds."

"They don't smoke opium?"

"Not to my knowledge. Their religion forbids it."

"By the way, how many deaths have there been since yesterday, do you think? According to our reports, the fighting is heavy around the North Station."

"A few hundred. The Reds have solid firepower, with their union militias. The February rebels are supervising them. Very determined people, survivors who know what awaits them if they're captured. They are fighting with their backs to the wall. But you can trust Du's men—they're also very resolute. The Green Society doesn't fool around when it's a matter of honor and money."

"In any case, the honeymoon between the Nationalists and the Communists is over. They say Chiang Kai-shek is a blood brother of Du, that they belong to the same tong."

"The fact is that the two fellows have been together for some time already. By the way, did you know that Chiang Kai-shek is getting married? The bride is supposed to be the youngest daughter of Soong, the banker."

"The end of the Reds in Shanghai, you say? It looks like it. Not surprising—those ideas have nothing in common with the Chinese temperament."

The hotel room, small and bare, hidden under the roof, had two doors, one of them for making a rapid and discreet getaway. In the event of an alert, Li was supposed to run down a back corridor and escape over the neighboring terraces, with an expert skill he'd have to acquire by himself. The hotel, which was more or less a family affair, had about fifteen rooms, and the whole staff was armed and dedicated to the cause.

The man who was waiting for Li, on the evening he arrived there, was by far the most important one, in his opinion. Many others had passed through the room in the course of the day, reporting from hour to hour on the situation. But it was with this man alone that the new arrangements were to be decided upon.

Chou En-lai. An old comrade from his Paris days, from the demonstration in Lyons. The man with whom Li had been working for months on his revolution. At the age of twenty-nine, Chou was the head of the party in Shanghai and, like Li, was one of its most prominent leaders.

It was dark when he finally showed up, his face more emaciated than ever, drawn, his eyes wary beneath his heavy, worried-looking eyebrows, though he was usually so much in control of himself. The two men embraced briefly, then sat down before a steaming teapot.

Chou spoke in a flat, tense voice. Shortly before noon, during the final assault, he had barely managed to escape from the Commercial Printing building. His three hundred defenders kept firing until they ran out of ammunition.

"Gu Shunzhang was also able to get away. He's safe," he added.

Li, relieved, breathed more easily. He had recruited Gu two years earlier, during the massive anti-Japanese strike in 1925. Gu had excelled in organizing pickets. He had become the head of the Party's workers' sections. It wasn't surprising that he'd escaped. A professional magician, Gu performed, in greasepaint, on the garden terraces of the big Sincère store in Nanking Street. Afterward, he went back to his hideout, the New World nightclub, where he melted into the crowd. Gu was valuable: he'd been trained in techniques of insurrection alongside Soviet comrades, and had returned from Vladivostok only a few weeks before the uprising.

The fact that Gu was still alive was, however, the only good news. The protest demonstration against the crackdown, which began around noon in Tsingyun Street, had certainly brought out tens of thousands of people. All the lower classes of Djabei were there, with their wives and children, carrying a petition to the headquarters of the Sixth Division of Chiang Kai-shek's army.

"It was a slaughter. First, they opened fire with a machine gun at San Detai, and then they chased people down with their bayonets, pursuing them even into their own homes. A hundred deaths, at least."

Near the Longhua barracks, south of the French concession, there was a rumor that execution squads were firing practically nonstop. The prisoners were marched into the barracks in columns or brought by the truckload.

In the course of the morning, several hundred men from the Green Society had used iron bars to take over the offices of the Commercial Printing club, the headquarters of the General Labor Union. Shortly afterward, they announced the creation of the Workers' Union. The army had banned the General Labor Union, which had been directed by Communists since Li Lisan had founded it in 1925.

Chou En-lai had no news of his superior, Wang Shuhua. The latter had not been seen since he'd imprudently accepted, two days earlier, an invitation to dine with Du Yuesheng. For Chou, there was no doubt that he was already dead. Li was visibly shaken. Wang had succeeded him as the head of the General Labor Union eighteen months earlier.

In two days, the fighting had left at least four hundred dead in the Communist ranks and at least a thousand prisoners who were to face execution squads. Martial law was in force in Shanghai's streets, which were cut by the army's roadblocks and patrolled by the Green Society's teams of hired killers.

As for the general strike protesting Chiang's crackdown, it was valiantly observed by a hundred thousand workers, but that was not enough. Now it was every man for himself.

The civil wars that were ravaging China had finally come to Shanghai. The blow came from a source the Communists had not expected it to come from: their ally, Chiang Kai-shek, the leader of the Northern Expedition. Sun Yat-sen's successor thus put an end to three years of collaboration with the Communists. They were too burdensome, too demanding, too dangerous. In March, the Reds had shed their blood— 320 killed, 2,000 wounded—in order to open the gates of Shanghai to Chiang's forces. In April, what they got in return were bayonets.

The most surprising thing, however, was Moscow's determination to hold on to the alliance with Chiang at any price. The latest orders from the Comintern were clear: no break! The Communists and the right-wing Nationalists had been at war for several weeks, but in Stalin's view, the man on the rise in China was Chiang Kai-shek, and no one else. In Moscow, Trotsky, before going into exile, had excoriated the "Chinese Napoléon" whom Stalin found so appealing.

The Green Society had changed sides. The sworn brothers of the tong, the ones with whom the Communists had been forced to compromise in order get into the Shanghai factories, the ones who had become Communists or pretended to, workers and foremen, longshoremen and mechanics, tramway drivers or women working in the textile mills, all of them members of associations in provinces near Shanghai, the people crowded into the lower-class neighborhoods of Jabei, Putong, and Nantao, where the great Shanghai tong was even more popular than the communists.

That was a lot of betrayals for one day. The two men separated after working out the final orders for retreat. The rest would be decided in the Central Committee, which was supposed to have an emergency meeting. At present, there was a price on their heads; they had to think about saving their skins. "My wife, Deng Yichao, is supposed to give birth any time now," Chou said before slipping out of the hotel and disappearing into the Shanghai night.

Outside, Japanese marine units, supported by British machine guns, were venturing into the Chinese zone outside the concession in order to help run down the Reds and eliminate the last snipers. *Lang hu, cheng chun:* the wolves and the tigers had fled the city. Li Lisan fell into a dark sleep of mourning, filled with crowds whose endless clamor seemed to have borne him, spinning like a straw in the wind, in the turmoil of the past six years, since the day he had returned to China.

# 5

It was the afternoon of December 10, 1921. The *D'Artagnan,* an old liner beloging to the Messageries Maritimes, had come into the port of Shanghai after sixty-five days of slow travel from Marseilles. A blast from the ship's horn gave the signal for a sudden commotion on the docks. Several hundred Chinese, most of them students, had agreed to meet in order to welcome the "Hundred and Four," as the press called them. The student-workers exiled from France, bruised by police batons in the Lyons occupation, had been told to go make their revolution elsewhere.

Li had never forgotten the acclamations that welcomed them as they disembarked. The return to China put an end to the delays of the crossing, to the feverish discussions punctuated by long maritime reveries and bouts of seasickness. Very soon, Li was introduced to Chen Duxiu, the dean of the faculty of arts at the University of Beijing. Now commissar for education in Sun Yat-sen's southern government, he had wanted to meet this not very cultivated but brilliant young man who had distinguished himself in France by his courage and his passionate oratory.

Li was ready for action. He knew the factories in France, and Chen Duxiu assigned him to Chinese labor. The Communist Party was only four months old, a few hundred quarrelsome intellectuals and not a single proletarian in its ranks.

Then things moved very quickly. A rapid visit to his family, to his mother and father, to the wife he'd never loved; a brief dive into the city of his childhood, Liling, drowned in the cold, wet mists of winter, lost among the hills of Hunan, dotted with ponds of silent water. It was time to listen to stories about the area, to meet old pals and schoolmates, and to make new friends in the evenings, sitting in cheap restaurants lit by candlelight, around a bowl of yellow, steaming wine.

Hunan had hardly recovered from the tea crash. The Russians, its best customers, had stopped buying since they had become Soviets. Pockets of famine were numerous, and the local warlord was cruel and taxed the people heavily, Li's companions assured him.

It was there, in December, that Li saw Mao Tse-tung again. He was now the principal of a primary school in Changsha, the provincial capital. Li had met him briefly six years earlier, when he was a student. One fine day in the autumn of 1915, Li had been struck by an announcement in the *Ta Kong Pao,* the local newspaper. Under the mysterious pseudonym of Twenty-Eight Strokes, the author of the strange announcement was looking for companions who were "animated by a true patriotic flame," and asked them to meet with him in the library of the Normal School. Li, who was not yet sixteen, had gone to the meeting and half opened the door. There was only one person in the room, a student a few years older than he, sitting at a table piled high with books. Mao looked up at the intruder.

Their eyes met and Li, who was expecting a meeting, saw only an advanced student at the Normal School. Without saying anything, he closed the door and went timidly away.

This time, six years later, the two men had much to say to each other. Mao had almost come to France as well. Li's misadventures in the "country of the Law" reassured him: other countries were the domain of barbarians. Only Russia interested him, because of its Bolshevist revolution.

At twenty-eight, Mao was the head of the Party in the province. His long, greasy hair, his loquacious, vaguely esoteric remarks, the seediness of his traditional robe full of rips and tears, put on over a pair of pants of uncertain color, and even the somewhat sour odor that emanated from his body reminded Li of the Taoist monks he'd met on the rural roads of Hunan in his childhood. Mao was one of twelve men who had, eighteen months earlier, issued a clandestine proclamation of the existence of a Chinese Communist section of the Moscow International, which had itself scarcely emerged from Lenin's coat sleeves.

Li had been recommended to Mao by Chen Duxiu, the head of the Party. This young man of twenty-two, who had just come back from the factories in France, knew a great deal about the methods of agitation and labor organization. Red labor unions were his specialty: at Le Creusot, his French friends had told him about the turbulent birth of the new CGT.* Li knew the rudiments of the art of the strike, the tract, and the demonstration. His idea of workers' schools pleased Mao. Li could talk endlessly on the subject. Establishing a workers' school in the evening, run by Communist teachers, would make it possible to kill three birds with one stone: first of all, they could teach workers and their wives to read and write: second, they could establish contact between the Party and the proletariat; and third, they could recruit party members by taking in the best ones, the avant-garde.

The principal of the primary school in Changsha didn't object. By common agreement, Mao and Li decided that the school would be established in Anyuan, about ninety miles from Changsha.

An immense coal mine spreading over hundreds of acres had made Anyuan the site of the largest concentrations of workers in China. Far from Shanghai, in the hinterland, the ancient village in the green foothills of the Wugong Mountains sheltered a new population in its shacks made of wooden planks. Its inhabitants—small farmers who had been ruined, day workers, craftsmen or village shopkeepers despoiled by soldiers—had become miners as a result of the civil war and repeated famines.

In deep pits dug into the flanks of the mountains, about twenty thou-

---

*The Confédleration Générale du Travail, a French labor union formed in 1895.

sand Chinese of all ages, from children to grandfathers, naked as jaybirds and using picks and their bare hands as their only tools, sweated seven days a week to extract the black gold for locomotives' boilers. These steam-powered monsters had begun to crisscross the country, triggering terrible panics, and the tall blast furnaces of the steel mill in Hanyang, on the Yangtze, spit forth strange and heavy smoke. China provided the capital for the Hanyeping mine, the engineers were German, and the salaries were distributed less regularly than the blows with a bamboo stick that rained down on the backs of miners who didn't work fast enough. In the summer, Anyuan was an oven, and the tenacious mists of winter froze the men's bones, but those who had a job and were able to support their families were envied.

Despite being under the jurisdiction of the neighboring province of Jiangxi, Anyuan was still only just the other side of the border with Hunan, almost across from Liling, less than thirty miles, as the crow flies, from the town where Li was born. Virtually no one spoke Mandarin there, and the Hunan dialect was as commonly heard as on the other side of the Lian River.

At the end of December, Li established his headquarters in Anyuan, in a mud hut where he lived alone, jammed between the neighborhood of the miners and that of the railroad workers on the Anyuan–Chu-chou line. All he had to start with were two or three names of anarchist school-teachers, potential supporters, and a few Chinese dollars that the Party had given him to set himself up. He felt good there, as if all the energy he'd stored up in the course of his peregrinations had finally found something to work on. He immediately went to work, a flame burning within him whose existence even he did not suspect. Moving from gambling joints to opium dens in the evenings, and to shopkeepers and neighbors in the mornings, he brought the good word to the miners. By February, he had rounded up six bold men.

In March 1922, the first workers' club in China was formed in the backroom of a tavern. By April, a few dozen miners were learning to read and write at the same time that they were discovering bits and pieces of Marx's *Communist Manifesto*.

On May 1, with three hundred members, the club of miners and railroad workers, decorated with red cloth like a bride, was formally inaugurated, to the sound of fireworks. In June, it moved to a new, larger location provided with chairs, a few tables, and, above all, blank paper, which had been found in Pingxiang, the neighboring town. On the blackboard and with awkward brush strokes on the precious paper, the miners of China discovered the new alchemy of "wages, price, and profits."

Li had become a schoolteacher. After the lesson, the young intellectual eagerly told the proletarians from Anyuan, who were often fascinated by, and sometimes incredulous about, the factories in France or the workers' revolution in Moscow. His audience agreed: China's misfortunes were caused by soldiers and foreigners.

"And by the bosses. They are strong only because we are weak!" Li insisted. "China's honor can never be reestablished without a powerful workers' movement. And power comes from organization!"

The miners in Anyuan liked this loudmouth who didn't mince words. His name had begun to be known in town, and as far as Pingxiang, and it was known to the police and the local warlord as well.

"A Nationalist troublemaker, like so many others in the country," the police chief commented philosophically.

"An oddball, too," the notables pointed out. He had been seen walking in the streets of Anyuan with a woman on his arm, in the Western fashion.

"Westerners have brought us this fashion, as well: women are now acting modern and no longer walk behind but alongside the man. It's indecent, this way of behaving in public, to take each other's arm, to touch each other."

Even the young miners in Anyuan were a little surprised when they saw the young couple going by.

Li had fallen in love with her almost instantaneously. It happened in the train that was bringing them back from Beijing, where he had been sent on a short mission, a few months after his arrival in Anyuan. Her slender cheekbones, her lively, laughing eyes, her light skin, and her astonishingly direct manner had conquered him. Li Yichun was going back to her native province of Hunan. She was going to visit her family after a long stay in the capital, where Li had run into her at a friend's home.

She was scarcely twenty years old, but it was the first time that a young woman in his own country spoke to him with such ease. During the long train trip, sitting across from him in the jolting compartment, she had talked freely and openly with this big, gangly young man in his long robe of black cotton; he had a craggy face, but it was lit by a rare enthusiasm. The young woman had no difficulty in understanding what his shining eyes meant.

Li had a son that he'd almost never seen, and a wife he had not chosen. His refusal to live with her had been categorical. Since the wedding, she'd lived in the paternal home in Liling.

Li's long period of celibacy in France, the solitude of the hovel in the suburbs of Anyuan, and the vigor of the spring of 1922 made him bold for the first time. The young woman told him she was the eldest of seven daughters. Li Yichun had been lucky—her father was a wealthy, educated man in Changsha, very open to modern ideas and curious about the West. So she had been able to study in the new schools, the ones where girls learned the same things as boys: mathematics, history, geography, and even foreign languages. She admitted that it was new and rare. Li Yichun also thought that Chinese women were "absolutely concerned" with political matters. Moreover, hadn't she herself participated in the movement, in May 1919?

The more she talked, the more revolution finally took on charm for Li Lisan. Full of enthusiasm, the beautiful woman supported "free union" and even free love, an idea that had been discussed far into the night among the young Chinese in Le Creusot and elsewhere. In Beijing, she lived with Yang Kaiming, to whom she had been married with her own consent, "in the Western fashion." She also knew Mao Tse-tung well; in fact, he was her brother-in-law. He had married Yang Kaihui, her husband's youngest sister. The two families were linked by the friendship between the fathers, two convinced supporters of modernity in the province.

At the end of the trip, Li Yichun never went to see her family. She fell into Li Lisan's arms, left her husband, and moved to Anyuan with her new flame. A few months later, she gave him a son.

In August, shortly before the strike began, they had had to share their hovel with another couple. Liu Shaoqi and his wife, He Baozhen, had come from Moscow, where he'd received almost a year's training in Communism. Sent to Anyuan as reinforcement for Li Lisan, he was a year older and also came from neighboring Hunan. Reserved and courteous, Liu came from a well-off peasant family, from the gentry of the Chinese provinces. Although his wife's talkativeness tended to stir things up a bit, his austere devotion to the cause made it easier for the two couples to live together. As the single concession to preserving privacy, a curtain was hung to separate the hovel's only room into two parts.

The mine was in turmoil. The Workers' Club now had seven hundred members. It had set up a consumers' cooperative and a library and organized leisure activities before electing, in assemblies of activists, dozens of officers.

On September 10, 1922, the salaries that were owed to the miners, who were supposed to be paid weekly, had not been paid for a month. The Hanyeping mine was disorganized administratively, and such delays were common. But for weeks, Li had been covertly organizing a sophisticated system of delegates from the mines and workshops. The list of grievances was finally ready.

On September 14, the strike began. In front of the main entrance to the mine, hundreds and then thousands of miners gathered at the time when hiring was done. Carried away by his enthusiasm. Li began to speak, and talked himself hoarse before the crowd of blackened faces. Then he set off a roar of applause by shouting: "Before, we were beasts of burden; now we want to be men!"

The work stoppage was sudden and massive. The company's officers sent out telegrams asking the military to declare martial law and send in troops—without success. Li demanded that negotiations be opened and hid in a small farmhouse surrounded by lookouts. Messengers brought him reports about the negotiations being conducted with the mine's management, while Liu Shaoqi took Li's place as representative of the Workers' Club at the negotiations.

On September 17, the company agreed to pay the miners, including back wages. It promised a raise, recognized the statutes of the Workers' Club, and even accorded it a monthly allocation of two hundred Chinese dollars. And most important, the foremen deep in the mine had to put away their bludgeons. Beatings were abolished.

In Anyuan, Chinese proletarians had their first victory. In four days, the miners had won out. The press, which had followed the affair, recognized that this was a first. The news traveled throughout the country and then reached Moscow. In the Comintern, eyebrows were raised: "A Chinese *workers' movement?*"

That day was like a rebirth for Li Lisan; it was the proof that he was on the right path. The class struggle's role in the race for progress was not only praised by Western theorists, but also *worked*. Berthier, at Le Creusot, had told him . . .

THE MINERS IN THE WORKERS' CLUB ALMOST CARRIED HIM ON their shoulders when he returned to Anyuan. A few days later, to show clearly that Li was an honored man, he was inducted into the local tong, one of the secret lodges that were everywhere in the country. Remnants of the secular struggle against the Manchu rulers, the Ch'ing, the tongs formed an invisible but omnipresent network that united peasants with workers, and the latter with foremen and even government officials, all in opposition to the state. Many of the tongs had turned into criminal organizations, like the Green Society. Li didn't care, and in his thirst for solidarity, he drank chicken's blood and opened a vein to mix his blood with that of a sworn brother in the presence of a witness. He would soon make them revolutionaries, too, he thought.

Li left Anyuan in March 1923, fifteen months after he arrived there. Liu Shaoqi stayed behind to take care of the miners' union that had been founded after the strike with the men in the club. The Party sent Li to Hankow, one of the three cities which, along with Wuchang and Hanyang, were clustered on both sides of the Yangtze to form the powerful city of Wuhan. Riveted to its river, more than five hundred miles upstream from Shanghai, this industrial and commercial center, the last stop for freighters coming up from the Pacific, had a Nationalist heart.

Like all Communists, Li carried in his pocket a membership card for the republican party, the Kuomintang. The latter was the umbrella for all the varieties of nationalism, on the right as well as on the left. Moreover, hadn't its founder, Sun Yat-sen, just publicly allied himself, in January 1923, with Moscow? The young republic of the Soviets held out its hand to the man who had brought down the last Chinese dynasty. Sun Yat-sen had seen his dream of a republic collapse almost as soon as it was born in 1911, and the country torn asunder by warlords. In 1923, he hoped to reconquer it from Canton, in order to lead it along the path of the Three Principles: Nation, Democracy, and Prosperity. Russian advisers from Vladivostok had landed by the dozens in the ports of Shanghai and Canton in various disguises and under the purblind eyes of British intelligence agents or of their colleagues in the French police.

The Soviets' advice was given in the form of orders: the Chinese Communists must, by means of a vaguely schizophrenic mental gymnastics, ally themselves with Sun Yat-sen, join his party, and defend the Three Principles of the People, while at the same time conferring with each other and developing the Bolshevist, workers' influence of their own party.

When Li arrived in Hankow, an odor of terror filled the city. The troops of the warlord Wu Beifu, the master of central China, had just put down a strike by the railroad workers on the Hankow-Beijing line. Four union leaders had been decapitated by saber on the platform of the station in Kiangan, before the eyes of their comrades, after they refused to order the men to go back to work. Fifty others had been executed by firing squads or killed as early as the evening of February 7, around the train station.

Everything had to be done over, and from now on clandestinely. Ten months after he arrived in Hankow, Li had fulfilled his mission: the workers' clubs, under cover of various pretexts and activities, were once again bringing together the rebellious elite in the steel mills of Hanyang, the railroad workers, and the rivermen; and the Kuomintang's republicans were grateful to these young Communists for restoring their party's popular base, even if at the same time, surreptitiously, the ranks of the Communists were also visibly growing.

In January 1924, Li suddenly made his appearance at the heart of the Chinese political scene. In the hall in Canton where the Kuomintang's convention was being held, everyone had piously listened to the opening speech given by President Sun Yat-sen. "Dr. Sun" had saluted the alliance with the Soviets and excoriated Western imperialism, while at the same time stressing that Communism was inapplicable to China, and then called for reconquering the country in order to put his program into effect. The next day, the party veterans, the anti-Manchu revolutionaries of 1911, were jolted when they saw the young delegate from Hankow stand up in the middle of the hall and launch into a diatribe against the party's old-fashioned ideas and its halfheartedness about mobilizing workers. His remarks were lively, articulate, filled with a heat that warmed the bones of the oldest delegates. As for the young people in the Kuomintang, Li captivated their attention.

Another young man, the delegate from Hunan, continued with the same brio, but with more respect for Dr. Sun. Mao Tse-tung repeatedly quoted the father of the republic but in support of very different views. He talked at length about the feudalism of the countryside.

The two young men were thus the stars of the weeklong convention. In the corridors, the party veterans squabbled a bit about these garrulous young pups who talked as if they knew everything; just who did they think they were? But the Kuomintang and its leader agreed: "We have to listen to this generation of May 4, 1919. Its enthusiasm is precious." So precious that this first Kuomintang convention made room for the Communists: they began to codirect the reorganized party with their Nationalist allies.

That evening, at the home of Mikhail Markovitch Gruzenberg, known as Borodin, Mao Tse-tung and Li Lisan were scolded. The head of the Soviet advisers in China told them that the Communists had to show a little more unanimity within the Kuomintang. The two men from Hunan protested that their views were identical.

Later on, Borodin told them about his tribulations as the son of Lithuanian Jews and an agent of the Comintern. He had been imprisoned by the czarists, then exiled to America; after that, he had traveled to Valparaiso and Mexico City, and, after missing the October Revolution, had returned to Moscow in 1918. In Canton, where he'd set up the Whampoa Military Academy, on the banks of the river of the same name, he'd been nicknamed "the Lafayette of China." Borodin, who loved this venture as a Soviet proconsul with which Lenin had entrusted him, liked the image. But the Chinese were not Americans, and here, nothing ever seemed to be resolved.

Two months later, Li Lisan moved again. He left Hankow, and arrived at the central train station in Shanghai, a felt hat on his head and dressed in a worn Western-style suit that made him look like a modernist student. In his pocket was a new assignment from the party. In general, he was supposed to do the same thing he'd done in Hankow and Anyuan, but on a larger scale and more powerfully: he was to found the workers' movement in Shanghai and, if possible, launch a revolution. The result went beyond all expectations.

Li was not very familiar with Shanghai, which was voraciously absorbing the destinies of 2.5 million of his fellow citizens, most of them coming from the neighboring provinces. Under the protection of the Yangtze gunboats moored in the port, fifty thousand Europeans and several thousand Japanese exercised imperial sovereignty within their concessions at the center of the city.

In the evening, in the streets of the hybrid city, at least thirty-five thousand prostitutes plied their trade under paper lanterns, while their pimps lay dreaming and sucking on bamboo opium pipes as they burped after a business dinner. In the concessions, especially in the French concession and in the international one, people liked to pretend they were in Paris. Old whores from Pigalle crossed the ocean to "renew themselves" in the "Pearl of the Orient."

Shanghai had to have a soul, and Li set out in search of it. He went straight to the international concession, in Weihaiwei Street. With its tramways, rickshaws, automobiles, water carriers and other coolies, the crowd was hardly less fantastic than in the Chinese zone. Alone, Li felt totally free and ready to double his stake in his political commitment. He didn't speak a word of the damned Shanghai dialect, which was incomprehensible to other Chinese—as was his own local dialect in Hunan— and there were very few among the lower classes of the city who spoke Mandarin, *guoyu,* the national language.

In Weihaiwei Street, at the Party's liaison office—a discreet place that also served as a welcome center for new arrivals—the comrade in charge was at loose ends, but he was fortunately a student, one of the three hundred at Shangda, the Party's university in Shanghai, which had only two departments, literature and social sciences. Literature had been given to leftist teachers, while the social sciences were entrusted to the

Communists. The students studied historical materialism, the history of the labor movement, and political economy. About twenty of them constituted almost half the Party members in Shanghai. But there was not a single proletarian. Borodin and the party leaders had decided that this time they were going to put all their chips on the Chinese workers' capital. Under the noses and in the faces of the powers, a movement of any size was certain to have an international impact: the press in Paris, London, and Washington was eager for stories about the metropolis on the Pacific, and Moscow even more. Hence the foreign correspondents had set up shop there, far from the diplomatic languor of Beijing, which had become provincial and melancholic since the end of Manchu rule.

Better yet, the foreign concessions offered Chinese revolutionaries excellent refuges from the henchmen of the military potentate who ruled the city and the area around it with an iron hand.

THAT EVENING, LI SET DOWN HIS BAGGAGE AT NUMBER 307, AN anodyne house in Minhou Lane, only a few steps from the Bubbling Well in the international concession. Situated close to the university, the place was convenient. Its occupants, all people who could be counted on, spent most of their time at Shangda, as teachers or students, so that there was a kind of Bohemian atmosphere mixed with sudden flashes of militant fervor. A few weeks later he moved to Yangshupu, the most densely populated neighborhood in the city, in the Chinese zone. There, not far from the port, in a little two-story house, a dark and dirty hovel, he wound up the mechanism of his revolutionary clock, which had so well proved itself.

First, Li launched a four-page rag filled with misprints and printed with the discreet aid of the linotypists at Commercial Printing. A bastion of anarchist humor, the *Shanghai Worker* was born. It began to circulate covertly and soon became a new sign of recognition in the workshops, in the textile mills, and on the docks. Li wrote most of the articles himself; they recounted, in very simple language, anecdotes about factory life picked up here and there, and developed in all registers the themes of putting the homeland back into Chinese hands and abolishing exploitation.

In September, the girls working at Nanyang, the largest Chinese cigarette factory, began a wildcat strike. There were several thousand of them, mostly very young girls who worked ten hours a day under the con-cupiscent eyes of foremen who forced job applicants to sleep with them. The strike failed after a few days, but in the meantime, the first clandes-tine labor union in Shanghai had been born. Li took advantage of the opportunity, and hanging out day and night around the factory in Huad Street with a small group of comrades, made the first promising contacts.

Toward the middle of October, the first school for workers was cre-ated. The neighborhood chosen was Xiaoshadu, to the southwest of the city, where tens of thousands of working families were crowded into hov-els constructed of scrap materials alongside refugees from the civil war who had ended up in shacks or even on the street.

Underneath its poverty-stricken and indifferent appearance, the neighborhood was crawling with the most diverse associations, the most extensive of which brought together people from the same province, often from the same town. In the evening, far from the lights of the concessions, the people uprooted from the rice paddies of Zhejiang, or those who had escaped the soldiers' raids in Jiangxi, gathered in makeshift taverns to talk about the latest rumor of a coup d'état in Beijing, or the uncertain out-come of the last battle between two warlords in a remote province.

The workers' school won clear approval from parents in the neighbor-hood, who wanted to provide for the education of their children. A student at Shangda, Liu Hua, as conscientious as he was poor, was given the role of teacher, which he quickly came to like. A small rented building was suffi-cient, along with a few desks and benches. And while Liu was teaching the children how to make their first brush strokes, Li and others were having intense discussions with their parents. Before long, these became an evening course for adults, which was soon attended by so many people that it was necessary to break them into two groups. After class, they remade the world while listening to the man from Hunan explain with his usual fervor that the imperialists had to leave China, that the warlords had to be defeated, and that the people must take their destiny into their own hands.

Just as in Anyuan, this led to the creation of a workers' club. Every day off, in the school's rooms, the club brought together workers in the neighborhood for long discussions in which precious ties between one fac-tory and another, one branch and another, were woven to form the fabric of a new solidarity. As a result, the investigations into the condition of workers carried out in the Party's daily newspaper, the *World of Labor,* began to acquire substance, and its descriptions became more extensive, precise, and concrete.

Li traveled back and forth between the school and his stronghold in Yangshupu in order to launch, together with few others, a labor union for mechanics that had hardly fifty members. But they knew how to read and write, and this was a precious asset. For weeks, Li was active all day, and stayed up late at night reading, by the light of his oil lamp, extracts from Darwin, Marx, or Lenin translated roughly into Chinese.

At the last large meeting of Party members in Shanghai, he had noticed with some alarm that the approximately forty participants were almost all government workers or students.

One cold, rainy Wednesday afternoon in February, the usual classes at the workers' school were not held. It had been learned that workers in Putong, on the other side of the river, had been beaten by their Japanese foremen. Liu Hua, the frail teacher, accompanied Li to NWK, an enormous conglomerate of Japanese textile mills that the people of Shanghai called by their numbers: Number 1, Number 2, and so on.

The incident had taken place at Number 8, on Gordon Road. In front of the gates, they found troubled workers who told them what had happened; some of them were very angry. It had all started on February 1, when about forty young men learned that they were being fired and replaced by girls, "temporary workers." So-called apprentices, these girls were bought from their families at the price of a few chickens. NWK exploited them free of charge for three or four years, their only salary being lodging in a dormitory and two meals a day. Up until then, this had been the usual practice, and led only to brief skirmishes in the factories. A few smashed machines and the young workers ended up leaving, furious.

This time, they had sent a delegation of a few of their comrades to demand their pay. The only response was a squad of Japanese foremen in their navy blue uniforms who beat them with clubs before handing them over to the English police in the international concession.

The following Monday, several thousand workers at NWK gathered in front of the factory and formed a procession. At its head was carried a banner on which Liu Hua had quickly sewn the slogan DOWN WITH THE JAPANESE WHO BEAT THE WORKERS! Several hundred members of the Workers' Club and others from Yangshupu had come along with Li to help the workers of Putong. They headed for the northwest section of the city, on the Suzhou road, where the other NWK factories were located. As they moved forward, work stoppages took place along the way, and the procession grew larger, joined by shopkeepers and curious onlookers. The ordinary people in Shanghai were nationalist and didn't like the Japanese and their gunboats, any more than they liked the Japanese marines who were always marching, uniformed and hieratic, through the city's streets.

A week later, NWK's forty thousand workers, male and female, were on strike. On Sunday, a new demonstration marched toward the Toyodo cotton mill, in the Chinese zone. The crowd climbed over the hastily closed gates and fights broke out between the demonstrators and the management, which included a few White Russians. There were already hundreds of demonstrators inside the compound when a Model T Ford came out of the administrative building, carrying on its running boards Japanese foremen who started hitting demonstrators with their billy clubs. But the car got wedged in the crowd, whose anger was so great that under the hail of avenging punches and kicks, one Japanese was killed and two others were left for dead. The workshops were wrecked, and the whole neighborhood was in an uproar. The next day, an association supporting the strikers was founded. Its teams fanned out through the city. Li and Liu Hua started a strike newspaper, pamphlets were circulated, delegates were elected everywhere. Strike pickets appeared, patrolling the neighborhoods, while the students at Shangda, asked to contribute, were exercising their oratorical talents in teams of two or three on every street corner.

THE JAPANESE BOSSES GAVE IN. DEFIED AND HUMILIATED, THEY signed a rather vague agreement on February 28. Liu Hua had to surreptitiously renegotiate the rehiring or indemnifying of the fired workers. But in the streets, tens of thousands of demonstrators began shouting "Down with imperialism!" or, more often, "Shanghai for the Shanghaians!"

The international press, and especially the American, put the "labor unrest" in the Pearl of the Orient in their headlines. Concerned, the Shanghai press itself focused on the affair; the Western papers tended to see in it the work of "communist bandits." The Chinese papers went over to the other side: the republican *Minguo Ribao* opened its columns to a vibrant call for demonstrations made by "those who are undergoing all sorts of ill treatment on the part of foreigners and are forced to strike. . . . The honor of the nation is at stake at a time when the Japanese treat us as less than nothing and as stateless slaves."

Above all, other workers' clubs were formed. Li carried the torch constantly, working like a demon in every part of the city.

In the spring, the embers were still hot. In the teahouses, in May, people were still telling for the hundredth time the story of February, and everyone swore he had been there.

For weeks, Li had been driven by a single idea: he wanted to make the coming May 4 a solemn commemoration of May 4, 1919. The Party was unanimous: in six years, this date had become a symbol throughout the country, the symbol of the day when its youth had risen up and saved China's honor. For the "young leaders" of the Party, as the Soviet advisers called them, May 4 was the origin of everything, their coming into the world. Its only rival in Li's memory was his tenth birthday, when he cut off his braid in joy and defiance at the announcement of the fall of the Manchus.

Li Lisan's revolutionary machinery was once again running at full tilt. The Party's formerly stammering propaganda now crackled in its pamphlets, small occasional papers, and on walls covered with calls for a strike and an uprising, smeared on under cover of night, clandestinely. The membership rolls were growing, and the skeletal staff of the Communist offices could no longer handle the crowds. The whiplash of February had awakened partisan spirit in their ranks, which had been dulled by official collaboration with the Kuomintang headquarters.

On May 1, 1925, the Shanghai police forces—English, French, and Chinese—noticed little more than a predictable agitation led by small groups of students and workers speaking to crowds at street corners.

On May 4, the workers at Number 8 once again stopped working, this time demanding salary increases. In the following days, the strike spread to other NWK factories.

On May 15, a crisis occurred at Number 7. The night crew that arrived that Friday evening at the factory gates, which had been closed by the management, broke in by force. As it moved forward, it ran into the turbaned Sikh guards and the Japanese foremen. The latter panicked, took out their pistols, and opened fire. Ten workers were wounded, seven of them seriously. Among them was Gu Zhengshong, a member of the Workers' Club, who was taken away in a coma, having been hit by four bullets. The workers retreated to the neighboring factory, Number 5, where they destroyed the workshops. The police from the international concession moved in and made arrests. No Japanese foreman was arrested. When Gu Zhengshong died two days later, the news was censored in the press, on the orders of the British police. At Gu's funeral at Djabei on May 24, skirmishes broke out after the ceremony, while the Chinese part of the city rumbled with vengeful rumors and patriotic indignation.

Li Lisan and the party leadership then turned up the heat to the maximum. On May 28, before the Central Committee, Li argued, along with Cai Hesen, for moving to a political strike: he insisted that the opportunity was unique. The warlord, busy fighting to the north of Shanghai, had relaxed his police pressure on the Chinese part of the city. As for the foreign powers, and first of all Japan, they had now focused the population's aversion on themselves. And then, two days earlier, on Saturday, hadn't there been the opening of the trial of the five students arrested for distributing pamphlets urging solidarity with the NWK workers? The date for the people's rendezvous was set.

Over the following forty-eight hours, passersby gathered until late at night on street corners where teams of speakers from the universities or workers' clubs were taking turns haranguing their audiences. On Saturday, ten thousand people marched behind banners demanding the abolition of the Unequal Treaties and the end of the extraterritoriality of the concessions. At the head of the procession, university and high school students marched in support of their indicted comrades. They were followed by postmen, railroad workers, woodcut makers, carpenters, bank employees, teachers, and workers for foreign companies. The demonstration was supposed to move through the streets of the international concession and reach the courthouse. It was a daring plan: people called that "pulling the tiger's mustache."

A few red flags flapped in the spring gale: messengers went up and down the procession; the clamor of the crowd echoed off the walls of the buildings in Nanking Street; at the windows, Chinese and foreigners looked on curiously, incredulously: it was 4:30, and on the sidewalks, the shopkeepers were quickly closing up their displays, many of them in order to join the demonstrators.

Li was marching with his friends from the Workers' Club. For the first time, he felt the heart of the city beating in unison.

The docks of the Bund had not yet come into view when the British police charged. His Majesty's servants roughly bundled off several dozen students, the first rounded up in the general confusion. The demonstrators were melting into the crowds, mixing with the customers of the large Xinxin and Daxin stores, when a shout went up: "To the police station!" After a moment of hesitation, the demonstrators regrouped and marched on the police station in Luza, farther up Nanking Street.

Inside the station, the chaos was almost as great as it was in the street. The hundred or so students arrested, highly excited, were shouting slogans and insults. They hit out at the policemen who were beating them with their billies as they tried to put their prisoners in their cells. Outside, confronted by the threatening crowd, the handful of Indian auxiliary troops nervously shouldered their rifles and waited for orders. His Majesty's officers, McGowan and Edwardson, the chief and deputy chief at the police station, consulted for a moment before going out and barking, "Fire!"

At the third salvo, Li was carried off by the screaming crowd that fled through the narrow streets amid countless oaths. He had not had time to see the thirteen young bodies on the roadway, surrounded by fifty wounded marchers dragging themselves through their own blood.

That same evening, at eight o'clock, Li went to a meeting of the Party's leadership at the home of Zhang Guotao, one of its twelve founders. His house in Baoxing Street, at the heart of Djabei, was often empty and served as a meeting place for the Communist leaders. That evening, there were eight of them. Besides the host, there were Chen Duxiu, the founder of the Party; Cai Hesen, Li's comrade in France; and Liu Shaoqi, who had left the mines in Anyuan four months earlier.

They wasted no time on pointless indignation. They had to launch immediately a general strike of the people of Shanghai, of all the Chinese, whether merchants or workers. A mad wind was blowing over the city, which was ready to do anything to avenge the affront. In Vallon Street, in the French concession, the head of the great tong, Du Yuesheng, had already called an emergency meeting of the representatives of the powerful Chamber of Commerce, which brought together the upper crust of the new commercial bourgeoisie, and of the Kuomintang, the Nationalist party. The former cursed their subjection to the fierce competition of the Japanese, while the Kuomintang demanded a major response together with their Communist allies. Du swore that he was patriotic and announced that he was prepared to close the brothels and gambling houses in the concessions. As for the Communists, Du was familiar with them as well. He had heard of this Li Lisan ever since Anyuan.

In the Temple of the Celestial Empress, the Chinese employers voted to strike alongside the labor unions. Fifteen hundred persons solemnly adopted a resolution calling for a boycott of Japanese and English businesses, including the tramways. Violators were to be shot.

That evening, before several hundred workers' delegates, Li launched the Shanghai General Labor Union. He denounced at length the "assassins of the Chinese people" before holding his audience spellbound by talking about the immense force that was rising up.

"We must create the General Labor Union, here and now!"

In the abstract, the idea was leapt at by the enthusiastic assembly. The delegates voted for a general strike in the foreign factories and mills, with the fusion of all the workers' groups into a single organization. Once again, Li had acted forcefully, on the spot. More than his large stature and his bony physique, it was the naturalness of his extraordinary determination that was impressive. A crisis galvanized his almost instinctive sense of tactics, and this gave his speeches an almost messianic intensity. In one evening, the dream of sending the Chinese masses to conquer their sovereignty and building a powerful labor organization on the scale of

Shanghai—a dream that would have seemed chimerical only a few months earlier—suddenly seemed within reach. The revolution, clearly, proceeded only by forcing the hand of fate.

The next day, the General Labor Union held its first congress. Li was elected president, with much applause and little disagreement. The position was highly political: at a time when the nation was trembling with indignation, the people wanted a leader who would also be their spokesman in dealing with merchants and employers.

Everywhere, Chinese shops were rolling down their shutters. Du kept his word: foreigners found the New World inexplicably closed for several evenings in a row. During the daytime, the tramways and buses were almost empty. Electricity was repeatedly cut off, and telephone employees didn't show up. The Chinese students in the schools run by missionaries disappeared. Those at Saint John's University, the most upper-crust in the city, also marched in the streets. Soon the tellers' windows in Chinese banks closed, and even servants started telling their Western employers that they could not work. Dinners in town suffered; a breath of panic passed over the mistresses of houses in the international concession. The French were envied by the English, the Americans, and the Japanese: the Chinese protest spared France, which had kept its distance from the incidents. The merchants in the French concession closed their shops only one day, June 5. In the war of nerves that was heating up, the most irritating thing to foreign ears was no doubt the constant hum of the Chinese part of the city, where life was pursuing its normal course, contrasting with the fall in the activity in the concessions, those suddenly besieged citadels.

LI LISAN SPENT THESE DAYS RUNNING FROM MEETINGS TO DEMONstrations, punctuated by long sessions of consultation with the representatives of the Chamber of Commerce, the delegates of the Kuomintang, and Du's "sworn brothers." Like them, he was traveling around the city in a large automobile driven by a chauffeur and surrounded by bodyguards standing on the running boards, big men who had been made available to him. A federation of organizations of workers, merchants, and students was founded, bringing together under one umbrella everything in Shanghai that counted in the way of corporations and popular associations coming from the most diverse places. The movement was determined to retain a peaceful character. Li prohibited any act of revenge against foreigners. The strike's goal was to hinder their activities and their supplies, while minimizing the difficulties for the entrepreneurs and the Chinese population.

Nervousness was growing among the Westerners and the Japanese. The phantom of the Boxer Rebellion, the war that had inaugurated the century by launching the masses against the concessions, hung over the city. The Volunteers, a group of militiamen consisting chiefly of White Russians, went back into service and made an increasing number of armed patrols through the streets, often venturing into the Chinese zone. A curfew was imposed after eight in the evening. Gunboats sent as reinforcements were anchored in the port, while Japanese and American marines landed and took up positions at intersections. Chinese were forbidden to go into Nanking Street and the vital zones in the concessions, and they were subjected to searches. Foreign troops took over Shangda, the Red university, and all other institutions of higher education were also closed. On June 12, a dozen British police, accompanied by two hundred Japanese and American marines, went into the Chinese zone aboard armored vehicles and arrested a few students. Almost everywhere, incidents occurred during the almost daily roundups.

At night, these roundups were often deadly. The police in the concessions opened fire at the slightest sign of rebellion. By the end of June, there had been sixty deaths and more than three hundred arrests.

The whole country was in the grip of a gigantic convulsion. On June 19, a strike in sympathy with Shanghai was begun in Hong Kong. On June 23, a demonstration brought to Canton several thousand students, workers, and cadets from the Whampoa Military Academy, where Soviet instructors had for the past year been training the officers of the Kuomintang's Nationalist army. When the procession reached the Shakee Bridge, British and French police on the other side of the canal that separated the Chinese part of the city from the international concession on the little island of Shameen opened fire with machine guns. There were 42 dead and 117 wounded. The response was a long exodus of longshoremen and factory and mill workers, more than a hundred thousand of whom left Hong Kong for Canton, paralyzing the British port for eighteen months.

The French and Americans distanced themselves from London, which they regarded as dangerously inclined to go all the way. Germany, which had lost all its rights in China, discreetly sympathized with the new Chinese patriotism. In Moscow, *Pravda* saluted the "formidable anti-imperialist mobilization of the Chinese workers" and "the indefectible united front" formed between the Communists and the Nationalists.

But in Shanghai, the movement was crumbling. Li sensed that the merchants were hesitating. None of the conditions for the resumption of work had been accepted. The British were not moving an inch. The Chinese Chamber of Commerce, which wanted to reduce the movement's demands, was already talking about negotiating the rehiring of the strikers, without sanctions, by the foreign enterprises. Li tried desperately to maintain the fragile unity, but on June 26, the merchants went back to work. They had saved face by accepting the conditions Li had fought for: the continuation of the boycott on British and Japanese products and contributions to the strike fund. The students left on vacation, except for those from Shangda, who had moved into the shacks in the Chinese zone and were more active than ever.

On July 6, the Westerners cut off the electricity to the Chinese factories. The blow was heavy: tens of thousands of workers were thrown into the street, joining the two hundred thousand strikers. Funds were beginning to run short, and Chinese businessmen had to be forced to make their contributions. The strikers were now getting only twenty cents a day, as compared with almost double that amount in June. Soup kitchens were set up in working-class neighborhoods, and whole families crowded into them.

The strike held out all through July. Li initiated the move back to work by letting it be known that work could resume in the factories whose management satisfied the workers' demands. The British and the Japanese were informed; a line was thus thrown out to them. On July 12, the Japanese employers, with the representatives of NWK at their head, agreed that the two foremen responsible for the death of Gu Zhengshong should be brought back to China to stand trial. The family was to receive ten thousand Chinese dollars in compensation. Bearing arms would be prohibited in the mills and factories. As for the labor unions, they would be recognized as soon as the Chinese government published a law to this effect.

The workers hesitated and dissension appeared. In Djabei, at the offices of the General Labor Union, where Li had set up his headquarters, he was warned that death threats had been made against him. The police in the international concession were beginning to take a keen interest in him. So was Du. The head of the Green Society had realized that the Communists were drawing great benefits from the movement: the little people of Shanghai now regarded them with respect and liking. The General Labor Union, with more than two hundred thousand members, covered the whole city and drained off considerable amounts of money. But its head had strange and very inflexible ideas. Du had different ideas, in particular regarding labor unions. The Kuomintang, for its part, was divided between its left wing, which worked hand in hand with the Communists, and its right wing, which distrusted them and did not appreciate their competition.

On Saturday, August 22, Li was in his office on the Baoshan road when someone came in to tell him that a certain Zhao Zhonghua was asking to see him. It was still early and the building was half-deserted. Li vaguely recalled this union activist, who had not been seen for some time. The man came in, and after a few marks of fulsome respect, he launched into confused remarks from which it emerged that he had committed unsuspected errors. While he was speaking, his eyes, straying from Li, seemed irresistibly attracted to the window. A sixth sense alerted Li to the danger. He leaped to the window, where he saw groups of people he didn't know moving slowly toward the building. By their poorly hidden clubs and the expressions on their faces, he was easily able to recognize lumpen, toughs and killers from the favorite haunts of the Green Society. Sometimes they made excellent Communists. And they were always dangerous. Li hurried to ask Liu Shaoqi to summon the workers' guard. Shaoqi hardly had time to leave before about a hundred assailants, taking advantage of surprise, attacked, breaking windows and knocking down the door of the building. Li's only avenue of retreat was over the roofs; he slipped out a window and onto a terrace next door before disappearing into the saving jumble of Djabei's narrow streets. He reappeared an hour later, once the offices of the General Labor Union had been retaken after a memorable battle with clubs and knives, which miraculously left only two wounded. The building was wrecked, but the strike chest was intact. That same evening, at the head of a solemn delegation, Li broke with age-old Chinese courtesy and made a loud, resounding protest before the city's authorities.

But the time for retreat had come. On August 25, the workers returned to NWK and the last Japanese factories. On August 30, it was the turn of the British textile mills. Tramway workers and postmen in the international concession followed suit. In the presence of representatives of the Chamber of Commerce, the English agreed to pay the strikers' salaries, and especially to restore electricity to the Chinese factories. Servants went back to work in the concessions, those who had not been fired.

For everyone, the "cyclone of May 30" left an unforgettable memory. For months, in Yangshupu and Xiaoshadu, people argued over whether the whole thing had been properly conducted. But no one would have denied that it was well-founded. This time the foreigners had been really scared.

The ranks of the Communists had grown as never before. Li and his comrades no longer found themselves at the head of a small army of three thousand men, undisciplined and often illiterate, but exercising an irresistible attraction on talented minds, from workers to students and soon to artists as well.

Among the Communists, there was much discussion of whether the movement could be compared to what happened in Russia in 1905, whether revolution, especially the worldwide revolution, was close at hand or far away, whether the alliance with the Kuomintang was still justified, and often whether the Soviet advisers, the comrades sent from Moscow, really understood China.

One thing was certain: the bourgeoisie had been the first to give in to the foreigners. And whether they were Communists or not, everyone agreed with pride that it was the first time since 1919 that China had experienced such a jolt, such a blazing up of hope.

★　　★

IN THE CHANCELLERIES, BALANCE SHEETS WERE DRAWN UP. THE crisis had been expensive, even if it hadn't turned out too badly. Not only was China prey to a chronic anarchy among military rivals, but now it was infected in its turn by the Communist virus, and right in the middle of its flagship city, Shanghai. The question was whether this was a passing fancy or a fatal flu.

Li had come out of the turmoil deeply moved and transformed. At twenty-six, he was a recognized popular leader and owed his position solely to his total, unrelenting commitment. Carried along by the nationalist wave that had submerged Shanghai and was now splashing over China as a whole, he had pulled the tiger's mustache and had even ridden its back all through these days, trusting in some principles and a lot of intuition. His oratorical talent had convinced the city's richest businessmen to ally themselves with him for a time. He had crossed swords with them to delay the time when they would inevitably go their separate ways. On his arrival in Shanghai in 1924, a year earlier, the Communist Party was a tiny student group. It was now the most important labor party in the city, if not in the country. The one preferred by young people, the one most discussed among the intellectuals, the most effervescent one elsewhere.

Li raised the stakes again. Anyuan had engaged him to the revolution, Shanghai celebrated the wedding. If history responded so vigorously to his appeals, if the people stood up so heroically against its evils, wasn't it because the advent of a Red China, as Red as the young Russia of the soviets, was on the horizon?

The killers were waiting for him at the exit from the wedding ball. The name of Li Lisan was on everyone's lips, and his description was in every police station. His bodyguards no longer left him alone. They were four big, husky fellows from the port, expert in kung fu, quick with a knife, and crack shots, who watched over the young leader as they would have over a newborn child. All of them were former members of the Green Society; in the factories and the working-class quarters, relationships between the sworn brothers of the tong and the Communists were often cordial.

In Beijing, a man was impatiently waiting to make the acquaintance of this Li Lisan, whom everyone described as an unmatched agitator and organizer. Li Dazhao was the first to have introduced Marxism into China. A librarian at the University of Beijing, thirty-eight years old, he had discovered Marx in Japanese and translated Lenin into Chinese. Years afterward, he continued to enjoy great prestige, but in the capital there were still only a handful of Communists. The echo of the Shanghai uprising of May 30 had agitated the sleepy old capital for a few days, but the streets around the deserted Forbidden City had quickly resumed their normal activities.

Beijing had changed hands again, and the new master, Feng Yuxiang, a Christian general with a Herculean physique, was having his troops baptized with fire hoses. For the time being, he enjoyed the favor of Moscow, which was providing him with advisers and armaments in exchange for his tolerating its protégés.

At the end of August, Li took the train, by himself, to the capital, where he intended to plead the union's cause with the new authorities. He was especially curious to meet Li Dazhao; the man was an intellectual and moral authority on the level of Chen Duxiu, with whom he had founded the Party four years earlier.

Li's stay in Beijing quickly turned into a fiasco. Returning from a long discussion with Li Dazhao, Li noticed at the last minute three sinister-looking men waiting for him near the Celestial Peace Hotel. Instinctively, he took to his legs, the killers on his heels. He ran quickly, or once again he was lucky, and ended up finding refuge with Li Dazhao.

The next day, he was taken to the inconspicuous shack of a railroad worker in the Changxing neighborhood, not far from the train station. But he had hardly time to take a breath before the shack was in turn being watched by other threatening lumpen in rags. Like an accursed capital, Beijing, the City of the Emperors, was turning out to be a fatal trap for the excessively famous provincial. Li had to be evacuated in the middle of the night. Li Dazhao's son came to get him with a squad of railroad work-ers, who had Li get on the locomotive itself, which had been brought onto an isolated track especially for the occasion. As he shoveled in the coal, the grinning engineer turned to his clandestine passenger and told him his name was known even there. Later, dressed in new clothes, Li got back on the train. Li Dazhao's sons, at his side, had orders to take care of the hero until he was back in Shanghai.

The hunt was on. Soon, Li had to retreat to Hankow: Shanghai had also be-come too dangerous. An arrest warrant was waiting for him, delivered by the commandant of the place. Back in the city after a military campaign in the north, the satrap intended to set Shanghai's affairs in order. On September 18, the General Labor Union was outlawed and its offices closed by the army. Roundups and arrests were made in the workers' suburbs. Those who could went underground. The experience of the Green Society veterans, who were experts on the shadowy side of China and artists in secrecy, proved to be in-valuable. The Soviet consulate distributed its advice via its men, all of them used to carrying out missions in White zones. On Huangpu Road, the GPU's comrades operating on Chinese soil decided that it was high time to set up *tchons*, the Communist Party's combat units. It was lucky that the name Tschasti Osobovo Naznatchenia, the special units, sounded just right in Chi-nese. The *tchons* were required to show limitless devotion to the cause and be good shots. Every Russian Bolshevik knew it: the October Revolution, the taking of the Winter Palace—it was the *tchons* that had done it.

LI WAS HIDDEN FOR THREE DAYS WITH DAI LIFU, WHO BELONGED to an old family of Manchu aristocrats, and no longer needed to prove his respectability and liberal ideas. Some friends put about town the rumor that Li was ill and had been hospitalized. Policemen and soldiers lost pre-cious time searching every medical center in the city, looking for the "demon from Hunan."

Made up to look older and disguised as a peasant, Li gave them all the slip on board a steamer going up the Yangtze. Forty-eight hours later, he set down his bag on the dock at Hankow, feeling pleased and relieved to be back in the old river city. Not for long: the games of hide-and-seek with the police began again with renewed vigor. Li learned to live with his bag always packed and ready underneath his bed. A traveling salesman for the revolution, he was carrying with him a few breviaries, and lots of certainties. The banks of the Yangtze had been traveled by missionaries for ages. Recently, many of those who came from the West, Christians who sometimes knew what martyrdom was, had been dying.

For the time being, the warlord of the central region, the potentate in the belly of China, Wu Beifu, was not playing games with the Reds. He even liked to have their heads cut off with sabers, in public. But the local police were not fond of soldiers, who were too predatory for their taste. In exchange for money and good meals, Li's security was bought without too much difficulty. Policemen and informants warned him in advance when raids were to be made; the raids were then duly made and reported to superiors.

One day, the soldiers gave strict orders to the police to get Li Lisan dead or alive. The man from Shanghai was regularly observed in various parts of town, in semiclandestine meetings where he spoke with a contagious ardor. The policemen wrote up a detailed report describing the assassination of the fugitive in a nocturnal brawl outside a dive. Two days later, the Hankow daily paper announced the news: the agitator Li Lisan was dead. The brief article, which was a sort of disguised homage to Li, mentioned his role in the great strike of the miners in Anyuan and during the upheaval in Shanghai.

The news spread like wildfire. Workers' associations, dismayed, organized a solemn ceremony in memory of the dead hero, attended by several hundred guests.

"My second death!" Li somewhat pensively joked in his hiding place, holding the newspaper in his hand. Previously, in Anyuan, a gazette had prematurely sent him to his grave. During the strike, the whole city was filled with rumors about the thugs that were pursuing him. The news reached Paris, and the ears of the Chinese students. Chou En-lai immediately organized a memorial ceremony for the "valiant comrade" who had fallen under the savage blows of the "militarists."

Whether it was in Beijing, Shanghai, or Hankow, the air in China had become too unhealthy for Li. Two months later, in November 1925, he sailed away. This time, he boarded a Soviet freighter that had come from Vladivostok to go up the Yangtze.

Li had been chosen to represent China in Moscow at the plenary meeting of the Comintern, where the elite of the world revolution were gathering. The summit was followed by the meeting of the Profintern, the Communist International of Labor Unions. Borodin, from Canton, had approved the choice of Li Lisan, the young genius of the terrain.

Li boarded the freighter with Cai Hesen, with whom he had shared the adventure in France right up to the explusion from Lyons, the boat from Marseilles, and the triumphal return to Shanghai. Cai, with whom he had laboriously deciphered *L'Humanité,* dictionary in hand, in Montargis. Since then, this man from Hunan with the sparkling eyes and the erudite verve, a fine writer and a clever politician, had been directing the party's weekly newspaper, *Avant-garde.* Passionately interested in theory, he proved to be a talented propagandist, and was one of the earliest leaders, a member of the first circle. Li, ten years younger than Cai, liked to tease, not without respect, this bookish man with little inclination to participate in street battles.

The two men left with their female companions. Xiang Jingyu was the only woman on the Central Committee. Slender and rather pretty, she had also been part of the group in France. There she had discovered, along with Cai, love and revolution. In Shanghai, she had turned out to be a very talented agitator. One of the instigators of the strike, she had brought things to a head in the Nanyang cigarette factory. Next, she had created the first women's column, which was very popular, in the major nationalist daily paper, *Minguo.* But the couple was not getting along well; Xiang, who was temperamental, had just gotten out of an overt love affair with another important Communist leader in Shanghai, Peng Shuzhi. The trip to Moscow was to some extent a trial of reconciliation with Cai.

Li Yichun, for her part, was rediscovering Li Lisan. She had given up hope of leading a normal life with this man who disappeared so often, without explaining, and often without even saying when he would be back. The three-week trip to Moscow seemed to them an infinitely long lover's idyll. Free union was not an empty expression; it had a price: their child, at the age of three months, had to be entrusted to family members. The revolution recognized neither fathers nor mothers.

However, on board the old freighter that was carrying them out to sea, toward the "homeland of the soviets," the four of them were caught up in a strange, intimate fever at the idea that they would once again be treading that mysterious earth whose name flashed like a beacon, the coded message of a new hope.

The Russians. They had heard them discussed at length by the hundreds of young Chinese who had already spent time in Moscow, living in the dark and shabby dormitories of the Communist University of the Far East, at the corner of Pushkin Boulevard and the Tverskaia. There, for the past four years, Russian Bolsheviks had been fabricating little soldiers and generals for the Chinese revolution. The accounts of those who came back from Moscow were enthusiastic or reserved, but they all agreed on one point: the food, in this holy city, was not only inedible but scanty.

IN THE EVENING, AS HONORED PASSENGERS, THE TWO COUPLES were invited to dine in the officers' quarters, where they made the acquaintance of the person in charge; the commissar was not in uniform and looked like an ordinary sailor. But the captain, seated next to him, seemed very worried and listened to him respectfully, nodding his head. The discussion, carried on through an interpreter, a young student of Russian from Shanghai, grew animated when the political commissar, opening a bottle of vodka, mentioned that the freighter did not always carry mineral ore alone, but also and often machine guns, and even their Soviet crews, who were on their way to China. A few toasts later, the commissar lifted his glass to the revolution and the beauty of the two blushing young women.

The passengers were greatly disappointed when the captain told them that the boat would not stop at Nagasaki; they were in a hurry, and he had to get back to Vladivostok as soon as possible. Li had dreamed of having a glimpse of Japan, that enigma for China, the insular and insolent neighbor that had been the master of modernity in Asia for the past half century.

In Vladivostok, the formalities were handled without delay. The pass delivered by Borodin had a rapid effect on the officers of the Red Army and the GPU who controlled, without any leniency whatever, access to Soviet territory.

THE NEXT DAY, THE TWO COUPLES BOARDED THE TRANS-SIBERIAN Railroad for the longest railway journey in the world: eleven long days through Siberia before finally seeing, as they crossed the Urals, the first distinctive signs of civilization. At the end of December, their eyes riveted on the train compartment's frosted windows, after passing through Irkutsk they saw hardly anything but endless forests covered with snow, with a scattering of sleepy *izbas* that immediately vanished from sight. Five thousand miles later, the heavy locomotive, draped with red flags, had finally stopped, with a sound of squeaking axles, in Moscow, safe and sound.

There, still feeling the rhythm of the bogies, they were thrown into a whirlwind of meetings, guided visits, and various kinds of ceremonies.

Before panels of hardened veterans of the revolution, Li had to recount over and over the movement of May 30, as it was henceforth called. The members of the Comintern, mostly Europeans, listened to this Asian with some curiosity, despite the hesitations of his interpreter. According to Li, matters in China were more complicated than elsewhere, but one thing seemed clear: the revolutionary question had now been raised in China, and this gave the semicolonial country a quasi-official existence.

Moving from committees to subcommittees, Li learned to manipulate the dialectic of the International, putting his heart into it in order to develop the party line, the result of a subtle alchemy between alliances with the national bourgeoisie and the workers to be organized, the peasants to be made to revolt, a communist party to be Bolshevized, and an army to be found. Not to mention finances and logistics.

Moscow was indeed, no doubt about it, the headquarters of the worldwide revolution. Strolling through this Western city's icy streets full of muddy snow, Li, in his rare moments of leisure, sought in vain to find in it the charm of Paris. However, the city was shaking itself and the first workers' towns had appeared. Four- or five-story, blocky buildings, thrown up in a hurry, with rough facades, like those of the neighboring factories. In them, the first Soviets were piled up in tiny apartments, but for the first time they had running water and toilets, while in the collective kitchens people kept a sharp eye on their family's store of potatoes.

Shiny new buses moved about on the boulevards, Leylands that had come straight from London and Renault taxicabs assembled in Boulogne-Billancourt. Two years earlier, before he died, Lenin had made fun of these capitalists and invited them to come in and help rebuild the exhausted country, swearing that in doing so they were braiding the rope that would someday be used to hang them. But the display windows in the GUM store had taken shape, and in the Sukharevki market the peasants from around Moscow were selling well and at high prices, under the interested eyes of the *nepmen,* the ostentatious nouveaux riches, and the militiamen on duty.

In the evening, the lobbies and rooms in the Hotel Lux, on the Tverskaia, a stone's throw from the Kremlin, were humming with delegations from France, Germany, Italy, Great Britain, and Japan. As members of the Comintern listened to the latest jokes circulating in this Tower of Babel, their raucous laughter resounded under the faded stucco and Roman marble columns of the old hotel, which had been converted into a dormitory for professional revolutionaries. A French delegate told how old Riazanov, the very abrupt director of the Marx-Engels Institute, had recently received passionate letters from an admirer, maliciously signed "Jenny," the name of Marx's wife. Titillated, the old man, despite his venerable age, was looking for the mysterious Comintern member who was so fond of him. Jenny was none other than one of the French delegates with a facetious sense of humor, it was whispered. A Polish delegate imitated the way his compatriot Piatnitsky, the Comintern's very stingy administrative secretary, who was inflexible regarding bills for expenses and a sworn enemy of alcohol, had fallen flat on his face one morning as he came out of his room into the hotel corridor. On the threshold of his door, tipsy members of the Comintern had treacherously left rows of empty vodka bottles, along with the bill.

But a few steps from the Lux, in the upper floors of the big apartment building on the Manezh Square, at the corner of Mokhovaia Street, the sanctuary of the International was humming with rumors about Lenin's successor. Things seemed to be going sour. The heirs had just attacked each other viciously under the chandeliers of the Kremlin, at the Fifth Bolshevist Party Congress, which had just ended when Li arrived in town. For months, the victors of October 1917 had been throwing themselves at the opportunist of left or right, depending on whether they leaned toward Stalin or Trotsky. The question was whether Russia should set out alone toward socialism, or instead stoke the fires of worldwide revolution. Or again, whether the alliance with capitalism was to continue, or whether they still had to deal with the peasants. The Zinoviev-Kamenev-Stalin troika wasn't getting along; the Georgian was making his moves on the chessboard while placidly waiting for his time to come. Trotsky, the military leader of October, decided against a second coup d'état in order to save the first one, and retired to his Olympus.

The muffled echoes of the battle were arousing curiosity and perplexity in the Comintern's phalanx. The Chinese section, like the others, had to examine the problem. Li was quickly reassured: the revolution was retreating in Europe, and was no doubt vacillating in Moscow, but no one denied that it was moving forward in China. "It's a matter of cycles!" Manouilski, a Ukrainian with a mustache and lively eyes who was head of the Comintern's executive committee and directed Russian diplomacy as if he were foreign minister, kept repeating. Familiar and jocular, Ma-nou, as the Chinese delegates called him, had taken a liking to Li Lisan: he was pleased by the revolutionary stature of this Asian. However, he found Chinese issues extremely confusing, and so he had entrusted this subject to his friend Borodin, his proconsul in Canton.

In Italy, the Communists had emerged defeated from the duel with the Fascists. The Blue Shirts and the Blackshirts paraded in triumph through Rome. In Berlin, London, and Paris, workers had put off the revolution until later on. Everywhere the old quarrel between reformers and revolutionaries, between socialists and Bolsheviks, had resurfaced and was raging. Punches, insults, and expulsions punctuated the fight, to the affected applause of the European intelligentsia.

Li had fewer worries. Russian affairs were certainly important, but difficult to decipher. He had come to Moscow borne on a revolutionary wave, a real one, and he knew somehow that it would not be the last one.

Timidly, he exchanged a few words with the French delegation, but interpreters were rare and his memories of French distant. Nonetheless, he thought he understood that the French labor union movement was still divided. Marrane, the head of the French delegation, was wide-eyed as Li told him, with many gestures, that he had fought his first battles in the forges owned by the Schneider family.

Manouilski said to himself that Li would be a good man to send to Amsterdam. That was where the Communist International of Labor Unions, the Profintern, had its headquarters, and they needed experienced leaders. The man seemed completely burned out in China. In Europe, he could still be useful: what police force would suspect that a Chinese was working for the Comintern?

Li refused. The offer didn't appeal to him at all. The very idea of a desk job horrified him. As tactfully as he could, he emphasized his lack of qualifications for the position, without concealing his desire to return to China. Back there, he intended to pursue what was for him his mission from now on. As for the police who were after him, he'd take care of them himself.

The leaders left it there, and in April 1926, Li got back on the train at the Kursk station, headed for Vladivostok this time. His friend Cai had remained in Moscow to fill out the Chinese delegation and to perfect his knowledge of Marxism.

Li had seen little of the country of the soviets during these three months. But he liked the virile, rather rough fraternity that still emanated from the members of the Comintern, guided by their handful of revolutionary celebrities. He enjoyed the passion shared among people coming from such different backgrounds, and savored the taste of resolute decision that always concluded the hand-to-hand battles of indefatigable dialecticians that enlivened these weeks of revolutionary forums. He had raised his hand for or against many resolutions, convinced each time that he was tipping the delicate balance of the revolution. The question of the Trotskyists had been the occasion for much talk, but it hardly mattered to him: like most of the Chinese delegates, he found the whole business too

Russian and hoped for a compromise between the heirs of October. Moved, he had gone with the crowd to Red Square for the ceremony of January 21, 1926, on the second anniversary of Lenin's death. The misery of the Russians, which nothing could conceal, he found rather reassuring: the country of the soviets was poor, but China was still poorer. But the Chinese ate better all the same, between one famine and the next.

Too bad for Marx: Europe was rich, but not revolutionary. It was time to turn to the Orient, where the German's predictions, with the help of the spirit of Lenin, were more likely to pass the test of history.

In his bag, Li was bringing a new treasure back to China: the *political line,* one of those diamonds of doctrinal purity long polished in the fires of dialectics and polemics, the holy grail of revolutionary miracles. Of all the "isms" Li had learned to distinguish, his favorite was internationalism, a faith discovered in France. He was leaving Moscow baptized and confirmed. The idea that China shared such a long border with the country of the comrades was almost sweet.

However, thousands of miles after leaving Moscow, neither the frozen monotony of the Siberian forest nor the endless rocking of the rails was able to calm an unfamiliar kind of pain in Li's breast. Li Yichun was not going on this trip with him. She wouldn't ever go on one again, at least not with him: she had fallen into the arms of Cai. Li's friend and comrade had failed to reconcile with his wife, but did not miss the opportunity to start a new love affair. Li Yichun, who liked romantics, had left Li Lisan for a reason similar to the one that had made her say yes to him four years earlier, abandoning forever her first husband. The child she'd had with Li was safe in the countryside, with his grandparents. In Moscow, the couple's final interactions, before his departure, had been difficult. Li Lisan subscribed to the liberation of women, free union, and free love. He found it more difficult to understand that his lover had left him for another man.

On the boat sailing for Shanghai, he looked for the last time at the cliffs of Vladivostok, thinking of the Chinese verses about great meetings on the road, the "great woven braid of destinies," before giving up his pain to the muffled song of the ship's propellers.

# 6

Shanghai was waiting for Li, proud and restive, buzzing with countless stormy rumors, vague conspiracies, and murderous nights. In the morning, the police auxiliaries picked up the bodies of foremen that had been left lying in the streets of Djabei or Putong, stabbed with avenging knives or shot point-blank with pistols by mysterious workers' squads. Dozens of strikes were going on in the city, whose workers were victorious almost half the time. Some of them demanded the suppression of corporal punishment or the dismissal of brutal foremen; others asked that apprentices be paid salaries, or that women giving birth be allotted a month's paid leave. An increase in food allowances was always unanimously supported. Sometimes a factory went on strike in order to obtain the liberation of workers who had been imprisoned. The General Labor Union was forbidden, and its activists were in Shanghai's prisons. Li Lisan's chief adjutant, Liu Hua, the frail student who'd become a teacher in the first workers' club, had been executed after his arrest. But a year after May 30, 1925, the movement's shock wave retained its power, and the mood in Shanghai was more rebellious than ever.

Li had no sooner resumed the infernal round of clandestine meetings than he escaped to Canton for a few days. There he was expected at the Third National Labor Congress, the one that was to give birth to the first pan-Chinese labor union, the cherished dream of fighters for the cause.

An honored guest on the main podium, Chiang Kai-shek, the young Nationalist leader, had just had himself declared generalissimo. At thirty-eight, he had eliminated, by a masterstroke, all the claimants to Sun Yat-sen's succession. Before a virulent cancer killed him in Beijing in March 1925, the father of the republic had pinned all his hopes on the Northern Expedition, the *Beifa:* the reconquest of the country, from Canton, and the subjugation of the warlords. Twelve months later, the Nationalist army, newly emerged from the barracks of the southern capital and trained by Bolshevik officers from Moscow, had a leader. Borodin and Galen (Vassily Blücher) were fully committed to Chiang. On the banks of the Pearl River, the young officers at the Whampoa Military Academy were eager to fight it out with the satraps who were bleeding the country. And then, perhaps, they would drive the English, the Japanese, and the French out of the empire.

On the platform, the generalissimo presented himself in uniform before the assembly of five hundred delegates. Many of them were tough cookies, he said, like their *shun li,* their younger brother. His modesty concealed an infinite mistrust of his Communist allies. He did homage to headquarters, the Kuomintang. In passing, he mentioned coolly that "the workers and peasants were already able to fight imperialism with their own forces, without having to count on the army," the army that he was soon to send on campaign. He reassured his audience by ending his speech by raising his fist and shouting, "Long live worldwide revolution!"

Li, like many of his comrades, thought it was high time the Communists regained their freedom and their flag. This alliance with the Kuomintang was absorbing a great deal of their energy. Thanks to the Communists, this bourgeois party now had a national popular basis. However, it contained a great many declared, powerful enemies of the Reds and a Russian-style venture. But Borodin's orders were categorical:

the alliance must be prevented from collapsing, at any cost. Only a united front could inflict blows on the adversary, whether Chinese or English. On the Kremlin's agenda, China's place was designated: "For the time being, the Communists must serve as the Kuomintang's coolies," Borodin kept repeating.

Li was elected to the leadership of the pan-Chinese Federation of Labor Unions, where he assisted a forty-five year old sailor, Su Zhaozheng, who had just joined the Communists. This man, who was from Canton, had sailed all over the world on the vessels of European shipowners. He had been involved in all the actions against the Manchus, alongside Sun Yat-sen, before starting dreaded strikes in the port of Hong Kong. He had humiliated even London's Foreign Office and Admiralty. The union claimed to have more than a million members, a third of the Chinese proletariat. Many of them dreamed only of taking up arms, so many blows were falling on them.

One in Canton, the other in Shanghai, the Su Zhaozheng–Li Lisan tandem had the effect of nearly doubling the number of strikes in the following months. The first anniversary of May 30, 1925, was celebrated by new strikes, waves of pamphlets handed out at city intersections, and a few attempted demonstrations, which were quickly dispersed.

At the same time, Li Lisan had to be protected: there was still a price on his head. The "prestidigitator," Gu Shunzhang, a specialist in undercover techniques, the head of the workers' squads, had a brilliant idea all his own: they would invent a false Li Lisan, a worker chosen for his resemblance to the true Li, a double to throw the police off the track. The stratagem worked marvelously, and Li was able to attend real meetings, half clandestine, while the double was making brief appearances in public here and there, surrounded by comrades and under the admiring eyes of the people of Shanghai. They thought they were seeing their hero of the preceding summer, and were delighted to see the police henchmen of Sun Zhuanfeng, the military potentate of the city, taunted in this way.

Li operated in close teamwork with Chou En-lai and Liu Shaoqi. Chou, after being in Paris and Berlin, had gone to Moscow for further political training. The Comintern had then sent him to Canton, where he had served as the political commissar at the Whampoa Military Academy before coming to Shanghai to help run the Party.

Before the end of the summer, the powers decided that it was time to make a gesture to calm the agitation: for the past year, with ups and downs, it had been going on almost incessantly. In the concessions, the atmosphere was oppressive. Barbed wire and *chevaux de frise* (barricades) had disappeared from the entry points, but women and children had often stayed in the country. At the end of August, the representatives of London, Paris, Tokyo, and Washington magnanimously announced that China would soon recover its sovereignty over the city's joint court. In so doing, they were agreeing to one of the thirteen demands of the May 30th Movement. Too little and too late, the gesture passed almost unnoticed. China had turned its eyes elsewhere, toward the south.

In July 1926, the Nationalist army's columns set out from Canton on the Northern Expedition. The reconquest had begun. Its objective was to take the Yangtze valley, some six hundred miles to the north, halfway to Beijing, and to drive out the satraps, who would not fail to try to bar their way as they advanced. Then, to hold the river basin, the femoral artery that divided the country into east and west. Conquering Wuhan, Nanking, and Shanghai was half the job; the other half was to take northern China and Beijing.

In a few weeks, the expedition began to look like a triumphal march. Even before the arrival of the republican soldiers, towns and villages often rose up, while railroad workers and telegraph operators sabotaged the lines of communication of the local military, who were roundly cursed for their cruel stupidity. Agitators infiltrated in small units preceded the troops and supervised the uprisings. The technique was familiar to the Soviet officers accompanying the expedition: they had all fought in the Russian civil war. The ease with which they advanced surprised them, however. Very inferior in numbers, less well equipped, the expedition's hundred thousand men made up for their deficiencies by their discipline and their conviction. Many students had donned uniforms and marched alongside peasants, craftsmen, railroad workers, and coolies. Along the way, the miners of Anyuan, the future military elite, put down their picks and joined the ranks of the Nationalist army by the hundreds, providing it with precious information about the traps laid in the region. Wu Beifu's troops, fighters feared by the civil population, dispersed even before the first shots were fired. *The Art of War,* a Chinese classic taught even in the Whampoa Military Academy, significantly expanded the chapter titled "The Enemy Changes Sides": as the republican columns advanced, soldiers who had recently signed up suddenly discovered that they were patriots at heart. They voted as a group, along with their officers, to raise the blue flag bearing a white sun, the standard of the Canton government. The most belligerent among them were subjected to brief but precise artillery fire on the part of Soviet crews. They soon retreated, leaving behind them modern equipment made in Europe.

Things moved so quickly that Changsha, the capital of Hunan, fell on July 11, without a shot having been fired, as a result of treachery on the part of one of Wu Beifu's lieutenants. The army then divided into three columns; two headed for the north and Wuhan, while the other, commanded by Chiang Kai-shek, headed northeast, toward Shanghai.

In August, after fierce fighting, the road to the Yangtze was opened, and the troops arrived at the gates of Wuhan, the function of three river cities: Hankow and Hanyang fell on September 7; Wuchang, sheltered by its thick walls, resisted for a whole month despite a regular siege and several assaults.

The Northern Expedition was beginning under good auspices. It remained for Chiang Kai-shek's column, which had stayed farther to the south, to seize Shanghai. The generalissimo was taking his time.

# 7

Li traveled to Hankow by riverboat. Coming from Shanghai, he found the old city still recovering from the shock of its liberation. The blue flag flew everywhere in the streets. From the other side of the Yangtze, there was sporadic cannon fire: Wuchang was still holding out. The population was unsure about the victory: the fluidity of the civil war that went on and on, with its ebb and flow of armies, led it to be prudent.

As soon as Hankow had been taken, the Communist leadership, confronted by an entirely new situation, had sent Li in; the Shanghai-Canton-Wuhan triangle, the new tripod of the revolution, no longer had many secrets for him. He had given up a clandestine life in hideouts in the cellars and attics of the Paris of the Orient to participate in the establishment of a revolutionary order in a half-conquered, half-liberated city.

On October 10, 1926, Wuchang finally fell. Wuhan, with

its three reunited cities, became the new capital of the Chinese revolution, replacing Shanghai and Canton in that role. The whole political staff, including the Soviets, moved from Canton to the new provincial seat of the republican government, in the center of the country.

But Chiang Kai-shek, its leader, seemed to be reluctant to join in. He set up shop far from Wuhan, in Nanchang, the capital of Jiangxi, where he was completing his plan for an offensive to take Shanghai. He had observed from a distance the taking of Wuhan, and the Soviets were beginning to annoy him. These foreigners were clearly becoming too important in Chinese affairs, he let it be known. On the military level, the Bolshevik officers were handing out orders to the Chinese, often on their own authority; on the political level, by bringing the Communists into the Kuomintang, they had made it into a party that was increasingly escaping his control. In Wuhan, the Kuomintang's moderate left was even prepared to give the Communists two ministries in the provisional government.

When he was invited to visit the new capital, Chiang declined the offer. In Wuhan, Borodin, perplexed, frowned and drew up a plan for bolshevizing the republican officers. The idea was simple: execute all those who were hostile to the Reds, and win over those who were lukewarm. Chiang learned about it and accelerated his preparations for taking Shanghai. Soon he was engaged in secret negotiations with the Green Society and Du Yuesheng, who was a buddy of his, as well as with a few of the city's bankers who were well disposed toward him.

In the meantime, Wuhan was becoming very Red. Li was there, promoting the notion that workers ought to participate directly in the management of mills and factories. In fact, that was the only way to make them go back to work, since the strike was more or less general and spontaneous. Manifestos, petitions, and pamphlets abounded in countless public meetings. The fear that killers would suddenly appear had disappeared. Assemblies to which whole families flocked in a joyous disorder demanded a workday of ten hours rather than fourteen or even sixteen. It was proposed that workers should have twenty-four hours of rest per week and a minimum salary of thirteen Chinese dollars a month. The question of weekly rest led to a number of polemical exchanges. Some people, who preached moderation, suggested that one day of rest every two weeks would be enough. Others, more numerous, didn't understand this idea of stopping work, even for a single day, except for the New Year.

Li was a virtuoso orator, and the crowds loved what he said. It was as much a matter of dignity as one of face, or of the number of hours of work and the strength that had to be recovered in order to go back to it.

Wuhan soon formed its own General Labor Union, of which Li was immediately elected vice president, alongside a former worker at the Hanyang arsenal, Xiang Zhongfa, a hero of the railroad strike who had escaped Wu Beifu's sabers.

At the end of December, the union, the city's hotbed, claimed three hundred thousand members, bringing together all Wuhan's activists, sworn brothers of the tongs, anarchists, small groups of declared patriots, and idle youths.

The mood became insolent. Since they couldn't lay hands on the bosses, a few middle-management types and two or three foremen who were hated more than the others were led through the streets under a hail of gibes, dressed in outsized top hats, a kind of headgear that resembled the one worn by Westerners in the concession and that never failed to astonish the Chinese.

TWENTY-FOUR BRITISH, AMERICAN, AND JAPANESE GUNBOATS FULL of marines began to pour into the port of Hankow, having been sent up from Shanghai. Anchored on the Yangtze at a certain distance, they nonchalantly pointed their cannons toward the Chinese city, while in the officers' quarters telexes were coming in from the admiralties asking that plans be drawn up for the immediate evacuation of women and children: the Chinese mob had these unpredictable "fits." The missionaries along the banks of the great river had already had fatal experiences with these fits.

Telegrams were also being exchanged by Borodin and the leaders of the Comintern in Moscow. Stalin's and Manouilski's orders were still categorical: "*No soviets in Wuhan!* The time for a Bolshevist revolution has not yet come!" Li and the Chinese Communist leaders were asked to moderate popular enthusiasm.

At the same time, Borodin was trying to cripple Chiang Kai-shek. Moscow's proconsul wanted the general to yield to the party, which had control of the rifles. In the ranks of the republican army in Wuhan, the political commissars drew up lists of officers—the "Whampoa cadets"—to be "purged." The new republican capital was defying the generalissimo.

Of all the current slogans, the most popular was nonetheless the one that called for driving out foreigners. It was foreigners who had caused all the misfortunes that had struck the country for the past century. In front of assemblies, Li constantly demanded, as he had in Shanghai, the return of Chinese sovereignty over the concessions. The concession in Hankow consisted chiefly of Britons, by far the most arrogant of the imperialists. In Wuhan, in the teahouses, markets, and prostitutes' hotels, the events were the subject of lively discussions. The most clever drew a distinction between good foreigners, the Soviets and the Germans, and bad ones, the English first of all, who had seized part of the country. The Americans, who had no Chinese colony, surprised the Chinese by their naval and military activism on the Yangtze: their gunboats were as numerous as those of other countries.

On Monday, January 3, 1927, toward three in the afternoon, British soldiers on duty at the entrances to the concession suddenly noticed unusual movement on the square. From the adjacent streets there emerged a continuous flow of Chinese of all ages who gradually formed into little groups that turned their backs on the British. Soon it was a human wave, whose front lines were a few yards from the soldiers. Orders were given to assume combat positions, and messengers ran to report to the British consulate, a few hundred yards away.

Speakers harangued the crowd, which was beginning to sway back and forth. Cries were heard, then short tirades howled by a single voice, while the whole group made a dull clamor punctuated by a few shouted slogans. Li, in the middle of the crowd, was nervous. It was the first time that people here had demonstrated to demand the reestablishment of Chinese sovereignty over the concession. With him, in the crowd, were all the hard-liners from the General Labor Union and the Party's propaganda teams, but also merchants, students, families. The little people of Wuhan, crazy with curiosity since the liberation of the city, wouldn't fail to do something rash.

The messengers came running back, followed by reinforcements, and orders were shouted: "In position!" A few dozen young Britons and other subjects of His Majesty knelt down, their bayonets pointed at the crowd. A second line of soldiers stood behind them. But the officers, worried and perplexed, kept saying to each other: "Hold your fire!" The British lion was hesitating. The consul's orders were clear: they were not to shoot.

The confrontation lasted for long minutes, while the tension mounted. The crowd in front of the Hong Kong and Shanghai Banking Corporation building was now agitated by sudden movements and was literally touching the rifles. The clamor grew louder. The soldiers, frightened, made a few martial gestures, pointing their guns, making feints with their bayonets. An officer fired a pistol shot into the air, screaming, "Hold your fire!"

The bayonet blades cut twice into Chinese flesh, which bled heavily but not seriously. At the sight of blood, the crowd panicked, drawing back while the wounded people were taken away, amid agitation close to hysteria. The crowd then returned to shout insults at the front line of soldiers.

Li shouted in his turn. The British had their backs to the wall. Their gunboats on the river were the same ones that had opened heavy fire, four months earlier, on Wanxian, a large town upstream. From the ruins, the Chinese had recovered hundreds of dead and wounded. A lesson administered by the British Admiralty, in response to a few bursts of machine-gun fire suffered by a gunboat a few days earlier, during an evacuation of Westerners in danger.

The man of May 30, the hero of the black-faced miners of Anyuan, the man who had a price on his head everywhere, tried this time to calm the crowd. For his talents in feverish situations, Li had been called "the best speaker in the Party." Climbing onto a comrade's shoulders, he shouted out a diatribe against the imperialists' arrogance, turning the crowd's attention toward himself, giving a series of questions and replies in his hoarse, rasping voice that slowly calmed the fever.

Soon the soldiers retreated in order, their rifles still trained on the crowd, and took up positions behind sandbags and *chevaux de frise* (barbed-wire barriers) hurriedly placed at the entrances to the concession.

The face-off at a distance went on late into the evening, but people had passed from slogans to gibes. The cheek of people from Wuhan was famous, and the national repertory regarding foreigners was rich. All night, the city talked about the situation. The wounded had turned into fatalities, and their number grew larger as the night went on. The members of the General Labor Union deliberated until dawn.

BY NINE O'CLOCK THE NEXT MORNING, THE CROWD WAS BACK IN the same place, responding to an order passed along by thousands of mouths and ears. In no time, the *chevaux de frise* and sandbags had been removed and thrown aside. The British soldiers returned in a disorderly manner. After a moment of hesitation, as if surprised by its own audacity, the compact mass entered into the concession. Shouts and slogans resounded in the main street. After a few dozen yards, the excited crowd, delighted, completely absorbed in its jostling, slowed down. This was, after all, a Chinese street like any other. Stupefied, terrified by this violation of the rule of extraterritoriality, the Westerners—British, American, and German citizens—contemplated the advance of a native population. A German staggered, his shoulder lacerated by a knife. Windows were broken, shop displays overturned and immediately pillaged. But the whites the crowd met were subjected chiefly to insults and vengeful tirades. The order that Li kept repeating as he ran alongside the demonstration with the union men was that no blood, British or other, should be shed.

The procession arrived in front of the British Municipal Council building. There, accompanied by nervous or mocking shouts, the Union Jack was taken down while the Kuomintang's men at the foot of the flag-pole slowly raised the blue flag bearing a white sun, imposing a brief silence on the excited crowd.

The gunboats remained quiet.

At that moment, Li felt intuitively that an immense victory had been won. Raising his fist, intoxicated with daring, he joined the crowd in a long hurrah. The fight had been bitter and dangerous, and had succeeded at that cost.

Three weeks later, London gave in. In the British concession in Hankow, law and order were put back in the hands of the Chinese, without bloodshed. For the first time, the British lion was retreating, the Admiralty was giving up. Tired of fighting, the English were giving up territory they had conquered, as if strewing a first handful of confetti. Some five hundred women and children, His Majesty's subjects, were taken out to the gunboats; about a hundred Americans were also evacuated. The men gathered in the Asiatic Petroleum Company building on the docks, while waiting for the storm to pass and business to resume.

The news spread round the world. The newspapers had been reporting for weeks on the "madness on the Yangtze." They wrote at length about the "British loss of prestige." But in London, the British cabinet stood firm. The Foreign Office was categorical: after the gigantic wave of May 30, 1925, in Shanghai, this was no time for stupid firing into the crowd, but for a policy of conciliation.

From the people in Hankow, Li retained a cheeky expression he'd heard during those days, one he liked to use later on when speaking to crowds and in meetings: "The imperialists are paper tigers!" An orator's trick that always won over his audience.

Then the first reports from Shanghai arrived, announcing that the city was in revolt. On February 24, 1927, telexes were coming into Borodin's residence in Hankow, referring to fierce fighting between the workers' assault units, the *tchons,* and the troops of the warlord, Sun Zhuanfeng. The Comintern had sent its clandestine agents a few hundred old rifles and pistols. On February 25, Chou En-lai, panic-stricken, cabled that there was a massacre going on all over the city. The heads of dozens of comrades were strewn in the streets of Djabei, Nantao, and Putong or exhibited in cages hung from the street lamps. Death squads commanded by the northern satraps were using their sabers to kill passersby, at will. Chou reported that among the killers there were units of White Russians, the very sight of whom inspired fear. Terror had come over Shanghai. There was only way out of the massacre: Chou asked for authorization to put an end to the general strike.

Twenty miles from the city, the forward units of Chiang Kai-shek's army had not moved.

A month later, on March 22, Chou En-lai cabled once again from Shanghai: this time, the rebellion, the third one, was victorious! Only the White Russians were still resisting, in an armored train, near the North Station. The Westerners had barricaded themselves in their concessions, but were not intervening, officially, in this conflict between Chinese.

It was a few days before Li left Hankow to return to the liberated Pearl of the Orient. In Nanking, he'd taken leave of Voitinsky, Borodin's adjutant, and said farewell to Chen Yannian, the eldest son of the founder of the Party, Chen Duxiu. Sent on a mission to evaluate the situation in Shanghai, they were to finish their trip separately, for greater security.

Then the junk slipped away into the night, while Li listened, his eyes half-closed, still dazed by the clamor, to the imprecations of the old Yangtze boatman, who punctuated his remarks by spitting into the dark waters of the great river. Before long, he was ordered to put on a mandarin's garb, before setting foot on the docks. . . .

# 8

Li glanced at his watch for the hundredth time; it was almost midnight. In half an hour, he was going to attack at the head of his regiment, which consisted of hardly a thousand men. Around him, in the semidarkness of this summer night, the first of August 1927, twenty thousand soldiers were silently waiting under the stars, their weapons at their sides. In the distance, the dark shape of Nanchang could be seen, sleeping in the lazy loop of the Gan River. The old prefecture of Jiangxi had no idea what was about to happen. Tomorrow, if things went as planned, it would be the Communists' first capital. Long enough to cleanse themselves of the affront and to avenge the people who had died in Shanghai the preceding April.

Wearing his grayish-blue Kuomintang army officer's uniform, Li lifted his rifle, a heavy Russian model going back to the First World War. He had never fired a shot, and he wanted to go on the attack with this weapon, rather than with his Mauser, which he now always wore strapped to his thigh in its holster.

Nanchang! For two weeks, Li had repeatedly explained why it was necessary to take this city: to reply to Chiang Kai-shek, to his betrayal, to proclaim the revolutionaries' independence. After taking Nanchang, they would march victoriously toward the south, toward Canton, where the revolution would get a second wind.

In the three months since their crushing defeat at Chiang's hands in Shanghai, thousands of the Communists and their close or distant sympathizers had died—hanged, decapitated, shot, or buried alive—even in the smallest towns of the neighboring provinces. Their former ally's determination to subjugate them to the Nationalist banner had been pitiless. Borodin had had to leave China precipitously. Relying on little schemes, he had made errors all along the way. Moscow still couldn't get over the fact that its faithful ally Chiang, its favorite knight on the Chinese chessboard, had bitten the master's hand, while waiting to exterminate the master's servants.

In Shanghai, Li remained hidden for a week—a week of violence and terror that had elicited in him a deep, unfamiliar rift. Up to that point, in the firmament of ideas, the imperialists, both foreign and occupying, were in his view the absolute evil. But now a new general certainty had been imposed on him by the obvious fact of bloodshed, despite the widespread confusion that followed the massacre: in China, the class struggle was a civil war, one more war in addition to all those that had been fought since the fall of the Manchus. Chinese fighting Chinese, with an unparalleled ferocity, as if from the Celestial throne that had been empty for sixteen years, forgotten in the deserted Forbidden City, battered by the winds, a mysterious curse had fallen on the country. Or as if the lesson of the Taiping Rebellion, eighty years and 50 million deaths earlier, had proven to be completely useless. Stroking his rifle, Li remembered the words of the victor of the Russian civil war—Lenin's words—that the members of the Comintern repeated to each other while joking under the chandeliers of the Hotel Lux: Revolution is not a dinner party.

Below Nanchang's fortifications, the Communists had their backs to the wall that evening, and Li knew it. Of all the leaders of the revolution, he had the most rapidly understood that the battle for this city would be the first real one waged by the Communists in China. With this throw of the dice, they would finally win their freedom, ceasing to exist in the paternal shadow of the republicans, of the Kuomintang. Li had done everything he could to convince Chou En-lai and the others of this. Chou, who had escaped from Shanghai, had drawn from Li's idea a plan that seemed to hold together from a military point of view. Others had hesitated, worried about getting a green light from Moscow. Borodin's reply from Wuhan had come by telex: half fish, half fowl, the Comintern strongly urged moderation, without forbidding the action. Since April, the headquarters of the worldwide revolution had found it extremely difficult to follow the events in China. And especially to get to the bottom of them. Besso Lominadze, the twenty-eight-year-old Georgian who had succeeded Borodin, recommended prudence, without resolving anything.

In any case, Li didn't care about a *nyet* from Moscow. From the outset, he had not put much stock in the policy of cooperation with the Kuomintang. Russian ignorance of the rules of Chinese polities had cost the lives of too many good comrades. April in Shanghai, that bloody spring, had aroused a new fury in him.

Nothing was able to stop him: in two weeks, he had convinced the whole Communist leadership. First he had to rally his forces, including the troops faithful to the military leaders of the Northern Expedition. Around a city, if possible, where they would proclaim a political program. The ideal city was Nanchang, and no other. As for the program, they had to begin with the countryside, bring to heel the landowners and their militias, and impose a moratorium on farm rents until they could redistribute land to millions of poor people and bankrupt farmers. In the cities, they had to proclaim the eight-hour workday and a few pay increases. As for the rest, they'd have to see.

Since the revolution was still at an initial stage, they would take a broad view and continue to operate under the Kuomintang's banner—while waiting for the red flag, the only one that could raise the masses and to which a good half of the notables in the city would also rally. The *pronunciamento* would be made in the name of the father of the republic, Sun Yat-sen. His widow, a very beautiful woman of thirty-seven, was on the Communists' side and was outraged by the Shanghai massacre. Mme Soong Ch'ing-ling had broken publicly with Chiang Kai-shek, informing her future brother-in-law that she thought well of the Reds, those "ardent patriots."

LIKE HIS COMRADES, LI HAD SWORN THAT HE WAS NOT AFRAID TO die. He would go into battle without fail. He was prepared to stake everything on the assault, as he was on every assault. Afterward, if he survived, the venture would continue. To hell with prudence, in this land in turmoil: history would decide.

At half past midnight, as agreed, he received the order to attack. In a clatter of weapons, the troops, which had been given a pep talk, moved toward Nanchang. In a few minutes, they had reached the suburbs. Several bursts of gunfire broke out in the deserted streets, fired by the advance units. In the city, the troops commanded by He Long, Ye Ting, and Zhu De,* local generals who had gone over to the Communists, disarmed the garrison's three thousand men. Among men in the same army, that of the Kuomintang, it was quickly decided to negotiate rather than fight: the future was very uncertain.

In the morning, it was all over. The front committee, led by Chou En-lai and Li Lisan, wasted no time on victory banquets. They quickly decided to have a ceremony proclaiming the new revolutionary government. The population tried to figure out what was going on: Some Kuomintang armies had won a victory over other Kuomintang armies? The republicans were fighting among themselves now? Notables and workers' associations were quickly called together to listen to explanations. Chiang had betrayed the Kuomintang and the Communists were there to save the party, they said. The old people of Nanchang understood mainly that the future of the revolution and the country would be determined in their city. A few notables openly endorsed the Communists, others were prudently polite, while labor unionists, emerging from hiding, applauded.

A Revolutionary Committee was named to run things; its twenty-seven members brought together willy-nilly, more often on paper than in flesh and blood, the upper crust of the Chinese left in Shanghai, Wuhan, and Canton.

---

*After 1949, He Long and Zhu De were two of Mao's ten marshals. Ye Ting died earlier.

But this time they were flanked by military leaders, who were indispensable now that the revolution was taking the military route, straight toward epic.

On August 2, the people docilely attended the ceremony—a rather confused parade of troops—and listened, without understanding much, to speeches given for hours under a blazing sun, while little blue flags bearing white suns were handed out. Students and workers repeated a few slogans while Li warmed up the crowd with his speeches, though it hardly needed warming on such a hot August day.

The next day, Li, in charge of security, discovered a still more unknown aspect of the revolutionary epic: repression. In this prefecture of more than half a million people, lacerated by years of civil war, hatreds were strong and consciences often heavy. The chief of the local police and a few of his men, who had been in hiding since the entry of the troops, were flushed out along with a handful of leaders of the local tongs. After a quick trial, they were found guilty of having executed republican sympathizers and Communists in March, a wave of public assassinations that had bathed the city in blood.

Li himself led the firing squad. He knew how horribly so many of his comrades in Shanghai, Wuhan, and elsewhere had died. Accompanying the condemned men to the place of execution, he told himself that blood had a price and that scruples were no longer appropriate. When the officer turned to him, awaiting his order, after a moment he forced himself to bark *"Kai tsiang!"* ["Fire!"] in as martial a way as he could. For him, the sound of the shots echoed only the cries of his own martyrs, and he said to himself that the dead were avenged.

On the way back, he felt a century older. Revolutionary justice had been done. But the time when a dreaming adolescent in Hunan filled his school notebooks with poems was already so far away. . . .

Nanchang was no sooner taken than it had to be evacuated. The news was not good. A punitive expedition was already on its way to put down the rebels, coming from Tiujian, to the north, on the Yangtze. To the east, Chiang was massing his troops with the same intention. It was a tempting opportunity to have done with the old Communist allies. Within a few days, the city would be surrounded again, and for the Communists there was hardly any chance of winning by force of arms.

The Revolutionary Committee decided that its troops had to be preserved by undertaking a march of almost six hundred miles to the south, toward Canton. On August 5, a column of twenty-five thousand men left Nanchang, accompanied by hundreds of porters carrying heavy loads or pushing wheelbarrows on which were piled the odds and ends that accompany all exoduses. The soldiers had only thirteen thousand rifles and less than a dozen light cannons, and they had no assurance of being paid. But many of them were happy about this new maneuver; having been born in the province of Canton, they were returning to their native land, finally leaving these provinces where people spoke incomprehensible dialects.

The first day of marching was like a gigantic parade, a military shambles in which the troops, mixed with the civilians who were accompanying them, formed a compact mass stretching out over miles of dusty roads.

The notables who had decided to go along were in despair at not being able to find bearers for their palanquins. Along with the other civilians—anarchist teachers, radical craftsmen, Communist workers, and patriotic merchants—they got painful blisters on their feet after a few miles of walking. The soldiers, indefatigable marchers, soon left them behind. The heat was terrific, and only those with the most foresight opened parasols of oiled paper, while people began to worry about finding water. Too heavily loaded bags, which were becoming heavier and heavier, ended up abandoned by the side of the road.

In the evening, when they stopped for the night by the side of a river, Li and the other members of the Revolutionary Committee, harassed, lit a bonfire and burned all the useless castoffs and superfluous souvenirs. Watching the fire, they swore that they were thus demonstrating an iron determination. Afterward, they wondered whether it wouldn't have been smarter to keep all that stuff in order to trade it for food requisitioned for the immense column as it went on its way. Their provisions were meager, and their war chest insignificant.

On the following days, Li and his companions noticed that the villages they went through were practically deserted. Not being sure what to expect, the peasants preferred to leave when they found out that the troops were coming. As a result, morale began to suffer, and so did the numbers of the troops: at the morning roll call, desertions were making increasingly noticeable gaps in the ranks.

The column was broken into three parts, with an advance guard preceded by scouts who were to reconnoiter the cities and villages to be crossed. The reports were clear on one point: the local officials had all withdrawn before the arrival of the troops, for fear that they would be contaminated by this enormous Red virus on the move. So far as the others were concerned, poor peasants always referred the soldiers to a few other peasants who were less badly off than they were and who could provide them with food.

He Long's troops, very poorly disciplined, were accustomed to this sort of exercise. For years their officers had been following the young leader through the countryside around Hunan, where that hardened criminal, imitating Robin Hood more than Lenin, had built his legend. He Long, who had just turned thirty, traveled amid his men in a sedan chair, and feasted at dinner before going to sleep, always with a pistol under his pillow. A highwayman ever since he had killed a customs official at the age of sixteen, he was endowed with a rare military flair that had attracted attention in Canton, where he had been entrusted with the command of one of the elite units.

In the evening, he often invited Li, Zhang Guotao, or Chou En-lai to explain this communism he found so intriguing. He had long approved of taking from the rich to give to the poor. In his own way, he'd already taken a great deal and given a little of it to the poor. But to make that the banner of China as a whole! Listening late into the night around the campfire, perplexed or impressed by the brio of his comrades' demonstrations, he ended up agreeing with them.

The days went by, and the following days were even more difficult. The ragged troops, their throats parched under the blazing sun, crossed *li* after *li*,* hugging the rivers or laboring up the steep grades of the Tai Shan Mountains. Canton, like a mirage, was increasingly assuming the uncertain contours of a promised land. But the ordeal was forging ties, breathing a new realism into the group without its knowing it.

---

*The present Chinese mile. At the time, the *li* was equivalent to about six hundred yards.

★ ★

ON AUGUST 19, FIFTEEN DAYS AFTER IT HAD LEFT NANCHANG, THE cohort stopped and took up position at Ruijin; the advance unit's reconnaissance teams had sighted the first enemy formations. Massed at Huichang, less than twenty miles away, they had been sent there by the other Kuomintang, that of Chiang's republicans, in order to bar the expedition's way to the south.

In Moscow, *Pravda* incessantly praised the epic of this new "army of partisan workers and peasants" which, according to *Pravda,* was seeing the Chinese masses rise up as it moved along to drive out the British imperialists. Stalin silenced Trotsky by referring him to the Chinese comrades' revolutionary exploits, an exemplary proof that the Comintern's line was the right one.

On August 20, the torpor of the countryside around Huichang was broken by the first shots exchanged between the two armies. Clever plans had been drawn up by both sides, all of which failed. The Twentieth Army, commanded by He Long, was supposed to launch a frontal attack, while the Eleventh Army, under Ye Ting, was to go around the enemy and make a surprise attack on its right flank. In order to succeed, the maneuver required the two attacks to be made at the same time. But since they had no maps, the calculation of the distances to be covered was approximate at best: Ye Ting arrived late. He Long took the shock alone, and the first waves of the assault were cut to pieces by the Nationalists' machine guns. All the reserves soon had to be thrown into the battle to avoid a disaster. When Ye Ting finally made contact, he in turn was met by troops who held their ground. The enemy flank, solidly entrenched, inflicted severe losses on the attackers.

The battle quickly turned into a free-for-all. Between shots fired at each other from only a few yards apart, the opposing officers exchanged insults. Amid the fury, cries and weeping were sometimes heard; some of these officers knew each other, since most of them were cadets at Whampoa, the Canton military academy. Sitting on the same benches, united in a common dream, they had all listened to the advice given by the same Soviet instructors. This only made the fighting even more savage.

As darkness fell, after a final bout of hand-to-hand combat at the end of ten murderous hours of fighting, the advance stopped at the foot of Huichang's walls. The Nationalist troops retreated during the night.

THE COMMUNISTS BURIED THEIR DEAD WITH FULL HONORS, SOME five hundred men who would never see Canton again. Gritting his teeth and hiding his feelings as well as he could, Li counted the four hundred or so moaning wounded who had survived the machine-gun fire and who were now his responsibility. The few doctors accompanying the march were in despair at the magnitude of their task, the shortage of medical supplies, and the absence of nurses.

Li had not seen much of war before the assault on Nanchang. While he was already familiar with the crackling of gunfire, he had never participated in the bloodbaths that constitute real battlefields. Assigned to the general staff, he had avidly followed the development of operations, attentive to the military men's precise and vigorous language, before going toward the front lines to make use of his Mauser.

Late that evening, around the campfires, he listened to the officers and men, who were shattered by the violence of a battle such as they had never seen before, but who were proud of their victory. They agreed with Chou En-lai: an army had been born.

The next day, He Long, whose fidelity had been severely tested during the battle, pledged allegiance to the Communist Party. During a ceremony at Ruijin, in the presence of Zhang Guotao, Li Lisan, and Chou En-lai, the former criminal, a sworn brother of the Gelao tong and leader of the group, made a solemn oath to support the worldwide revolution. Tense and a little awkward, he also promised to do better in matters of discipline. After drinking many gulps of hot wine at the banquet that followed, he proposed a toast to the Red Army, which he had the pleasure of commanding, along with Ye Ting and Zhu De.

THE COLUMN RESTED FOR TWO WEEKS AT RUIJIN. ALMOST A THOU-sand women, having heard that men had gathered there, came to join them. Many of these were war widows who had come from the neighboring province of Fujian to escape the poverty there. Country women with big feet, because their feet had not been bound during their child-hoods in order to increase their dowries. They volunteered to carry the wounded on makeshift stretchers, as well as the army's odds and ends. Their arrival raised the men's morale.

The expedition resumed its march to the south, more determined than ever to seize Shaoju and Shantou, on the coast, the last obstacles on the road to Canton. The first group to leave Ruijin was made up of the best combat units; its task was to secure the road and to take the two cities as soon as possible, without waiting for the rest of the troops. The second group included major figures on the Revolutionary Committee and all the civilians who had left Nanchang. The third group, under the command of Li Lisan, was given a battalion to protect it, and brought up the rear of the army, taking care of the sick and wounded, and handling logistics.

Deployed over about twenty miles this time, the column set out in the intense heat, crossing silent and unfamiliar terrain cut by narrow gorges and rushing rivers in which stretchers overturned without warning. At the head of more than two thousand troops, Li, who was two days behind the rest of the expedition, had halted his usual methodical indoctrination of the men at stopping points; they were too tired, and he had to keep them from becoming rebellious.

After the men had exchanged a few words when they awakened under the open sky or in abandoned farmhouses, the march pitilessly asserted its rights, and everyone fell silent. Li moved forward like an automaton, waiting like all the others for the blessed midday nap. Le Creusot, Anyuan, Shanghai, and Hankow were far away, and getting farther at every step. Lacking newspapers or radios, he seldom learned what was going on else-where. In September, couriers informed him that Mao Tse-tung had failed to take Changsha, the capital of neighboring Hunan. The "Autumn Harvest Rebellion" soon turned into a disaster. Even though the peasants, armed only with lances and a few rifles, had risen up and managed to take and hold Liling, Li's hometown, for two days, they had to evacuate it quickly when the Kuomintang's troops arrived. Mao was leaving to take refuge, along with at least a thousand men who had survived the fighting, in the Jinggan Mountains, on the other side of the border with Jiangxi province.

Peng Pai, who, like Mao, had built his reputation on peasant affairs, was traveling with Li. Three years earlier, he had been the head of a "peasant soviet" near Canton, and he was eager to return to it; he had been driven out after terrible massacres on both sides. Like some of his comrades, he couldn't see what had led Mao to engage in such a poorly prepared operation: Mao, who a few months earlier had declared that they had to "support the peasants' excesses" against landowners, and that the latter were, on the whole, no more than "rotters." Stunned, the Party leadership in Wuhan had told him to try to be more subtle.

The political defense office of which Li was in charge was supposed to collect information regarding the regions they were traveling through. The task of this group of about five hundred men was not easy: the peasants, suspicious, fled whenever its emissaries arrived in the hamlets along the route. There were very few peasant associations that had a representative on site. Their stories were all alike, telling of unpaid farm rents, accumulated debts, disputed lands, sometimes the last peasant revolt before the troops' arrival, or anti-Bolshevik militias founded by landowners. As the Red columns approached, these militias decamped. Their pigs and rice reserves were requisitioned and used to feed the troops.

One day Li decided to accompany one of these expeditions, in order to take the pulse of the local population. With a small escort, he left the column and set out on the country roads. After walking for an hour, they fell into an ambush: shots fired from nearby clumps of trees forced them to hit the ground. They immediately replied, shooting blindly and taking cover in a thicket. Li, lying in a ditch, emptied his pistol in the direction of their assailants without seeing them. Then there was a silence, and the two sides began to observe each other. An officer came up to Li and told him that they were surrounded, but that in his opinion, they were not greatly outnumbered. No trace of a hostile army had been reported in the area. They could just be highwaymen, wandering derelicts, deserters from a lost or conquering army, so many of whom were moving through the Chinese countryside, or even a residual band of peasant rebels protecting their village.

Li began the dialogue. From the thicket, he launched into a long declaration in which their peaceful intentions were made clear. After a silence, another, more succinct tirade was shouted from a copse not fifty yards away. No one understood anything, but a soldier who was a native of the country asked in the local dialect whom they were dealing with. Negotiations started in earnest, initially at a distance. Soon, Li suggested that they sit down and talk. Two hours later, about twenty ragged soldiers who had been looking for something to steal in the Jiangxi countryside fell in line behind their new leader, asking what there was to eat.

The troops arrived in Changting, a large, sleepy town on the banks of the treacherous Ting River. Li requisitioned a hundred junks and almost four hundred sailors to transport his people to Shanghang, some sixty miles downstream. The river was a safer route; it would give his men a rest and win them time. Li, who knew nothing about the ancestral rules of the river, started dividing up the boatmen as he saw fit, depending on whether they looked young, strong, old, or weak, assigning them to junks that were not their own. Then he gave orders to put the wounded officers and officials in the boats of the young, vigorous boatmen, leaving the rest in the hands of the older ones. This was an error; when they came to the first rapids, the young boatmen, who lacked the skill of their elders, caused a naval disaster that almost cost the lives of many passengers. Several junks broke up on the rocks. Fortunately, it was summer, and the river was low: people were barely saved from drowning. The old boatmen, whose eyes were sharp and whose hands were steady, went on far ahead, furious about their junks and grumbling about their unusual cargo.

Soaked, the others had to bivouac along the banks of the river, while waiting for the old boatmen to come back to help them. Li had to have the mariners' long tirades translated into the dialect of Fujian before deciding that he had no choice but to reimburse the owners of the junks that had been destroyed. He ruminated on this lesson while the flotilla descended the Ting's muddy waters toward Shanghang.

Less than a month later, the column was marching through mountains and valleys on its way toward the south, an enormous, hesitant, disparate, caterpillar-like column whose men, divided up into three components separated by dozens of miles, were melting steadily away as a result of desertions.

However, among these men setting off in pursuit of an uncertain future, a new chemistry was being born: by talking with the political leaders, the soldiers were becoming familiar with the subtlety of the doctrines, while Li and his men were learning from the generals the rudiments of the art of war, tactics and strategy. And also how to sew buttons on their trousers, oil their rifles, and keep an eye on the commissary.

At the end of September, sitting on his mount, a recently requisitioned mule, Li contemplated from a hilltop the narrow, luminous line that ran along the distant horizon. The Pacific. Before his eyes, like a promised land, the green plain stretched out as far as the coast. Farther on, he could see Shantou, the port. Waves of Chinese had embarked there to go overseas, the first generations to flee a land on which a curse had been laid. Weary of war, the city let itself be taken by its new conquerors almost without firing a shot. The expedition's advance unit set up its headquarters there a few days before Li arrived in view.

WHEN CHOU EN-LAI CAME TO MEET LI NEAR SHANTOU, HE LOOKED embarrassed, and carefully examined his comrade, who was coming toward him perched on his mule, his face tired but proud. After congratulating him, Chou cleared his throat and admitted to Li that he had organized a memorial service for him, the second one after the one in Paris. In fact, in the column's advance units, there had been a rumor that Li had been killed in an ambush.

"Here's to my third death!" Li cried, lifting his glass at dinner that evening, amid joking about this phantom of the revolution.

The euphoria didn't last long. Access to the promised land, the gate that controlled the road to Canton, was locked up tight. Closing off the exits to the west, the Kuomintang's armies were advancing by forced marches toward the Communist troops. The coast, which the latter had been waiting for as if it were their deliverance, was turning out to be a net, a deadly trap. Isolated, far from the port, Zhu De's troops were deployed to protect the north flank. With most of the troops, Ye Ting was facing the enemy formations that were taking up positions hour after hour in the hills to the west and the south, cutting off the way to Canton. In a few days, the encirclement would be complete. This time, everyone felt the battle would be decisive.

An emissary arrived from Hong Kong carrying in his pocket a new political line. Zhang Tailei, one of the twelve founders of the Party, announced to the stupefied leaders of the expedition that they must avoid combat, and head for the Haifeng district, farther south, in order to proclaim there a republic of workers' and peasants' soviets, equipped with a Red army. The new directive had just been issued by the Comintern, which had lost almost all contact with the realities in China since its flock had left Nanchang three months earlier. Stalin and his men were finally recognizing that a disaster had occurred in Shanghai the preceding April and that the alliance with the Kuomintang was over. Republicans and Communists must henceforth fight it out to the death, speeding up the headlong rush of history.

But as far as concrete matters were concerned, the expedition's leaders were informed that they must not expect any help from the Soviets. In addition, one political line taking the place of another, they were all blamed for the Nanchang affair. Li and Zhang Guotao were called back to Shanghai, where the Party leadership had set up a secret headquarters again.

Defeat put a sudden end to the nascent polemic. On September 30, five thousand Communist troops attacked fifteen thousand entrenched, well-trained, and well-equipped republican forces waiting for them in the hills of Tangkeng. For two days and two nights, wave after wave of the expedition's soldiers were cut down by the republicans' machine-gun fire as they desperately tried to break through. Two thousand of them died without having seen Canton again, clutching a handful of their native province's sacred earth.

The next day, everything collapsed. Pursued by the enemy, leaving hundreds of wounded behind them, the soldiers retreated in disorder, haunted by bitterness, exhaustion, and bloody visions. Li and the other revolutionary leaders quickly left Shantou, taking the minimum with them, while the fleeing soldiers urged them to run, as they were, because the enemy was coming. After having given their last orders and consulted briefly with each other, Li, Chou, Zhang Guotao, and the others separated, some heading south, some west.

Li and Zhang took shelter in a local peasant's house, where they removed their uniforms and put on civilian clothes, after having given their weapons to their host. When night came, they set out silently to march through the mountains, accompanied by an officer, a leader of the Young Communists, and a guide. In the morning, they reached Tiazugang, a small coastal port, and entered the town separately, pretending not to know each other. They spent the day nervously killing time and waiting for the return of the guide, who had gone to find sailors who would take them to Hong Kong for a price. The guide's intuition and experience allowed him narrowly to avoid engaging pirates who fully intended to slit their throats at sea, once they had deprived them of their last dollars. Toward ten in the evening, they fell asleep, exhausted, hidden on board a fisherman's junk sailing for Hong Kong.

In a discreet hotel room in the British colony, Li wrote a long report on events since the taking of Nanchang. With bitterness, he wrote of the humiliation inflicted on the expedition, punctuating his narrative with acid remarks on the amateurism that had presided over this "simple military adventure." He told about the army drifting along the roads for weeks, all alone, cut off from any outside information, and finally defeated. But he also asked his audience not to forget the "precious lessons of the revolution of August 1," when the Communists took an irreversible step in Nanchang and set out on the road of war.

For defeat had become foreign to his character. The disaster suffered in Shantou could only be a reversal, one more reversal, since China was involved in a general combat in which no one yet had the last word.

A few days later, disguised as an elegant businessman dressed in new clothes and freshly shaven, Li left Hong Kong on board a steamer going up the coast as far as Shanghai. The Central Committee, the secret leadership of the Party in Shanghai, was waiting for him.

At the end of 1927, clandestinity was required in Shanghai, on pain of death: the price of Chiang Kai-shek's peace was the terror visited upon Communists since April. A shadow war, fought without mercy, with denunciations exacted by torture or payment, and betrayals. As a result, the Party's activists were becoming thugs. The best allies of the Kuomintang's secret police were Du Yuesheng and the men of his Green Society, whose opium dens were full all the time. The French concession had become the favorite refuge of Communist managers. There, Police Commissioner Fiori and his proverbial tolerance were less feared than the British police of the international concession, where His Majesty's officers closely cooperated with their Chinese colleagues in pursuing the Reds.

It was in British territory, however, that Li took up lodging, along with Zhang Guotao, in a furnished apartment in a quiet house behind Chongtsing Road, one of the hideouts the clandestine Party apparatus used for its leaders. The place was safe, no doubt by virtue of the adage according to which the enemy won't look for you in his own house. But they had to fool people. After having perfected his role, Li presented himself as a bank manager, the younger brother of Zhang, who had come to Shanghai to get medical treatment for a nascent tuberculosis. They prudently played their roles, loudly referring to each other as "older brother" and "younger brother."

The days went by, and reduced to inactivity, the two men soon realized that they had been put under house arrest by the Party.

The meeting with the new supreme Party leaders was not very pleasant. The founding father, Chen Duxiu, had been removed from office, with the Soviets' approval, shortly after the assault on Nanchang: violently attacked for his "right-wing opportunism," he had paid for the years of alliance with the Nationalists and for the final disaster. His replacement, an amateur poet and former newspaper correspondent in Moscow, was more familiar with smoke-filled rooms than with tough action, but he was ideologically virtuous. Qu Qiubai had been told by Moscow to deal with the Nanchang affair and Mao's peasant uprisings. Li experienced Communist sanctions: he learned that he had been removed from his functions in the political bureau, along with Zhang Guotao, Chou En-lai, and Cai Hesen. Of the four, Chou came off best, and was assigned to direct "military work" in Shanghai and the Party's secret services. Li and Zhang were vaguely accused of having opposed the Comintern's directives. In addition, Li was blamed for the collapse of the labor unions in Wuhan after he had left the city.

It was a bitter pill to swallow. The risks taken, the sacrifices accepted, the heroism on the battlefield—none of that mattered to the political leaders: only victory counted. "The winner is made king, the loser is a bandit," Zhang Guotao kept saying to Li in their room that evening.

Li suppressed his indignation. He was stunned to find that during the whole expedition the Party's little decision-making machine had been running at full speed under Moscow's impetus and without even consulting them. Without any assignment, he paced for weeks like a lion in his cage, killing time by indulging in a new pastime, going to see films in the protective darkness of the first movie houses in the French concession.

At the beginning of December 1927, Stalin and Manouilski had a brilliant idea: they would launch a new Communist insurrection in China. In Canton, this time, and especially on a date that would coincide with the opening of the Fifteenth Bolshevik Party Congress. Perfect for sweeping away the protests of Trotsky and his supporters, before expelling them and throwing them in prison. They who had been ironically mocking, for months, the misadventures of the Chinese revolution and its Soviet strategists—they wouldn't dare criticize a nascent workers' insurrection.

On December 11, at 3:30 in the morning, the old trading center on the Pearl River was awakened by a regiment of cadets in revolt and several hundred "Red guards," veteran strike pickets armed with twenty-nine Mausers and two hundred grenades. They shot a few reluctant officers before launching, in the predawn darkness, a surprise attack on key points in the city.

The insurrection was promptly carried out, and the headquarters of the military police as well as the central police station were taken after a short exchange of gunfire. In the morning, only the headquarters of the army's general staff was still holding out, solidly entrenched behind its machine guns, while the Bolshevik cadets and the labor pickets took up positions at intersections. A dozen "delegates" emerged from hiding and proclaimed the existence of a "soviet of delegates of workers, peasants, and soldiers," while barricades were being hastily thrown up at the entrances to the city.

All the political prisoners were freed, swelling the meager ranks of the rebels by about a thousand volunteers. Cars were requisitioned and teams of young propagandists fanned out in all directions through the city to announce the good news: the revolution had finally triumphed, and the red flag was replacing the blue banner of the Kuomintang. After Nanchang, Canton woke up as the Red capital of China. In the workers' suburbs, students shouted that all debts to usurers would be canceled, decreed freedom of the press and of opinion, and swore that soon they would be living in the houses of the wealthy, which had moreover to be immediately expropriated.

They were wasting their time. For years, the Cantonese had been hearing such things. Confronted with this change, the last in a long and painful series of such turnarounds, the population remained stubbornly indifferent, even hostile and fearful. The machine-gunning in June 1925, the summary executions and disappearances in May 1926, as well as the countless echoes of the country in flames had chilled the soul of the city, whose heart beat in time with the uneasy rhythm of commerce.

At noon, despite pressing invitations, the mass meeting in the center of the city attracted only three hundred people. The shopkeepers had prudently rolled down their shutters, but the railroad workers, boatmen, and factory employees stayed at their jobs, almost as usual. A few typographers, mechanics, and rickshaw men joined the rebels on the barricades, but in a few hours the Cantonese communards were beginning to look like Mexican desperadoes.

QUICKLY RECOVERING FROM ITS NOCTURNAL SURPRISE, THE Kuomintang army began to fight back. At the center of the city, the general staff headquarters of the army held on behind its machine guns. The expected reinforcements soon arrived. British, Japanese, and Chinese gunboats took up positions on the Pearl River, their cannons pointed toward the places where the Communists were concentrated.

From his command post at the Soviet consulate in Canton, Heinz Neumann, a German whom the Comintern had sent from Moscow to supervise the insurrection, cabled his delighted chiefs to tell them of the latest "victory of the armed Chinese proletariat." This revolutionary bureaucrat had hastily thrown together a plan for insurrection and found Chinese coolies to carry it out. Ye Ting, the general who had survived the Shantou disaster ten weeks earlier, had been able to reach the city a few hours before operations began. Perplexed, he had given his opinion as a military man: it was at best a hazardous bet, since the enemy, this time, consisted of forty-five thousand men scattered around Canton, fresh and ready for action, well armed and trained by Soviet advisers. Those facing them were mainly civilians, perhaps three thousand men, armed with odds and ends, massed behind makeshift barricades, without any artillery.

Zhang Tailei, who had long served as Borodin's interpreter before being named head of the Party in Canton, carried out his orders without questioning them. The Party was mobilized, with all the energy of a clandestine organization adrift. But the political unknown, and it was an important one, was the popular uprising. Only the latter could bring about a military miracle.

On December 12, in the early afternoon, the republican cannons fired their first salvos in the direction of the barricades, while small infantry units attacked in the suburbs. Fierce street fighting began. In the firing, one hardly heard the thundering of the Chinese gunboats that joined in the concert, covering a landing of troops with a heavy barrage on the city, to the applause of the defenders holed up in the Kuomintang's headquarters. Fires were spreading in several quarters, adding to those set by rioters. On the barricades, the Communists, workers and cadets, were attacked or harassed from behind by armed civilians, members of Canton's tongs, who were powerful, declared enemies of the Reds.

The next morning, at around ten o'clock, the regiment of cadets, hardly a thousand men, succeeded in breaking through the barrage around the city and escaped. Heinz Neumann and a few Soviet advisers, their faces black with gunpowder, begged the guards of the Western concession to let them through so they could take refuge there. They were grudgingly allowed to come in. At noon, the Communists holed up in the central police station, the seat of the "soviet" of Canton proclaimed the preceding day, were completely surrounded. Two hours later, their ammunition having run out, there was not a single survivor in the building. Zhang Tailei, the son of a Cantonese shopkeeper and the first Chinese Communist to have set foot in Moscow, seven years earlier, had died on a barricade a little further on, his weapon in his hand. The Kuomintang's blue banner once again flew over the city, and Chiang Kai-shek congratulated his soldiers.

The fighting went on long into the night, street by street, alley by alley, house by house, down to the rebels' last cartridges: no Cantonese would have bet a cent on the life of a captured Communist.

After iron and fire came terror. The Nationalist soldiers, left to themselves, cleaned out the workers' areas, denunciation after denunciation. Almost five hundred rebels were killed, and there were more than two hundred summary executions of various adversaries. Young women with short hair were particularly sought out, raped, and their bodies piled up by the hundreds in the streets of the city. The subordinate officers were clear: that masculine-looking Western haircut was the sign of a dangerous radicalism. The Soviet consulate was taken by republican troops and then looted. The five officials who still remained there, including the vice-consul, were dragged out in front of the gates and shot down on the sidewalk, without further ado. Four days later, there had been more than five thousand deaths in Canton, and the stench of dead bodies plagued the city, as well as a few journalists who had come to report on the events.

In Moscow, people were jubilant. The news of the latest Chinese insurrection was not, of course, very good, and was therefore kept secret. But that wasn't what was important: Lev Davidovich Bronstein, alias Trotsky, had been expelled from the Bolshevik party, KO'd by Joseph Dzhugashvili, known as Stalin. The war of Lenin's succession was over.

When the train finally pulled into the station in Canton, Li went pale as he looked out the car's window. The platform was crawling with soldiers running in every direction as officers barked at them. The doors were thrown open and the sound of boots echoed through the corridor as the soldiers started checking the cars and the passengers.

Li looked at his suitcase in the baggage net. It was filled with ultra-confidential Party documents and propaganda, hardly covered up with a piece of cloth and a few shirts. He was alone in the compartment. It was a bullet in the nape of the neck or the executioner's saber on the station platform, if he was lucky and it was a quick death. Once again, in a few seconds, the dice were going to be thrown on the green felt. The door to the compartment opened, and a Kuomintang subordinate officer came in and asked for his papers. Li handed him the documents, good-quality forgeries. The soldier asked this young merchant, elegantly dressed in the old-fashioned way in a black tunic of fine silk, where he was coming from and what he was doing in Canton. Standing at this full height, Li replied, coolly but respectfully, that he had business to do for his employer in Shanghai, a banker.

"Textiles," he explained.

The soldier glanced around and pointed to the suitcase.

"Samples," Li said, moving as if to show him what was in it.

Textiles didn't interest the officer, who signaled that he could get off the train.

ON LEAVING THE TRAIN STATION, HIS SWEATY HAND GRIPPING THE suitcase, Li, very pale, walked straight ahead before collapsing into a rickshaw. Before his eyes, the traces of the preceding week's fighting were still visible. Whole blocks of houses had burned. He pressed the suitcase to him as if it were a precious toolbox. As soon as the news of the disaster had become known, the Party had sent Li to Canton. Shattered, the leaders in Shanghai had gone in search of a revolutionary troubleshooter. Someone who could rebuild the Party machine under a regime of terror. The mission was very dangerous, and there were few volunteers. Li, under fire for weeks for "deviationism," was stifling in his apartment, locked up with Zhang Guotao, and sick of having to shout "dear elder brother" to his comrade every time a visitor showed up.

As soon as he learned of the uprising in Canton, he had rebelled. Through the intermediary of some rare clandestine emissaries, he had let it be known that he was immediately available to resume the fight. The anger of the man of May 30 was already feared, while the current leaders, tormented intellectuals, were prostrated by the defeat. Chou En-lai, for his part, knew they needed a man of action and courage. Suddenly exonerated by his accusers, Li was declared "secretary-general of the Party for the Canton region" and sent there to observe the disaster. His mission consisted of surviving and reestablishing ties, since he couldn't raise the dead. At the Canton train station, he had won the first set, having escaped the police and soldiers. It remained only to get to the secret address where he was going to have to begin rebuilding on these smoking ruins.

The clandestine meetings with the survivors were tumultuous. Everything had to be begun over again from zero: the class struggle, the imperialists, the labor unions, the worldwide revolution, the ups and the downs. A stubborn Leninist, he rubbed salt in the wounds. If the revolution in Canton was in mourning, that was surely because "errors were made right here," he kept repeating. Several meetings of survivors turned into psychodramas. Li made decisions with the determination of a surgeon on the battlefield: a few people were expelled from the Party, the rest were saved. Since Nanchang, the laws of war had been imposed: any defeat was only a temporary reversal. The dead, he told this bloodstained group, were martyrs. Respect for their souls required the continuation of the combat, not capitulation. But in his report to the Party leadership in Shanghai, he harshly criticized the amateurism of the Comintern's adventure in Canton.

By January, the Party had been reorganized. Several dozen cells formed of widows, brothers, or friends of the martyrs, and often recent orphans, were more or less functional. They were supervised by tough cookies who had survived the barricades and gone underground, furtive phantoms in the burned ruins of Canton who constantly changed hideouts.

In April, when he was on the point of being arrested, Li once again escaped to Hong Kong. He found the British colony singularly restful after weeks of playing a dangerous game of hide-and-seek in the streets of Canton. The bloodhounds working for the "department of social affairs," the Kuomintang's secret police, were always on the go. Even when flooded with cables from the Chinese authorities demanding that they arrest Communists, they worked more phlegmatically than the colony's British officials. At tea time, they awaited without impatience the reports from Chinese police auxiliaries and from the army of informers.

A warrior monk, Li had made Hong Kong his monastery, where he continued constantly to transmit directives, advice, reports, and analyses regarding Canton and Shanghai.

Mukden-Harbin. The trains headed straight into the immense plains of Manchuria. The locomotive announced its gallop to the north by blowing its whistle. After twenty-eight hours, braking as it descended the foothills of Mongolia, it would turn westward. Then the engine driver could relax, with his elbow on the windowsill, as he set his course for the Soviet frontier. With a little luck, after Harbin, the last city in Chinese territory, they would see, if the weather was good, the summits of the Yinggan Mountains, still wearing their winter snowcaps. On the Mongolian plateau and then in Siberia, there would be the endless rhythm of the train wheels, day after day, forest after forest, until they arrived in Moscow.

In 1928, spring was late in coming. Li opened a pack of cigarettes, his tenth, perhaps, since leaving Hong Kong a week earlier. This time, he hadn't had to put up with freighters and seasickness; the trip, after a stop at Port Arthur, was now made by rail all the way. Food was not always available, but there was plenty of tobacco. Li smoked a great deal, in the modern way, buying packs of cigarettes and not rolling his own. Since the boycotts of foreign products, he bought, out of proletarian spirit, only Chinese brands.

There were several dozen people, camouflaged under various identities, making the trip to Moscow to participate in the Sixth Congress of the Chinese Communist Party. The organization's elite was invited to the capital of the worldwide revolution. There, they could speak freely, without worrying about betrayals or police raids. None of them had any doubt that history—their history—had arrived at a turning point after 1927. The revolution's first steps were bloody, and they had to be cleaned up. The war was total, the enemy powerful and devious, the prisoners doomed to torture or disavowal. Many, some of the best, had already fallen; their deaths had fanned the flames of the survivors.

In his car on the Trans-Siberian Railroad, between naps, Li slowly pulled his thoughts together. As if he were going to examine his conscience, he tried to put in order what he had experienced these past few years, before making his first return to the Jerusalem of communism. His doubts with regard to the Comintern, and the good sense of its envoys, were immense. But his conviction that the solution to the Chinese problem was international remained intact. However, the news about the worldwide revolution was not good: in Europe, no insurrection was imminent. The news that came from Moscow, still rarer, referred to a "majority" and an "opposition" within the single party, which were at dagger's points over the Chinese issue as they were over everything else.

He also felt a pang in his heart. In Moscow, he was very likely to run into Li Yichun, his ex-companion who had left him to run off with his old comrade Cai. The mother of his son, whom he had not seen for months and who was growing up somewhere in the Hunan countryside with his grandparents and amid the spasms of civil war. Pressing his nose against the window of his compartment, he thought melancholically about those brief, idyllic months in the little house in Anyuan, surrounded by blackfaced miners. That was five years ago, already.

As on his earlier trip, on waking up Li was struck by the sight of Lake Baikal, along whose shores the train was slowly traveling. The brilliance of its water under the morning sun, like the azure of a Mediterranean lost between steppe and forest, made him blink his eyes. Soon they would come to Irkutsk, more than four days before reaching Moscow.

Joseph Stalin watched the tall, lanky Chinese come into his office, and examined him with interest. The Georgian was glad to see in flesh and blood this revolutionary whose name regularly came up whenever Chinese affairs were discussed. That face, that prominent jaw, those rugged features, that almost aristocratic air, those slightly ironic eyes below the stiff, black hair: so it was him, the man of May 1925 in Shanghai. He had already seen his picture, taken by an unknown photographer and published in the newspapers at the time. The Comintern's services had attached the picture to the file that Stalin had reviewed just a few minutes before telling the young man to come in; according to the report, he was twenty-nine years old. In the picture, Li, taken at relatively close range by the photographer, was haranguing a crowd that had risen up against the common imperialist enemy: "The Chinese Revolution on the March" might have been the caption under the picture, which seemed to have been taken from an Eisenstein film.

The Chinaman, the report said, had not proven unworthy: a fiery temperament, an unmatched taste for action, a limited but efficient tactical sense, stupefying courage and devotion. He was not of proletarian origin, alas! But he wasn't an intellectual either, thank God.

No, Stalin said to himself, the man in front of him was an intractable bear, capable of moving heaven and earth in the Middle Kingdom. He'd fired the shot; the French had thrown him out, the police had always failed to get him; he'd started strikes and uprisings everywhere he went. And in Hankow he'd even reconquered a bit of Chinese sovereignty from the British. An engineer of the revolution, in short. No reported penchant for the Trotskyists; the only thing he was interested in was clearly to gain power in China, rapidly.

AFTER A FEW POLITE REMARKS, STALIN, IN ORDER TO SOUND OUT his man, quickly began asking him questions, one after another. He, Stalin, was soon going to turn fifty, and no one was going to put one over on him: underhanded tricks, attacks on banks, prison, clandestinity, treachery, ideological quarrels, and, from the rear lines, battlefields—he knew all that better than anyone.

Chinese affairs had not been a lucky area for him up to now. He had even been completely wrong in his predictions: Chiang Kai-shek was not the Russian knight on the Chinese chessboard, and the scoundrel, who had been brought up in Soviet military academies, had tricked him.

Contrary to all expectations, Moscow's preferred general had shot down the revolution's best troops. The Trotskyists' ferocious mockery on that subject was still ringing in his ears. Besides, the International's affairs were going badly everywhere that summer of 1928. In Great Britain, the workers, tempted for a time by the Communists, were turning away again toward the Labour Party, while in Germany the Weimar bourgeoisie was growing fat. At this rate, Stalin repeated, socialism was going to have to be built in a single country.

China and the violence of its sudden reversals were giving the experts in the Kremlin headaches and cold sweats. A year earlier, Stalin had declared, during a delicate meeting concerning Chinese affairs with Bukharin in the presence of the Italian Palmiro Togliatti* and the Frenchman Treint: "We have sufficient authority over the Chinese masses to make them accept our decisions." Since then, he felt that he was completely exposed. For months, the Comintern's Far East office had had to conceal from Communists around the world the truth about the carnage in Canton. Heinz Neumann had been sent back to Moscow, where Borodin was doing penitence in his dacha. For Stalin, the Comintern's envoys were cretins. The telexes from Shanghai and Beijing tried to follow the inextricable convulsions of the Chinese dragon, but every prediction turned out to be too hazardous. One thing was certain: the massacres were continuing at a brisk pace. The most recent cables from the Soviet consulate in Shanghai referred to more than twenty-five thousand executions of Communists and their sympathizers officially announced since January. And that was without counting the thousands of anonymous deaths in peasant insurrections. Even czarist Russia hadn't dared do that much, and that left Stalin pensive.

The Chinese Communists were not making his task easier, either: their congress, which had opened in the capital in mid-June, had turned almost immediately into a general row. Two weeks later, the eighty delegates, divided into several shifting blocs, were still involved in astonishingly bitter personal quarrels, fed by tenacious resentments. Officially, the question was whether the line followed for the past five years had been a

---

*Head of the Italian Communist Party from 1931 to his death in 1964.

good one, and what the next line should consist of. But the settling of accounts kept going on, and it did not spare the Comintern. The delegation from Canton, the most numerous, had harshly attacked Li Lisan and the severity of the measures he had taken after the disaster. The assault on Nanchang was bitterly debated, the peasant uprisings still more bitterly, and the delegates shouted "Putschist!" and "Adventurist!" and "Opportunist!" at each other while trying to determine precisely who had been responsible, and for what.

For hours on end, harangues and counterharangues succeeded each other at the rostrum, under the fascinated and somewhat weary eyes of Nikolai Bukharin, the president of the International, and his lieutenant Mikhail Fortus, alias Pavel Mif, the head of his Chinese bureau. The Russians couldn't make head nor tail of all this in Bolshevist terms, and tried to calm the debates by offering their good offices in the wings. Their task was difficult. Mif, a Ukrainian, gave Stalin detailed reports on the congress's events, having the interminable exchanges translated for him by his protégé Wang Ming. This young Chinese was one of the "students" at Moscow's Sun Yat-sen University, of which Mif was also in charge. It wasn't a sinecure, either: the Chinese "students" in Moscow, a good thousand apprentice revolutionaries, tended to lean toward Trotsky and against Stalin—when they weren't protesting against their living conditions and poor teaching, even going so far as demanding that they all be taken immediately back to China. He resolved to straighten out this group of undisciplined Orientals, with the help of the NKVD's* policemen. Pavel Mif, who hadn't been much moved by a brief stay in Wuhan, had ended up secretly detesting China and the Chinese.

STALIN THEN TURNED TO CONVERSATION TOWARD THE ADVANCES and retreats of the revolution. Li could hardly understand how one could elaborate theories about the retreats. In his view, the revolution could only more forward. Especially since Moscow had given it a capital. At most, a few temporary setbacks might have to be endured. Anyway, wasn't China a second laboratory of world revolution, stuffed with com-

---

*People's Commissariat for Internal Affairs, the forerunner of the KGB.

bustible material, and whose many advantages Li enthusiastically laid out for the master of the Kremlin's curiosity?

Lenin's successor couldn't resist teaching this awkward young man a lesson, by telling him that "even receding tides make waves." Li liked the poetry of the remark, and the two men spent a long time examining the waves of the revolution and the difficulty of gauging the hollows and the crests, especially during a storm. Stalin even drew him a picture.

Both of them were landlubbers, and they agreed that the trend was undeniably revolutionary, but that from now on urban and peasant insurrections had to be better combined with the development of the Red Army in the countryside.

"And we have to build a *true* Bolshevist party!" Stalin insisted. For him, lack of discipline and quarrels were a childhood illness of the Chinese Communist Party.

STALIN, LIKE LI, WAS IN NO MOOD TO MODERATE THE COURSE OF things. On the contrary, his left flank being freed up by the defeat of the Trotskyists, he was getting ready to strike a blow at Bukharin on his right. This would be easier, but in order to do it he had to bring to heel the International and the young Communist parties in Europe and Asia, to make them march "class against class" for the defense of the "homeland of Socialism." According to *Pravda,* the latter was threatened, in this summer of 1928, by a mysterious and imminent imperialist attack. London had still not reestablished diplomatic relations with Moscow, which had been broken off two years earlier. Anyone who was preaching moderation in Paris, London, or Berlin would henceforth be labeled a "right-winger," "social traitor," or even "social-fascist."

The Trotskyists were still the most dangerous enemy. Stalin asked about Chen Duxiu. The founder of the Chinese Communist Party, overthrown by the new generation a year earlier, was pining away in Shanghai. He was living there under a false name, like a leper, at a clandestine address no one dared approach. Stalin regretted that the old Chinese fighter had declined his invitation to come to Moscow "to explain himself." Chen Duxiu had understood that Moscow had approved or even made the decision to remove him. For him, everything had already been

said. Stalin feared him because of the tutelary hold he had on Chinese mil-
itants. What if he were to decide to support that strange idea of Trotsky's:
demanding elections in China and holding a constituent assembly in order
to decide the fate of the country?

Li, who had never read the Trotskyist literature, agreed immediately:
elections in China, joint assemblies with those killers in the Kuomintang,
that could only be suicide or capitulation! Reassured, Stalin became jovial,
filled his pipe, and started telling about his adventures as a young man.

Two hours later, Li left the room, ushered out by guards into the
silent corridors of the Kremlin, which were deserted at this late hour. He
was taken back, still under escort, to the Hotel Lux, where it took him a
long time to go to sleep. Stalin, for his part, said to himself that he liked
this young man; he was more straightforward, less devious than other
Chinese, who clearly were no match for him so far as their taste for action
went. That Chou En-lai was a good worker, to be sure, but he was difficult
to figure out. Li Lisan had enthusiasm and authority; he might be just the
man to lead the Chinese Party at a time when it needed fighters.

But first, Stalin had to find a bona fide worker, a man of proletarian
origin, a real one, in order to give him star billing with the title of
secretary-general. Proletarianizing the leadership was of capital importance for propaganda. Studying his files, he picked out the name of a former longshoreman, Xiang Zhongfa. Limited intellectually, but his class
origins and his service record were impeccable. With Xiang, flanked by Li
Lisan—to exercise the real power—and Chou En-lai—for administration—the Chinese Communist team could get back on the road.

Stalin returned to more urgent matters. In the summer of 1928, there
was no lack of them: in the countryside, there were the peasants to put
down; in the cities, the trials of "bourgeois specialists"; and there was the
idea, which had to be examined, of opening work camps throughout the
country.

At the Party congress, the Chinese delegates finally agreed, after a month
of debate, to condemn "opportunism" and "putschism," and to meet again

to prepare the next wave of insurrections, which should take place soon, since the crisis in the worldwide revolution was becoming more serious. As a result, at the congress the Comintern began the hunt for "right-wingers." Ernst Thälmann, the German party chief, announced that the Nazis in Hamburg and Berlin were far more dangerous than the socialists. Echoing him, Qu Qiubai, who had lost his title as head of the Chinese Party in the battle, but whose Russian was excellent, told an audience of the "professional revolutionaries" from all over the world that the danger in China lay in right-wing scruples. Those who hesitated to launch an immediate attack on Chiang Kai-shek, the White terror, and their imperialist allies were flirting with treason.

When it was all over, some of the delegates went back to China, and some remained in Moscow. Li, Chou, Xiang Zhongfa, and Cai Hesen took the Trans-Siberian Railroad back to Vladivostok, where they boarded separate boats. Chou was almost captured by the Japanese secret police on the boat from Port Arthur to Shanghai. In Moscow, the Chinese delegates who had remained resumed their incessant political battles within the Comintern. Exhausted, the Finn Otto Kuusinen told them: "Stalin is the highest authority over China! He would like to know how the Comintern is going to provide instructions for the Chinese party!"

# 9

In October 1928, Cunningham,* the British consul, cabled the Foreign Office in London from Shanghai to report a "sharp rise in communist activities" in the city. The Reds were still there. Apparently, they were in hiding, but their clandestine print shops were running at full speed. The factories were flooded with Bolshevik propaganda, while it was said that there were many conflicts between commercial employees and their employers, and even among the employees of foreign banks. For the time being, the concessions were without mail because of a strike of thirty-seven hundred Chinese postal workers.

The postal workers had been famous ever since they had been seen in their green uniforms on the barricades the previ-

---

*Not to be confused with the American consul in 1927, whose name was also Cunningham.

ous March, during the Shanghai uprising against the warlord. They had participated in attacks on the armored train held by the White Russians, near the North Station. On the day of victory, they had even flown the Chinese flag over the post office, at the heart of the international concession.

For the past few weeks, Cunningham noted, not a day had gone by without an incident, and sometimes a sudden demonstration, which was immediately dispersed.

LI WAS SPENDING ONE OF THE MOST UNPLEASANT WINTERS OF HIS life. In the damp cold of the port, between the cellars and attics of Djabei or Putong that served him as hideouts or meeting places, he was nonetheless secretly weaving a new network. Chou En-lai had taken military affairs in hand. The Party now had well-placed spies in the Kuomintang's police force, and even in its most secret departments. The shadow war was raging, and the *tchons,* the Party's killers, were doing their job: Red terror against White terror. It was a tight contest against the Chinese, British, and French police. With the Green Society's men, the war was total, and more vicious to boot: Du Yuesheng's henchmen controlled all the public places. Often, in broad daylight, shots rang out at an intersection or on a sidewalk, and a man, shot down at close range, fell to the ground while others, holding guns in their hands, raced away, shouting a few slogans as they went: the Reds had struck the Greens, which made the score even for the week. In the suburbs, more foremen died a brutal death, and every strike quickly led to skirmishes between opposing groups armed with iron bars, knives, and sometimes pistols.

The network woven by Li, Chou, and their men was much tighter than the earlier ones. The party was completely reorganized. Clandestinity was not something for the soft, the faint of heart, the uncertain. There not being much more than a thousand of them in the city, the activists met in groups of two or three at most, taking infinite precautions. Fearing their neighbors, losing real or supposed tails, surreptitiously circulating tracts and pamphlets. Always threatened, often tracked down and captured, sometimes dying under torture in the cellars of the Longhua barracks. Some of them cried out, but said not a word.

★   ★

LI HAD BECOME SIAO BOSHENG, AN ANTIQUE DEALER WITH A SHOP
in the French concession. His previous flamboyant outbursts and provo-
cations in public were no longer appropriate. Even the pleasures of love
took on the bitter and furtive taste of clandestinity.

His passion for Li Yichun, a young man's luxury, was over. Since then,
Li had been sharing his life as a hazardous phantom with one of the six sisters of the beautiful Li Chongsan, a Party comrade. He had three children
with her, Li Jing, Lili, and Xie Zhipei, whom he seldom had occasion
to see.

The only comrades who survived were the ones who were courageous or who betrayed the Party. Discreet, unrecognizable behind his
neutral glasses with elegant Mandarin frames, Li had grown, as had Chou,
a little goatee, which was supposed to serve as a disguise. Rarely in the
shop, the antique dealer Siao Bosheng moved about the city, often dressed
in the European fashion, wearing a boater on his head in order to melt
into the fashionable crowds. As he went to meetings by complicated
routes in order to lose the men tailing him, three invisible bodyguards
kept within a few yards of him. The antique shop was losing a lot of
money, but the funds provided by the Comintern, although they were
meager, were enough to cover the costs.

Li's determination was fierce, and the powerful twist he gave the
Communist apparatus made more than one comrade crack. In the spring,
a quarrel with Cai Hesen broke out; the ideologue, entrusted with North
China, was beginning to revolt against Li's curt, imperative directives. But
this friend from Montargis days, the elder brother who knew his Marxism
so well, the bookish fellow who had seduced Li Yichun, no longer
impressed the man who had survived Nanchang and Canton: to survive in
clandestinity, the party had to transform itself into a disciplined, silent,
and efficient machine, run by energetic managers and speaking with a single voice. Neither accusations of authoritarianism nor theoretical quarrels
about rich peasants moved Li. The clash between the two men was brief
and violent, in proportion with the esteem they had for each other. By the
end of spring, Cai, exhausted by Li's vitality, was labeled a right-winger

and sent back to continue his cherished studies in Moscow. The Comintern found him "work" in Chinese affairs.

In June 1929, at the second plenary meeting of the Central Committee, held with elaborate precautions in a suburban hotel, Li was henceforth the uncontested head of the Party. Xiang Zhongfa, the nominal secretary-general, had had to go to Moscow in March for further training. The former longshoreman's courage and devotion were not in question, but the man could hardly read a newspaper, and he found the indispensable theoretical texts still more difficult to decipher.

Li, who was now familiar with dialectics, began to make use of his political imagination. The new holder of the revolutionary holy grail since his return from Moscow, he communicated to everyone his vision of a world he thought he could interpret and foresee. His tone was severe, his lyricism sober, as he appealed to the Party members' souls. From his hiding place, he called for a "battle for freedom," writing article after article, distributing directives to his comrades. He set forth, and proposed to resolve, "numerous current tactical problems" one year after the congress in Moscow. In June, he reviewed the world situation. "The revolutionary crisis will grow," he swore. Echoing Stalin's predictions, he assured his readers that the collapse of the capitalist world would lead to war. It was a "grave illusion to believe that American imperialism was going to help Chinese capitalism to develop itself." This young capitalism would in any case find Japanese imperialism blocking its way. As for the rest, Li noted that China was still embroiled in civil war and beneath the foreigner's heel; neither Chiang Kai-shek's victory nor his Nanking government had brought peace. The country north of the Yangtze resounded with artillery fire and the sound of boots. In the south, the Kuomintang's generals, and first of all Chiang himself, were settling old scores and fighting among themselves. The warlords were thick-skinned, and they already had heirs.

FAR FROM SHANGHAI, IN THE SOUTHERN PART OF JIANGXI PROVINCE, lost in rugged mountains covered with forests, Mao Tse-tung and Zhu De were languishing with the remainder of the troops who had survived the peasant uprisings. With two thousand men, living in sordid poverty, surviving with the help of the population and by levies, the two men were leading the Red Army. He Long was wandering about his familiar countryside in northern Hunan, at the head of a thousand soldiers. The former highwayman had gone back to his local legend as the Knight of the Blue Forests.

Li ordered them all to regroup and avoid attacking large cities. They were to assemble in a single region and launch land reform, under the direction of a soviet government. Then Li commanded them to "begin a guerrilla war, extend the soviet zones, and organize the Red Army." Six armies were already fighting over the country. China could well accept a seventh, he thought.

The situation, in short, was excellent. "We can discern signs of a new revolutionary wave," Li wrote. It was time to "prepare ourselves for armed insurrections." The Party was raising its head again and morale was increasing, despite the disasters and massacres. Or because of them. In the country as a whole, its members had risen from forty thousand to seventy thousand in the course of the year. The Communists were still the depositories of part of the people's hopes. Labor agitation continued; it now remained only to give it political goals.

By adroitly combining, when the time came, urban insurrections with attacks on the cities by the Red Army, the revolution would move ahead. As for the Party, it had to be given an iron discipline, the kind that makes armies victorious.

Telexes started flooding into Moscow again. The young Soviet Union had lost its consulate in Shanghai; the shutters of the great and imposing building on the Bund had been closed since the events of April 1927. The Comintern had had to send Russian radio operators, trained to operate clandestinely, in order to receive, encode, and decode messages. With the laconic curtness of telegraphed dialogues, the communications between the conspirators in the worldwide revolution had taken on a military tone. The radio operators were well-trained specialists recruited in the ranks of the Russian GPU. They also served as liaisons between Chinese Communists, making use of various kinds of commercial or journalistic cover. In the evenings, when they were not explaining the secrets of their codes to the Chinese, they made the rounds of the concessions' cabarets—the Casanova, the Venus Café, or especially the Majestic, where both the orchestra and the girls were Russian. The girls were often former bourgeois, sometimes bankrupt aristocrats who had ended up in Shanghai ten years earlier, after the civil war. Prostitutes or hostesses, they hummed "Pleasure, gin and jazz!" while serving up all three, bewitching the somewhat oafish Muscovites, Reds they would hand over to the police at the first opportunity.

AT THE OTHER END OF THE TELEGRAPH LINE, PAVEL MIF WAS FAITH-fully reporting to Stalin, accompanied by Wang Ming, his interpreter. Detested by his peers, Wang was not only expert in the Russian language but also the best student of dialectics at Sun Yat-sen University. With his group of "students," consisting of about thirty thugs who had recently become Stalinists, he had begun a reign of terror at the university, with the blessings of the rector, Pavel Mif himself. The first operation of liqui-dating young Chinese Trotskyists, kept secret, had begun with general beatings on the campus. Soon a second wave was to be launched, this time with the GPU's police. There were more than two hundred arrests one evening in the dormitories, and one suicide. A few one-way tickets to Siberia concluded the operation.

In the little world of the Chinese in Moscow, the measures taken by Li Lisan were the subject of much commentary. Wang Ming found little to object to in them; he had just finished writing a pamphlet glorifying armed insurrenctions. Xiang Zhongfa, the half-illiterate longshoreman, had a tendency to fall asleep during theoretical discussions. He was delighted to see his name appear in *Pravda*, accompanied by his title, "secretary-general of the Chinese Communist Party," and a flattering "authentic proletarian." But the young Wang Ming, at twenty-four, was privy to the secrets of the gods of the revolution, and he envisaged the future the way one envisages one's own career. Mif had promised him that he, too, would soon leave Moscow and go back to Shanghai. The Party needed young men like him—men who thoroughly understood Russian.

Stalin, impatient, demanded results. He had to have a revolution quickly, somewhere. Telexes came into Shanghai asking Li and Chou to turn up the heat.

In October, the holy of holies, the Executive Committee of the Third International, sent a solemn address to the Central Committee of the Chinese Communist Party. In Moscow as well, people were certain that China was experiencing the beginning of a revolutionary wave. It was henceforth official.

In Shanghai, Li was crossing swords with the Trotskyists, a few somewhat crazed students who'd come back from Moscow and who wanted to fight for holding general elections and calling a constituent assembly. In August, Chen Duxiu, who had been sidelined for two years, had come out of his long internal exile, ending his sullenness to give overt support to Trotsky's theses. This veteran communist was a formidable danger and threatened to derail the Party machine. Stalin had sensed that the Trotsky–Chen Duxiu alliance was beginning to emerge. In mid-November 1929, the sacrifice was decided upon, and the Chinese Communist Party excommunicated its father. Li Lisan conducted this expulsion without flinching, writing an implacable indictment of all the real or supposed crimes of Trotskyism in general, and of its Chinese variant in particular. Stalin breathed more easily; the Party was clearly in good hands.

But not for long. Concern grew again on the other side of the Urals when the cables sent by two employees of the Comintern were read. August Thalheimer and Heinrich Brandler, sent to Shanghai to supervise their Chinese comrades, were perplexed. Since their arrival that summer, the two German Communists, in disgrace back home, had been trying assiduously to follow the tribulations of revolutionary Marxism in the land of Confucius. Like their predecessors, the two experts did not speak a word of Chinese and knew almost nothing about Chinese affairs. Silent and pensive, they spent their time sitting side by side in the smoky garret where the Politburo secretly held its meetings, trying to understand what was going on.

Chou En-lai, who spoke a little German and Russian, occasionally did the two Cominternians the favor of providing a few magnanimous summaries. When they thought they had understood, Marx's two compatriots immediately objected systematically to the decisions that had been made, raising all sorts of erudite questions of principle. After several such exercises, Li lost patience and decided that he had two "useless morons" on his hands.

Comrades Brandler and Thalheimer then realized that the head of the Chinese Communist Party was not only touchy but also not very open to hierarchical arguments. To the great pleasure of his Chinese Politburo, which loved his holy rages, Li brutally snubbed the two men before moving to the following point, indifferent to the protests of the Comintern's representatives. Li considered himself just as much a Cominternian as they were, and treated them as equals. When tempers flared, Li sharply reminded the Germans that they were there, after all, because they were right-wingers in bad odor with their Party, and because the Comintern lacked enough competent personnel. And that this was the time to fight to the death the "right-wing spirit," as the Comintern and Stalin were repeating daily. A diplomatic incident was barely avoided; the two experts reported to Moscow that there had been "disrespectful" and "undisciplined" treatment by the head of the Chinese Party, whose leader was displaying "nationalist" behavior.

On the Shanghai-Moscow telegraph line, the Russian radio operators, tapping into these barbed exchanges, jumped when Li Lisan demanded, in a surprisingly direct way, that the two Germans be simply recalled.

HIS EYES GLUED TO THE REVOLUTION'S BAROMETER, WHICH WAS STUCK on "storm," Li observed his country, attentive to the slightest rift. In September 1929, fierce and murderous fighting had broken out between Chiang Kai-shek and Zhang Fakui, a southern leader who had earlier been his ally. The generalissimo, head of the Nanking government, still did not enjoy unanimous support. In October, the dukes and lords of the north had formed an opposing coalition and crossed swords with him in their turn. Anarchy was in full swing, and not decreasing. The Northern Expedition had done nothing to change this, and the Shanghai and Canton massacres still less.

In November, the young Soviet Union, China's former protector, attacked it. Soviet troops in Manchuria fired on those of the local satrap, who had tried to make a show of force. In the Kremlin, Stalin insisted on the treaties between the Chinese emperor and the czar being observed; they allowed the Russian East China Railway to pass through Chinese Manchuria on the way to Vladivostok, Russia's great port on the Pacific.

This shortcut of about six hundred miles along the rails of the Trans-Siberian Railroad was a tempting prize.

Thus a Chinese military feint ended up provoking a campaign lasting several days, a Soviet war lesson administered by a connoisseur: Vassily Blücher, alias Galen, the Russian general acclaimed by his Chinese soldiers on the Northern Expedition, had struck hard. Expelled from China along with Borodin, Blücher, who was familiar with campaigns in the Far East, was sending a signal to the army of the mikado, who was financing the Chinese troops in Manchuria: Russia did not intend to be weak. But Chinese blood had been shed by the rifles of the Red Army, and public opinion in Nanking, Shanghai, and Beijing pointed an accusing finger at Moscow.

Li swept the affair aside: if necessary, the Chinese revolutionaries would stand shoulder to shoulder with the heroic Soviet soldiers against the threats that weighed on the young homeland of the Soviets. Japanese troops, their rifles at their sides, were observing from a distance. The mikado's infantrymen, massed in Korea, were fully equipped and ready for action. Mukden, the ancient capital of Manchuria, was teeming with spies from Tokyo, Moscow, and elsewhere.

Farther to the south, in a comfortable villa in Tientsin, a somewhat blasé twenty-three-year-old man was languishing. Pu Yi, the last emperor of China, the last scion of the Ch'ing dynasty, was settling disputes among his concubines and dreaming of a constitutional throne.

In January 1930, the Politburo met and echoed the Comintern's call for action: "We must act on the instructions of the International and immediately begin to prepare the masses" for armed insurrection. On this subject, Li had already taken more than one salaried prophet of the International literally. The Party machine was enthusiastic. Every strike was a pretext for intense propaganda in favor of a general uprising, the fourth one. The one Shanghai had long been waiting for, and which was to bring victory and freedom. At the beginning of March, Chou En-lai left for Moscow to engage in the final consultations. On March 5, skirmishes broke out between the police in the

French concession and women cotton mill workers on strike. The police had not appreciated the chamber pots the demonstrators had thrown on their uniforms. When the *tchons,* armed with iron bars, broke a policeman's rifle, the police, who had been recruited in the French colony of Annam, opened fire in Admiral Bayle Street. The workers carried off one dead and five seriously wounded. On March 8, International Women's Day gave rise to a few feminist demonstrations. After a short time, the women workers won out, and victims were compensated. At the same time, tramway drivers in the British and French zones and employees of Shanghai Power were holding nocturnal meetings in vacant lots in Djabei and Yangshupu to plan the next strike. In the Pathé factories, the strike was cut short by the hiring of twelve White Russians.

While rotary presses were being turned by hand in cellars, Li undertook to transform the Party into a tiger ready to leap across the country at any moment. Starting in April, members had become conspirators, reorganized into action committees to build up slender stocks of weapons and draw up plans to take over their cities. They were prepared to die, like earlier martyrs, provided that this time was the real one. The Party had a leader, and a hail of instructions was putting the battle units in position.

Li concocted a simple and sturdy scenario: May Day would be marked by as much agitation as possible, which would be continued until the anniversary of May 30, 1925, which would not fail to redouble popular feeling. In April, he announced in *Red Flag,* the Party's clandestine organ, that the situation was now "directly revolutionary."

The grand gestures in the street brought together a few hundred brave people. At the China Omnibus Company, a strike of seven hundred drivers and conductors was launched, and soon joined by fifteen hundred tramway workers. The Party urged all of them to be "prepared for the bloody struggle against the capitalists." On May 13, three hundred strikers attacked in broad daylight the trams on Ferry Road and dismantled the throttle levers after a few fights and several shouting matches. Arrests started to be made in large numbers; Police Commissioner Fiori, in the French concession, soon counted a hundred. His British colleagues had already made more than three hundred arrests. Some of them were fine catches, such as the sixteen agitators arrested on April 29 at the Shanghai Power workers' club on Yalu Road, as they were preparing for May Day. Three days before, the French had rounded up thirty-six agitators at one time. All of them were handed over to the Chinese police: many, who had long been identified, were immediately executed in the Longhua barracks. The others went to rot in prison for a few years.

Chou En-lai and Kang Sheng transformed the party into a clandestine bunker, airtight and walled in. But there would not be a general strike on May 30. Their hearts were no longer in it.

LI MOVED ON. THE WHITE TERROR WAS STILL MURDEROUS, BUT ITS days were clearly numbered. Moreover, the news from the Red armies was good, even excellent in this spring of 1930. The regroupings had been carried out more or less well, and the soviet zones had been extended to about twenty cantons in the rural hinterland of Hunan and Jiangxi.

In the belly of China, sixty thousand men had been gathered together, half of them equipped with rifles and ready to fight. Hardened criminals, agricultural day workers who had been idled by the civil war, factory workers and craftsmen, city dwellers who had fled the sabers of the police and ended up in the countryside, dreamers lost in dogmas, they formed a disparate but willing group. During long instructional meetings, Communist officials inculcated the virtues of discipline in these *déclassés*, half guerrillas, half soldiers. In their state of raised consciousness, they pitilessly tracked down so-called rich peasants and rural nobles, making them "return their ill-gotten gains" and arousing fear and respect among the local populace.

Seen from Shanghai, Mao Tse-tung and his men seemed to be doing good work, despite the difficulty Chou En-lai had in contacting them. Li particularly liked the reports that had reached headquarters. In January, Mao had warned that "China as a whole is sitting on a tinderbox, ready to burst into flames." Citing a proverb, Mao added that like Li, he had no doubt that "a single spark can start a prairie fire."

This was also an exercise in self-criticism. Six months earlier, Mao had sworn that within a year he would take the whole province of Jiangxi and its capital, Nanchang. Now he recognized that the time was a little short. But "Marxists are not oracles," the former teacher explained. This time, "it is enough to glance at the workers' strikes, the peasant uprisings, the soldiers' mutinies, and student strikes that are growing everywhere, in order to understand that the spark will soon come."

Poetically, he added that the revolutionary wave was there, "like the disk of the sun whose burning rays are already piercing the shadows of the Orient, visible from the mountaintop."

Li then gathered in Shanghai the insurrection's general staff, a few dozen delegates from the Red and White zones, military men and civilians. Mao, who hated Shanghai, refused to come. The Red Army was nonetheless honored there, and its leaders helped put the final touches on the plans for action. When the secret consultations were concluded on June 4, 1930, the goal was to found a "Chinese republic of soviets" as soon as the insurrection succeeded. The date was even set: it was to be proclaimed on November 7, the day of the Bolshevik victory in Saint Petersburg thirteen years earlier.

Then Li wrote his political testament. In two days and one night, he sketched out a turbulent picture of the world in which he predicted, with a vivid clarity borrowed from Lenin, that "it is in China that the volcano of the worldwide revolution is the most certain to erupt," and that the subsequent earthquake would shake the whole globe. The Chinese revolution had an "international mission" that could only provide an heir for the October Revolution. The time was ripe, Li swore. In June 1930, world capitalism, deeply affected by the financial crash, was "on the brink of collapse." Moscow was trumpeting its final fall. The homeland of the soviets had proclaimed the advent of the "third period," that of imminent Bolshevik victory throughout the world.

The revolutionary wave was up? Point noted, Li replied. Here in China, "any incident can start the great fight." It would set the Japanese, the British, and the Americans to fighting for supremacy in Asia. China was the country where all the imperial ambitions converged, the geometric point from which the flames of the worldwide revolution would spread. The war that would not fail to follow would be "cruel." Convinced of what he had observed over the past few years, Li stressed that "all means will be used to get rid of the Chinese revolutionaries." What did it matter? The country was there, impatient to do battle with the enemy, eager to put an end to exploitation. For "the workers do not lack the desire to make a revolution, but only a revolutionary consciousness." And above all, people should not count on the apparent lethargy of the masses: if the occasion presents itself, "they can be mobilized at the speed of light." In the suburbs of Shanghai and Wuhan, didn't one hear it said that "when the hour of the insurrection arrives, tell us, and we'll come running"? And Li, the secret clockmaker of history, jumped at the opportunity: "We must tell people boldly that the time is coming and that they should organize!"

Everywhere in the country, "famine and war are putting tens of thousands of people on the roads, casting them into cold, hunger, and death, and none of the leadership cliques is capable of saving China or reunifying it!" For every Chinese, for every patriot, there was "no longer any other choice" than revolution, which would build a new world, freed from oppressors and foreigners.

The rest was a matter of preparations. Experience had shown that workers could not win by themselves. Moreover, urban combat was "more cruel and more intense than combat in the countryside."

Therefore, the revolution had to be combined with the Red Army. They had to target an urban, industrial center on which they would march while the people there staged an uprising. Wuhan was ideal, but too risky for the time being; it would be better to start with one or two neighboring provinces, where the enemy, busy fighting in the north, was thinner.

In passing, Li warned Mao that he had to break with the guerrilla mentality, that peasant habit of occupying a city for a few hours and then retreating as soon as it looked like the enemy was coming back. It had to give way to a Red Army worthy of the name.

Li asked everyone, old and young, to go to their battle stations. He did not forget Moscow, which he enjoined to tell the world about the battle going on in China. And to give them the help they needed.

Putting down his brush, Li reread the document with the care he would have given to a Mandarin examination, murmuring, in response to

Mao's prairie fire, the ancient verses: "And we shall water our horses in the great river!"

More perplexed than ever, the two Germans of the International cabled Li's message to Moscow. When Li discussed the operational plan he envisaged, they went pale. He was asking Stalin to make internationalism equal to the stakes, and to occupy Chiang Kai-shek and the northern warlords by staging a military operation. A little march through Manchuria for the young and valiant Soviet army would make things much easier for the revolutionaries south of the Yangtze. Blücher, who was commanding the Soviet troops on the border and was familiar with Chinese affairs, would easily understand this. For him, it would be a Northern Expedition in reverse, in short. It would start from the banks of the Amur River and move down toward Beijing.

So far as troops were concerned, Li offered an idea: there were hundreds of thousands of Chinese immigrants in eastern Siberia, whom the Soviets had only to arm and send to reconquer their own country. Most of them had fled war, poverty, or famine; according to him, all they wanted was to take up a rifle.

As for the military initiative, he counted on Blücher to make it a proud one. After all, this was the much-heralded worldwide revolution that was on the march. It well deserved a bit of daring.

In Moscow, the leaders of the International were torn between stupefaction at the nerve of this Chinese and fear of the Kremlin's ire. Li's line was impeccable. None of Stalin's men could find anything to object to in it. Only the diplomats were startled: a Soviet military initiative in Manchuria would immediately turn into an overt conflict with the Japanese. Since 1905, the general staff had preferred to avoid such a conflict. So the answer regarding the military initiative was no.

Li exploded with anger. He sharply reminded Stalin that the Chinese Bolsheviks had supported him when the Soviet army had fought Chinese soldiers in Manchuria six months earlier. Li was not far from railing at the homeland of socialism. The Russian telegraph operators in Shanghai, cabling ciphered messages to Moscow, thought they discerned a new crisis. The Comintern's utility was harshly questioned, openly defied, even called upon to prove that it was not compromising with the right-wingers. Draped in his dignity, Li assured the Soviets that if that was the way things were going to be, he would not hesitate to choose the Chinese revolution over the country of the soviets. At the very least, the insurgents would be satisfied with a few shipments of armaments. Machine guns were rare, and artillery nonexistent, except in the hands of the enemy.

IN THE COMINTERN'S CORRIDORS, PEOPLE WERE WHISPERING, "LI Lisan has gone mad!" Pavel Mif suggested to Stalin that this insolent fellow was a "semi-Trotskyist." For months, Li's behavior had been bordering on insubordination. Comrades Brandler and Thalheimer's reports were disastrous. Instead of filling management posts in the Party with those who "had returned from Moscow," as planned, Li was taking a sly pleasure in sending these young Chinese students, freshly graduated from Sun Yat-sen University, to do organizational work in the Shanghai factories. There they were risking arrest and death, like everyone else. Li did not have a great deal of esteem for these intellectuals imbued with the Russian language, virtuosos in dialectic, but with little experience under fire. Wang Ming had exasperated everyone as soon as he arrived in Shanghai. With his precious manners, the young expert from Moscow barely concealed an erudite arrogance. More seriously, he seemed incapable of putting up with clandestinity. He had gotten himself arrested by the police at a meeting of labor agitators two weeks after he came to Shanghai, and getting him out of jail had cost the Party several thousand dollars in bribes paid to the Sikh policemen in the international concession. Wang had given his prison guards the address of a comrade who could be contacted to pick up the money. Not only had he forced the Party's hand, but he had set his own price for his freedom. When Chou En-lai and Kang Sheng, who were keeping a sharp eye on security questions, put the whole matter before Li, Wang Ming was censured for having "failed to observe political vigilance and gravely deviated from the discipline of clandestine work." Li had then sent him to a cigarette factory to give his classes as a revolutionary proletarian.

Wang had confided his bitterness to the two Germans. Brandler and Thalheimer sympathized with him: Li was *ein groBes Problem*. . . .

Soon, all Moscow's faithful would be there, like Yang Shangkun,* who came from the Red capital to aid Wang Ming. Twenty-eight of them had made a Bolshevik pact among themselves in the dormitories of Sun Yat-sen University. All of them were young Chinese devoted to Stalin.

Pavel Mif was counting on them to bring this Li Lisan fellow to heel. For the time being, the Party was behind Li. Even Chou En-lai, on reboarding the Trans-Siberian, assured the sorcerer's apprentices from Moscow that the situation in China was eminently revolutionary. The exact date depended on the circumstances. Chou had been a big hit when he addressed the delegates to the Soviet Communist Party's Fifteenth Congress, shortly before leaving Moscow. Stalin wanted this exceptional favor shown the foreigner: to speak before the top leadership of the Russian Communist Party. He had personally given the signal for applause after Chou had finished his speech. Chou had assured his hearers that China was soon going to give birth to a revolution. Stalin, his eyes lively and triumphant, had scrutinized the disciplined audience.

From one end of Russia to the other, portraits of Lenin's heir, painted by revolutionary artists, were multiplying at an accelerating rate. But in the villages of the Ukraine and the Volga, the harvest was disastrous. Ten years after the civil war, famine and death were on the prowl again. Collectivization was moving forward with giant steps.

ON JULY 23, 1930, A NEW TELEGRAM FROM MOSCOW CAME INTO Shanghai. As was its habit, the Comintern had carefully weighed its words. The International recommended the "reinforcement of the Chinese Red Army so that, depending on the political and military circumstances, one or several industrial centers might soon be occupied."

Li heaved a sigh of relief: he had won. The key words had been uttered. "Soon" came quickly: on July 27, Communist troops entered

---

*Future president of the Republic of China after the events in Tiananmen Square in 1989.

Changsha, the capital of Hunan and dear to the hearts of the Party's leaders. At the head of his eighteen thousand men, Peng Dehuai occupied the old city without much difficulty, since its defenders had retreated farther to the north. The first phase of the plan had gone well.

In the city, the welcome was rather cool. Changsha, which had been drowning in violence for ten years already, had ended up casting the same opprobrium on all the uniforms and armies that occupied it. Peng Dehuai, thirty-two, was from Hunan and a fervent partisan of Li Lisan. A man of the same stamp as He Long, the former highwayman, at the age of eighteen he had led a group of peasants in his canton in appropriating a landowner's stock of rice, and then joined the first army that came by. In the army he had found a family before winning his spurs in the service of Sun Yat-sen. An officer with character, he had broken with Chiang Kai-shek after the rift in April 1927 and taken his regiment with him, joining Mao's and Zhu De's forces. For this veteran of the Northern Expedition, taking Changsha was almost a matter of military routine. Peng proclaimed on the spot the advent of the "soviet government of the three provinces": Hunan, Hubei, and Jiangxi. Next, he had called for cheers for the name of Li Lisan, who was designated president of this new Red republic.

For Li, in hiding in Shanghai, the conquest of Changsha was a good sign. In Moscow, they were holding their breath as the teletypes came in.

THE SECOND PART OF THE PLAN FAILED. IN NEIGHBORING JIANGXI, Mao and Zhu De broke off the battle before Nanchang. By a telegram signed by Li Lisan a few weeks earlier, Zhu De had been promoted to commander in chief of all the Red armies. Mao was his first political commissar, the direct representative of the Party's top leadership to the army. Orders from Shanghai.

They had arrived in front of the fortified city on July 29, under the blazing sun. Their columns had traveled on foot from the mountains in the southwest through half the province, raising thousands of peasants who were more or less volunteers along the way. The news of the fall of Changsha in neighboring Hunan on July 27 had raised morale. It also inspired Mao to write some verse for the occasion: "A million workers and peasants have risen up / Sweeping through Jiangxi, straight toward Hunan and Hubei / To the sound of the poignant accents of the International / A savage whirlwind comes down from the sky." The few Kuomintang troops met along the way had prudently retreated to take refuge in Nanchang.

On August 30, 1930, precisely three years after it was born, the Red Army found itself once again at the foot of Nanchang. Mao and Zhu De launched a first assault. The city had little artillery, and its population was terrorized by the soldiers. At the end of twenty-four hours of indecisive skirmishes at the approaches to the city, Mao and Zhu De, who still favored guerrilla warfare, decided to abandon the attempt.

The troops were ordered to withdraw, and they headed north, in the direction of Wuhan. The triple city on the great river was the third stage of Li Lisan's plan. It was supposed to be taken after Nanchang and Changsha. Only the keys to Wuhan, taken while waiting to acquire those to Shanghai or Nanking, would give national legitimacy to the Communists.

Too bad for the plan, Mao and Zhu De had decided. For them, the revolution could move forward no more quickly than a column of men who were weary, always hungry, and as skinny as their mules. Down there on the banks of the great river, they would water their horses while waiting for a military windfall.

During this time, in front of Changsha, the American gunboat *Palos,* which had come up from the Yangtze, opened fire on the city. After Great Britain, the United States, claiming to protect its citizens, was blocking the Communists' road. Anchored at a distance on the Siang River, the escort vessel bombarded the city using its sole cannon, firing deadly and incendiary missiles without being able to see its targets. The British, Japanese, and Italian gunboats had, however, already evacuated foreigners from the city. Uneasy in the old merchant city, poorly supported by the population, Peng Dehuai's troops had been sorely tested, while the Kuomintang was massing its battalions for a counterattack.

Peng soon learned the news of Mao's and Zhu's failure at Nanchang. He realized that he was going to take the brunt of the counterattack all by himself. Nine days after he entered Changsha, he gave the order to evacuate the city. Already warned regarding the danger that would accompany the return of the soldiers who had been driven out, hundreds of civilians went with the Communists when they retreated.

For his part, farther north, He Long was leading his men by careful steps toward Wuhan, preferring not to wait for a hypothetical junction with Mao and his men.

IN SHANGHAI, MARTIAL LAW WAS INSTITUTED IN THE FRENCH CON-cession because of serious strikes. Consul Koechlin asked Paris to send reinforcements. The Reds in the city were on a rampage. The concession was covered with barriers, barbed wire, and sandbags guarded by sol-diers. France was in its turn ostracized for the "massacre of July 21"—an incident in which the concession's police had beaten strikers and that had turned out badly. One death and a number of wounded were deplored. The Red labor unions demanded reparations. The police were on edge and the memory of May 1925 was on everybody's mind.

The Chinese police auxiliaries and their informers were categorical: Li's hand was behind this new climate of rebellion. Despite official reports, the informers were sure that the demon had not died in a brawl in Hankow: he was living in town under countless pseudonyms. Unfindable and elusive, it was he, the leader of the Reds.

On August 2, it was reported that more than fifteen hundred strikers had assembled on the playing field at the Western Gate, despite martial law. The following day, the news that Peng Dehuai had taken Changsha brought at least a thousand people into the streets in the center of the city. The reports on the consul's table were unanimous: the crowd was chant-ing "Let's follow Changsha's example!" The city was flooded with clan-destine tracts. On August 5, the same people were demonstrating and shouting "Down with the French police!"

Since then, incidents had been breaking out almost everywhere, even far from Shanghai. If there was no popular uprising, China's cities were witnessing an increasing number of actions instigated by the Communists. Consul Koechlin was baffled. Reinforcements would be welcome. The Chinese jumble was certainly indecipherable, but still menacing.

★     ★

LI LISAN WAS NOT GIVING UP. THE NEW NORTHERN EXPEDITION turned out to be far more uncertain than the first one, but the battle was on. With the Party's general staff, he decided to put together a new assault on Changsha, regrouping and concentrating their forces this time.

At the end of August, the armies of Peng Dehuai, Mao, and Zhu De had effected their junction. Disciplined, the soldiers were carrying out Shanghai's orders. But the generals were sullen. "The damned artillery!" Peng grumbled. He still lacked that modern weapon par excellence, even though Moscow was constantly promising to provide it. Forever, Soviet advisers had been telling Chinese officers that artillery alone could make the difference. In fact, the troops, which were ready for any kind of hand-to-hand fighting, were afraid of being caught under an artillery barrage. Since the bloody harvests of the autumn of 1927, Mao had been a partisan of returning to guerrilla warfare. The cities were always dangerous and far away. Shanghai's emissaries arrived in the military camps only after five days of harassing travel, and Soviet radio operators were rare.

At the beginning of September, Peng, Mao, and Zhu started out with more than thirty thousand men to make another assault on Changsha. Within the ramparts, five Nationalist regiments, which had hastened to repair the city's defenses, were waiting for them. In the streets, the Kuomintang's army, fearing a Communist fifth column, had massacred all the opposition. Soon the Red columns, armed this time, arrived within range of Chinese artillery.

To the north, on board gunboats anchored in the Siang, elegant officers of the Western marines exchanged courteous formal visits before examining maps of the region: recently, the evacuations of Christian missionaries had been increasingly difficult.

On September 13, 1930, Mao, Zhu, and Peng disengaged before the city. The second assault never took place. In hastily dug ditches around the city, the men had been facing each other for a week under the burning sun of the Hunan summer. The Nationalist republicans, who had taken up fortified positions around the city center, had cannons and assured supplies. The Communists had a few obsolete artillery pieces and empty mess bowls. The machine guns facing them did not encourage attempts to approach the city. The retreat was made in good order toward the south, along the now familiar roads, to the relief of the besieged city.

On the way, the young Red generals wondered whether they had disobeyed or simply respected military science.

The announcement of the retreat from Changsha struck Li like a freight train. This time, the defeat was complete. The news coming from other cities was no better. Nowhere had the actions led to insurrections. The spark that was supposed to ignite the worldwide wildfire had gone out.

In Shanghai, Consul Koechlin lifted martial law. They'd dodged the Red bullet. The summer had been hot and agitated, but now they could breathe again. The Chinese were strange, their ways of doing politics so confusing.

As usual, the repression was cruel. In Changsha, even more heads rolled under the sabers. Mao's wife, Yang Kaihui, who had been living there alone for the past two years, was arrested along with their two sons, Mao Anying and Mao Antsing, aged seven and four. The mother was executed in public, but the two boys were saved.

In Moscow, in the Comintern's meetings, Pavel Mif rubbed his hands: the time had come. It was now clear that the Chinese were not capable of handling their affairs by themselves. The commands of Moscow "students" could now make their entrance on the stage. Pavel Mif wanted Li Lisan's head. After those of Chen Duxiu and Qu Qiubai, he would offer this one to Stalin as a trophy.

Mif and Manouilski spoke to the Guide, who approved. This Li Lisan was too temperamental and had no real army. He lacked flexibility and his insolence was unlimited. The Chinese revolution was spinning out of control. The telegraphic correspondence in June had stunned the Center. Especially when, in reply to Moscow, Li Lisan had demanded the pure and simple recall of the two Germans. In July, Russian diplomats had gaped in stupefaction on seeing his telegram asking them to join in the great summer offensive. Stalin had listened, incredulous: not satisfied to consider himself a revolutionary leader, this thirty-year-old Chinese was inviting him to engage in a military venture. It was high time to remind him who had made him king.

Besides, he must have been mistaken when he gauged the wave. "Bring him to Moscow, then," Stalin said jovially. "We'll teach him to be flexible."

As soon as the world press had reported the Communist failure to take Changsha, Mif had a severe condemnation of the events in China sent to Shanghai. A week earlier, *Inprecor,* the official organ of the International, had paid homage to the city's fall, which opened "a new chapter in the Chinese revolution: it is the first time since the insurrection in Canton in December 1927 that a major industrial city has fallen into the hands of revolutionary workers." In its next issue, the paper had to announce the failure. The announcement did homage to the Chinese Communists' "great step forward for the soviet movement."

These repeated blunders annoyed the head of the Chinese bureau. Previously, in its number for March 22, 1930, *Inprecor* had published in its obituary column the news of the death of a certain Mao, an obscure Communist peasant leader. Li, who knew about announced deaths, had made ironic remarks about this in Shanghai in the presence of the two German advisers, who were strongly suspected of having fed the rumor.

THE FIRST SKIRMISH TOOK PLACE IN SHANGHAI ON SEPTEMBER 24. Before a meeting of the Central Committee called at Moscow's request, Chou En-lai had explained the Kremlin's complaints, and then immediately taken his stand on Li Lisan's side. To be sure, his comrade was responsible for "sporadic tactical errors," but in no case was he guilty of a "political error." His line was the right one, and moreover, "the revolutionary situation in China was becoming more acute every day." The proof of this was "the wave of workers' uprisings and peasant wars that are spreading from the villages to throw off the yoke of the Kuomintang!" The result was there: "We now have fifty million Chinese under our control!"

If there had been a problem at Changsha, Chou explained to the other Party leaders, "that was because the Red army is not yet completely a Red army. Born out of peasant guerrilla warfare, it has to move beyond it in order to become a powerful and centralized army, the main force in the war."

And Chou interposed himself between Li and his attackers. He sternly asserted that there was "no question of tolerating expressions such as Lilisanism" in the ranks, as Moscow suggested.

The Chinese leaders approved. Kang Sheng, who was reponsible for secret operations and served as Chou's right-hand man, stood with him. The last Red labor leaders in Shanghai yielded. They had been quarreling heatedly with Li for months, but he was one of theirs.

ON READING CHOU EN-LAI'S REPORT, PAVEL MIF WAS LIVID WITH rage. Li had gotten off with a "perspeciacious self-criticism," which was praised by Chou in his report. After Li's defiance, the way he had thumbed his nose at Moscow. The Chinese party was hunkering down. Ungovern-able. It was a crisis.

Stalin was angry: they had to take drastic action, and even use force to get rid of this Li Lisan. Mif's plan was simple: put his own men, the good ones, in charge of the Chinese Party. They were young—much younger than Li and Chou—but they had had *serious* training in Moscow. Pavel Mif could count on about thirty of them who were already there or en route, all of them reliable and devoted. Rector Mif's Sun Yat-sen University had done its job well. At the end of autumn 1930, it had just closed its doors. The military academies had taken over, along with the mysterious Lenin Institute for Party officials.

Stalin, smoothing his mustache, looked at Mif with his piercing, sar-castic eyes: "Pavel, pack your bags. You're going to Shanghai. You are directly responsible for the operation."

# 10

L ike a will-o'-the-wisp dancing over black, frozen water, the white light of the moon danced on the lapping waters of the river. Silently, the junk slipped between the freighters that were also heading for the mouth of the river and the open sea, the Pacific. Li Lisan sniffed the sharp air full of spicy spray, the last effluvium of China emanating from the shore, a dark mass of deserted docks on which stood idle cranes. For once, the night was clear over Shanghai. Li shivered. The parade of docks faded out, and rice paddies could be glimpsed in the distance, behind the dikes. A timid siren rent the darkness and made him jump. He heard the muffled, rhythmical complaint of a steamer's engines as it passed the junk, which pitched in the silvery wake of its screws laboring the river. Li was reliving his first departure, eleven years earlier, amid the joyful cries of his comrades, headed for France, straight toward Enlightenment. He lit another cigarette, as if to protect himself from the cold.

At the mouth of the river, they had a rendezvous with a Russian freighter anchored at sea, which was going back to Vladivostok. From there, he would take the train to Moscow again, the endless ride through Siberia. It occurred to him that this time he would be traveling through snow. The December air was glacial, and this departure felt a lot like exile.

STALIN'S INVITATION HAD STRUCK HIM LIKE A LIGHTNING BOLT. THE Comintern had unleashed its powerful machinery. An imperious cable from Moscow had made him an anti-Leninist. Him, the hero of Anyuan, Shanghai, and Hankow, the conqueror of Nanchang and the founder of the Red Army, the spirited, intrepid orator whose name had been circulating around China for the past seven years, a phantom mocking death and its henchmen. Pavel Mif had insisted that *Li Lisan is anti-Lenin!* That label had already won countless people a bullet in the nape of the neck. After sending the cable, Mif had left for Shanghai to complete the operation of getting things back in hand. His boat would pass the one Li was waiting for.

The Kremlin's assurances were clear: Li was to go to Moscow to study and reeducate himself. He would have plenty of time to "study." The idea left him pensive; he didn't much care for academies. But he had hardly any choice. Leaving clandestinity was equivalent to a death warrant, with a price on his head and the Chinese, British, and French police after him. If he continued to defy Moscow—Chinese Communists against Russian Communists—his sole ally would become an enemy.

Chou En-lai and the others had finally given in: the movement's survival was at stake in the Kremlin. The Chinese Party could not be led by an anti-Leninist and a semi-Trotskyist. One evening, in a Shanghai attic, all eyes turned toward Li Lisan. He had understood. His comrades were silently begging him. Stalin had won. He would go to Moscow.

The Guide of the worldwide revolution had signaled the end of Chinese insolence. Following Berlin and Paris, Shanghai had yielded. The Kremlin's men, the ones who had returned from Russia, took over.

The news he'd collected hurriedly before leaving was the worst. In Fujian, Mao was executing hundreds of soldiers and officers of the Red

Army who were loyal to Li. The Red warriors were eating each other alive. There had been a rebellion in the ranks, brought on by a general who accused Mao and Zhu De of running away at Changsha. At the moment that Li's junk was moving out to sea, the affront was being washed away in blood. People spoke of thousands of executions. The savagery of Mao's reaction had stunned Chou Enlai and the others. The Party was asking itself: What happened, then, in front of Changsha's walls? Had Mao and Zhu run away from a fight? Was the city impregnable, was Li's plan so audacious? Peng Dehuai and other generals had expressed doubts.

In Shanghai, after the summer's brief revolutionary outburst, the police had regained the upper hand and were waging a pitiless war.

The wind was propelling the junk, whipping the oiled mats of its sail. Li lifted his eyes toward the stars, as a flight of dead souls accompanied him. He saw again the faces of his comrades, those who were close to him and those who were anonymous, who had fallen under the machine-gun fire in the sunny fields of Hunan and Jiangxi, or in the fetid cellars of the barracks, under torture, awaiting final deliverance. His people. Rough and stubborn to the point of fanaticism, or touched by the grace of ideals, blind poets lost in the sun of radiant futures, fierce, often brave nationalists, steeped in dreams, thirsty for vengeance. Setting out on the adventure, they had already inflected China's destiny.

The junk passed at a cable length's distance the last light marking the beginning of the ocean. Li filled his lungs with air. At least in Moscow, he would no longer have policemen on his back. He could move about without fear, without bodyguards in front or in back of him. No more antique dealer disguises, no more parts to play. The dull terror of the tracked animal was over. In the country of the comrades, "the streets were safe and the avenues were cut in freedom," the poets said.

Once again, he had not had time to say good-bye to his family. His father and mother, guilty of having produced such a son, were threatened with death down there in Hunan. He hardly knew his children; he would have to keep away from them at any cost, since they were no doubt under surveillance by some servant on the police payroll. Their mothers, the two Li sisters, were in deep hiding, the mute tomb of adolescent loves.

THE WATER WAS BLACK BENEATH THE MOON. LI DREAMED HE WAS taking the southern route, toward France, the land of Napoléon Bonaparte, that man whose eternal youth fascinated them all. The glacial reflection of a little wave alongside the junk, a silvery wink from the moon, forced him to smile wanly. "The waves . . . one has to know how to gauge the waves. . . ." At least he had learned a Russian word, recently: *pod'em*—waves.

The sailor tugged at his sleeve in order to tell him that the Soviet freighter had come into view.

# II

September 1933. From the windows of the Lenin Institute, near the Arbat, Li could see the roofs of Kitai-Gorod, the old Chinese quarter behind the Kremlin. Pensively, he realized that three years after leaving China for Moscow, he had still not understood the mystery of this quarter that had nothing Chinese about it but its name. In its dirty, narrow streets, one met all kinds of Siberians, Caucasians, even Koreans. But very few Chinese. It was whispered that most of them had disappeared along with private enterprise a few years earlier. Since then, Moscow had a shortage of dry-cleaning establishments, which had been transformed into implausible workers' cooperatives with many red flags and banners flying over their doors.

The whole city, moreover, was decorated. Single red flags attached to the windowsills of anonymous apartments, bouquets of red flags at the entrances to offices and factories. Or lined up like a parade along the columned facades of the buildings housing the new regime. Flags and banners, deluxe banners—dark-red velvet with letters embroidered in fine gold—or neighborhood banners in white cloth, barring the roads and the sky with their virile, painted-on slogans: DEATH TO ENEMIES OF THE PEOPLE! LONG LIVE STALIN'S FIVE-YEAR PLAN! Between the flags and banners, portraits, thousands of portraits of the Vojd, the Chief, stared at the passerby with benevolent but still slightly mocking eyes. From one street corner to another, one might run into portraits of the Chief's closest associates, the powerful People's Commissars—Mikhail Ivanovich Kalinin, the president, or Kliment Yefremovich Voroshilov, the First Red Officer. Near Pushkin Square, going up Gorky Street, one found them all together, the Chief's portrait a little elevated over the others. The regime made a great display of itself. The revolution also exhibited its philosophers. Crowds of anonymous artists, requisitioned by the state, carefully painted thousands of square yards of oil portraits of the faces of Marx and Engels, some of which might be more than eight yards high. Throughout the country, the portrait factories displayed, like other factories, plans, scores, and elite workers imbued with socialist emulation. Now the smallest hamlet, the tiniest handful of *izsbas* in the depths of the Russian forest, had its portrait of the two German philosophers. Beyond, as far as the remote villages of Kazakhstan or Armenia, people went to bed after spending the evening under the learned gaze of the new masters. In the streets of Moscow, the billboards of the time of the New Economic Policy, bearing slogans with jovial plays on words, had disappeared beneath the new icons.

Tentatively, haggardly, the capital was putting on a new skin, as if a giant hand had torn it away from the makeshift torpor of the 1920s to climb astride the century. It was time to make a leap forward! Only one more year, and the first five-year plan would be complete. It was pulverizing the world records of capitalism, banners, newspapers, and radios proclaimed. Already, Moscow was trembling on its foundations. The walls of Kitai-Gorod had fallen, and beneath the surface, day and night, an underground army was drilling, digging, welding, constructing miles of tunnels as broad as avenues. A subway in Moscow? Better yet: a legacy to humanity. A worldwide challenge that the country of the soviets would accept at any cost, and do it in record time to boot. Subterranean palaces, a feat that would make Paris, Berlin, New York, or Tokyo pale. It was trumpeted day after day in the streets, where faceless voices, virtuous or triumphant, constantly came out of loudspeakers at intersections, reading a long list of *oudarniki,* outstanding workers, before launching into "The International" again. In April, Komsomols had been recruited in large numbers. Thirteen thousand adolescents were sent as reinforcements to lend a hand to the workers digging in the entrails of the capital. Their tools on their shoulders, their red scarves carefully knotted over their white shirts, their heads held high, and their eyes full of pride, Young Communists marched through the streets, parading before photographers and the *komsorg,* the monitors at their sides, attentive to the slogans and as uneasy as shepherd dogs. Every shovelful dug in the subway was rewarded by a place in the epic, and, Komsomol's honor, the thing was worth an oath sworn before the nation.

Moscow, the city where the proletarian was king, was setting out on the conquest of the automobile. Taylorism was behind schedule here, and the only automobile factory in the country, ZIS, "the Factory of Stalin's Name" in Simionovski, the old working-class quarter in the southwest part of the city, was ordered to catch up. In five years, the number of its workers had increased from fifteen hundred to thirty thousand. It had to catch up with Renault in Boulogne-Billancourt, catch up with Ford in Detroit, catch up with the great powers' tons of iron, enter the age of machines. The Party liked big concentrations of workers, and large construction projects as well. The architects of the proletariat were putting the final touches on the plans for a new Moscow, cutting straight through the network of narrow streets in the old city in order to open up majestic new avenues. *Pravda* was making the workers dream by suggesting that there would soon be thousands of automobiles on these avenues, just as in America. But under the windows of the Kremlin, around the Metropole, the regime's palace, the horse-cab drivers bellowed and cracked their whips to move their skinny horses between the trams and trolleys. Stubborn, the old Russian drivers still called their customers *barin* (gentleman), cursing under their breath the *tovarichtchi* (comrades) in their taxis, and complained about the first traffic jams. At intersections, they shouted abuse at the traffic officers—all of whom were now women! The male police officers in Moscow were spending a considerable portion of their time in classes with their colleagues at the GPU.

The architects wanted to see the capital double its surface area, surround itself with forests and parks, and limit its population. The newspaper *Moskovskaia Pravda* proudly announced that Soviet housing had lodged 60 million workers in one year, in new three- or four-story apartment buildings built of concrete. These apartments had gas, electricity, sewers, and even telephones and radios, the newspaper told Muscovites. Socialism was achieving great feats, and the paper published many reports on the pleasure of cooking for eight families in a common kitchen.

Li Lisan was bent over that day's *Pravda,* which was spread out before him. The paper was examining once again the consequences of the Nazi victory in Germany. Since July 14, the Reich had been put under a one-party system. Its new leader, Adolf Hitler, had won the elections held six months earlier. He was opening prison camps that the Gestapo was filling. In the Comintern, all this made people think. Up until the last minute, the German Communists had made a common front with the Nazis against the socialists. All the party officials knew that in Hamburg the head of the Red militia and that of the Brownshirts called each other on the telephone to make plans: the Reds would attack the meeting of those dirty socialists on the right side; the Brownshirts, on the left.

When Hitler was elected, Stalin decided that the democracies were ephemeral, and decreed that the revolution was still more imminent. At the moment, the Comintern was working to win the freedom of Georgi Dimitrov, its representative in Berlin, on whom the Führer and Hermann Göring had pinned the Reichstag fire. "Free Dimitrov!" demanded banners and loudspeakers everywhere. At his trial, Dimitrov had swept away the accusation "like a Danton!" and the people had risen up as far away as New York. The Bulgarian was a great success, and the newspaper swore that on his return to Moscow he would be given a triumphant welcome.

Alongside the article, Li deciphered the Cyrillic characters celebrating the tour of the Soviet Union currently being made by Édouard Herriot, the former prime minister of France. This was the first visit by a Western leader—a statesman, a Frenchman of letters, and an unhesitating "bourgeois reactionary." The mayor of Lyons wanted to see for himself what was going on. In Paris, in London, in Warsaw, people spoke of a famine that was once again ravaging unfortunate Russia because of the witch-hunt for kulaks launched by "Monsieur Stalin." The father of the French Radical Party (which was in fact more centrist than radical) had taken his walking stick, entrusted himself to the good offices of Intourist, and was traveling around the country of the soviets accompanied by an imposing delegation of curious people that delighted *Pravda*.

Li smiled ironically. Édouard Herriot had also traveled, in his way, to the Orient, twelve years after the expulsion of 104 young Chinese who were occupying a government building in his fine city of Lyons.

M. Herriot had come to a clear conclusion: People in Paris, London, and elsewhere were deceived. *Pravda* was exultant: "He had categorically denied the lies of the bourgeois press regarding a famine in the Soviet Union!"

On the same day, the *New York Times* confirmed Herriot's view. Its Moscow correspondent, Walter Duranty, was furious: "Talking about famine in Russia today is either an exaggeration or malicious propaganda." In Kuban—where, according to some people hunger was at its cruelest— the star reporter on the Soviets, who had won a Pulitzer Prize in 1932, had seen only "chubby babies with plump calves." At the same time, praised for the exceptional quality of his views, the American confided in private to the British ambassador that in his opinion, 7 million people had probably died of hunger.

As for Édouard Herriot, he observed that "the harvests are decidedly admirable: they don't know where to put all the wheat." Wherever he went, he had seen "only prosperity." Lyrically, he commented: "Here one sees the kolkhoz's vegetable gardens, marvelously well-irrigated and cultivated; there, loaded with grapes, vines grown from French rootstocks. . . ."

Even if a reactionary says it, thought Li. In the meantime, the cafeteria at the Lenin Institute served inedible food, and no one dreamed of complaining about it. At least the cafeteria was being supplied. Outside, as soon as the sun was up, the lines in front of empty shops stretched out into the distance. Just as they did in front of the soup kitchens in New York. But photos like that did not appear in *Pravda*. In the spring, rationing was reintroduced. It was severe, and the black market in coupons was in full swing. At the institute, there was a rumor that in October the municipality of Moscow would raise intellectuals' bread ration to six hundred grams a day. The Chinese at the institute liked to talk about the good news: the two daily broths would be thicker, the doctrine was in the clear. The future was radiant, but so far as eating was concerned, the present was difficult. Rumors flew about the stubborn refusal of the kulaks and others to hand over their harvests, their lands, and their personal property to the Bolshevik shock troops sent to collectivize the countryside. "Move forward toward 100 percent collectivization!" In unison, the press had been singing for the past three years the praises of the Komsomols' heroism in the villages, helped along by the indefatigable officers of the GPU. The Young Communists were making the saboteurs of the harvests give up their ill-gotten gains, while "the sword of the revolution was liquidating the kulaks as a class."

The country was murmuring that hordes of hungry peasants, who sometimes even indulged in cannibalism, were taking over trains and advancing on cities in the Ukraine, the Volga, and the northern Caucasus. Around a barricaded Moscow, the countryside was dying. Along with Leningrad, Kiev, Vladivostok, and a few other urban centers, it had been proclaimed a closed city. All through the month of July, increasingly frequent roundups had been carried out on the streets of the capital. Without warning, militiamen and Chekists would stop people and check their papers. Those who weren't carrying their *propiska* were immediately arrested and taken away, often never to return. Five thousand gypsies had disappeared in this way during August alone. As a result, the rare collective restaurants no longer had orchestras in the evenings, the last remnant of the glory days of the NEP. The press called this "hunting down déclassé elements." The *propiska* was equivalent to a residence permit and protected the citizen from wandering avengers in the countryside. For the past eight months, Li, like all Muscovites, had never gone out without his new internal passport, his authorization to be there. Leaving your *propiska* at home could change your destiny in the space of an hour. In Simionovski, at the ZIS workshops, people told the story of a worker who had gone down to buy a pack of cigarettes: Vladimir Novojilov, a model worker, had ended up in the Urals, near Magnitogorsk, without ever going to say good-bye to his wife and children. Others landed in Ukraine, in Dnepropetrovsk—no one knew quite where. Magnitogorsk, where a hundred thousand men were building a dam "such as the earth has never seen" that would bring the country into the age of electricity; Dnepropetrovsk, where the Soviet steel industry was taking root, in a muddy forest.

IN THE SAME MONTH OF JULY, THE CHIEF HAD A TRIUMPH. THE whole official press displayed his photograph in his new summer uniform. The Vojd struck a relaxed pose, his pipe in his mouth, sitting in a rattan chair on the deck of a boat, dressed in a sober white uniform jacket and loose trousers stuffed into leather boots. With his old friend Sergei Kirov, the head of the party, Stalin had inaugurated the canal between the White Sea and the Baltic, the Belomorkanal. A trip of a few hours through the locks, very restful after dealing with the problems in Moscow, on which the Chief worked unrelentingly. The gazettes invited Muscovites to come see the candles burning late into the night in the windows of the Kremlin. Behind these windows, the "colossus of steel" was drawing up his plans under the moon. The construction of the canal had been completed in record time. On the first of May, 1933, almost 150 miles had been dug in only twenty months, through rock and swamps. Under the supervision of the GPU, 300,000 "enemies of the people," with only rags to protect them against temperatures as low as twenty below zero, had worked on it, using picks, shovels, and wheelbarrows as their sole tools. A hundred thousand anonymous people had died of the cold and exhaustion, at the rate of 170 a day, or about 660 per mile.

On the boat, Stalin was enjoying his pipe and respite from a busy life. Six months earlier, he had buried his second wife. The dead woman haunted him, those close to him whispered. His eyes a little mad, Stalin had told Kirov, "She left me as an enemy!" Kirov was petrified. He, too, remembered only too well the evening when Nadezhda Alliluyeva, at the end of her rope, had shot herself in the head. She had slammed the door at a dinner at the Voroshilovs, after a final argument. She left Stalin a ten-year-old son, Vassily, and a five-year-old daughter, Svetlana. Afterward, Stalin had proven still more intransigent regarding delays in constructing the Belomorkanal. The GPU, sympathizing with him, had done its best. An old dream of the czars: the Baltic fleet was finally connected with the White Sea. On the site, the engineers, *spetzy* of the old school, whispered among themselves that with less than five meters of draught and this kind of mud, not even a miniature submarine could get through. The Chekist heads of the project didn't care and shut up these enemies of the people: the important thing was to complete it successfully in accord with the standards.

Instead of battleships or destroyers, another passenger boat passed through the canal during the month of August, loaded with writers, and with Maxim Gorky in person at the helm. A hundred men of letters on a cruise: Stalin was sure at least half of them would celebrate the "Great Helmsman's" exploit and compose for him one of those sweet odes that he liked so much. Soon a writer's union would have to be founded. Before the ship carrying the novelists and poets had passed through, the banks of the canal were carefully cleaned. On the bridge, Maxim Gorky, who had just come back from a long stay on the isle of Capri, off Italy, had remained silent and pensive.

Li yawned. In the sky, the birds of Moscow, enormous hooded crows and grayish-black jackdaws, cawed as usual as they dived down toward the rooftops. The September light was soft and the sounds of the city were muffled on the upper floor of the Lenin Institute. The thick walls of the Comintern's little fortress, rebuilt in the manner of Le Corbusier, didn't let in much that was going on in the outside world. Here, in a light and spacious universe, everything was filtered, both men and ideas. On the ground floor at 25A Vorovskaia Street, Chekist sentries kept a sharp eye on all the entrances. In the auditorium, about forty young men and a few women, the Chinese section of the Comintern's training school for party officials, were attentively listening to a speech. Some were recent arrivals from Shanghai or Manchuria discovering for the first time the country of the soviets; others had been living in Moscow for years. All on scholarships, they were lodged, fed, and laundered by the International. On arriving, they had had to hand over their passports to the official of the Department of International Liaisons, the OMS, an auxiliary of the GPU. They also had to give up their identities: the agents of the worldwide revolution could have only noms de guerre, aliases, pseudonyms. Looking forward to winter, even their shoes were exchanged for Russian boots. The scholarship was small, but the country was poor. The dormitories and rooms, with two or four beds, had no showers, and only rather unreliable toilets. The important thing was that they were heated during the winter.

Everything was paid for by the OMS, old Piatnitsky's very secret empire. A stingy, cunning Polish revolutionary, Piatnitsky was against alcohol, and nothing escaped him: supplies, logistics, finances, false papers.

The Comintern's cadets completed a short, nine-month course of study, while others did a longer, two-year course. Each of them had carefully filled out a biography, several pages of detailed questions about what they had done with their lives up to that point. The bio exercise required memory—one had tell about one's childhood—as well as considerable attention. What one said had to be thoroughly weighed, in response to questions such as "What do you think of Trotskyism?" "Is your companion a communist?" or "Are there government officials in your family?"

On the upper floors there were, in addition to the Chinese section, the French section, the noisiest one; the Italian section, only slightly less noisy; the German section, full of exiles; and the Japanese section, furtive and discreet—about fifteen sections in all, depending on the season. In the institute's corridors, one met the stars of the worldwide revolution, who had come long enough to give a lecture or a course on doctrine, or a pep talk to the cadets. They were the heads of powerful or minuscule communist parties, from all over the world, in Moscow temporarily or for a prolonged residence, as a land of asylum or a rearguard position. For the cadets, some of these visitors, such as André Marty, were living legends. He was the hero of the Black Sea mutineers, the model

Cominternian after whom Leningrad had named a naval shipyard. Marty supervised the French section for two years, between visits by Jacques Doriot, Maurice Thorez, and Jacques Duclos. Palmiro Togliatti* had taken up quarters there: Rome was Fascist. They all liked to go to the institute, a short trolley ride from Manezh Square. There, at the foot of the Kremlin, they had their offices, in the long, hushed corridors of the imposing Comintern building, the *headquarters,* the center of the Center, the cyclopean eye of the revolution.

In the auditorium, a strident exclamation proceeding from the podium made Li jump. His successor, the new head of the Chinese Communist Party, Wang Ming, had launched into a long peroration on the battle of "class against class," a recipe for worldwide revolution for the past six years. Bourgeois against proletarians: Wang Ming could talk endlessly on the subject before the audience. Holding a degree from Sun Yat-sen University in Moscow, he manipulated dialectics like an exercise: in the West, capitalism was collapsing; here in Moscow, socialist was triumphing; and over there in China, the Kuomintang's fascists were losing nothing by waiting.

Li remained silent, crossing and uncrossing his arms as he waited his turn. When Wang Ming spoke, he had to be there. His presence was indispensable to the ritual. The new head of the Chinese Communist Party irritated him. Wang was a coward, a courtier, and Li had known it from the start. No one at the institute was unaware that Wang Ming had hastily returned from China in the summer of 1931—a scarcely disguised flight from Shanghai, where he found the air unbreathable. He didn't want to breathe the air of the underground in Jiangxi, either, where Mao and his men were holding on. In Moscow, Wang had his comforts and access to the Kremlin. Stalin had made him the king, or rather the duke, of China, after having swept Li Lisan off the chessboard. Everywhere, Stalin was methodically placing his own men at the head of communist parties.

---

*Head of the Italian Communist Party from 1931 to his death in 1964, just as Thorez was head of the French Communist Party from 1930 to his death in 1964.

Young men, with flexible minds. Maurice Thorez, at thirty-three, for the French party, or Togliatti, forty and already a celebrity. Wang was certainly the only Chinese with whom Stalin could converse directly in Russian. He was a good interpreter, and more docile than Li. At twenty-eight, Wang represented the new wave of Bolsheviks; he regarded Li Lisan, six years older than he, as an old-timer.

The young leader detailed the urgency of instigating vigorous urban insurrections in China's large cities. Li said to himself that the time had come: Wang was soon going to shake his fist and conclude with a resounding "Long live the worldwide Bolshevik revolution!" The audience would reply mechanically with a brief and sonorous *"Wan sui!"** Then the question of Li Lisan would be brought up.

*"Wan sui!"* Like forty samurai, the Cominternians of the Chinese section shouted their cry, promising ten thousand years of life to the dictatorship of the proletariat. Wang savored the effect of his words, ran his fingers through his hair, and adjusted his glasses before lighting one of his expensive Kazbeks. Rolling the cigarette sensuously on his bottom lip and lowering his inquisitive eyes toward the audience, he sought his victim's eyes.

"And now, comrades, I think it is time to come to the question of Comrade Li Lisan. The problem, as you know, is fundamental for the ideological purification of the party. To put it frankly, in the course of his last self-criticism, Comrade Li Lisan did not seem to me truly sincere. He said that he has already admitted having followed an anti-Leninist and putschist line, but . . ."

In the audience, there was a low hubbub mixed with relief, as if they were approaching a recreation period. This had been going on week after week for months. The forty students were waiting only for this moment. The ceremony could begin. All eyes turned toward Li, who was sitting a little to the side. Li coughed, uncrossed his legs, and pretended to listen to Wang's severe criticisms.

So his last self-criticism had not been sufficient, as usual. He accepted the blow and sighed. Never mind. After almost three years of this, the exercise no longer had any secrets for him. As soon as he'd arrived, in 1931, Manouilski—the governor of the International and a "close comrade" of

---

*"Ten thousand years of life!"

Stalin—had taken his case in hand. The insolent Li Lisan, the daredevil, was going to have to begin, willingly or unwillingly, a long process of political introspection. Li was called to Comintern headquarters for "discussions" before a commission of comrades. Alongside Manouilski, anonymous men in leather jackets sat behind thick files; they were officials of the International's Far East Bureau, and they looked at Li as warmly as a raptor looks at its prey. He was given an interpreter but no attorney, and the clash was fierce. Li the orator almost got the best of his opponents, cutting the ground out from under them by admitting from the outset the military failure at Changsha and the seriousness of the Communists' situation in China. Very quickly, he pointed out that the least that could be said was that mistakes had been made on both sides, and that Moscow had also erred. At the end of several exchanges of remarks, the commission, stupefied, realized that it would have to fight it out with Li. Manouilski, who had studied at the Sorbonne, made a cunning counterattack. "You recognize your errors much too quickly, Li Lisan! No, no, you have to dig into the deep causes of your errors!" Discussions and negotiations. Li wanted to argue, justify, protest, insisting on showing that he had applied—and with what enthusiasm!—the International's general line. That he had obeyed, on the essential points at least, Comrade Stalin's orders. No, he nourished no particular animosity toward Comrade Stalin. To be sure, they had no doubt both been poor generals, and he himself might have attacked too soon, or too late; who knows? But wasn't it Stalin himself who demanded quick results? Were the Comintern's telegrams ambiguous? Certainly he had quarreled with the two German envoys. But confound it, what queer birds they were! And right-wingers, to boot. Yes, the revolutionary waves, the *podiem,* they were debatable . . .

What? Him, an anti-Leninist? A chauvinistic nationalist? A semi-Trotskyist? Insults? Li was shaken, got confused. Nothing helped. The more he talked, the more he seemed an annoying witness. The time for debating was over. No more epic clashes over the course of the revolution! No more passionate discussions and subtle compromises at congresses, like those at the Moscow congress in 1928, when the Soviet comrades interposed themselves between opposing Chinese groups. Stalin was a Jacobin, there was only one center of the worldwide revolution, right there under the windows of the Kremlin. Hero or not, Li Lisan would be brought to heel.

Manouilski wanted humility, much more humility on the part of this proud Chinese. Of that, among Cominternians, among peers, Li was incapable. He demanded to see Stalin. Manouilski told him in no uncertain terms that the Vojd had other fish to fry. It was a matter of Bolshevik discipline; he had defied Moscow, wanting to draw it into a worldwide revolution on the Chinese schedule, thinking the Comintern had a destiny. In front of him, Li had a troika, a revolutionary tribunal, endowed with full powers. Next to Manouilski, the wily Piatnitsky was waiting his turn. The men in leather jackets fired questions at him, questions about dates, numbers, names. In the land of the Cheka, merely being accused of anti-Leninism could put you before a firing squad. As for the Trotskyists, Li knew how sensitive Stalin was on that subject. "Counterrevolutionaries!" Manouilski pounded his fist on the table. He drove the point home: "And you know what we do to counterrevolutionaries, don't you?" But Li was still only a semi-Trotskyist. That looked like a half-open door.

The confidence and fraternal frankness Li had been determined to show his comrades in combat in Moscow were swept away by a terrible unease. Manouilski knew all about him and showed him that. Without a passport, without money, Li was at his mercy. If he slammed the door, he would be doomed to a slow or rapid—but in any case certain—death. It was an unequal fight, and the troika of investigators was becoming increasingly aggressive, taking turns bullying him hour after hour. The next day, the session resumed: day after day, the same thing, over and over.

One evening, exhausted and alone in his room, he finally understood that all they were asking of him was to kneel before the Kremlin. Li had known defeat only before the walls of Shantou and Changsha. He had come to Moscow certain that he would be able to dissipate the misunderstandings. But it was not a matter of the number of cannons, of strategy or political line. It was time for kowtowing, for prostrating himself before the emperor, beneath the sabers, time for the ancient bow of the sons of Confucius before the master.

Not without difficulty, the oak made itself a reed: Li yielded. Little by little, he retreated, arguing, exasperating the men in leather jackets.

Manouilski finally forced him to make a declaration in Chinese and in Russian, a nine-point *protokol* several typed pages long, for the archives of the department of party officials. The young Chinese leader admitted that he had shown an "inexcusable attitude and a lack of respect toward the Comintern's envoys." That he was "entirely wrong" as a theoretician of revolution; in particular, he had believed that "the insurrection in China would be the beginning of the worldwide revolution," and that to support it, the land of the soviets "would adopt an offensive policy against imperialism." That his instructions were "premature, adventurist, and dogmatic." That such errors were "essentially a repetition of Trotsky's theories." In short, that he had "failed to adhere to discipline" and that "his greatest error was to have brought the Chinese Party into conflict with the comrades in Moscow."

No reference was made to the fits and starts of the Chinese revolution or the blood of the martyrs in Shanghai, Canton, and elsewhere. Empty gestures. In the *protokol* listing Li's errors, the epic was lost in the depths of a dialectical labyrinth in which "right-wing views were hidden behind left-wing behavior" and vice versa.

Let the cannon of doctrine thunder! This Chinese was going to be plastered with "isms" as no one had ever been before. Li, who swore only by the International, was guilty of *chauvinism;* Li, the doctrinaire gogetter, was guilty of *opportunism;* Li, who from the outset had blazed the way for Marxist insurrection in China, was guilty of *putschism.* But dialectics performs miracles, and Manouilski needed a strong rope to hang the man: the "Li Lisan line" was born. It was to appear in manuals, in the chapter about the dark years, for the edification of the coming generations.

THE DEFEAT APPEARED TO BE SEVERE AND TOTAL. MANOUILSKI TOLD Stalin how Li had ended up signing his own political death warrant. Stalin congratulated the Ukrainian; the errors of the Chinese revolution were no longer his responsibility. Trotsky could rail and rage all he wanted, in his exile. The guilty man was now identified. He was Chinese; that was more natural.

A tactician all the way, Li had nonetheless obtained one important concession: his errors had related clearly only to the three months—

Manouilski claimed six—preceding and following the assault on Changsha in August 1930. In a final bit of indignation, he won the right to compose a paragraph of his own at the bottom of the document, a kind of final out-burst: "The Comintern," he wrote, "has not understood the conditions in China, nor has it understood that loyalty to the International was one thing, and loyalty to the Chinese revolution quite another." And he warned: "I cannot say that in my heart I have fully understood my errors, nor that I shall not repeat them in the future. I dare not say that." He con-cluded with a salute: "But I will employ all my courage and my strength to correct my errors, and I will oppose the incorrect tendencies in the Chinese revolution, in accord with the Comintern's instructions."

One more death for Li Lisan, still crueler than the three others. So even in the inner circle of the comrades, this world was full of fatal pit-falls. It seemed to him that he was drinking the revolutionary grail down to the dregs.

Carefully reread and checked, the document was sent to the propa-ganda office, and from there to the printers. Every Party member was supposed to examine it, for it was now necessary to "extirpate the roots of Lilisanism," whether they were in China or in Moscow. Manouilski would see to that. His men in Shanghai had completed the putsch with guns in their hands: a month after Li's departure, they had brought together the leaders of the Chinese Party and forced the installation of Wang Ming as its head, along with his student friends from Moscow. The method was pure GPU, and Pavel Mif, sent by Stalin to direct operations on-site, knew his subject thoroughly. Chou En-lai, obliged to confess his faults and swear before the Kremlin's envoy that he was not a "Lilisanist," experienced the worst humiliation of his life. Shortly afterward, a provi-dential denunciation allowed the police to arrest about twenty of the lead-ers who had opposed Moscow's power play, and who were meeting in secret in a Shanghai hotel. They were all executed in the Longhua barracks a month later. The Chinese Party henceforth had a Bolshevik leadership of a different kind.

MONTH AFTER MONTH, IN THE GRIP OF AN IRON HAND, LI HAD HAD to bow. Impossible to get away, to leave Moscow. He might as well bend.

Since then, penitent, he had been pulling on his chain. In the cosmopolitan salons, the Cominternians were making fun of Lilisanism, the latest heresy and the final childhood illness of Communism, Asian variant.

Wang Ming was writing learned and polemical articles about Lilisanism, with the approval of Stalin, whose "just leadership" had saved China from disaster. For a time, Li nourished the hope that he might one day be allowed to reply in writing. Manouilski quickly made him see that he would only aggravate his own case by doing so.

An excluded leper without any assignment, Li was sent to the Moscow Artillery School. In addition to a little of the military art, he'd begun to learn Russian, alongside other foreigners. But the worst happened with Wang Ming, a few weeks later. The self-criticism moved from humility to humiliation. Like a bear-baiter, Wang, displaying his trophy, started exhibiting Li in meetings, and the latter had to recount his errors over and over, ad nauseam. Impatient to take over the reigns of the revolution, Wang had never pardoned Li for having sent him to a factory as soon as he had arrived in Shanghai from Moscow.

Wang was so relentless that Li soon became a master of the art of self-criticism. The cadets at the institute listened to his remarks with the liveliest interest. A new genre, self-criticism was in fashion in Moscow. Stalin had set the rules four years earlier. The most important thing was "sincerity," he said. Since then, three hundred thousand members had been driven out of the Party, despite praiseworthy but vain attempts at *samakritika*. The Party was strengthening itself by purifying itself, the Vojd explained. The Chinese cadets, like the others, were told about the vagaries of the "general line" adopted by their Russian big brothers, and invited to join the movement. In Li Lisan, the younger generation had a choice morsel: his self-criticism opened up a majestic panorama of the gunpowder days of the Chinese revolution. When he confessed that he had overestimated or underestimated something at one stage or another of the action in Anyuan, Shanghai, Canton, Wuhan, or Nanchang, he was still talking to them about the country, distilling the lessons taught, inviting them to reflect on the "objective conditions." A new Chinese oratory art, *ziwo piping* (self-criticism), was taking shape.

This time, Li said to himself that he would speak to them about the errors made during the Nanchang uprising and the long march to the south that ensued. He knew that would annoy Wang Ming, who had had, to his disgrace, nothing to do with the birth of the Red Army. When Li's turn came, he stood up and turned toward the audience before addressing them: "Comrades!" As usual, he went on to salute the perspicacity of his young successor, who was "perfectly correct to raise the question" of his left-wing opportunism. "And moreover, in my last self-criticism, I understimated an important point. When we decided to launch an assault on Nanchang . . ."

Sitting in the audience, one of the cadets was looking closely at the man speaking in a low, strong voice with a strong southern accent. Zhang Bao recognized that tall, lanky silhouette, that willful chin, those rugged features beneath stiff, black hair. He had seen them in a photograph published years before in the American press: a man atop a makeshift podium, speaking to a crowd in Shanghai. Here in Moscow, every cadet knew the legend of the hero of the 1925 uprising, the mines in Anyuan, and the demonstrations in Hankow, but they hardly said a word to him. One would have to be very curious or very imprudent to spend time in his company. Since Zhang Bao had been observing Wang Ming's circus, he had kept saying to himself: "This guy is treating him as if he were his mother-in-law!"

But the more Li performed his self-criticism, the better Zhang Bao liked him. Clearly, the man had committed errors, and he was paying for them. His humility was composed of heartfelt passion and intelligence when he mentioned those who had fallen on the field of honor, obeying his impetuous orders as a young, enthusiastic leader.

"And that is my fault!" he stressed each time, amid an awed silence that even Wang Ming didn't dare interrupt.

Zhang had been in Moscow for eight months, and he liked Li's sin-

cerity. He had left China to study in the United States, where he had discovered Marxism. Life in Moscow was harder than it had been in New
York, where he had worked for the head of the American Communist
Party, Earl Browder, before coming to the Red capital. He found the
atmosphere in Moscow strange. He would have liked to feel enthusiastic
about constructing socialism, but his inadequate knowledge of Russian did
not allow him to read the newspapers. The Marxism taught by the
Russians at the institute was robust, but it seemed a little incomplete after
the elegant exchanges he'd had in the classrooms of the University of
Wisconsin. Fortunately, there were the practical exercises: writing pamphlets, composing posters, putting together a clandestine newspaper,
writing speeches and giving them. Soon he would go to acquire work
experience in a factory, alongside the glorious Soviet proletariat. Zhang
dreamed of being a journalist someday. And no doubt he would also go to
the south, to the Black Sea, to learn about agitation among the sailors and
longshoremen there before being sent back home to China, ready to die
for the cause.

Li finished his self-criticism; one or two zealots raised their hands to make
a brief speech relating to what had been said, and then the session was
over. When everyone else had left, Zhang Bao put on his cap and went
toward Li, who had remained alone. He greeted Li and introduced himself. Li, stunned, looked at Zhang's extended hand, the first one he'd seen
in a long time.

"I liked your self-criticism, comrade," Zhang went on, with a broad
smile. After a pause, he added in a low voice: "It's strange, you'd think
Wang Ming detested you."

"I know, this guy treats me as if he were my mother-in-law," Li sighed.

The two men laughed and decided to go have a drink at the Hotel Lux.

"Tell me about the United States," Li said, once they had gotten past
the Chekists at the entrance to the building.

"No, tell me about China," Zhang replied. "It has been so long since I
left. . . ."

CHAPTER

# 12

Hurtling down the Urals, the Trans-Siberian locomotive joyfully blew its whistle to greet the great white milestone erected amid the pine trees to mark the passage from the East to the West, from Asian Russia to European Russia. Elisabeth Kishkin sighed with pleasure and abandoned herself to the languid magic of the countryside that had already been passing before her eyes for six days and thirty-five hundred miles. Still four days and four nights in the train, and then she would be in Moscow. Siberia, blanketed with winter snow, was behind her with its infinite procession of deserted plains sprinkled with bright or dark forests. Lisa was glad to be returning, in this month of March 1933, after spending two years far from her family and friends. The Soviet Far East was fading away, and along with it, her memories of Vladivostok and the shores of the Pacific.

She had gone so far away, at the age of seventeen! She had

hardly finished her schooling in Moscow when she had left her worried mother to "construct socialism" at the other end of Russia, like millions of young Soviets. The first five-year plan required it, and the Party made a vibrant appeal to youth: "Leave the cities! Go build and edify on the whole of Soviet territory! Tear the country out of ignorance!" And spread the good news: the classless society is on the horizon. In Moscow, despite excellent grades, Lisa had had to halt her studies after completing her secondary education, at the age of fourteen. She had learned a little about literature, geography, mathematics, and grammar. In 1928, because of her execrable class origins and despite her late admission to the Pioneers, she had been sent to a vocational school. Her mother, the widow of an aristocrat, kept a low profile and survived by doing sewing at home. Lisa was barred from attending the university. At the Moscow Publishing School, she was delighted to receive her first salary: twenty-eight rubles a month, a pittance that had allowed her to put a little meat in the soup once a week. Above all, she had learned all about typography, how to set up a page, choose titles, bind books, to make them look good. Since she was a child, she had been dreaming of the vastness of the East, on the other side of the Urals, and she was asked to go to Khabarovsk, to take a job as a technical editor for a press in a remote city thirty miles north of the Chinese border. After hesitating a bit, she responded to the Party's call, along with her friend Claudia: together, the adventure would be more fun. The girls climbed on a train, and six thousand miles later they set down their bags in a dormitory-hotel—shabby, but heated—in the large commercial town.

Everything was constructed of planks and logs, even the sidewalks. Situated at the confluence of the Amur and Ussuri Rivers, at the northern end of the Manchurian plateau, Khabarovsk had muddy streets and harsh winters, and was populated by a mixture of Russians, Chinese, Koreans, and Siberians.

Lisa's job, her first, was at Far East Editions, which published books and propaganda pamphlets in Russian, Chinese, Korean, and Japanese. Like all publications in the country, they were under the complete control of the Party. Lisa met Chinese there for the first time, fellow workers at the press or the editorial offices. Young men, often cultivated, and all trained at Soviet schools. Most of them had come down from Kitaiskaia, a citadel perched on the shores of Lake Baikal where the Soviets trained men for clandestine combat—including printing. Others had received their instruction as professional revolutionaries in centers run by the GPU or the Red Army in Krasnoyarsk, a Siberian capital, or in Khabarovsk itself.

Dying of curiosity, Lisa was delighted to be making these new acquaintances. At seventeen, she found them terribly romantic. Stories about China seemed far away and complex, but captivating. Told by agreeable people, they became familiar. The Chinese at Far East Editions spoke Russian fluently; they were named Chiang or Liu, but called themselves by names such as Smidovitch, or ones that sounded Georgian, like Enuikidze. Enuikidze played a very good game of tennis, and soon Lisa was holding her first racket on an improvised court at Far East Editions.

In 1931, famine had hit the area with unprecedented violence. In the cafeteria, they managed thanks to special supplies provided by the Red Army: fish, always the same, morning, noon, and evening, for weeks and months, dried fish boiled in water. Lisa and Claudia swore that if someday they had enough to eat, they would never touch those cursed *navaga* again. However, on Saturday nights they still found the strength to go to the dance hall in the only workers' club in the city, where the Komsomols, emaciated and unrepentant, met to dance waltzes, mazurkas, and polkas to the sound of the accordion and violin, an inseparable tandem warmed up by contraband vodka.

In Khabarovsk, Lisa said farewell to her childhood. The work was hard, but stimulating. A virtuous young Soviet, Elisabeth Kishkin decided it was time to enter Komsomol. Admitted with great difficulty into the Pioneers in Moscow, despite her confounded class origins, she had finally become *normal*. Of course, she mustn't think about becoming a Party member. That elite was recruited solely among children of bona fide, handpicked proletarians, and subjected to years of probationary examinations. But at the press, everyone assured her that it was easy to get into Komsomol, and at her age it would be quite natural. Claudia, more well-behaved, preferred to keep her distance: the meetings of the Young Communists, especially on Sundays, didn't much interest her. But Lisa liked to make herself useful: constructing socialism, what could be more

noble than that? As a schoolchild, she'd been taught that "laboring humanity, in a hurry to reach communism via the socialist stage, was seeking
everywhere to overthrow capitalism." She wrote up her application for
admission and went through the process of initiation, reading and studying carefully Stalin's *Principles of Leninism,* and filling out her biographical
questionnaire, at length and without erasures. The verdict of the elders,
the Party officials at Far East Editions, would soon be made. It was prudent, but standard: she would be an apprentice Komsomol, on probation,
because of her dubious class origins. The waiting period was symbolic: the
officials were much too busy pursuing the vertiginous objectives of the
plan to spend much time giving young people political instruction.

The day on which she was finally admitted, she took an oath before
the Party and the red flag, and under the benevolent eyes of a troika composed of the director, the party secretary, and the labor union official at
Far East Editions. The secretary concluded the ceremony with the habit-
ual speech calling upon young people to be vigilant against the "Trotskyist
vermin" and the "enemies of the people" who were causing famine to rav-
age the country of the soviets.

AT THE END OF A YEAR IN KHABAROVSK, LISA AND CLAUDIA WERE
sent to Vladivostok, five hundred miles farther south. In the great port on
the Pacific, standing on the city's cliffs and looking out toward Japan, with
her back to China, Lisa, caught up in the magic of the ocean, thought she'd
arrived at the end of the world.

Arm in arm with Claudia, she wandered through the Chinese quarter
of the city, exploring recesses where no militiaman dared to hang around,
a network of narrow streets where fifty thousand people were crammed
into poorly heated three-story houses built of wooden planks, from which
buckets of dirty water were thrown without warning. Next to sidewalk
barbers, the two friends enjoyed fritters, bowls of noodles, or *mantu,*
steamed filled buns that helped them forget the *navaga.* Despite the food
shortage, the Chinese in Vladivostok were in no hurry to go home. Having
arrived before the Bolshevik Revolution, they had drilled wells for the
city and sold the water to the Russians. Every day, Lisa bought two pail-

fuls at the street corner. The Chinese worked in transportation and the mines and cut wood in the nearby forests. In town, they were cobblers, dress designers, or dry cleaners. Around the city, they carefully tended their truck gardens and sold the only vegetables still available in Vladivostok; they had become increasingly rare as the GPU collectivized the surrounding area.

The two young women could not stay in this neighborhood for long. A smuggler's den, the place had a bad reputation, and the sickly sweet odors of opium lay on the air along with other pestilences. Gambling was banned throughout Soviet territory, but Vladivostok, in the Chinese manner, was waiting for the GPU while mah-jongg pieces clicked fatalistically behind every door in the evening. When young white women passed by, they were laughed at by Chinese prostitutes with hard eyes—tall, badly made-up girls from the north who had sold everything in the turmoil in Manchuria. Having crossed the frontier, they were trusting in their last customers.

Lisa and Claudia shared a room in a local house. In the evening, after work, there was nothing to do except walk along the cliffs or the port, no place to visit or go. Except for the Saturday night dance at the workers' club, which served neither drinks nor food, Vladivostok offered few distractions. Lisa had made some friends, an unusual couple she'd met soon after her arrival. They were both employees at Far East Editions: he was Chinese, she Russian. He called himself Nicolas Vassiliev and had married a Jewish woman, Salda Leferova.

Lisa liked the work, gladly agreeing to return to the print shop in the middle of the night to make a last correction. But Claudia soon became homesick for Moscow and decided to go back. Lisa remained alone in Vladivostok a few months longer, completing her contract. Never had she received such a salary: 250 rubles a month, like a good factory worker. But in the state store, potatoes were 10 rubles apiece. At the rate of twenty-five potatoes a month, Lisa ate her meals in the refectory, often no more than a piece of black bread and a glass of tea, and then went quickly to bed before she began to feel hunger pangs. Now a confirmed proletarian, she did not renew her contract. She wanted to see her mother and her brother.

Between Omsk and Ekaterinburg, the train stopped with a long screech of hot axles. Another one of those unanticipated stops in the middle of nowhere, on a plain or in a forest or in some unknown station. Sometimes one had to wait for hours while mysterious goings-on took place at the head of the train, the locomotive heaving its sighs of impatience. Behind, there were about fifty sleeping cars, compartments carrying four persons, who took the opportunity to stretch their legs in the corridor, to make a little conversation or get some boiling water from the samovar at the end of the car.

Lisa saw a train coming in the opposite direction. Pulled by a worn-out locomotive, freight and livestock cars, some of them with their doors open despite the icy cold, passed by a few yards from her eyes. Huddled inside, Lisa glimpsed the pale faces of hundreds of men, women, children, old people, their features immobile, their eyes haggard, staring or frightened, fixed on the Trans-Siberian.

"*Kulaki!*" someone in the compartment said.

"*Muzhiki,*" an old woman muttered, making the sign of the cross.

Lisa looked at the faces slipping past and suddenly her heart froze: they all had that inexpressible stamp of people who live on the land, leathery skins that only harvests or frost in the sun can furrow, the infinite humility of people who get up at dawn and go to work. Their ragged garments, the cloth wrapped around their feet in place of shoes, the old men's beards—these did not lie: for months, millions of men and women from the Russian countryside had been put into trains, stuffed in to the point of suffocating, and sent in endless columns of railroad cars to distant lands and a menacing fate. Silence fell, and the passengers went to the windows. A convoy of phantoms, a train of the damned, peasants passing by as they looked on, the Russian people's slow farewell to itself. The people deported from the countryside in the Ukraine, the Caucasus, or elsewhere left behind them an immense shroud in which lay 7 million beloved people, dead as a result of hunger or execution.

In the mass, faces suddenly came to life, cries were heard, muffled by the sound of the rails and by the windows. A mother held out her child, like a supplication. Some shouted the names of villages; addresses, perhaps. Others wept in silence, motionless, watching the train full of free people disappear into the distance. Between the livestock cars, at regular intervals, was a car in which soldiers, wearing the bluish-gray uniform of the GPU, watched over their cargo, their rifles on their shoulders.

Deportations of kulaks! Lisa remembered when the Vojd had announced this step to the whole country, two years earlier. Since leaving Vladivostok, she had seen at least a dozen such convoys of "rich peasants" sitting at a distance in train stations, under heavy guard. But she had never seen enemies of the people at such close range. Moved, Lisa thought they looked strangely like the people themselves.

The train slowly got under way before beating its rhythm on the rails again, resuming its endless run toward Moscow. In the compartments, silence reigned. After many long miles, Lisa drove out of her mind the look of the deportees and plunged back into her reveries. In Moscow, she had to find work in a print shop, quickly. She felt comfortable about taking on a new job. The trade no longer scared her. Above all, she had heard about evening courses one could take after work. Claudia had told her that as a proletarian, she would have the right to prepare herself for the university entrance examination in the capital. It was hard, but some people passed. Coming out of the Urals, Lisa, her nose glued to the window of the compartment, told herself that she would really like to become a geologist. Then she would be able to travel all over the country and turn over every bit of land.

Before going to sleep, she thought with a half smile that she had definitely had a good trip. Being a young Soviet woman opened the doors to adventure. She recalled her first job when she first arrived in Khabarovsk, at Far East Editions: a propaganda pamphlet to set up, to correct, which was supposed to be published simultaneously in Russian and in Chinese. The title—she remembered its big Cyrillic characters— still made her smile: *Against Lilisanism!* Puzzled, she'd looked up what it was about. Isms—at her age, Lisa knew a whole series of them: Leninism, Trotskyism, opportunism, deviationism. The Bolshevik lexicon went on forever, feeding the press new expressions every day. Stalin, who had read everything, had founded Marxism-Leninism. But "Lilisanism"?

Lisa had asked her fellow worker, Enuikidze: "What's Lilisanism?"

"Ah!" the Chinese grunted, with an embarrassed smile. "That's complicated, it's still not very clear. A long story. It comes from Li Lisan. He was the head of the Party, a Chinese revolutionary, a comrade who did great things, and committed grave errors as well. He opposed the Comintern; he claimed that it didn't understand anything about China. He stood up to them, but he ended up acknowledging his mistakes. Now every comrade has to study his errors attentively. It seems he's living in Moscow at present."

On approaching the capital, Lisa had forgotten the battles fought by Chinese leaders. But Elisabeth Kishkin was arriving, pleased with her adventures, happy to rejoin her family and friends, and certain that she had loved this Far East, which she had passed through like a mirror.

# 13

June 1936. Stretched out in the grass, a sprig of dill between her teeth, Lisa smiled as she watched her husband out of the corner of her eye. The sun was warm and the *shashlik* were sizzling on the fire. The picnic promised to be delicious, with white bread and even some pickles. On all sides, pines and heather surrounded the dacha, hidden in a clearing outside Moscow. The summer would be as warm as anyone could want. Muscovites had resumed their summer commutes: in the city during the day, in the country in the evening, in the cool of the dacha. The air was so good there. And the electric train, the Elektritchka, brought its groups of workers and government employees from the Kazan station. From the station, everyone walked to his little wooden cabin, rented by the month or a gift from the authorities, depending on one's rank, and surrounded by a bit of countryside. Far from indiscreet ears, they spent the evening among friends, around meat grilled over a wood fire and sprinkled, on good days, with a few shots of vodka; on Saturdays, they hoed the garden or watered the potato plants. Stalin had recently reauthorized vegetable gardens. In them, potatoes reigned supreme: the ones they'd had to swallow these past few years were often so rotten that Muscovites had gone into gardening with a passion.

Lisa looked at her husband and smiled silently: five months since she'd married him, and she was still stunned by her own daring. She loved his slender silhouette, his tall stature, those vigorous features in a calm face, his jet-black hair. Li Lisan looked over at her, and their eyes met; he returned her smile. Alongside him, Zhang Bao, as usual, was remaking China. While they were talking, the two men, dressed in the Soviet manner—white shirts with open collars, a proletarian cap on the backs of their heads—were preparing a fricassee they knew how to make, using three vegetables and two bits of meat. Lisa was amusing herself by imagining them as the kind of Chinese she'd seen in the engravings of her childhood, with braids and pointed hats. The two friends' ability to hold long discussions under any circumstances astonished her. She liked their language, that confusing music with melodious sibilants, punctuated by loud exclamations when they got excited.

She heard a female voice call out *"Nietchevo!"* behind her: Zhang's wife, Nadia, had come back empty-handed from her hunt for mushrooms. Dressed in an elegant white dress gathered at the waist, the young woman went up to Zhang, her empty basket on her arm, and gave him a quick peck on the cheek before kissing him on the lips. Zhang blushed and gave her a luminous smile.

A handsome couple, Lisa thought. The four of them, Nadia and Zhang Bao, Lisa and Li Lisan, were easier on the eyes than the other Russians seated on the benches of the Elektritchka they rode morning and evening. In town, on Gorky Street, the two pretty Russian women on the arms of these Chinese men intrigued more than one passerby. But the porters in the Hotel Lux knew the two couples well: Lisa and Li Lisan had gotten married in the hotel the previous February. A little party in a room on the seventh floor, room eighty-four. Cominternians sometimes got married, and the GPU's porters noted down their comings and goings, including their schedules.

Zhang had noticed Nadia at a dance a year earlier. Li Lisan had met Lisa at the home of common friends who had come from Vladivostok, a Russo-Chinese couple. The two Asians were both struck by a *coup de foudre,* but the two women had not let themselves be persuaded so quickly.

"A Cominternian is a bird on the branch!" the two young Komsomols kept telling each other in private when they were talking about flirting.


LISA KNEW. SHE SAVORED THE MOMENTS SPENT WITH LI ALL THE more because she had no idea what the future would bring. The man could disappear at any time, without warning, for a secret mission in China or somewhere else. She would never know anything in advance—and not afterward, either. She mustn't ask any questions, he kept telling her, mischievously. Secrecy was the rule in revolutionary work. Even the wives of Red Army officers didn't understand. The Cominternians were perhaps the cream of the revolution, but they were too unpredictable to make good husbands.

Li had been such a gallant fellow! However, their first meeting had been like a shadow play. Li, wedged in their hosts' sofa, had hardly opened his mouth. He remained impassive and lost in the music of the Russian language as he listened to Elisabeth Kishkin telling stories about Vladivostok and Khabarovsk. A ravishing young woman, gay, innocent, observant. Li plunged into the blue of her eyes, cursing his timidity in the language of Tolstoy, his so rustic Russian. He could barely decipher and articulate the language of the regime. The other language, the Russian of ordinary mortals, was charming to hear, but difficult. Filled with countless traps, with *r*'s so hard to roll on a Chinese palate. A mouthful of cactus when the time came to speak to a desired young woman. Li had jumped slightly when, stupefied, he had heard Lisa, involved in her story, make a blunder in front of him with an incomparable grace.

"And in Khabarovsk, we published this pamphlet, *Against Lilisanism!* That's how I learned a little bit about the history of the Chinese Communists. . . ."

Candidly, Lisa had added a few puzzled remarks about this Li Lisan and his terrible errors. He was living in Moscow, people said.

Li Lisan, on the sofa, had paled. He fell silent, and Nicolas Vassiliev and Salda Leferova, their hosts, had suddenly changed the subject. Not without difficulty, Li had retained his mask. This young Komsomol didn't know his true identity. He couldn't hold it against her; when he came in, he had introduced himself as Li Ming.

His nom de guerre in Moscow. No one was to know who Li Lisan was, except the authorized people in the Comintern. On entering into penitence, he had changed his name, relieved to slough off an accursed skin. "Li Lisan" had sounded for too long like a man wanted for the Kuomintang's firing squads. They had failed, but Stalin had not; Stalin had had him roasted on the grill of self-criticism in exile. With "Li Ming," Li had recovered a degree of anonymity. Long enough for a precious evening among friends in Moscow, talking about everything except politics, making the acquaintance of Russians who asked discreet and benevolent questions—unlike those of the interrogators in leather jackets. For the rest, he knew he would always be Li Lisan. Without malice, Elisabeth Kishkin, the smiling young Komsomol, had caught him up. Li was overwhelmed by an unfamiliar feeling. He had loved women, Chinese women, shared the lives of some of them for a short time. Fleeting, almost adolescent love affairs, always pursued in partial or total clandestinity. A taste of bitterness, four children he didn't know, who had disappeared, swallowed up by the belly of China and the life of a nomad on the run. Lost in the blue eyes of the young woman, he was submerged in the sensual freshness that emanated from her and felt that one thing was sure: life was giving him a second chance.

As he left, he promised himself he would see this Lisa again, explain to her someday that Li Ming was a beautiful name. In Chinese, it made him a son of light. In any case, he would try to tell her that, in Russian. On the doorstep, he made her understand that he would very much like to see her again, wrote down her telephone number, and disappeared.

"Not very talkative, that fellow," Lisa, intrigued, had concluded. In the course of the evening, he had seemed to her to be very absent.


THE FOLLOWING DAY, LI MING HAD PICKED UP A PHONE IN THE Hotel Lux to hear Lisa's voice again. He invited her to go with him to the theater, or to a movie. Active and concentrated, Lisa had found a job in a print shop on her return from Vladivostok. She was sharing a *komunalka* room with her mother at Red Gates. Above all, she had decided to prepare herself to enter the university, which meant three years of unremitting work in evening courses, after work, to bring herself up to the required level. The invitation made by this tall, rather timid Chinese man came at the right time, and she accepted, delighted to be going out. At their third meeting, she found him charming and honest. At her side, one on one, he had found his tongue again. Without telling her who he was, he had modestly told her, in his broken Russian, about his adventures in China. He did not explain that he was the man to whom Stalin had devoted a few words printed in Khabarovsk: he had had responsibilities, that's all. For the rest, Li admitted that he was champing at the bit in Moscow, having recently been confined to an office in the labor union international, the Profintern, from which he dreamed of returning to his own country and taking his place in the battle. One evening, he told her that he'd committed serious errors back there in China, that his memories were haunted by dead souls, and that his solitude was a burden to him. But in her presence, he said, he felt like a new man; he was constantly thinking about her. Lisa timidly changed the subject to her approaching examinations. But now she knew his heart and took pleasure in their rendezvous, their walks in Gorky Park, along the banks of the Moscow River. Soon, sitting close to him on a bench in Pushkin Square, she corrected his Russian, laughing as he looked at her with desperate eyes.

And then, one day in September 1934, he'd disappeared. The preceding day, out with friends, Lisa had visited him in his room at the Hotel Lux. They had found Li packing his bags. He was about to leave for the Black Sea, in Crimea, he'd mumbled, looking embarrassed. He had to rest in a sanatorium on the coast, near Sochi. Surprised by such a hurried departure, Lisa had noticed the pair of boots Li Ming was getting ready to put into his bag. High felt boots, covered with *botfur,* the kind of fur worn by hunters in Siberia to protect themselves from the bitter cold.

"So, like that, you're leaving for the Black Sea beaches?" she had asked, slyly.

As they went out, her friends had told her again: one mustn't ask Cominternians questions. The less one knew, the better.

"And he doesn't even know when he'll come back!" Lisa had sighed, with a pang of bitterness.

For eleven months, there was neither a telephone call nor even a letter. No more Li Ming; the bird had flown from the branch. Lisa would have liked to forget him, had she not discovered his true identity one evening in 1934, with the same friends at whose home she had met him. The conversation, about this and that, once again turned to Lilisanism, but this time the name of Li Lisan was uttered as if he were a friend.

Out of the blue, Lisa suddenly frowned and asked: "Li Lisan, who is he? Do you know him?"

Nicolas Vassiliev and Salda Leferova had turned toward her, embarrassed. The joke had lasted long enough.

"Yes, we know Li Lisan. And you do, too, Lisa. Maybe even better than we do," Salda added, bursting out laughing.

Her husband went on: "You know Li Ming? Well, there you are: Li Ming and Li Lisan are one and the same person. Now you know."

Stunned, Lisa took in the news. So Li Ming was the famous revolutionary leader who'd been pilloried in the pages they'd printed in Khabarovsk! That Li Lisan, whom she'd imagined as an old, bearded man with a severe look, surrounded by books. The pamphlet said nothing about the man, and here he was, none other than this attentive and jovial Asian, this young man who seemed to want to hide his pain, courting her, opening doors for her, effacing himself behind her, taking her arm in the street. Suddenly she remembered that photo, an anonymous picture she'd seen in a newspaper, in which a young Chinese was haranguing a crowd. A photo that had struck her, as an adolescent, because of the painful passion she read on his face.

The image of Li Ming superimposed itself on the picture, and all at once, Elisabeth Kishkin, overwhelmed, felt that her destiny was being made. Life was unpredictable, Russian proverbs said.

Six months later, at Red Gates, the telephone rang. His voice. *Li Ming!* Overjoyed, happy to be back in Moscow. He excused his silence, assuring her that she was the first person he had called. That he'd thought a great deal about her, all these months he'd spent in complete solitude.

"In Sochi, at the sanatorium?"

Li had mumbled a confused explanation, but Lisa had interrupted him, laughing: "I know: one must not ask questions. . . ."

They quickly resumed their walks, during which she teased him about disappearing and his mysterious airs before granting him a first kiss on the banks of the Moscow River, in the warm sunlight of the summer of 1935.

There was no nap under the trees the afternoon of the picnic. A storm was coming on, and the heat was oppressive. After night fell, Nadia and Lisa discussed the relative advantages of raising a son and raising a daughter. The two men talked for a long time, wearing serious expressions on their faces. Li Lisan and Zhang Bao were now journalists in Moscow.

Li had emerged from his purgatory. The collapse of the Communists in China had been so dramatic after his departure for Russia that in the Kremlin it was feared they might disappear altogether. In September 1934, they had come to get him at the Profintern for an ultrasecret mission. All lines of communication between Moscow and the Chinese Communists had been cut. Stalin and the Center were sending their instructions into the void. The agents at the listening post in Vladivostok, run by the Red Army, were categorical: "All radio contacts cut off. Last reports catastrophic, series of multiple betrayals. Numerous Party officials arrested and executed. Popular support nonexistent. Destructive police raids." Since the police raid of June 14, 1934, no further communication had been received. The last seven radio operators in Shanghai had been captured, along with forty-five officials, in their hideouts in the French concession.

Stalin was furious: he had to read the bourgeois press in order to know what was going on in China! Manouilski was embarrassed. No more little schemes, this time. The disaster was almost total: the Chinese Communists had disappeared from the cities. There now remained only rural guerrillas, surrounded by Chiang Kai-shek's forces, and a handful of cantons renamed Soviet Republic of China and defended by a dubious Red Army, sixty thousand men equipped with odds and ends and led by Mao Tse-tung. To Moscow, Mao was an obscure regional leader who had taken refuge in the hills of Jiangxi and was not fully accepted in China, even by Chou En-lai. Liaison was provided by Otto Braun, a German Cominternian. Disguised as a Jesuit, he had managed to cross Chiang Kai-shek's lines in September 1933. As a makeshift military instructor, he was teaching the Chinese about trench warfare against a government army ten times as large and equipped with heavy artillery.

Stalin and Manouilski agreed that day that only one man was capable of getting them out of this mess: Li Lisan. The Comintern had only to send him to reestablish liaison. They would notify General Berzin, the head of the GRU, the Red Army's intelligence service, of Li's mission.

Li had never gone to the shores of the Black Sea or to a sanatorium. He had gotten back on the Trans-Siberian Railroad and then turned off toward the south, in the direction of Alma-Ata, in Kazakhstan. There, at a secret Red Army base lost in the desert, near the Chinese border, Soviet military men had put him in front of a powerful radio transmitter. At his side worked a radio operator, Liu Changshen, who was proud of his young nephew in China, a Communist general by the name of Lin Biao. Vladivostok could no longer hear radio signals from Shanghai, and Alma-Ata was supposed to reestablish contact with the guerrillas in Jiangxi. Like a physician, Li, moved, had begun to listen through his earphones to the heartbeat of the Chinese patient: where the devil were they, the comrades back there? In Moscow, firsthand information was scarce.

On a lucky day at the beginning of October 1934, just after Li's arrival at the military base, a radio operator picked up a cable sent from Jiangxi: Otto Braun announced that the Chinese Red Army was going to try to break out of the encirclement, and that Mao's men, facing annihilation, were going to start moving, heading west. That will be a long march, Li said to himself, worried by this message of distress that took him seven years back into the past, when, after Nanchang, they had made their way under fire as far as the defeat at Shantou.

Since that message, there had been nothing more, except a lot of static in the headphones. The radio waves were silent. Some absentminded person, back there, had mislaid the codebook. The telegraph operators were silenced, and transmissions to Moscow were once again interrupted. But on October 14, the Long March had begun. Like the other march, it was overloaded with equipment and possessions. Thirty thousand civilians and ten thousand porters trudged alongside the eighty thousand troops. The printing presses alone weighed tons; they were dismantled and carried on bamboo sticks. Every battalion dragged along its own sewing machines. The books followed, a cortege of porters laboring under the works of Marx and Lenin as they climbed through the mountains of Hunan toward the Guangxi plateaus. The column had plunged into the belly of the country. Pursued by government troops, thinned by massive desertions, it was under surveillance by the Kuomintang's biplanes, which dived out of the sky with their machine guns blazing. At night, by torchlight, the human caterpillar crawled silently through the mountain defiles, undulating like the tail of a furtive dragon. At dawn, beside the path, the enemy that was following the column picked up the abandoned equipment, cast off along with propaganda pamphlets by the Red troops in order to lighten their loads.

The codebook, probably mixed up with the texts on Marxist-Leninist doctrine, had gone into the ditch. Without the codes, they'd had to reestablish contact with Moscow directly, by radio. The Soviet officers didn't like that, but they had no choice. There was no question of speaking Russian over the airwaves and asking that the Comintern's envoy be put on the microphone. If they intercepted the conversation, their enemies would be overjoyed. They needed a Chinese to speak to the Chinese. A message would certainly attract the attention of a Party radio operator, who was listening to the right frequency: "Hello, Li Lisan here, calling from the Center, do you hear me?" Everyone knew Li Lisan, and the Hunan accent and dialect were unmistakable.

Li had put on the headphones, dying of curiosity. Who knew, with a little luck he might be able to get in contact with Mao. According to the latest news in Moscow, his compatriot in Hunan was supposed to have been sidelined as well before the beginning of the march. Too Chinese, in the opinion of Otto Braun, who no longer spoke much to the "president of the Soviet Republic of China." The two men, on their mules, argued in silence at the head of the procession.

In the spring of 1935, military communications were being reestablished, but the situation was not much clearer. The march continued, zigzagging through the country, fleeing this time toward the north, forcing its way against enemy resistance and through a hostile natural environment. But Otto Braun remained mute, and for good reason: the Chinese Communists had changed leaders and were in no hurry to inform Moscow. In January, during a halt in a mountain village in Guizhou, Mao had taken over the direction of operations and silenced Wang Ming's friends—the ones from Moscow, the alumni of Sun Yat-sen University, as Otto Braun himself was. In Zunyi, Chou En-lai had gone over to Mao's side, this time. The Russians would be informed later about these internal affairs. In this situation, they were powerless.

For Mao, what was urgent was to reach the yellow lands of Shanxi, the protective grottoes of Yan'an, in the far north of the country, as secure as their native cradle. Up there, they would dress each other's wounds, their backs to the country of the soviets.

On returning to Moscow, Li had been named to head the Chinese section entrusted with translations at International Workers' Editions, and as editor in chief of the new organ of the Chinese Communists. After years of penitence, this detour via publishing and journalism seemed to suggest that he was on his way back into the Party's good graces. Not a single Communist newspaper was still appearing on Chinese soil. Shanghai's clandestine printing presses had gone, along with the last writers. The clandestine Communists and their friends in the city had all been arrested and their hideouts identified. The Party, deprived of a central organ, was silent. A voice had to be found for it in exile.

Stalin and Manouilski chose Li Lisan to be this voice. Hard to control, but popular with his own people. He had paid for his daring long enough. Young Wang Ming was a good interpreter, but as president of the Party, he'd impressed no one since he'd been in a cushy position in Moscow. Stalin asked this greenhorn finally to accept Li's self-criticism, and the ax was buried. When the situation got desperate, Wang Ming even came to ask Li's advice. The Chinese exercise in keeping face was delicate, but Li clung to his credo: errors, to be sure, but always in the service of the revolution. To get a return ticket to China, that was still the simplest formula.

Li assumed the direction of *Save the Homeland* with jubilation. Finally, he had a job. He chose Zhang Bao as his assistant, and with the help of a dozen writers, he started enthusiastically producing a periodical of eight (soon sixteen) pages, written in Moscow, printed in Paris, and distributed clandestinely in Europe, the United States, and China.

Success came rapidly, and Chiang Kai-shek was worried: in Paris, after his diplomats intervened, the French authorities got involved and threatened to seize the weekly. It quickly reappeared under another name, the *Time of National Salvation*. The trick was the same: the paper's foundry proofs, set up in Moscow, arrived at the Soviet embassy in Paris every week in the diplomatic pouch, and were then transmitted to French Communists. The Communist network's Chinese printers, in the thirteenth arrondissement, took care of the rest. Within a year, circulation had risen to more than twenty-five thousand copies. From dry cleaners in Brooklyn to Shanghai postal workers, the question was "What do the Communists say?"

In June 1936, they changed tone. The slogans of class war had been retired for a year. In Europe, it was "All united against fascism!" In Rome, Mussolini, riding high, was puffing out his chest in front of crowds and saluting his victorious soldiers. Back from Africa, they sang the "Song of the Ethiopians": Addis Ababa had fallen in May. In Berlin, Hitler was in a good mood: the Rhineland had been remilitarized in March, without firing a shot. In Paris and Madrid, popular fronts were bringing socialists and communists together at the gates of power.

Seen from Moscow, the current situation was exciting, but Li's and Zhang's eyes were turned toward Asia. Back there, "fascism" was Japanese. In Tokyo, the government, in the hands of the military, swore only by the greatness of the yellow race and the sphere of coprosperity. Hirohito, the young emperor, yielded to the army, which was developing its plans for conquest. In Moscow, General Berzin, the head of Red Army intelligence, sent his best agent, Richard Sorge, to Tokyo. Sorge was a Cominternian, an expert on Asia who was working under a solid cover as a correspondent for the *Frankfurter Zeitung*. He was familiar with Shanghai, where he had taken funds to Li Lisan in 1930, during a long mission in China. "Comrade Johnson" was also familiar with the Lux. One night, in the hotel bar after his return from Shanghai in March 1933, he had made Li like German Cominternians a little better. Sorge wanted to write a book about Chinese agriculture, a subject Li was afraid to talk about. Berzin did not give Sorge the time to write it. From Tokyo, Sorge was cabling observations that were reassuring for Moscow, but alarming for China: the general staff of the Japanese Imperial Navy wanted nothing to do with an attack on the Soviet Union or an invasion of Siberia. Tokyo was aiming farther south, toward Beijing and Shanghai. Sorge made it clear that the generals of the Rising Sun were in the mood for conquest.

Stalin was scanning the horizon on which the hurricane was approaching. This time Japan seemed on the point of swallowing up China. The matter was of no small importance, at the very gates of the Soviet Union. Up to that point, he had been untouched by the fate of China. In Moscow, the Japanese conquest of Manchuria had aroused only the usual "Hands off the Soviet Union!" In Vladivostok, Blücher had been promoted to the rank of marshal, and was watching, along with General Mikhail Tukhachevsky, the Soviet border. Blücher knew the Far East well, and he also warned that war was imminent. Japan's disciplined, mechanized armies had already methodically conquered Manchuria. On September 18, 1931, the Japanese took Mukden, the former Manchu capital. At the age of thirty, Hirohito offered Pu Yi, the last of the Manchus, a chance to regain a throne. Pu had to be coaxed: "the Emperor of Manchukuo" sounded rather provincial, like a return to the starting point for the Ch'ing dynasty. But at twenty-five, he had the future before him: if everyone else was taking a piece of the Chinese pie, why shouldn't he do so, too?

Four months after Mukden, during the night of January 29, 1932, the guns of Japanese cruisers woke Shanghai with a jolt: General Hideki Tojo's* marines were landing to put down a local warlord undisciplined by the Kuomintang. The era of the Yangtze gunboats, the frail old tubs of the colonial regimes, was over: the artillery shells that were falling on Wusong and Djabei, the ancient Chinese quarters of the docks, were fired by monstrous steel ships that had come from the Pacific with flags flying.

---

*Tojo was head of the Japanese government from 1941 to 1944, and was responsible for the attack on Pearl Harbor. A war criminal, he was executed in December 1948.

The Westerners, immured within their concessions and powerless, observed the Rising Sun's proud Imperial Navy through binoculars. In Tokyo, the generals had predicted four days of combat. It took Tojo's marines six weeks to silence the last Chinese snipers in Djabei, which had been razed by naval artillery supported by airplanes. Richard Sorge, who had seen it all, cabled Stalin that the Chinese soldiers' resistance was stupefying. Militarily, they had to count on the Kuomintang against Japan. The Chinese masses had taken refuge in the international concessions, leaving several thousand dead and wounded behind them.

In Moscow, Li and Zhang surveyed the history of their country in vain; never had China fallen so low: a Japanese invasion! The news was overwhelming.

They had to wait until the summer of 1935 before they could regain a little hope. The Communist International held a congress in July, the first in seven years, and the elite of the worldwide revolution came to Moscow for the event. Li and Zhang had to move out of the Lux in order to make room for these noisy visitors who had come from every continent. The capital was transformed into a vast international garden party in honor of the "authentic representatives of the worldwide proletariat, defenders of the homeland of socialism." Under the marble columns of the House of Labor, Stalin's name was applauded by five hundred delegates from sixty-five countries. But although Togliatti shouted from the rostrum, "We address ourselves to you, Comrade Stalin, you who have been able, along with Lenin, to forge a new kind of party . . . ," the Vojd did not deign to appear. The Comintern's plenary sessions bored him. On the podium, Manouilski smiled modestly when his name was chanted, several times a day, by the audience. The delegates did not know that this congress was the last one for the International. But they gave a triumph to Dimitrov—who, during his trial for the Reichstag fire, had caused Hitler to lose face—and applauded him when he announced the new line: "Sweep fascism, and with it capitalism, from the face of the earth!"

The plan was simple, from now on: united fronts everywhere. The Communists were going to have to learn to extend their hands and act more humbly.

Afterward, Li, who had taken part in the congress's work, had joyfully accepted his new assignment. Anything rather than remaining inactive. Every one of his requests to return to China had been turned down, even the ones addressed to Stalin. He was offered the directorship of the new paper, and he grabbed it. Forgetting the indignant agitprop of the 1920s, he adopted with relief the new, more tangible credo. In the columns of the *Time of National Salvation,* he sounded the death knell of "the fatherland in danger." This time, he could be a patriot and a Stalinist at the same time. Setting aside resentments, a whole page was devoted to the peace offer made to the Kuomintang, the sworn enemy. Chinese on the right and on the left no longer had any choice: the invader was there, entering the gates. A united front against Japan, then. Wang Ming was worried: What about the class struggle? Li reassured him, Stalin was only preaching the childhood of art. Japan simplified everything. One thing was certain: they were finally going to fight.

Zhang Bao and Li Lisan tirelessly examined the problem from every angle: the Communists had everything to gain from it, there was no doubt about that. If Chiang Kai-shek rejected a united front, he would look like a traitor conspiring with Japan. If he accepted, he would have to let up on the pressure, the White terror. Communists and Nationalists would become partners once again, faced with a common enemy. After all, wasn't it Chiang who had treacherously broken the first alliance in Shanghai, eight years earlier, during the Red April of 1927? The Communists would cease to be nomadic, hounded outlaws, and Mao could receive help and armaments.

Zhang knew nothing about Mao, and Li told him what he could about his compatriot from Hunan. His two sons, Mao Anying, twelve, and Mao Antsing, nine, had arrived in Moscow. After the execution of their mother, Yang Kaihui, they had wandered around for two years, orphans abandoned to the streets of Shanghai, before being picked up and sent to Moscow. One day, Lisa saw Li coming into the room in the Hotel Lux, holding the two boys by the hand: "Mao's sons!" he joyfully cried before handing them over to Lisa to take care of for the day, until they could be put in a boarding school. They spent the afternoon jumping on the bed, paying no attention to Lisa's protests, chattering to her without being able to understand her.

In Montargis in 1920, Li Lisan (first row, fifth from left) with his "student-worker" comrades, many of whom were to become communists. They spent several weeks in Montargis, studying French. Afterward, Li Lisan worked at the Le Creusot foundry, where he met his first French communist activists before being expelled back to China. *(D.R.)*

At the age of twenty-six, Li Lisan is already a prodigious agitator. In May 1925, four years after being expelled from France, he launched a wave of national protest here in Shanghai after British soldiers fired on a student demonstration (thirteen dead). The Chinese Communist Party is four years old. *(D.R.)*

Lisa (in the middle, at the right) with Komsomol friends at the printing school in Moscow, at the beginning of the 1930s, before her departure for the Soviet Far East. *(D.R.)*

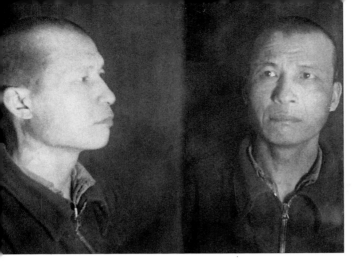

Anthropometric photos of Zhang Bao taken at the Lubianka, the seat of the NKVD, after his arrest in March 1938, during the Great Terror. After two years of interrogation and torture in prison, he is sent for a long trip through the Gulag. (D.R.)

Nikolay Ivanovich Yezhov, who tortured Li Lisan, Zhang Bao, and millions of other people. Nicknamed the "bloody turnip" because of his short stature (five feet), he orchestrated the Great Terror between 1936 and 1938, made the extraction of confessions by torture a general practice, and had at least a million Soviets executed, as well as thousands of foreigners. Millions of others—the "zeks"—were sent to the Gulags. Stalin's faithful instrument, Yezhov was sacrificed in December 1938 and replaced by Lavrenti Pavlovich Beria. Tortured by his own henchmen, Yezhov died on February 4, 1940, in a Moscow prison. (AFP)

Li's daughter Inna was born in 1943, after the winters of war in Moscow. Her mother is worried, her father delighted but torn; after fifteen years spent as a hostage in Moscow, Li Lisan was finally able to return to China and rejoin Mao. The photo was taken in 1945, just before his departure. Lisa wondered if she would see him again. (D.R.)

Li Lisan has gone back to work, this time in a general's uniform and under a false name. In Harbin and Mukden, he is leading, with Lin Biao, the Red delegation to the three-party talks with the Americans, who are trying to prevent the resumption of civil war between the communists and the nationalists. (D.R.)

On arriving in Harbin in 1947, Lisa finds it difficult to recognize her husband disguised as a general! The nationalist press is not deceived: This General Li Mindjan looks like a twin brother of the famous Li Lisan of the 1920s, who was thought to have died in the Soviet Union! (D.R.)

Li Lisan cannot be changed: Since the miners' victorious strike in 1922, the working class has been identified with him. Here, in 1949, in Harbin, at the pan-Asiatic meeting of the labor unions, he has been elected to a key post: the vice presidency. (D.R.)

Lisa (at left) has left Moscow along with Inna (at bottom) to rejoin her husband in Harbin after a long trip on the Trans-Siberian Railroad. The young, beautiful Sung Weishi (at top) accompanies her; an actress and director, she is returning to China, dreaming of producing Chekhov in Beijing. Lin Biao fell madly in love with her. She died a tragic death during the cultural revolution. At right, Lin Li, another friend on the trip, who was to become Mao's interpreter. (D.R.)

October 1, 1949. The communists have won the civil war, and Mao Tse-Tung proclaims the People's Republic of China on Tiananmen Square. Li Lisan is third on Mao's left. He has given a lot for this victory. This photo was rapidly to disappear from circulation. (D.R.)

In homage to the 1920s, Li Lisan is naturally made Minister of Labor in the first cabinet of the People's Republic of China. His first assignment: the Beijing rickshaw men's strike. (D.R.)

The Minister of Labor likes to play with his children: Alla, his second daughter, was born in 1947 in Harbin. At home, the family speaks Russian, and invites for dinner old friends such as Marshal Chen Yi, the Minister of Foreign Affairs, also a veteran of France. *(D.R.)*

Nadia and Lisa: two women, two destinies. *(D.R.)*

Li Lisan's family still doesn't fit the mold. In 1964, Inna (holding her father's arm) is more rock 'n' roll than Maoist. Kang Sheng, the Chinese Beria, the all-powerful head of the police, warns Li Lisan: "Your daughter dresses like a decadent Westerner!" *(D.R.)*

The pleasure of growing old together at the seaside, where Lisa and Li Lisan forget the capital and its intrigues. Back there, Mao is cooking up his "cultural revolution." *(D.R.)*

Probably the last photo taken of Li Lisan as a free man. He is sixty-five. Like a marathon runner, he has carried the revolutionary torch far to the east, from the Paris of the 1920s to Shanghai and Nanchang, from Moscow's prisons to Beijing in October 1949. Li Lisan likes to quote the poet's ancient verses: "And our horses shall drink the waters of the Great River." *(D.R.)*

In China, one terror is followed by another. Here, the three great architects of Maoism: Lin Biao, followed by Chou En-lai and Kang Sheng (behind, at right), brandishing the Little Red Book during the cultural revolution in 1966. *(AFP/New China)*

Li Lisan under house arrest during the cultural revolution in 1966. He defies the prohibition on going out and walks about in disguise in order to read the *dazibao* posted by the Red Guards. He has become a "reactionary," an enemy of Mao. Inna is a Red Guard, like all her friends at the University of Beijing. Her style of dress no longer leaves anything to be desired. *(D.R.)*

Chen Yi. Along with Zhang Bao, Li Lisan's best friend since France. One of the regime's ten marshals, this hero of the military campaigns that gave Mao victory was Minister of Foreign Affairs from 1958 to 1967. His frankness and humor made him appreciated by foreign diplomats ("China is much too heavy to be a satellite," he said, talking about relations with Moscow). With Li Lisan, he spends hours playing *go*. Overthrown by the Red Guards, he dies under house arrest in Beijing in 1972. *(AFP)*

Lisa, after eight years in solitary confinement in Tsinsheng, has been reduced to a shadow of herself. Here, after her release, in the summer of 1975 in her exile in Shanxi. Li Lisan has disappeared and she doesn't know what happened to him. Where have her daughters gone? Mao does not have long to live. The two young Chinese on either side of Lisa are her guardians. They are not hard on her. In prison, she experienced much worse. *(D.R.)*

On March 29, 1980, Deng Xiaoping, along with the whole Politburo, bows to Lisa. That won't bring Li Lisan back, but at least in China it isn't the way it is in the USSR: People know how to apologize. Lisa stares into space. *(D.R.)*

Elected to the Chinese People's Consultative Political Assembly, China's Russian grandmother now spends her time addressing minor problems such as those faced by local schools, which are falling into ruins in every village, teachers whose salaries are not paid for months at a time, the fate of little girls. . . . *(D.R.)*

By June 1936, radio contact with China had been reestablished, and messages were getting through again. Moscow discovered that in Mao Tse-tung the Party had found a new leader in China. Wang Ming, in Moscow, was threatened. The Long March ended after a year, in October 1935, and the ten thousand survivors were resting in the grottoes of Yan'an, on Mao's orders. How long would they hold out? wondered Li and Zhang, who were always homesick.

Late at night, stretched out on the bed in the dacha after making love, Lisa teased Li Lisan: "So, tell me about the beaches in Sochi, the Black Sea, your stay at the sanatorium. . . ."

As he did every time, Li mumbled some evasive and embarrassed words. Lisa was in love with him, and she, too, was dying to tell him the good news: in September, she would be going to the university. She had passed the entrance examination. The proletariat was fine, if you could get out of it. Li had told her over and over: "You should stop working and go to the university." Well, in the fall, she would finally be a student. She would learn French. She had asked to study English, but that was reserved for a better class of people, not for those who had gone to night school. Then she had asked for Chinese. Comrade Frumkina, an old Bolshevik woman who ran the Pedagogical Institute for Foreign Languages in Moscow, had cut her off: "No, no, no, Lisa! Your class origins aren't good enough! You're a Komsomol, yes, but you have been assigned to the French department, that's it."

Li reassured her: French was fine, and very international, too. Moreover, he remembered a French phrase: *Je t'aime.*

Lisa loved it when he talked about Paris, about France. She secretly knew that it was partly because he had been in France that he was here, with her. "But . . ." Those fur boots, on the sand at Sochi, weren't they a bit warm?"

Looking up at the ceiling, Li swore to himself that someday he would tell her what he'd done during the time he was gone. In Sochi, if possible. All lovers dreamed of going to Sochi.

# 14

Lisa greeted the spring of 1937 with relief. The winter had been a hard one for the Komsomols at the institute. She had not expected her entrance to the university to be like that. Hardly had she begun to plunge into the language of Molière than orders were given over the loudspeakers, several times a day, for all the students to assemble that very evening in the institute's main lecture hall. Three or four hundred of them sat facing the platform, where the leaders of Komsomol were wearing the grave faces they wore when something serious was up. The most belligerent of them opened the meeting with a violent tirade against enemies of the people, against whom everyone present had failed to be sufficiently vigilant. Naively, he said, they had thought the enemies of socialism were outside the party, the Komsomols, the unions, and the country. Wrong: they were *inside*. Invisible, often indistinguishable from good comrades. *Right here.* The country and all its organs were filled with people sabotaging the great Stalin's line, and they were showing that they had a fertile imagination.

The first time, all the students in the hall, stunned, had felt a chill run up their backs. On the platform, the institute's young Komsomol leader, aping his elders, thundered that the time had come to unmask the saboteurs. The hunt was on. It was up to everyone to designate an enemy of the people. Denunciations were welcome. The leadership, at least, was no dupe: it had a file on everybody. The sky was falling on the heads of the Young Communists. Everyone remembered some remark, some expression of doubt, some objection made here or there, for the pleasure of debating doctrine. Lisa had a hard time reconciling the announcement on the front page of *Pravda* in 1935 that socialism had finally been achieved in the Soviet Union with the lines waiting in front of perpetually empty stores. But Stalin was categorical: social classes had disappeared, history had made its decision.

For the Komsomols, the purges—the *chistka*—were reserved for adults, those who had already joined the party, or for engineers, specialists, and the countless counterrevolutionaries and saboteurs. Every September 3, all the Komsomols commemorated the heroic death, at the age of fourteen, of Pavlik Morozov, who had been made a hero of Soviet youth for having denounced his father, subsequently executed for having protected kulaks. In meetings, and in the pamphlet *To Be a Good Komsomol,* Lisa had learned how the boy had then been shot by peasants who wanted to avenge the president of their local soviet. During ceremonies, wearing her uniform with a red scarf, she tried to show as much enthusiasm as her comrades. But a strange uneasiness held her back when she was confronted by the destiny of the young parricide hero.

At the rostrum, other speakers had taken turns, and in the course of a harangue, one of the Komsomol leaders had suddenly shouted a name: "You there, so-and-so, in the audience!" The person named was a cunning devil, in fact, who deceived people. Who constantly swore that he had an unqualified admiration for the great Stalin. Now, there were proofs that he had always hidden his Trotskyist sympathies! That his father was a dog of a Menshevik!

The first person designated for prosecution couldn't believe his ears. He had to get up, go to the foot of the rostrum, and submit to intense questioning. After this, a young prosecutor heatedly demanded that the villain be expelled. In the audience, a claque cried, "Out with him!" and drowned out a few demurrals. Slowly, a forest of hands were raised hurriedly or hesitantly. Lisa, stunned, finally followed suit.

That evening, in the room in the Hotel Lux she now shared with Li, she talked about what had happened. Li was worried. Things in Russia were going sour. He, too, was lost in an abyss of confusion. In August 1936, he had learned, along with all Soviets, that Zinoviev, Kamenev, and Smirnov, three of Lenin's closest companions, had been shot after a resounding trial. Five days of sensational revelations to the world, in *Pravda,* regarding the "Trotsko-Zinovievist terrorist center." It seemed to Li that Stalin was surrounded by many conspirators. He advised Lisa to be prudent and discreet. The Bohemian life in the Lux was pleasant, but his young companion's class origins were not great.

At the institute, Lisa went back to her French studies, but the purge sessions continued in the same way all winter. The few people who had voted no at the first sessions provided the victims for the later ones. From one session to the next, the students, terrified, voted for the expulsion of their comrades, chosen on the basis of their Komsomol biographies or their parents' situations. Everybody was expecting to be next. Many of the students expelled did not attend courses the following day. The students in German were the most affected. The French section was spared. Soon, the directress of the institute, Comrade Frumkina, was arrested in turn. An old Bolshevik! The secret was whispered among students and professors, the most pessimistic predicting that she would be executed.

Everyone was focusing on personal concerns, and Lisa concentrated as best she could on her studies. Mme Krasnilkova's French classes provided her with a longed-for escape. She liked this Frenchwoman, who had served as a governess in an aristocratic Saint Petersburg family before marrying a Russian and making her living as a teacher. In a sweet, clear voice, she talked about the French novelists of the preceding century, while keeping a close watch on her fifteen students as they negotiated the minefields of spelling and grammar.

★　　★

FOR LISA AND NADIA, THE HARDEST THING WAS TO BE *ENTHUSIASTIC*. In the Komsomols, everyone was supposed to have inexhaustible reserves of this treasure of youth. The construction of socialism? It was a matter of enthusiasm! the Vojd kept repeating. The two young women still had enough for the May Day parades on Red Square, getting up at six in the morning and waiting for hours to the sound of accordions and songs sung over and over in unison; enduring sessions of adjusting the knot in their scarves, the forest of red flags flapping in the spring sunlight. Coquettishly, nervously, the young women were burning with impatience: was he really there? For sure? They were going to see *him* in the flesh? The Vojd appeared in public only twice a year, in May and in October. In rows of twelve, the gymnasts in front and the Stakhanovites behind, the female Komsomols, their white blouses ironed in impeccable pleats, passed in their turn before the Guide, twisting their necks to catch a glimpse of him at the right moment. *He* was really there, just a few yards away, smiling good-naturedly, waving his hand, looking a little oily, his eyes on the blushing young women, suddenly stretching out his arm to point at one or another of them, grinning, as if to say, "I recognize you!" You hardly thought you'd caught his eye before the *komsorgs,* feeling nervous, urged you to hurry: "Faster! Faster!" No matter; the next day, at the factory or in the university, everyone claimed to have seen him.

Since June 1937, Moscow had been pulling only for the Spanish Republicans. The Komsomols paraded under the summer sun, singing "O Bella Ciao!" The Italian song was all the rage at parties, the world smelled like gunpowder, and the proletariat had its international brigades, its world legion.

"LOOK AT THEM!" NUDGING NADIA WITH HER ELBOW, LISA NODDED toward Zhang Bao and Li Lisan walking side by side underneath the firs. Feverishly, the two men were making new projects for the future. "I sometimes wonder what life is like in China, don't you?" Lisa and Nadia couldn't help thinking about it: someday, maybe they would go there, after all.

Li no longer had any doubt: they were finally going to be able to leave the country of the soviets and go home. So far as their wives were concerned, the difficulty was great but not insurmountable: these days, the Comintern sometimes allowed wives to accompany their husbands. Zhang was less sure. According to the latest news, Mao, in the grottoes of Yan'an, had established a new communist way of life: men and women lived in separate dormitories. Couples who had survived the Long March could now be together only on Saturday nights. Zhang Bao couldn't imagine Nadia and Lisa getting used to that, if they happened to be able to join them in the new Communist base.

But the two men agreed that the die was cast. Since July 7, China and Japan had been at war. The Japanese beast had sunk its teeth into the tottering Republic of China. Near Beijing, on the Marco Polo Bridge, Japanese soldiers had attacked, on the pretext that one of their numbers, having gone to relieve himself, had been kidnapped by Chinese.

For Li and Zhang, it was imminent: they were going to return to their country to fight the invader. The two friends were not upset at the idea of giving up their work as journalists working in an office, confined to propaganda and translations. Zhang was not opposed to the idea of taking up arms, either. But he felt a little green, and dreamed of fighting alongside Li, who had already gone into battle with his Mauser, the favorite weapon of the Cominternians.

THE CRISIS OF DECEMBER 1936 HAD PASSED. IT HAD BEEN A TOUGH time, and once again it had taken all Stalin's might to bring the Chinese section to heel. A telex had come into Moscow, sent by Mao Tse-tung from the new radio transmitter in Yan'an. Chiang Kai-shek had been captured by his own generals. In Xi'an, an ancient imperial capital not far from the Communist base, the head of the Kuomintang had been commanded to stop the civil war and to oppose, along with all Chinese, the Japanese threat. Consulted regarding his fate by the rebel generals, the Chinese Communists, delighted with this windfall, were inclined to get rid of Chiang once and for all.

Stalin saved Chiang's life. Like everyone else, he was counting on the head of the legitimate government of the Republic of China, and not on Mao, to fight the Japanese. The Chinese Communists cut a sorry figure, holed up in their caves. For its part, the Soviet Union was entering the League of Nations: it was no longer a time for revolutions on command. Chou En-lai, sent as an emissary to the rebel generals, got them to accept the Comintern's order, which had been signed by Wang Ming in Moscow: Chiang was not to be executed. Freed at the end of a week, he had gone back to Nanking in a pensive mood and taken the government in hand again, after having ordered a few executions and solitary confinements.

As a token of his goodwill, Stalin had even returned Chiang's son, whom he had been holding hostage for years: Chiang Ching-kuo* had gone to study in Moscow in 1924. Since then, his father had not seen him again.

Li and Zhang found it difficult to accept Stalin's maneuver. In their view, a united front without Chiang Kai-shek would have been fine. But the Chinese section of the Comintern, like the others, had long ceased to have any voice in the Vojd's decisions.

Six months later, after the Japanese invasion of July 1937, Chiang accepted the new alliance with the Communists and ordered a cease-fire. The siege of Yan'an did not take place. Japanese troops were advancing on Nanking, the seat of the government.

At the newspaper, the staff members were packing their bags to go to the front. The future of the *Time of National Salvation* was in question. Li was still a member of the Chinese Communist Party's Central Committee, but he'd made up his mind to ask the Center for a transfer again. Rumors were flying. It was said that Stalin wanted to send Wang Ming to China, along with Kang Sheng, his right-hand man. Li wondered how things would go back there, between those two and Mao Tse-tung. He detested Kang Sheng, who had served under him in clandestinity, in charge of dirty tricks in Shanghai. In the self-criticism sessions, this man from Shandong, reputed to be cultivated, was always at Wang Ming's side, sizing up Li with mocking eyes behind his round glasses, pulling on his

---

*Stalin's hostage from 1924 to 1937, he became president of Taiwan from his father's death in 1975 to his own death in 1988.

long cigarette holder. Every time Li finished, Kang Sheng, then thirty-five, had taken pleasure in laying into his former boss, who was one year younger than he. In his high-pitched voice, he was a demanding prosecutor, always wanting the repentance to be more sincere.

Since then, with obvious reluctance, he had been forced to resume talking with Li about political matters. The two men, one as tall and thin as the other, hardly spoke, and avoided each other as much as they could. Kang Sheng sent his articles to the editor in chief of the *Time of National Salvation* by mail, and Li had nothing to say about his prose. However, in the sixth-floor corridor of the Hotel Lux, it was hard not to run into each other: Kang Sheng lived only two doors down from Li, with his wife, Cao Yi'ou. Lisa didn't like meeting the baleful eyes of this small, closed woman or the sardonic eyes of Kang Sheng himself.

Kang's activities in Moscow intrigued Li and Zhang. Because of his self-assurance, they assumed that Kang, the number two man in the Chinese delegation in Moscow, had access to Stalin, along with Wang Ming. Above all, it was no secret that Kang was always aware of "special matters." He lunched and often dined with the officers of the NKVD, with whom he had set up a "bureau for the elimination of [Chinese] counterrevolutionaries" in Moscow. He kept lists of names, and at the paper, everyone feared his vigilance ever since he'd unmasked a "Trotskyist spy," Wang De, on the staff. A communist leader in Manchuria who had taken refuge in Moscow, Wang De had disappeared one day, along with his wife, Tang Guofu, both of them having been arrested at their home by Chekists. A year earlier, in 1936, four young survivors of the clandestine struggle in Shanghai, who had come to Moscow to be trained as radio operators, had met the same fate. Kang Sheng had his favorites. A talented conspirator, he had even been credited with the revocation and arrest by the GPU of the directress of the Lenin Institute, Klaudia Kirsanova, who was nonetheless the wife of one of Stalin's close associates.

The atmosphere in Moscow was definitely poisonous, and Li and Zhang both asked to leave, even as simple soldiers.

At the dacha, the air was pure, but when the second great trial opened, in January, they could hardly believe their ears. After Zinoviev, Kamenev, and Smirnov in August 1936, it was now the turn of Grigory Pyatakov, the brains behind the five-year plan, the builder minister, formerly hailed for having "introduced reason into History against capitalist anarchy." According to *Pravda,* Pyatakov had confessed that he was in reality a "spy in the pay of Hitlero-German fascism." And so was Karl Radek, a founder of the Comintern and of the German Communist Party, another friend of Lenin's. And Grigory Skolnikov, the first Soviet ambassador to London, a veteran. And Leonid Serebriakov, a hero of the civil war. The NKVD and Andrei Yanuarievich Vishinsky had revealed a new plot to assassinate Stalin and throw the country into chaos. The affair was complex, but the evidence was damning: the accused had provided all the details. It was discovered that Pyatakov had made a secret trip to Norway to meet Trotsky in person, who had himself just returned from a still more secret meeting with Rudolf Hess, a close associate of Hitler's who had edited *Mein Kampf.* That Molotov had narrowly escaped an attempt on his life one day, when his driver had gone into the ditch. That the Soviet railroads were full of fascist agents, who were causing bloody derailments. That agents had infiltrated the chemical industry, which was subject to explosions as regular as they were mysterious.

Radek's statement before his judges made Li shiver. The former Trotsky supporter, a clever man with a good sense of humor who was considered the best Communist writer, had slipped into his public confessions a few sibylline questions. Ulrich, the head of the tribunal, with his shaven head, small, squared-off mustache, and unctuous voice, had also been startled when Radek said: "The question has been raised here whether we have been tortured during the interrogations. I have to say that it is not I who have been subjected to torture, but on the contrary, I have tortured my interrogators by forcing them to do a great deal of useless work" or "I was arrested, but I denied everything from the beginning to the end. Perhaps you will ask me why?"

The question had remained unanswered, and he had gone on to confess a long series of crimes of lèse-Bolshevism, aggravated by machinations in the service of Hitler, Hirohito, and Mussolini.

The reports on the trial in the press gave the facts a puzzling precision. Reading *Pravda* that day, Li had remained pensive when Radek warned that there remained "demi-Trotskyists, quarter and eighth Trotskyists" hidden everywhere in the country and in the party. "Demi-Trotskyist": Li had never liked that epithet, which had been in his file for the past seven years.

This time, the accused had a lawyer. On the seventh day of the trial, Ilya Braude, speaking for the defense, opened his plea in an expressionless voice: "Comrade judges, I will not conceal the fact that the defense finds itself in an extremely difficult situation, an exceptionally difficult situation." This jurist, whose fame went back to the time of the czar, could in fact "only share the immense indignation, the anger and horror of the whole population" confronted by such felonies confessed in the witness box. No, Braude was convinced of it: "The Comrade prosecutor is completely right!"

Even the accused men called for a death sentence. One of them, Chestov, a chauffeur of Molotov's who had attempted to murder him, uttered these final words before the court: "Proletarian justice must not, cannot spare my life. . . ."

Pyatakov finished his statement with his head bowed: "I stand before you, covered with mud, crushed, deprived of everything by my own fault, having lost my Party, having no more friends, having lost my family, having doomed myself. . . ."

Ever since the beginning of the trial, the state prosecutor, Vishinsky, had stolen the show with his sharp questioning laden with insults. When he made his closing summation, he could hardly control his indignation: what he had heard in the witness box reached "the depth of degradation, the extreme limit, the last frontier of moral and political degeneration!" He had seen "crime in all its horror." Stalin's enemies were, in his words, "Judases, traitors, spies, or scum." Even their confessions were unreliable, because "once we had unraveled the monstrous skein of crimes perpetrated by these individuals, we discovered that they were constantly lying, even though they already had one foot in the grave."

Vishinsky concluded in his favorite way: "A single punishment, death!" The Hall of Columns in the House of Labor had resounded with the same applause five months earlier, when, before Zinoviev, Kamenev, and the others, Vishinsky had cried: "I demand that these mad dogs be shot, all of them, without exception!"

Vishinsky, the jurist who founded the Soviet legal system and had been rector of the University of Moscow, had won his first death sentences for Russians ten years earlier, in 1928. In the Chakty trial, he had convicted "bourgeois engineers" accused of sabotage. The GPU had done the rest.

Even before the verdict was handed down, two hundred thousand Soviets, encouraged by the authorities, had invaded Red Square at night-fall, when the temperature was seventeen degrees below zero, to demand that the accused be put to death.

Vishinsky got almost all the death sentences he asked for. Radek, who had confessed a great deal, got away with his life—this time. Ten years in prison, Ulrich announced at three in the morning, then read in his dron-ing voice the list of the thirteen men condemned to death: Pyatakov, Serebriakov, Skolnikov, and the others. Four had been sentenced only to prison. In the witness box, Radek had turned toward his companions with an embarrassed smile. "What can I do?" the Comintern's humorist seemed to be asking, with a fatalistic shrug of his shoulders.

In the House of Labor, among some thirty VIP guests, the American ambassador, Joseph Davies, was delighted. This Vishinsky was "a great deal like the American attorney general, Homer Cummings, just as calm, impartial, lucid, and wise," the ambassador cabled President Roosevelt. "As a lawyer, I am deeply satisfied, and I admire the way in which he has conducted this trial." His British colleague, Lord Chilston, kept telling him that "we should be pleased that Yezhov has been named" the new police chief. Stalin had put him there "to clip the wings of the NKVD, that nightmarish organization." Moreover, at dinner parties Chilston was assuring people that Nikolai Ivanovich Yezhov would be Stalin's successor. A few Frenchmen and Germans winced: the Baron d'Uniac, of the French embassy, agreed with his colleague von Herwarth, an anti-Nazi aristocrat, that these trials looked like masquerades.

The news had gone round the world. Walter Duranty, in the columns of the *New York Times,* had sworn that trials like these couldn't be made up. The Soviet Union was teaching the world a new lesson, this time in law.

Everyone was noting similarities with the French Revolution. In Paris, people seeking to understand this new Russia were more inclined to speak of Robespierere, Danton, or Fouquier-Tinville than of Ivan the Terrible. In London, an important difference was pointed out: Whereas Danton and the others had used their trials to criticize those in power, the accused in Moscow competed with each other in making servile confessions that defied imagination. But the International Legal Association, which included some of the leading lights of the profession and had sent observers to the hearings, was serene: "We categorically assert that the accused were found guilty and sentenced in a completely legal manner. It was clearly demonstrated that there had been a connection between them and the Gestapo. They fully deserved capital punishment."

The International Human Rights League's representative, a lawyer named Rozenmark, gave his opinion: "We look for an error only when the accused denies his crime. Had Captain Dreyfus admitted his guilt, there would have been no Dreyfus affair."

Stalin was delighted. On the whole, the Westerners found his justice severe but fair. He liked Vishinsky's style. There was a rumor that the Vojd was attending the hearings in secret, hidden behind a curtain or maybe in the projectionist's booth, people weren't quite sure where. In the evening, he even corrected the text to be delivered by his public prosecutor, which was sometimes a little too soft for his taste. Chuckling, he added references to the accused as "degenerate rogues," "accursed reptiles," "mad dogs," "stinking carrion," or "manure." At the last trial, he laughed uproariously when Pauker, his faithful servant at the NKVD, just back from Zinoviev's execution, came into his office imitating the condemned man as he was led to his death, clinging to the arms of the two officers who were dragging him along, moaning, "I beg you, for the love of God, call Joseph Vissarionovich!" When Pauker, grinning, went on, making the Jew Zinoviev say, "Hear, O Israel, the Lord is our God, the Lord is one!" Stalin roared with laughter and begged him to stop. But what the Vojd liked best was for the doomed to die crying "Long live Stalin!" That homage was eternal. In a good mood, he lifted the ban on publishing Dostoyevsky, Russia's dark writer, and Moscow rushed out to reread *The Possessed*.

Vishinsky came out of the trials as famous as A. Stakhanov, the model communist worker. *Pravda* couldn't say enough good things about the prosecutor who was doing such a fine job of rooting out the hidden enemies of socialism. The Vojd decorated him with the Order of Lenin. Afterward, Vishinsky was finally able to move into his neighbor's superb dacha, which he'd so much coveted. Serebriakov was no longer there to live in it. But Vishinsky got no vacation. Stalin was indefatigable, and the accusation files were piling up by the hundreds of thousands in the NKVD's offices.

At the school for state prosecutors, the founder of Soviet law drilled into the new recruits that "a sense for politics is much more important than evidence and proof. When class instinct speaks, proof is not necessary: confessions suffice. They are the supreme proofs!" As for the methods to be used in obtaining confessions, Vishinsky deferred to the specialists.

In February, Sergo Ordjonikidze, Stalin's oldest friend, was found shot dead in his home the day before a stormy meeting of the Central Committee. In the Vojd's entourage, people often committed suicide, but each time the funerals were grandiose. Speaking before the leaders of the Party, Stalin had warned Yezhov: "Stop coddling your prisoners!" Bukharin, the Party's beloved child, Lenin's favorite, began a hunger strike. His name had been mentioned repeatedly in both trials. However, he swore in a written message to Stalin: "I'm terribly happy that all those dogs have been shot!"

In May, the first exiled Communist leader, the Hungarian Béla Kun, a veteran member of the Comintern, was arrested right in the middle of a Politburo meeting. On June 15, *Pravda* printed on its front page, without commentary, a list of military men who were guilty of crimes. At the head of the list was the leader of the Red Army, Tukhachevsky, a young marshal only forty-four years old—the modernizer of the Red Army, a proponent of tanks, parachutists, and airpower. He was a legendary hero of the civil war who had failed in front of Warsaw because of his deputy, Stalin: at the time, in July 1920, the future Vojd, on a whim, had driven toward Lvov and caused the battle plan to collapse. *Pravda*'s June 15, 1937, issue was exceptionally laconic, this time: Tukhachevsky had just been executed for conspiring against Stalin, along with Pyotr Yakir, the people's air force commissar, and others. To sit on the military tribunal and judge his chief, Vassily Blücher, marshal of the Far East, the strategist of the Northern Expedition in China, and Tukhachevsky's faithful second in command, had been urgently called back from Vladivostok. Once he was in Moscow, the matter had been settled within forty-eight hours. But it was said that Blücher was also in danger. Everywhere in the country, panic was spreading to officers and subordinate officers. In the barracks, the political commissars starting barking louder than usual, the NKVD was cutting broad swathes through the ranks, and people whispered that wives and children were also going before firing squads.

IN THE EVENING, AFTER RETURNING TO THEIR COLLECTIVE APARTments, worried Muscovites silently observed their neighbors' windows. At the end of the week, they counted the number of lights that had gone out, the dark windows, the apartments in which there was no longer any life. After dark, the NKVD's vans moved through the city, their sides camouflaged with advertising pictures. They were all heading for Lubianka prison. On Dzerzhinski Square, the facade of the enormous brick prison was lit by antiaircraft projectors, focused on the sentry keeping watch, a bayonet affixed to his rifle barrel, under the red flag flying from the top of the building. In the vans, alongside the drivers, subordinate officers in blue uniforms used their cigarette lighters to illuminate lists of names and addresses and a map of the city. There were endless lists of names, and there was no lack of work. But the bonuses were generous: these teams worked only at night. At dawn, Lubianka's men, the ones who worked during the daytime, took over.

UNDER THE PINES, LI AND ZHANG COULDN'T DECIDE: HAD STALIN gone mad, or was the revolution a dupes' game? Hitler had agents everywhere, and so did the Vojd. It was not news, of course, that friends could change into enemies, but Marxism-Leninism was clearly going to have to perform dialectical feats. Moreover, wouldn't Soviet citizens vote in December to inaugurate "the freest constitution in the world"? *Pravda* had published extensive extracts from the stunning list of civil rights that had been adopted a year earlier.

Foreigners were now threatened as well. After the trial, there had been arrests at the Hotel Lux. In April, Heinz Neumann, in exile and in disgrace, had left one night under escort by Chekists. He was also working as a translator at Progress Editions. Li Lisan noticed his disappearance; in December 1927, the German, sent by the Comintern to preside over the disaster, had given the signal for the rising in Canton. Five thousand Chinese died in order to have done with Trotsky in Moscow. Li sometimes ran into Neumann's wife, Margarete, in the Lux's corridors. She had lost her job at Progress Editions, and had been forced to move into the little house in the courtyard behind the hotel, which was already crammed with Polish women. Their husbands, Communist leaders who had fled Poland, had been arrested one after the other. In the hotel's corridors, the Cominternians now spoke to each other only in low voices. The news from Spain was not good. In May, in Barcelona, the NKVD's men had attacked other Republicans. The latest Russian joke about the fighting was an example of black humor: "Did you know that Teruel had been taken?" "Oh? His wife, too?" People laughed nervously.

Li wondered how long he could keep Lisa out of it, in her innocence as a young Soviet. He had always told her: "You have to understand that in my life, I put the Party first, and you second." She hadn't really liked it. But that's how virtuous men were.

# 15

The night of Wednesday, February 23, 1938. Outside, Gorky Street was covered with snow, swept along by an icy wind under a sky full of stars. On the seventh floor of the Hotel Lux, in Room 81, Lisa and Li Lisan, lying in their narrow bed, held hands under the covers, not saying a word. Soon it would be three in the morning, and they had still not been able to go to sleep. The long corridor was deserted and silent, but the carcass of the old building creaked from time to time. Muffled coughs were heard in neighboring rooms, as if night were unable to calm people's minds. Lisa closed her eyes and pressed her companion's hand every time there was a noise. People heard them coming from far away, in the stairway or at the end of the corridor. The footsteps, the footsteps of three men, always heavily booted, who made the stairs groan despite the heavy red carpet. The preceding day, Li had again held Lisa to him when, having arrived at the landing, the men stopped, suspended, silently hesitating. Everyone on the floor was lying stiff in his bed, holding his breath. Sometimes, they moved on toward the eighth floor. This time, they entered the corridor. Lisa had buried her face against Li's shoulder, trembling nervously. She knew what would happen next; it had been the same for months. The footsteps stopped in front of a door before one had finished counting them. Three loud knocks on the door, then the sound of the lock. People listened to try to catch the name of the person who opened the door, and then a voice thundered, the same one each time, curt and resounding: *"Order na arest!"* An arrest order. There followed a long bustling about in the resident's room, the sounds of voices. After an hour or two, the footsteps went away again, toward the stairway, four people's footsteps. As they left, a few people cried in the corridor: "I'm innocent!" Swearing, the Chekists hurried them along. Most of them went silently, holding in their hands a little suitcase containing their personal effects. Many had already prepared it for this purpose, and had been keeping it ready under their beds for weeks. Long after the footsteps had died away in the night, people started breathing again in the rooms. Soon it would be dawn, and the residents of the Hotel Lux would go down to the cafeteria to eat breakfast, with bags under their eyes and their faces pale and closed.

Walking through the corridors, they counted the gray seals affixed to the doors. Even the manager of the hotel, Gourevich, whom everyone knew, had disappeared. The Cominternians' ship was sinking as the NKVD boarded it. In the passageways, the International's men now saw only the faces of Chekists, who had taken up residence on the third floor.

LI KNEW THIS WOULD BE A LONG NIGHT. THEY ALWAYS CAME AFTER one in the morning, working through some list or another. Now hardly a night went by without hearing *Order na arest!* in the corridor. In bed, he tried in vain to keep calm, but he knew it was hopeless. His turn was coming, there was no longer any doubt about it.

That same day, they'd gone with Zhang Bao to say good-bye at the newspaper. They were not able to exchange more than few words, their throats tight. Zhang was one of the last members of the paper's team who was still free. The best of them, perhaps, and Li's only friend, for sure.

Starting in January, the other writers, those who had not been sent back to China, had disappeared one after the other. No trace of them, no explanation. The *Time of National Salvation* had ceased to appear. Manouilski was transferring the paper to New York, leaving Li and Zhang in a worrisome idleness. There was talk of hundreds of thousands of people behind bars. It was worse than after the assassination of Kirov on December 1, 1934. Everyone in the Lux remembered the earthquake that had followed that. The craziest rumors were circulating: a quarter of Leningrad's population was said to have disappeared as a result of Stalin's fury at the loss of his heir apparent. Since then, the Vojd seemed haunted by the shadow of Trotsky, whose hand he saw everywhere. The former head of the Red Army, who had taken refuge in Mexico, had long since been defeated. But as in a nightmare, his agents, his spy centers, his saboteurs were still popping up in large numbers, despite the lethal whirling of the sword. At the outset, Li had politely applauded, along with all the foreigners in Moscow, when the NKVD discovered the first conspiracies to assassinate Stalin. Applauded with enthusiasm; vigilance was necessary. But the multiplication of these conspiracies over the past two years had puzzled him, as had the arrests at the newspaper and at Progress Editions. These sudden and massive disappearances, for months, these trials of Communist heroes, one after the other, defied logic. Did Stalin know about all this? Was he really behind these new purges? Wasn't it the NKVD and Yezhov who were going too far? The highest levels of the young Soviet state had become impenetrable, unreadable. The torrent of official explanations didn't help; on the contrary, now the Party was telling people that "the closer we come to socialism, the more bitter the class struggle gets!" Three years earlier, Stalin was announcing that the construction of socialism was completed, except for a few details. In the streets, one was always seeing banners that read LIFE IS HAPPIER, LIFE IS GAYER! STALIN.

Neither Li nor Zhang understood much about theory, lately. In low voices, taking countless precautions to avoid being overheard, they ruminated on the puzzle: whether they were Russians or foreigners, all Communists were Stalinists, good, devoted Stalinists, obedient to the Vojd. But that made no difference. The whole city, the whole country was trembling as the roundups were carried out. Twenty-one years after the revolution, a new Red terror was striking the country, still more implacable, but totally inexplicable. Li was familiar with terror, with its odor of cold savagery, of violent death. He was familiar with the White terror, the thousands of people executed in Canton and Shanghai, the military chaos in the cities.

Moscow seemed full of order and calm. But night fell like a curtain on a stage, a minuscule stage lit by spotlights, and surrounded by an immense labyrinth of opaque wings. During the daytime, when one was visible, there was enthusiasm, but when night came, there was fear, a nameless, permanent tension deeply twisting people's minds until it became routine.

When the first Cominternians fell, Li told himself that at least one thing was clear: he and his were henceforth undesirables, if they weren't doomed.

"IF ONLY THEY COULD COME AND ARREST ME AND SEND ME BACK TO China!" Lying in his bed, Li silently cursed the Russian land that was holding him as mud clings to one's feet. In November 1937, he had gone to see Wang Ming and Kang Sheng, on the day before their departure for China. Li, who was supposed to go back with them, had thought he was really leaving. The plane was supposed to make the first air connection between the Soviet Union and Yan'an, the new capital of Mao's soviet. A feat of Russian piloting. But around Li, Wang Ming and Kang Sheng had seemed embarrassed. Kang had looked him up and down one last time and then said, in a pinched tone, "Impossible, you're staying in Moscow." They needed him here, not back there in Yan'an, he said. The orders had been countermanded at the last minute. Confronted by Li's anger, Wang Ming had ended up asking him to stop questioning the Party's orders, as usual. That was not a Bolshevist attitude. The next day, Li's successor and his companion had flown back to China without him.

Since then, the days had been ticking by in a slow countdown as he watched for the slightest good news, in vain.

Almost four in the morning. Li was floating in an agitated half-sleep, dreaming of tall junks sailing over dark waters, when he heard distant steps coming up the stairway. When they came to the landing, the steps immediately started down the corridor. Lisa sat up and pressed herself against Li. Soon the men were there, in front of the door. Li and Lisa's hearts fell when the room resounded with the three blows of a fist on the door. In his pajamas, Li went to open it.

"Are you Li Ming?"

"*Da.*"

"*Order na arest!*"

There were only two men, this time. Before him, Li saw an officer of the NKVD in his winter uniform. He unfastened his brown cape, letting Li glimpse his pale-blue uniform, and handed him a piece of paper. His other hand was on his gun. Behind him, a young Chekist, his cheeks red from the frost, stood holding his rifle so it could be seen.

"Are you armed?"

"*Nyet.*"

The orders were clear: always check first to see if the enemy of the people had a weapon. Especially in the Lux, since a Cominternian had committed suicide with his revolver and another had jumped out a window into the hotel courtyard while he was being arrested.

They came into the room and closed the door behind them. The officer had Li sign an arrest form. Then he asked him to get dressed, forbade Lisa to speak, and started a systematic search of the room's fourteen square yards. Lisa had to get up, trembling, while the officer, aided by the Chekist, turned over the bedclothes and mattress. Finally, he went to stand in front of the little bookcase. It held about fifty books, including Lisa's French textbooks. Slowly, silently, the officer flipped through each book, the revolutionary ones and the others, before making two piles. Li and Lisa, seated side by side on the bed, watched him, powerless. The officer grumbled when he came across Li's notes in Chinese, not knowing what to do with these exotic scribbles. Two hours went by in this way, with the watchful Chekist barring the door. Then he authorized Lisa to pack a bag. Biting her lip to keep from crying, she put together some warm underwear and a change of clothes, a toothbrush, toothpaste, and a little soap. Li had not packed a bag. When the officer signaled to him to go, he put the bag under his arm, numb and shattered. At the door, he took Lisa's face between his hands, looked as deeply into her eyes as he could, an intense and brief look, and, while giving her an awkward kiss, whispered in her ear: "Lisa, I beg you, go see Chen Tanqiu* and tell him that I have done nothing wrong. Not against the Soviet people, nor against the Party. I am innocent."

*"Davai!"* the officer shouted in the corridor. Li turned his tall silhouette as slowly as he could, and then disappeared down the corridor, followed by the two Chekists.

Lisa closed the door, then went to throw herself on the bed before getting up again to scribble on a piece of paper what Li had said. Furtively, she opened the door again and ran to knock at a room two doors down the hall. A terrified face appeared at the half-opened door and Lisa held out the message, whispering, "Li Lisan has been arrested. He asked me to give you this." Chen Tanqiu looked at the young woman for a moment and then grabbed the message before shutting the door without asking anything else. He was thirty-eight years old, the same age as Li, and had knocked about in every corner of the Chinese revolution. A refugee in Moscow for the past fifteen months, he was trying to write his memoirs about the birth of the Chinese Communist Party, sixteen years earlier. He was one of its twelve founders.

Still frightened by her own daring, Lisa hurried back to her room and rolled up in a ball on the bed, falling into a kind of trance amid the mess left by the Chekists.

At the bottom of the Lux's staircase, in the great vestibule adorned with Greek moldings, Li cast a last look on the red marble of the colonnades and the scenes of combat between Sparta and Athens.

*"Davai!"* the officer behind him shouted. Li moved forward, passing the sentry box at the entrance to the hotel, where the Chekist day concierge was just taking over from the night concierge.

His bag under his arm, he went out into Gorky Street, paralyzed by the icy cold. The city was still asleep, but the smell of baked bread was already emerging from the old Philippov bakery.

*"Na lieva!"* ["left!"], the officer said. Li adjusted his cap, buttoned the

---

*He was to be executed in Xinjiang in September 1943.

collar of his coat, and started down the street in the direction of the Kremlin. He knew where they were going: Lubianka, twenty minutes' walk from the hotel. The snow squeaked under their footsteps. Li went along as if sleepwalking, saying over and over to himself: "I've been arrested." He was going to experience his first imprisonment since the business in Lyons, seventeen years earlier, when France had expelled him with blows from a rolled-up cape. A Communist prison, this time. History was certainly inexhaustibly ironic. Strangely, he felt almost relieved. He was no longer afraid, no longer felt that unending fear of the days, nights, weeks of waiting, powerless, for them to come and get him.

At every step, urged on by the two Russian policemen, he exhaled a cloud of steam into the frozen air. This time, too, he would come out of it all right. This could only be a mistake. They would soon find out that he was Stalin's guest, a member of the Central Committee of the Chinese Communist Party. No, the Soviet police couldn't really want to harm him. Moreover, given internationalism, it was not for Russian policemen to determine his fate. After all, his comrades in China had kept him on the Central Committee. He had not committed any infraction that Yezhov's men could reproach him with. A semi-Trotskyist, perhaps? That business had been buried long ago. There would surely be some comrade in the Comintern who could dissipate the misunderstanding.

On Pushkin Boulevard vans were roaring by. The officer who was following Li grumbled as they passed: his motorized colleagues had been busy as well, at the wheels of their black vans. In these vans, made to look ordinary by signs announcing that they were delivering meat, vegetables, or fish, eight to twelve cells held the NKVD's latest captives. After midnight, until early in the morning, their nocturnal travels constituted the only automobile traffic in Moscow.

The NKVD was overworked: too many prisoners, too few vans. The Cominternians from the Lux were walking to Lubianka. They passed by the Petrovski passage on their right and came out on the deserted Kuznetky Square. Li saw the light of the five giant red stars that had just been put up on the towers of the Kremlin.

"*Davai!*" barked the officer, in a hurry to get back to the fold. Soon they arrived within view of Lubianka. The People's Commissariat of the

Interior was bathed in the pale light of three searchlights focused on the facade of the building, under the metallic eye of Feliks Dzerzhinski, the founder of the Cheka. His bronze statue seemed to be watching eternally over the work of his heirs. Given an order, Li, headed toward the back of the enormous building of dark bricks, looking up toward the scattered lights that were burning all night in the windows. At the foot of the walls, an unfamiliar fear rose within him, destroying his remaining confidence. In front of the heavy door, the officer ordered him to stop long enough to be checked by the guard. Li overcame a slight shakiness, and the sentries opened the enormous doors. In the interior courtyard, he glanced at the six stories above him, then at the bit of still dark sky, before going into the building of the interior prison.

He followed well-lit corridors with bright, clean tiled floors that emitted the acrid smell of disinfectant. Guards were bringing in new arrivals, giving curt orders, hurrying along fearful, hesitant prisoners. Corridors came off broad stairways going down toward the basements, while others went toward the upper stories. The Chekists took Li to a registration window, where he had to fill out a long questionnaire before depositing his bag, his watch, his papers, and his money. An official in a blue uniform had him sign in and gave him a receipt for all his property.

They climbed the staircase toward an upper floor. After passing through more corridors, he saw a door open in front of him, the door of a darkened cell. A hand pushed him toward a human mass, dark and silent, from which there emerged a few faces, their eyes blinking in the light. The mass hardly moved when the door slammed shut, throwing the room back into darkness. A few inches in front of him, eyes were trying to see him: anonymous eyes in countless faces whose breath he could feel, about a hundred people perhaps, standing up, crushed together in a room of twenty-five square yards. Lubianka had been designed to hold two hundred prisoners; it now overflowed with at least a thousand enemies of the people. The air smelled of sweat, and the heat produced by the bodies was suffocating. Li felt very weary. He had not imagined prison like this.

A murmuring composed of dozens of people whispering rose in the cell, as if conversations had been interrupted when he arrived. Around him, voices were soon asking, "*Russki?*"

"*Nyet. Kitaïski*," he finally answered. In a low voice, he was told that in theory, talking was forbidden, but there were Germans, Poles, Bulgarians, Yugoslavs, and others in addition to Russians. There was another Chinese over there, at the back of the room, inaccessible for the moment.

"Comintern?" a voice asked. Mistrustful, Li did not reply. Who were all these people in this prison?

The human mass moved a few steps at regular intervals: each person was taking his turn to sit for a moment against the wall at the back of the room. There must have been at least three people per square yard. They explained to him that here he was in the "kennel." One of Lubianka's admission rooms. There were about a dozen similar ones on this floor. No windows, no ventilation. People got out only for interrogation and transfer to other prisons. Some people said that executions took place in the basements, others that Lubianka was only a place where prisoners were sorted. In order to sleep, one also had to take one's turn: it was impossible for them all to lie down at the same time. Many people drowsed sitting back-to-back, their knees drawn up under their chains. As for toilets, you often had to wait more than a day, until a guard took you down to the end of the hall.

After a few hours of slow rotation, Li found himself alongside Yi Sinchao, one of the writers for the newspaper. Li knew him well. He had disappeared a few weeks earlier. In the dark, the young man told him about the interrogations, showing his face and lips swollen by the blows he'd received. Li refused to believe it. Not that. Not on the part of a Communist police force. In Chinese, sure that no one could understand them, the two men talked about their distress. As if it had been an old revolutionary saying, Yi Sinchao reminded him that policemen were all the same.

Above all, he told him that the NKVD's men claimed to have discovered a new plot to assassinate Stalin. With him, Li Lisan, playing the role of ringleader.


THREE DAYS LATER, IT WAS ZHANG BAO'S TURN. ACCOMPANIED BY the concierge, the men in blue banged on his door at two in the morning. Zhang tried to keep calm. For months, gnawed by an inexorable depression, he, too, had only been waiting for this moment, repeating to himself day after day without believing it: no, not me.

# 16

"Confess!"

No, he wouldn't confess.

"Confess!" Wolfson, the investigative commissar, cried for the hundredth time, walking up and down in front of Li Lisan.

He would not confess, because all that made no sense at all and broke all the rules.

But on this sixth night of interrogation, Li was having great difficulty discerning the rules. Moreover, he could no longer hear, see, feel, anything but his legs. Swollen legs that hurt, hurt like hell from having held him up, in his stubbornness, for hours on end, his torso and nodding head battered with blows. His arms hanging alongside his body, a few inches from the wall—it was forbidden to lean against it—he swayed back and forth and had only one, single desire: to sleep.

Wolfson wouldn't let him go before dawn. He interrogated him only at night and did not stop until morning. He went back and forth in the bare room, his hands clasped behind his back, only a few buttons on his uniform undone, belching threats and insults for an hour, sometimes stopping right under his nose to hiss to him, in a suddenly oily tone, looking down at him: "You'll sign, you stupid bastard! They all sign! Stop trying to be clever!" Li remained mute. Wolfson was running this duel, but by keeping silent, by closing his ears to his tormentor, he was regaining some strength, long enough to put one or two ideas in order, while waiting to see what would happen next.

On the desk, amid the files, alongside the pistol prominently displayed, he saw once again the little wooden calendar that showed the date, still on the previous day's page: Sunday, March 13, 1938. They had transferred him from Lubianka to Lefortovo, the Moscow prison reserved for interrogations.

Wolfson finally sat down behind the desk and took a calmer tone, holding out to Li a bundle of typed papers: "Sign! You sign and you sleep. The others have confessed. Travin told us: you're the ringleader."

Li glimpsed through a cloud the bundle of papers being held under his nose. All at once, he wanted to do only one thing: sign. Wolfson was right, after all. Sign this bunch of stupidities and sleep. His whole body was urging him: *Rest, and we'll see about it afterward.*

He glanced at the barred window, masked by a blanket. Dawn was late in coming; it must be four in the morning. Still another hour at least to hold out. Afterward, they would take him down the corridors to the cell and would let him collapse on his cot. Perhaps one of his cellmates would even massage his legs; they knew what it was like, coming back from an interrogation.

As on the preceding days, he would go to sleep, his head on fire. Fifteen minutes at most. Then would come the peremptory signal to get up, haggard, suffering, and forbidden to close his eyes or stretch out all day long. At ten in the evening, like the others, he would lie down, panting, on his cot, once he had swallowed the bowl of soup and the piece of bread that sharpened his hunger rather than satisfied it. They would let him sleep half an hour, maybe an hour.

And then, around eleven, they would come get him and it would start all over. At each session, Wolfson kept repeating the same thing: he had time. He was feeling great, he'd slept very well. "Didn't you?" Several times, when Li had come into the office Wolfson had not even lifted his eyes from files. For a good hour, he would remain working on his interrogation records, taking notes, lighting cigarettes, putting them out, digging around in the drawers of his desk, drinking his tea, clearing his throat as Li stood in front of him, immobile, silent, secretly praying for a glass of water.

"So, are you going to sign?"

Sleep. Li would never have thought that dreaming, that waste of time, was so carnal, so imperative. Nor that being deprived of it would be so painful. This time, he felt that he no longer had the strength, that he was going to sign. His brain on fire, he took a deep breath and, in a thick gurgle, said, "All right, I'll sign, but only if you transmit my statement of protest."

Wolfson made him repeat his words in order to be sure that he had correctly understood, before sinking back in his chair, a broad smile on his face: "Ahh, at last!"

AND NONE TOO SOON. THIS CHINAMAN HAD BEEN FIGHTING HIM from the beginning. Normally, hardly a week of interrogation, just long enough to get acquainted. But anyway, Chinese, Russians, Germans, Czechs, or Koreans, they all ended up signing. Sooner or later, no matter who they were. All his colleagues agreed. This time, Comrade Wolfson, a member of the Party for years, a former top Komsomol, a certified investigative commissar since 1932, was working on his first foreign case. The Chinese plot was his meat. His more experienced colleagues in the NKVD had told him how much difficulty they had with the Germans. All those Communists who had fled Hitler. Hundreds of people arrested who had to be made to confess. They all refused to admit that in Moscow they were spying for the Nazis. They were usually disciplined, those German Communists. But even when they were told that it was in the superior interest of the Party, they refused to confess. Some of them had to be torn to pieces before they would sign their confessions.

The Chinese case was very complicated as well. They were always complicated, these Oriental matters. But Wolfson was sure they were like all the rest: by depriving them of sleep, they went almost mad. After a few nights, they would sign anything. A few beatings, a couple of blows with fists or blackjacks, would speed things up, too. Some techniques cracked the hardest nuts very quickly. At the NKVD's school, Wolfson's fellow investigators were categorical: the toughest enemies of the people were often the Communists themselves. Since his graduation in 1932, Wolfson had come to the same conclusion: over the past months, he had tortured all kinds of Russians, but especially Communists.

In one of the mood swings he could make in the course of a session, Wolfson had told Li, before giving him his first beating, the joke the investigators told: "In the GPU's school, I was shut up in an office with only a table. They put a chair leg in my hand and told me: 'You won't get out of this room until you've obtained a complete confession from this table.' "

So far as he was concerned, Wolfson said, he would more than once have called in his colleagues next door. Giants with hard fists, who went at you with Russian swearwords—competing to see who could come up with the best set of oaths, the finest series of obscenities—to work up the courage to carry out their work. They hit as if they were deaf, with centurion's blows, often, and didn't stop until ordered to do so. Wolfson had to keep an eye on them. Some of his fellow investigators let them do what they wanted to: urinating in the face of the prisoner after beating him, or plunging his face into a basin full of spit. The shrewd ones often cracked when that was done to them. For this Chinaman, it wasn't quite clear why, the order was not to be too hard on him during the interrogation. His "cooperation" was needed.

In any case, if things went badly, the doctor on duty was there at the end of the corridor, and he passed through the interrogation rooms, making rapid, detached diagnoses. He had only two: "You can continue" and "No, that's enough for that one, take him back to his cell."

"ALL RIGHT, I'LL SIGN IF . . ." HE WAS BEGINNING TO COME AROUND, this one. But he wanted something in return for his signature, he negotiated over and over: a "statement of protest" to be transmitted to the authorities.

Wolfson thought for a moment, put his elbows on the desk, and then looked at Li with a broad smile. "All right. I promise you that your statement will be included in your file and transmitted."

Damn! They all asked for the same thing: to write to Stalin, to Yezhov, to Molotov, to others, to the big shots, to the bosses. Always to complain and swear they were innocent, that they were completely faithful to the Party. It didn't matter; he would put the letter in the file. His superiors would decide, that's all. Yezhov didn't have time to waste on the tens of thousands of letters from prisoners. He was too busy, day and night, working over long lists alongside Stalin, Molotov, and Kaganovich.* In a few months of "accelerated class struggle," the four drinking partners had already drawn up more than 324 lists composed of forty-four thousand individuals.

At the moment, all Investigator Wolfson wanted was a signature at the bottom of the document. The bosses required it: without a signature, the prosecution would take longer, and in any event unsigned confessions made the troikas mad. The three military judges had an average of ten minutes to devote to the defendants who appeared in front of them. And they, too, had quotas to fill. The verdicts were always the same: shot; eight, ten, or twenty-five years in prison; further investigation. Comrade Wolfson had hundreds of files to investigate after he'd finished with the Chinese one. In the Lefortovo prison, as at Lubianka, people worked in shifts twenty-four hours a day. Questioning went on constantly with teams of investigators relieving one another. The NKVD asked a lot of its servants; always had. But the work was worth it: these days, with night pay, salaries had tripled.

At the beginning of the spring of 1938, Investigator Wolfson was approaching the summit of his career. Stubborn, feared by his victims, he had won his superiors' confidence. At Lefortovo, he had been put at a crucial point in the chain: the extraction of confessions. Near Lubianka, the seat of the government offices, and in Moscow, far from the provinces. Far from the lousy province where he had first won his spurs in the GPU, dealing with peasants, a few years earlier.

At present, Wolfson was trying not to get too lost in the Chinese names, in the sketches. On his sheets of paper, he drew a circle around the names and connected them all to each other, as he had been taught to do. Not that behind each of them there was an individual. Impossible to pronounce, these names, and even harder to remember. Fortunately, among

---

*Lazar Moiseyevich Kaganovich, Communist leader and supporter of Stalin.

these Chinese, some had a borrowed Russian name, and that made it easier to get a handle on them.

Travin, for instance. His real name was Sung Shengwei, and he was a member of the newspaper's staff. Wolfson had been working on him for weeks. In a few days, he, too, would be ripe. Long enough to put the final touches on the file.

FOR THAT NIGHT, THAT WAS ENOUGH. TOWARD SEVEN IN THE MORN-ing, back home, Wolfson could happily tell his wife before going to bed, "It's over, he's signed, that Chinaman!"

Li staggered toward the stool in front of Wolfson's desk and collapsed more than he sat down. Wolfson handed him the bundle of papers and a pen.

"You can read them, if you want," he said wearily.

*"Nyet,"* Li breathed in reply.

No question of reading this horrifying tissue of fabrications, of accusations each more grotesque than the next. With a trembling hand, Li scribbled his signature at the bottom of the document without even glancing at it.

Wolfson had won the first duel. Li was going to be able to sleep for a few hours.

Assassinate Stalin? Spy for the Japanese? Prepare terror attacks in Moscow? Hang out with Trotskyists? In a troubled sleep, Li saw himself the protago-nist of Wolfson's deadly tales. He had spent the first hours of the interro-gation listening, openmouthed, to Wolfson reciting his lesson: "Your case is simple. We know everything about you. You are directing in Moscow a Trotskyist counterrevolutionary network that is engaging in espionage on the territory of the Soviet Union for the benefit of Japanese fascism."

The first time, Li had made him repeat what he said.

*"Chto—What?"*

"To deliver your information, you go through the Chinese embassy in Moscow. Your friends in the Kuomintang. Your contact with them is the embassy's attaché, its number two man. His name is Simen Zhonhua."

"What are you talking about?"

"We know about your network. It's Zhang Bao and all the other people on the staff of the paper and Progress Editions. We've arrested them all."

Li wasn't sure whether he should laugh or cry. Very quickly, he understood that this was not a joke, or else something about Russian humor escaped him.

He still remembered everything about his first interrogation, on the evening of his arrival.

"Your name?"

"Li Ming. That is, Li Lisan."

"You should know."

"Comrade, I'm a member of the Central Committee of the Chinese Communist Party, and I want to . . ."

Li went no further. Wolfson jumped out his chair and shouted at him, only inches from his face: "Shut up!" He came around the desk, took him by the collar, and threw him to the floor. "If you ever say *comrade* to me again, I'll punch your lights out!"

Since then, Li had addressed Wolfson as Citizen Chief. As a prisoner, he no long had the right to utter the word *comrade*. He'd been told that once and for all.

"That word is reserved for those who are worthy to use it," Wolfson explained, calmly returning to his chair.

"Citizen Chief, I am a member of the Central Committee of the Chinese Communist Party, known under the name of Li Lisan, and I beg you to authorize me to write to Stalin in order to inform him that . . ."

Wolfson jumped out of his chair again and shouted at him, calling him a dirty bastard who dared to utter the Vojd's name, when he had only one idea in his head: to assassinate him!

For hours, night after night, there was a complete misunderstanding. Neither Wolfson nor Li wanted to listen to anything, to give in on anything.

After these stormy exchanges, Wolfson became calm again and told Li in a fatherly way how things stood: "You're a Cominternian, right? So you know the international situation? Don't you agree that the Soviet Union, the homeland of socialism, is threatened by Hitlerian and Japanese fascism?

"Yes, of course."

"Good. We're looking for agents. Are you refusing to help us?"

"No, but . . ."

"You can help us. Besides, you're a good Communist, I've seen that in your file."

And then Wolfson came back to the subject. "So you know them, the Trotskyists . . ."

"I have known some, yes . . ."

"Tell us what you know about them."

"Well, it seems to me that I've already told you everything I know. I've had a chance to talk about that on several occasions, and it's completely clear that I have fought Trotskyist ideas as hard as I could. . . ."

Wolfson looked annoyed and explained to him, as if he were a child: "No, what we want is your testimony; you must tell us that you are the leader of a Trotskyist network and that you were recruited to engage in es-pionage, you understand?"

Li didn't understand, and Wolfson had to help him a great deal. Li shouted angrily at Wolfson, and in his broken Russian, even launched into dialectics. No matter what he said, Wolfson shouted back the same thing: "Confess!"

Finally, Wolfson had had enough and warned him: "If you go on like this, we're going to hit you."

After his first beating, Li began to understand that he was not being tortured to make him tell the truth, but to make him tell lies. Hour after hour, blow after blow, from scream to scream, all that seemed less and less important.

Wolfson liked to have a head start in interrogations. He would open the next session with a jovial "So, the last time you recognized that you were recruited by Li Dadjen . . ."

"I didn't recognize anything at all, and moreover, I protest against the illegal methods . . ."

Soon, Li stopped protesting. The loudmouth became grim, swollen with bruises and mute, hardly paying attention to what the Citizen Chief was saying. A moment came when Wolfson asked him to sit down on the stool in front of him. His body broken, Li decided that it was time to negotiate. Wolfson liked that. Carefully, he explained the key to the affair: "It's simple, no one believes in witnesses' depositions, but everyone believes the confessions of the guilty. That's why you have to help us. To help Soviet power." Like all the investigative commissars, Wolfson liked to cite the work of Vishinsky, the prosecutor's Bible.

Li fell into an abyss of perplexity. "I will never shame myself by making false depositions."

Wolfson sighed and shook his head. "I'm going to be frank with you; I've already ordered the interrogation of several other Chinese who've been arrested, so that they will testify against you. They will say that you are the leader of the Trotskyist network. We're going to force you to confess. Don't imagine that we're going to take it easy on you."

Li no longer imagined anything of the kind. Looking blankly at Wolfson, he murmured, "I don't know what you're talking about."

Wolfson called in the toughs and Li said, "I demand three days to think about it!"

"No, one day will be enough," Wolfson replied.

The next day, Li asked Wolfson for some paper. Sitting on a stool in front of a table in the interrogation room, he began scribbling furiously in his clumsy Russian two pages explaining why Trotskyism was the least of his concerns and that he couldn't think of anything he had done wrong in that regard.

Wolfson called in the toughs again. Li was given another beating. Then they picked him up and sat him down on the stool. Li finally said, "Tell me what you want me to write."

"Write: 'In 1930, I was recruited by a Trotskyist organization. I came to the Soviet Union to pursue my Trotskyist counterrevolutionary activities.'"

"No. Out of the question. If I write that, I am attacking the reputation of the Chinese Communist Party."

"All right, then. Identify the person who recruited you in Moscow."

Li remained silent. No name came to mind. Wolfson helped him again: "Well, you must know some member of the Chinese delegation at the last congress of the Comintern, someone who has been arrested?"

Li understood: Li Dadjen, the only one of the delegation who was still in Moscow. He had in fact disappeared a few weeks earlier, arrested at his home.

"Go on, write. You were recruited by Li Dadjen. Then you connect all the facts together, you put in a few details, you invent a little, and you write me a good deposition."

DURING THREE SESSIONS, SUFFERING FROM TERRIBLE HEADACHES, Li had tried to write his first crime novel—a few sheets that Wolfson carefully corrected, watching over Li's shoulder, advising him on spelling and grammar, helping him out when he couldn't think of a place or a date: "You have only to put down that you met at such and such a place" or "It doesn't matter, leave it blank, we'll fill it in."

Li had no taste for crime literature. Moreover, it had a very real lethal taste about it. In his new cell, there were almost two hundred people, but they all agreed that in the basements of Lefortovo, executions were constantly being carried out and the doors never stopped slamming. On the third day, toward three or four in the morning, Wolfson gave up and started studying the papers on his desk, falling half asleep on his stacks of interrogation files. Sitting at his table in the corner of the room, Li had glanced at the man, and surreptitiously picked up his pen and changed the subject. With fewer hesitations, he wrote a quick letter of protest addressed to Wolfson's boss, Citizen Chief Yezhov, head of the Soviet police and a close friend of Stalin's.

Then he put down his pen and waited. He would not write another line. Getting up, Wolfson took the sheets of paper without looking at them and put them in the file folder before having him taken back to his cell.

On March 13, Wolfson opened the session with a torrent of insults, handing him back his papers. But by six in the morning, he had accepted the deal and Li was finally able to sleep.

When Li woke up, he remained motionless on his cot, his eyes closed. What now? Wait for what would happen next? Never had he been in such an unequal battle.

# 17

At the general meeting of the Komsomols, Lisa got up, trembling, when her name was called. All her friends, her fellow students at the institute, were there, sitting as if they were at a theater, except that they weren't smiling. The meeting had been announced with great solemnity, and everyone knew what to expect. When Lisa received a special summons for this day, she'd understood. A few days earlier, she had met, at her own request, with the leaders of the Komsomol. Weeping, she had told them that her husband had been arrested, even though he was a virtuous Communist.

"We'll look into it," the officer in charge had replied, not at all surprised. There were lots of arrests everywhere in the country.

They looked into it.

"Comrades! Today, we have met to study together the problem of Comrade Elisabeth Kishkin, who is here before you," the young Komsomol leader at the microphone began. On the platform, he was flanked by the usual prosecutors. "It is imperative that we adopt a measure of exclusion with regard to her. Lisa is married to a spy working for the Japanese, a Trotskyist, an opportunist against whom the police of the Soviet state have had to take steps. As you know, comrades, the country is living under the double threat of Hitlerian fascism in the west and Japanese fascism in the east. . . ."

And the harangue continued, as usual, everyone pretending not to miss a word, knowing in advance how it would turn out. In any case, there was never any attorney. No one was crazy enough to defend the accused. Out of the corner of their eyes, they looked at Lisa, who strangely enough was not holding her head low but seemed to be staring with astonishment straight into the eyes of the Komsomol leaders. Lisa, the best student in her class, despite her deplorable class origin. Unbeatable in French. Since the beginning of the 1937 school year, she'd gotten the best possible grade, five out of five, on every test. Lisa, who had begun to read Stendhal in the original in front of everyone.

At the end of the diatribes, the little leader, following the rules, asked Lisa if she had anything to add.

Lisa cleared her throat and said simply: "I've spent two and a half years with my husband, side by side with him. I have never seen anything that had to do with the things you've just talked about. I can't believe what you've told me is true. We'll have to await the conclusions of the investigation for his problem to be clarified. If the judicial system says he is guilty, then we'll see."

A deathly silence fell over the hall. It was the first time that a person who had been expelled had engaged in such insolence. *Lisa was openly contesting the accusations made by the Party organs!* That was just like her. Her naïvete would be her undoing. To her comrades, who were intrigued by her love affair with the mysterious Chinese man, she willingly admitted, a smile on her lips, that she was "an internationalist at heart." Her friends liked her for that, for the candor that seemed to be defying the world with her blue eyes, with her ingenuous remarks.

The proudest of her friends limited themselves to a resounding *nyet* when asked whether they objected to the sentence passed on Lisa. Many of them vowed to do better and went further in self-accusation. Others publicly renounced their love affairs. In town, tens of thousands of women were no longer anything but "wives of enemies of the people." A new status, a very precarious one, with which one had to learn to live from one day to the next. To start repairing the damage, the Party strongly advised divorce.

Lisa was twenty-four years old, and she had no intention of hiding the fact that she loved her husband, despite the fact that he was Chinese.

On the platform, there was a moment of embarrassment, and then the Komsomol leader nodded to an acolyte, signaling that he could go to it. Standing up, the accuser started screeching at Lisa, pointing his finger at her: "Comrades, did you hear that? Elisabeth Kishkin has just admitted that she is guilty! She supports her husband! She protects him! A Japanese spy! A Trotskyist! She dares to doubt the heroic work of the organs of the dictatorship of the proletariat!" Responsible for sounding the death knell, the young prosecutor caught his breath. Then, resting his two fists on the rostrum, looking intently at the audience, he added in a lower, more somber voice: "She is his accomplice, that's evident. Ideologically, she is on the same side as her Trotskyist spy husband. We must expel her! I call for a vote!"

His final cry was given as an order, an order everyone in the hall was waiting for. They wanted this to be over, so they could hurry home. They wanted to forget these meetings that were so hard on their nerves, to throw themselves into their books, to escape.

The man presiding over the session went back to the microphone and immediately said, "Who is for exclusion?"

Lisa, standing at the foot of the platform, hardly looked around her. Immediately, as if in unison, the usual forest of hands silently went up.

"Who is against, or abstains?"

No one, of course.

Lisa went up to the platform and solemnly laid down her Komsomol membership card. She left the room, her lips pressed tightly together. She was followed by her comrades, who were relieved not to have been the one accused this time.

Since Li's arrest, Lisa had been going four times a week, after her morning classes, to stand in front of Moscow's prisons. There were five main prisons in the capital—Lubianka, Lefortovo, Butyrki, Taganka, and Sokolniki. In front of each of them, she found hundreds of other women and very few men, lined up on the sidewalks in endless processions in which everyone had to keep his place. There were a number of foreigners of all nationalities among them, but no Americans, French, or British. Despite the four or five hours' wait in line, shivering in the icy cold, silence or furtive whispers were the rule. The lines were so long that they bent back on themselves several times. They were kept under surveillance by soldiers in the pointed caps and heavy, pale-blue overcoats of the NKVD's troopers, their rifles slung across their chests.

There was a line of lucky women, those who had found their husbands, sons, brothers, or fathers, to whom they brought the only thing authorized: money. A maximum of fifty rubles a month, with which the prisoners could buy tobacco and onions. Among the women, a few bits of information circulated. The veterans, those who had been coming to the prisons for a year or more, passed good ideas on to the others. Such as coming every two weeks with twenty-five rubles rather than once a month with fifty. That sometimes allowed you to get a little news.

"Has he been sentenced?"

"*Nyet*. Next!"

Still being interrogated, then, and so in theory still alive. They came back in their turn, in alphabetical order.

The other line, the one in which Lisa took her place, was far longer. In it there were only women who were still trying to find out where their men were. At Lubianka, as at Lefortovo or Butyrki, she had to show her *propiska* and give Li's administrative name. Every time she had to repeat: "Li Ming! It's a Chinese name. Is he here?"

And every time, in front of the window, Lisa closed her eyes and was afraid to hear the answer once again. It had been the same one for weeks, barked, after a moment of silence, from an opening so narrow that the official behind it could hardly be seen: "*Ievo nietu!* No one by that name here! Next!"

The day after she was expelled from Komsomol, Lisa went to her classes as usual. Sitting in her seat, among about fifteen other students, she had met the eyes of her French professor. A brief, tender glance, accompanied by a fleeting smile. Mme Krasnilkova resumed her lesson where she had left off the last time. While she was speaking, Lisa saw a little note arrive on her table, then a second, then a third, passed discreetly from hand to hand. Holding them hidden in her lap, she unfolded them. Anonymous, scribbled messages: "We are on your side. You were very courageous."

This was balm for her heart, and she found it difficult to hold back her tears. Moscow doesn't weep! the poets kept repeating. But her friends were soon preaching good sense to her: "You have to forget him! You're young, you can find a Russian!"

In the evening, Lisa was consoled by her mother, with whom she was living again in the little room in the *komunalka*, the collective apartment at Red Gates. Two days after Li's arrest, the officials at the Hotel Lux had asked her to clear out. She'd returned to the little building in the hotel's courtyard, an old house known as the NEP wing, reserved for women and children of arrested Cominternians of all nationalities. The place was jammed. Most of the women were waiting their turn, and spent days looking for their husbands. A few of them risked everything and desperately tried to get their passports back from an embassy. But at the exits of the consulates, the NKVD's men were watching in their black cars, ready to pounce. Doing that sort of thing was tantamount to espionage. All the Polish women in the house had been taken away during a single night in September 1937. The NKVD had had to load up a bus to take them to Lubianka. Their children were sent to orphanages.

In the little house in the hotel's courtyard women and children struggled along, together with a few grandmothers lost in the turbulence of this country with strange customs. When they were not lining up in front of the prisons, the residents of the place were selling at the flea markets, for a handful of rubles, the clothes they'd brought from abroad and their last precious bits of personal property. Lisa had shared a room with two German women. There she also met Nelly, the daughter of Antonio Labriola, a philosopher who had been a friend of Engels and who had introduced Marxism into Italy. Nelly had been born in Naples, of a Russian mother, and had taken refuge in Moscow after Mussolini came to power. At thirty-five, she had married in Moscow the head of the Italian Young Communists. The man, hardly older than she, had been arrested.

An invalid, he walked with crutches and was awaiting execution in Lubianka. Nelly was desperately trying to get news of him from Togliatti, the Comintern, and the prisons.

Lisa lived in this building for three months before getting out of a place that was so exposed to the roundups of the men in blue. She went back to Red Gates to live with her mother, who was getting along by doing housekeeping and sewing. In the sixteen-square-yard room, the walls were thin, and they had to keep their voices low when they talked about Li Lisan. Now that she was the wife of an enemy of the people, Lisa experienced a little of what her mother had endured after Lisa's father's suicide in the summer of 1918.

In the evening, when Lisa was weeping silently in bed, her mother, Praskovia Kishkin, gently told her: "If you love him, you mustn't leave him. You have to help Li Lisan." She, too, was attached to this tall Chinese, so idealistic and such a hard worker, so obviously in love with her daughter. An unexpected son-in-law, but one who had shown her in return an almost filial affection.

# 18

Taganka prison, Thursday, October 26, 1939. Lying on his cot, Li Lisan was reading and rereading the words scribbled on the piece of wrinkled paper: "I'm continuing my studies. I'm living with my mother. I think about you. I'm waiting for you." Marvelous Lisa. Not only had she tracked him down, but she had succeeded in getting a message through to him. Laconic and powerful. Holding the letter tightly in his hand, his eyes closed, he let his tears flow in silence, seeing her eyes, her Madonna's smile under her bright eyes, telling him to hang on.

In twenty months in prison, he had learned the double, triple language of the penitentiary administration, such as the formula "Condemned prisoner without permission to correspond." When the families of enemies of the people heard that, they knew what to expect. It was pointless to stand in line in front of the prison any longer: the person you were looking for had been executed.

There, Lisa's seventeen words were written on the back of an administrative form that Wolfson himself had handed him during the last interrogation, accompanied by a curt "From your wife." Was this the beginning of permission to correspond?

"I'm waiting for you." The pretty handwriting in blue ink whispered to him that he was perhaps going to escape death. How the devil could she wait for him, when even he was not clear about his fate, when his life in this confined, mad universe hung by a thread? "I think about you." Modest Lisa. So she still loved him. The NKVD's men were surely tormenting her for that. He had feared for her. Many of his cellmates' wives had been arrested. But nonetheless, the police had authorized Lisa to write him this note. A sign that something was happening in his case.

She'd found him again. She hadn't abandoned him. That, Li Lisan had known for more than a year, since the day in August 1938 when, having just been transferred to Taganka prison, a warder had called his name behind the slit in the cell's door, at the time when money was distributed. His heart had leaped; he couldn't believe his ears, and his companions had had to scold him to get him to hurry up and take his turn.

In the corridor, the guard had made him sign a receipt and a register book, which gave him the right to fifty rubles for that month, the maximum. Enough to buy tobacco, onions, or carrots, to take a few vitamins and ward off the threat of scurvy.

"It's your wife who's sending it to you!" the guard muttered, his nose in his register book.

Since then, every two weeks, he felt the tenacious solidarity of his Russian wife. Here she was writing him that she still loved him, that she would always love him. This woman had entered his life once and for all.

Of course, he couldn't reply. He had paper and pen, however, right there at his side. His only weapons. Lisa's words had fired him up. For three days he had been writing, page after page. He had almost finished. Li reread the date as the ink was drying on the paper. He had only to put his signature at the bottom of the document. Thirty pages written in Russian, in small characters, in dense lines covering the whole sheet, without a millimeter of margin. Li had written down his final plea. His last will and testament, if his judges so decided.

He signed it and, after a moment's reflection, added a postscript in which he insisted that a copy of the document be sent to the president of the International, Georgi Dimitrov. In other words, to Stalin. And to Manouilski, who served as Stalin's majordomo in the Comintern. And to the head of the International's Party officials service, if there still was one after the execution of old Piatnitsky, whose limbs had been broken during his interrogation. And also to the Chinese Communists' delegate in Moscow. Who knew? Maybe there still was one, who would someday tell about Li's misadventures in Stalin's country. It was a matter of protocol, but no one must be forgotten. More than six hundred days in prison had taught Li about the severe, touchy formalism of the Soviet death machine, which was nevertheless so unpredictable.

He was still alive, and was surprised by it every morning. Of the thirty or so Chinese at the newspaper, only one was still free, an NKVD man to whom Kang Sheng had given his lists of names before going to join Mao. Most of the others had been executed. Wolfson made no attempt to conceal this fact. Travin, whose real name was Sung Shengwei, had been shot in the nape of the neck in May 1938, eighteen months earlier. Shen Fufang, called Konos, had died in a cellar of Lubianka prison on August 22, 1938. Li Dadjen had followed on December 10. Lin Dake had disappeared into Siberia, along with Krymov, aka Guo Shaotan.

Perhaps Zhang Bao was still alive? Before being transferred to Taganka fourteen months before, Li had made a discovery: they were in the same prison, Butyrki, the largest in Moscow with its thirty thousand prisoners for two thousand places. A former fortress, where Li had spent the terrible winter of 1938, a few floors away from Zhang. They had seen each other from a distance coming back from a walk, two by two, hardly long enough to glance at each other. Zhang looked like a dead man in his ragged clothes, his head hanging. They were forbidden to say anything to each other. The escort was pitiless with those who tried to send messages or call names in the corridors when the prisoners were going to the showers, which happened once every ten days, whole rooms of two hundred at a time. Since then, he'd had no further news, and he heard Zhang's name only in Wolfson's interrogations.

The system in Taganka prison, an old, three-story building in the Prole-tarski quarter, was even more severe than that in Butyrki. But above all, there were more common criminals there. Dangerous men, who didn't share anything and ruled over everything in their cells. People who killed political prisoners and were feared more than the warders. In the summer of 1938, encouraged by the NKVD, they had wiped out hundreds of real or supposed Trotskyists in their cells, along with other enemies of the people who were beaten to death or had their throats slit. Radek, the high priest of Soviet journalism, sentenced to ten years in prison, had died there in a cel-lar, without even the honor of the regular bullet in the nape of the neck. In front of Moscow's five great prisons in the searing summer heat, the air was heavy with blood, and the only notification received by the families waiting outside were these engraved words: "Died as a result of a heart attack."

It didn't take Li long to recognize that he was dealing with the under-world. Since his days in Shanghai, he quickly spotted criminals, whose total scorn for anyone who didn't belong to their world, and whose hatred for intellectuals and revolutionaries, were almost familiar to him. Sentenced for murder, rape, or theft, career criminals or novices, they alone knew why they were there. Their sentences were lighter, but their hierarchy and internal rules were far stricter: they stuck together in a united front against all the others, with the prison administration's tacit consent. The NKVD took a perverse pleasure in putting them in the same cell with idealists and dreamers, who were paralyzed by the savagery and determination of these men. As soon as they came into the cell, they were immediately deprived of all their property, including their shoes. They were beaten to a pulp if they made the slightest protest. Out of the two hundred prisoners in a cell intended to hold twenty-five, there were at least twenty *blatnoi* sitting on the corner of the pallet, flaunting their sumptuous tattoos and playing cards for the overcoat of some political prisoner. Surrounded by his courtiers, the *starost*, the leader in charge of the cell, had spotted Li as soon as he arrived. "Hey, slant-eye," he cried, "come over here and tell us what you're doing here!"

The *starost* and his henchmen looked Li up and down, suspiciously. "He's not a nigger, he's a slant-eye, all right," the *starost* observed. Not a guy from the south, a Georgian, a Chechen, or an Uzbek. Not a Kazakh, either, despite his high cheekbones.

Li told them that he was Chinese and a "fifty-eight." Right after his name, the number was the second thing he'd had to recite before the warders for the last twenty months: "article fifty-eight," anti-Soviet agitation. In a few words, he explained who he was: wrongly accused of Trotskyist conspiracy, and so on. The *starost* and his men had laughed at him. Always the same song, these fifty-eights. They, the fifty-nines, common criminals, chanted in unison their favorite joke: "It's clear, it's an obscure case!" The political prisoners' torments moved them not at all.

Li had not talked at length about his misfortunes. He had more important things to tell them. He suggested that he, too, belonged to the underworld in his own country. He told them how the tong in Anyuan had made him a sworn brother after the miners' successful strike. When he heard that, the *starost*'s ears pricked up. The slant-eye showed him the scar on his wrist, the cut he himself had made in order to exchange blood with his witness after the ritual bleeding of the chicken. He told how his bodyguard, Gu Shunzhang, the Shanghai illusionist, handled his Mauser. "Ah! a Mauser! Helluva gun!" A legend among criminals. Or how the opium trade occupied the feared men of the Green Society, who were sometimes their friends and sometimes their enemies. The *starost,* like all imprisoned criminals, liked stories. They broke the monotony of the place. He wanted to know all about the tongs. Li embroidered as much as he could.

This Chinese was less like those stupid political prisoners, those depressed intellectuals who spent all their time telling everybody they were innocent, when they weren't bitching about "that swine Stalin." In the underworld, the most perspicacious ones recognized Stalin as one of their own running the country. Many of them had a rough affection for the Vojd.

But the slant-eye was henceforth untouchable. No one in the cell would steal his ration of bread, his soup, or his tobacco, on pain of severe punishment.

The months went by in the anxious routine of the prison. Li, still in custody, talked little with his companions in misfortune, confiding only guardedly. The world had become a minuscule, hermetic, and threatening universe, from which reason alone had escaped. When ordered to go to sleep under the lights that were kept on all night, everyone lay down on their sides, so jammed against each other on the immense wooden pallet that they had to turn over together, or wait, while being eaten by thousands of lice, harassed by legions of bugs.

Between two waves of interrogation, Li had been able to read all the books available to the prisoners, an old collection of Russian literature still allowed by the prison rules. By the anemic glow of the only lightbulb, he'd plunged into Tolstoy and Dostoyevsky, on the best level of the pallet, the middle one, far from the stinking slop pail. As a young man, Li had prided himself on having eyes as sharp as a tiger's; now he had become so myopic that he had to ask for glasses.

When he wasn't reading, Li was writing, always squatting on his pallet. For the past few weeks, paper had been less tightly rationed: "Thirty sheets, no more!" the warder had bellowed the preceding day, through the slit in the door. A huge packet. A year earlier, it had been impossible to get more than three or four half-sheets. The soup was still just as thin, and they were still just as hungry, but there were little signs that the situation was improving in this month of October 1939. All the political prisoners, the ones that were still strong enough, were casting bottles into the sea, addressing their petitions to Stalin, Molotov, or whoever was responsible. Article 111 authorized them to do so. You had to insist, keep telling the warders, who couldn't take it anymore. No newspaper made it into the cells. The few bits of fresh news they got only from newly arrived prisoners. In this way Li had learned the fate of Bukharin, Piatnitsky, and a few others.

Pavel Mif had fallen, as well. Li wouldn't have bet a dime on his survival. He was said to be already dead. Li smiled bitterly on hearing mentioned the man whom Stalin had sent to China to bring him down, nine years earlier. For the past few weeks, Wolfson, his faithful interrogator, had never stopped questioning him about Mif. Over and over, Li had to repeat: "No, I've never had any relations with Pavel Mif, either in China or in Moscow. I met him the first time, briefly, in Wuhan in 1927, and a second time in Moscow, during the Sixth Congress of the Chinese Communist Party, in 1928. I had already left China for Moscow when he arrived toward the end of 1930. I don't know what he did in China, nor how he went about extirpating Lilisanism. No, I am completely ignorant of his counterrevolutionary Trotskyist activities . . . but I remember that when he was rector of Sun Yat-sen University, he organized the repression of Chinese students accused of Trotskyism, and had about a hundred of them arrested. . . ."

Li also sometimes wondered what fate Stalin had in mind for Borodin. He had never again seen the brilliant Soviet proconsul who had made China dance until the crushing defeat in Shanghai. But everyone in Moscow knew that as a notable, he had made himself a name in the press at the head of the *Moscow News,* the official organ in English. As for Manouilski, because he had offered up to Stalin hundreds of Cominternians' heads, he was still part of the Vojd's inner circle.

However, China seemed to bring the Russians bad luck. Wolfson had been nervous recently, even distracted. He had jumped the first time Li told him that he knew that Mif had been under arrest since December 1937.

"How did you learn that?"

"Wang Ming kept me informed."

"But who told you he'd been arrested?"

"A fellow worker in the Comintern, I don't remember just who."

Wolfson had not insisted on the point. He remained pensive for a moment, and then went back to his hobbyhorse: "All right, let's begin from the beginning. How long have you known Mif, where did you meet him for the first time?"

Li, standing in front of him, told his story over again for the hundredth time, using the same words, the simplest ones, the true ones, to the point of exhaustion. Wolfson wasn't even listening any more, sharpening his pencils or looking through the files on his desk. A war of attrition had one defect, so far as he was concerned: it bored him silly.

That was two weeks earlier. Since then, there had been no more interrogations, day or night; nothing. Li took advantage of this respite to recover his strength. This sort of thing never lasted very long, but a month, all the same, in the summer of 1938. Wolfson had had to take a vacation. At the end of August, the news reached the prisons that Hitler and Stalin had signed a nonaggression pact. The Führer and the Vojd had buried the hatchet. It was all over: the propaganda duels, the solemn antifascist parades, the writers, filmmakers, theater people, and scientists requisitioned to speak against the Brown Peril before the crowds. Too bad about peace: in the West, Hitler could fight it out with the bourgeois democracies. In the East, the Vojd drank a toast to the Führer's health. The hors d'oeuvre would be Polish, the main dish French.

In the cell, the political prisoners, all Communists, were stunned. But Stalin's surprise maneuver had shaken Wolfson and his colleagues in the NKVD: How could they reconcile the prosecution of "Hitlero-Trotskyists," jailed by the thousands, with the new instructions, such as the one that called for picking up everyone who expressed doubts regarding the end of the famous "antifascist combat"? As had these thousands of losers in the Spanish Civil War who had taken refuge in Moscow, the latest arrivals in the capital's prisons.

Wolfson disappeared again for four precious weeks because of an adjustment in the doctrine. But Li had been able to collect his thoughts, reorganize his defense, write protests, demand that the processing of his file be accelerated. The essential thing was to avoid madness and suicide. In Taganka, many prisoners had killed themselves by jumping over the guardrail, before the warders put up metal mesh.

When Li thought about it carefully, he realized that Wolfson's mood had changed after his trial. On that day, May 15, 1939, Li had gotten into a prison van that had taken him before the judges of the Military College. A crowded waiting room, guards, and a name shouted from the door at regular intervals. A few moments later, the prisoner came out again, found guilty and sentenced, his face livid. When his turn came, two soldiers led him into the room. Before him, a table draped in green cloth, below a majestic portrait of Stalin. Here and there, a few red flags in sheaves. Two smaller portraits framed Stalin's, that of Voroshilov, the head of the army, and that of another person, whom Li was seeing for the first time— Lavrenti Pavlovich Beria, who had replaced Yezhov at the head of the NKVD a few months before, according to the rumors in the cells.

He had no sooner sat down on the chair that was waiting for him than an officer came in: "Court rise!"

Three superior officers of the Red Army came in and sat down at the table, signaling Li to sit down as well. Behind them, a clerk had taken his place behind a small desk.

Without any preliminaries, the judge seated in the middle began: "The military tribunal of the USSR opens the trial of Li Lisan, known as Li Ming, who is accused of criminal acts subject, according to the terms of the criminal code, to the punishments provided for in paragraph 58 lines 6, 8, and 9. Accused, rise: do you plead guilty?"

His throat dry, Li replied *nyet,* before going on, in a steady voice, "I am completely innocent."

"How did you come to the Soviet Union?" the judge continued without reacting. "Be brief."

Li thought a moment and then replied: "By boat and train, at the personal invitation of the supreme Guide, Comrade Stalin."

The three men looked at the Chinaman and frowned. The presiding judge turned to his colleagues and whispered a few words in their ears, a worried look on his face. They had already judged hundreds of foreigners, slipped in among thousands of Russians. Chinese, Japanese, Germans, whatever, it didn't matter. They had to act fast, ten minutes per convict, as at the slaughterhouse. There were now only three sentences: death, eight years in prison camp, fifteen years in prison camp. Any other decision had to be exceptional and duly justified. A delicate balance was involved: eight years of camp was a good, reasonable, average verdict; there was no reason to skimp on handing it out. But there also had to be death sentences, many death sentences, so that the upper levels of the government wouldn't wonder about the Bolshevist severity of the tribunal. The officers of the Red Army serving as judges were overloaded with cases and the requirements of the police. The political commissars were keeping an eye on things. The preceding year, the NKVD had shot tens of thousands of military men over a period of six months. Officers, for the most part. With its Stakhanovist quotas, the Lubianka prison was always demanding more victims for its meat grinder and its work camps. Thousands of the latter were being opened, from Siberia to Archangel.

In making judgments, they had to go quickly, but carefully. Two months earlier, on March 21, 1939, Stalin had indicated that the purges were over. As an expression of his remorse, he had handed Yezhov over to the executioners. His own men had taken a perverse pleasure in putting the screws on their former boss, the bloodthirsty dwarf who had driven them so hard. Then the executioners had been handed over to other executioners. The investigative commissars had found themselves being questioned by their own former colleagues. Several hundred of them had ended up being shot in the nape of the neck in a cellar, as anonymously as nine hundred thousand of their victims since 1936.

No one knew whether Beria was going to put an end to this interminable game of Russian roulette into which the country had been plunged. The head of the military tribunal was burdened with this Li Lisan case, one of the few he had read through twice. Not only had this Chinaman, a bad customer, recanted all his confessions, but he had also methodically demolished, in writing, the statements in the file. To be sure, he wasn't the first prisoner to defend himself in this way, but the judge had an inkling that someone higher up would be waiting for him if he made a mistake in this case. He'd never heard of this Chinaman before, but the latter's revolutionary pedigree suggested that prudence was in order.

The head officer asked him why he had gone to Alma-Ata with the GRU's soldiers. Li had always told Wolfson that that was none of his business: it was an ultrasecret mission. To the judges, he replied that Party discipline, the discipline of "the glorious Bolshevik party," forbade him to reveal the details of his mission. Unless he received an express order to do so from the Party's legal authorities.

"Do you deny having committed acts of sabotage, having prepared attacks on the leaders of the USSR?"

"*Kliveta!*" Calumnies. Tall tales. Lies. Li Lisan denied the allegation with all the curtness he had learned from Wolfson.

With a gesture, the judge cut him off, and then asked the ritual question: "Do you have anything to say in conclusion?"

★    ★

YES, HE HAD SOMETHING TO SAY. LI HAD BEEN WAITING FOR THIS moment for fifteen months. In his worst nightmares, there were only endless interrogations, without the day ever arriving on which he could appear before a court, no matter what court. He had dreamed of having a defense attorney, but Wolfson and his fellow prisoners had undeceived him about that, telling him that he would be alone and that the court would make its judgment quickly, very quickly. He had rehearsed his declaration countless times, examining it, reexamining it, clarifying it, correcting it so that every word counted. As Stalin's prisoner, the hostage of a strange madness, he knew that here he was risking everything.

He told them that he was before them as a former head of the Chinese Communist Party, that he was still a member of its leadership, its Central Committee, elected by an assembly, an assembly held with Stalin's personal approval. That what was in his file had been obtained only through the "illegal methods" used by his investigative commissar. That his life mattered little to him, but that any attack on his person, physical or mental, would be an attack on, a falsification of, the history of Chinese Communism. A serious blow, therefore, to both countries, to both parties. The proof was that Wolfson had even tried to implicate in his *kliveta* Chou En-lai and other members of the Politburo who were currently serving in China. Whereas Stalin—and he could attest to this personally—had always made certain that the Chinese revolution was going well.

Standing before the Vojd's portrait, he had looked the officers at the table up and down, showing as much respect as he could. His Russian was no longer a problem, and even approached eloquence. His voice had grown a bit louder, until it took on an oratorical character. This speech could well be his last.

He was asking that Dimitrov and Manouilski be called when the presiding judge cut him off: "That's enough!"

The three judges stood up and went out of the room. The soldiers ordered Li to sit down. In the room next door, the three officers, after the usual consultations, agreed: they should be prudent. There was no question of sending this Chinaman to join his ancestors without a green light from the Center.

The minutes seemed long to Li as he sat on his chair, staring at the Vojd's mustache. He had time to remember that in China he had already died three times.

"Court rise!"

Behind the table, the presiding judge was brief: "Further investigation. Next!"

When Li reentered his cell, the *starost* congratulated him: "Further investigation? That means that they've had it! Don't know what to stick you with, or they're worried. You've won a few more months with us, slant-eye!"

Since the trial, Wolfson had been in a foul mood. They had to start all over, and his heart was no longer in it. Since the fascists had stopped being the enemy, Wolfson got mixed up in his grammar. Moreover, this Chinaman's case no longer interested him. The NKVD had nonetheless done a good job, succeeding in liquidating a whole "terrorist group," a whole "nest of spies." But not Li Lisan. This guy was a real drag. He'd signed his confession a hundred times, and a hundred times he'd recanted it the next day. Even the time he'd spent in the cooler hadn't helped. The informer he'd sent into the cell had come out saying, "There's nothing there. He's a Communist, a real one." Wolfson had known that for a long time, but he had to put everything in the file, confessions and recantations. That was the rule. A year earlier, the judges wouldn't have bothered about such little things. This damned Chinaman's stubbornness had made him lose time. It made Wolfson wonder if Li weren't protected, somewhere up there. Since Yezhov had fallen, everyone in the NKVD was worried. However, the new boss, Beria, didn't have a reputation for being a softy, either.

Almost the whole Li Lisan group had gone down. His accomplice, Zhang Bao, was still in Butyrki prison. A clever one, who had succeeded in slipping through the net last year, in extremis. Wolfson became furious just thinking about it. A moron at the NKVD, a secretary perhaps, had typed his name backwards on all the documents presented at the trial. Citizen Bao Zhang had been brought up for trial on June 24, 1938. He did not have a right to be tried before a Military College court, but only before a simple special commission, a troika that worked even more quickly. Despite all his denials, before he could say a word the Japanese spy Bao Zhang had been sentenced to eight years in a prison camp for reeducation through work. When his judges asked him if had anything to add, Zhang Bao had plunged into the minuscule crack in the case.

"A mistake has been made, citizen judges! I'm not Bao Zhang, he's another comrade. I know him! Chinese names, you know. . . . My name is Zhang Bao, not Bao Zhang! My family name is Zhang, his family name is Bao. . . ."

A confused discussion ensued, but the Chekists agreed: Chinese names were tricky, and all the files looked alike. Irritated, the head of the troika made an immediate decision: "Further investigation. Next!" His legs collapsing underneath him, Zhang Bao had been taken back to Butyrki, happy to have gained some time.

The troikas never went out of the courtroom for deliberations. When it recessed, having handed out a few death sentences and many years of work camp, the Chekists said to each other that in the case of that Chinaman, they had almost made a judicial error.

Li reread the thirty pages of his plea. Despite the erasures, it was written in good Russian. A cellmate whose native language was Russian had helped him with the grammatical subtleties. As for the style, the plea was in the tradition of Leninist flamboyance that he liked so much: concise, firm, and aggressive. As for the content, the citizen head officer could like it or lump it. Twenty months of torture had had no effect: so far as the original history of Chinese Communism went, no one was going to teach Li Lisan any lessons. Point by point, he demolished the whole of the indictment, established the facts, and threw out his challenge: if you lay a hand on me, you'll be attacking all Chinese, because you'll be falsifying their history. Kill me if you want, but no more *kliveta!* Your tall stories are too much, so enormous they would be silly if it weren't for the damned "illegal methods" employed by that monkey Wolfson.

Too bad about the mysterious Mordvinov: he'll get a good raking over the coals, this man whose name I don't even know, this unknown man in the Comintern who's been assigned to drag my name through the mud, this slanderer. Two days earlier, Wolfson had shoved in front of his nose the "Mordvinov note," one of the thousands of memos written for the NKVD. Mordvinov had wondered about Li's stay in France: "Didn't Li have friendly contacts with the French police, over there? How could one know that he didn't?" More serious still, Mordvinov had gotten involved in Chinese affairs. Li saw himself accused of having launched the insurrection in Canton in December 1927: "An adventure, a provocation, the defeat of the insurrection was programmed in advance!"

The insurrection launched in Canton at the date mentioned, with a view to making a memorable announcement at the beginning of the congress of the Bolshevik party of the USSR, the one where the Vojd would give Trotsky the coup de grâce. Five thousand Chinese had been killed for an imaginary Canton commune that had become legendary as fast as Neumann, the incendiary sent by Stalin, had fled the city in flames.

Li Lisan, the pyromaniac in Canton? No kidding! Stalin would laugh when he read that. Li would go Stalin one better: "And for starters, let's note that Mordvinov considers the Canton insurrection to be an adventure and a provocation." This fellow didn't know his Stalinist pantheon very well, Li remarked dryly; the Canton insurrection was officially a "heroic" revolutionary act on the part of the Chinese proletariat, cited in every Marxist-Leninist manual.

"Secondly, during the insurrection I was not in Canton, but in Shanghai, and I did not participate in it. Mordvinov is ill informed or ill intentioned. But it is true that immediately after the disaster, it was I who was sent to Canton to rebuild the Party on the still smoking rubble. It is no less true that there I cursed improvisation and dubious wagers on the military art in revolutions. That I alone held out against all the party leaders who claimed that the insurrection in Canton was a model of the art of insurrection. That one can even date from that time my first official row with Moscow, since in fact, once I was on the spot, I immediately sent a telegram to the Comintern, which I accused of having committed an extremely serious error in glorifying such a disaster. And that Chou En-lai ended up agreeing with my view. As for the difficult clandestine work carried on under the terror, it must have borne fruit, since a few months later, at the congress that designated me as head of the party, the Cantonese delegation was the largest of all. . . ."

As a matter of fact, wasn't that the "only Stalinist congress" of the Chinese Communist Party, as it is always proudly called? Li Lisan, the illegitimate son of the glorious Stalinist years? "Check your archives."

"Hostile to the Soviet Union?" Li Lisan? Come now. When Blücher attacked China in 1929, in connection with the Russian railroads in Manchuria, who immediately said, at the risk of seeming to be a traitor in the eyes of his compatriots, "Take up arms and defend the USSR, the country of the international proletariat, the faithful friend of the Chinese people"?

Even if this propaganda grated on the ears of Chinese workers, peasants, and soldiers. Li remembered it well: never had he felt so much in the minority. He was accused of betraying the nation, of being an "enemy of the homeland"! But at that time, too, he didn't stand for any nonsense when it came to internationalism, which had ever since been his muse, the source of his values and his optimism.

The Trotskyists? It was widely known that he had denounced and attacked that breed. They were partisans of "militarizing the labor unions," adversaries of the NEP, oddballs who demanded a constituent assembly in China while the terror was going on. And who but Li Lisan had rid the Party of them, back there? "Relentlessly unmasked" them, as the Russians said. Who else had gone so far as to commit parricide by expelling Chen Duxiu from the Party when he leaned toward Trotsky?

Moreover, "if Lilisanism were a kind of Trotskyism, then the Chinese Red Army and the Chinese Communist Party would be Trotskyist," and by 1939 people would know that, he whispered.

Later on, yes, later "my ephemeral success went to my head!" For six months. He acknowledged having flirted with "putschism" in the summer of 1930 by sending Mao and his troops to attack Changsha, and his own troops to attack Shanghai. He agreed that "putschism has brought great misfortunes and grave losses to the Chinese people." Yes, "I took the wrong road by opposing my devotion to the Chinese revolution to the Comintern's instructions." All that had been decided countless times and had led to his exile from China in Moscow. Even if, in secret, Li Lisan stubbornly still wondered why the devil Mao retreated that day under Changsha's walls, without fighting.

And what else? Li Lisan, his hand in the till? An "adventurer" who was supposed to have pocketed "30 million dollars" of the Party's money? After tall tales, insults? Just look at the accounts, comrades. That's an absurd slander, worthy only of scorn.

"But I now come to the most serious question—which is after all perhaps not so serious—namely, that Mordvinov is constantly trying to unmask me as a provocateur, a traitor, a saboteur, probably manipulated by foreign agencies, etc."

At this point, Li reread his document carefully. He knew that he was attacking the foundations of Soviet law. Wolfson had often brandished before him the articles of the Civil Code and Vishinsky's words! He had repeated so many times that they didn't need proof but confessions! And if he was now in prison and being tortured there, that was clearly in accord with Soviet law.

"The gravest accusations are truly grave only if they are confirmed by facts or proofs. A serious accusation without proof, without evidence, is only empty words." Perhaps such principles did not figure in any revolutionary manual, but Li had had time to absorb them.

Moreover, "such an accusation is serious not for the accused, but for the accuser. For it is obvious that he is a slanderer."

So, your honors the judges and other citizen leaders, let's sweep away the "soap bubbles": "The question is why Mordvinov made these false statements. Since I do not know who is hidden behind that name, this cannot be a matter of settling a personal score.

"But perhaps he did this with good intentions, in order to finish off the enemy? On seeing the name of Li Lisan, he may have pounced on it, saying to himself: There's one, a deviationist! An enemy of the people who must be done away with!"

Let's get serious: "It's clear that he has lost the ability to analyze historical facts in a reasonable way, as well as the patience necessary for studying them." If Stalin was behind Mordvinov, he would take that remark for himself, as an appeal to his proverbial wisdom.

No, "after my arrest, my case was heavily clouded, and it still remains so. That is because of the incorrect method employed by Investigator Wolfson in examining the case and the false testimony against me" by Mordvinov and other Travins.

No matter. If here people no longer respect anything, in China they still respect the dead. "If Lilisanism were connected with foreign espionage agencies, how could its lieutenants have died heroically? Such as Luo Dengsian, shot in Nanking by the Kuomintang? Or Qu Qiubai, executed by the Kuomintang two years later? Or He Chang, who died in combat" in order to cover the departure of Mao's Long March? The list was so long. . . . Li stopped there.

That was all he had to say. They had stolen everything from him, even his life, which hung by a thread. But they would not confiscate his history, his ultimate dignity amid hunger, lice, and criminals. A Communist he was, and a Communist he would remain. Martyrdom went with the territory: one could die a martyr beaten to death or before a firing squad. The unexpected thing was that the blows would be struck by Russian Communists. Cruel and twisted soldiers who only yesterday were embracing you in the name of friendship.

This was no time for meditations on doctrine. Here, he was wasting his time, and he was telling them that in China, people were waiting for him.

A final impertinence: "All that is only supposition, of course. I have no doubt that you will discover the Comintern's reasons by yourselves. If you feel the need to do so."


AT THIS POINT IN HIS PLEA, NOW THAT HE HAD SAVED FACE, THAT the truth had been reestablished, he had to save his tormentors' face. Not leave them humiliated. They were very sensitive about that. Modesty was in order, and every educated Chinese excels in that. For contrition, Li Lisan was unbeatable.

Citizen leader! I know that as a former deviationist, I have not sufficiently expiated my error before the Party and the Chinese people! Therefore it is normal that the Party and the NKVD suspect me and take

steps to check everything. . . . I do not claim, then, that my arrest was
the result of pure chance.

"But I see now, by your correct, genuinely Soviet manner of pursuing
the prosecution, by the detailed and meticulous manner in which you are
conducting the investigation, that you will soon succed in bringing the
truth to light."

Lucidly, Li added, on reflection: "Which is equivalent to saving my
life." He cared little about his life, of course. But every Communist knows
that there is no life outside the Party; it's like being dead.

Being a miserable worm, "I do not deserve the attention you are giving me. But since you are faithful to Lenin's and Stalin's internationalism,
you cannot allow the case of a soldier of the Chinese people to be dealt
with unjustly!" If they did, what would happen to the "great friendship
between the Soviet Union and the Chinese people"? The challenge was
implicit: if one of China's most famous sons died, innocent, in a foreign
jail, that would be tantamount to a state crime.

Li concluded by trusting in wisdom, which is often hidden in tactical
retreats: "If you are according so much attention to my case, that is
because it is closely connected with the Chinese Communist Party . . .
and if it appears that Lilisanism was unjustly condemned, that is very grave
for the Communist Party in China. For anti-party elements would take
advantage of that sentence to rise up against its current leaders, who have
committed the same error as I did, Lilisanism."

Stalin might well read it. Maybe he would even take it as his model.
Li took his pen, wrote the date, October 26, 1939, on the paper, and
signed it with his Muscovite pseudonym, Li Ming. Then he went to knock
at the slit in the cell door and, holding the sheaf of papers in his hand,
shouted, "Citizen guard!"

Three days later, during Li's interrogation, Wolfson seemed even more
nervous than usual. Point-blank, he asked Li: "Strakhov is in Moscow. Do
you want to see him?"

Li was stunned. Chou En-lai in town, there, outside those walls? He hadn't seen his cherished comrade, his former second in command, for years. It was as if a breath of fresh air had blown into the room.

"See him?"

Wolfson had given in. Obviously, his heart was no longer in what he was doing. This order received from the military prosecutor authorized the prisoner Li Ming to talk with a sidekick who was free. Wolfson understood: this order would be followed by others. He had lost. He wouldn't have this Chinaman's head. Li was sitting on his chair, looking intensely at him, lost in thought.

Instantly, Li said to himself that coming from Wolfson, this could only be a trap. Wolfson had already tried to get Chou En-lai thrown in jail the preceding year. He was using Li to attract him. No one in Moscow was safe from the tricks of the men in blue. There was no question of allowing Chou En-lai to fall into their hands through his fault. The breath of fresh air suddenly blew out of the room, and Li answered in a weary voice: "*Nyet*."

It was Wolfson's turn to be astonished.

# 19

L isa was lying in her bed, her mood as lugubrious as the wind blowing whirlwinds of snow around outside. Recently, at the institute, as at every factory, office, building site, or neighborhood committee meeting in Moscow, everyone was busy getting ready to celebrate the twenty-second anniversary of the revolution. Enthusiasm was to redouble as November 7 approached, trumpeted *Pravda*. But Lisa was dragging her feet. She was no longer a Komsomol, and ultimately, it was better that way: she had gotten over her expulsion. Her soul at peace, she watched her comrades at the institute wasting an incredible amount of time in boring meetings, listening for hours to their leaders speak and say nothing, before loudly applauding them. Endless applause, everyone standing up, even on the platform, each person taking care not to be the first to stop clapping his hands, watching the others out of the corner of his eye while waiting for the signal from the platform to sit down again and listen to the next speech.

That evening, however, neither Victor Hugo nor Maupassant could lift Lisa out of her depression. Nothing, except perhaps the stubborn memory of the sudden summons to Lubianka, two weeks earlier, around October 23. She'd picked up the telephone in the *komunalka,* frozen with terror. In the receiver, an anonymous voice, neutral and metallic, had said: "NKVD speaking. I am in charge of the investigation of Li Ming. I must see you. Please come immediately to Lubianka." And the man had hung up.

Very pale, Lisa told the news to her mother, who sat down on the room's only chair, as pale as her daughter. Lubianka! The very mention of that place triggered a mute panic in people's minds. All Moscow knew the saying: "You go into Lubianka, but you never come out of it."

Already in July, in one of the countless annexes of the NKVD, in Serenity-of-Sailors Street, Lisa, summoned, had almost fainted. There a man in blue behind a window had urged her to prepare winter clothes for her husband, without offering an explanation. Lisa had received the news like a blow of the hand: Li was still alive, that much was certain! But "winter clothes" meant Siberia. And Siberia meant that she would never see him again. Every wife of an enemy of the people knew that. Lisa had put warm clothes in a large four-cornered bag she had brought in the next day.

Stubbornly, she had eventually gone to an annex of the Military College of the Supreme Court, in Arbat Street. Sometimes, people said, they gave out information. There she found hundreds of Muscovites who had also come to get news. After waiting for several hours in the August heat, she was taken into the office of an official in military uniform. Respectfully, she said to him: "I would like to have news of my husband. He was arrested in February, last year, seventeen months ago. He is Chinese and his name is Li Ming, that is, Li Lisan. . . ."

The military man looked at her oddly. What the devil was this young, pretty Russian doing with that Chinaman? Grumbling, he looked through his registers, running his finger down endless lists, turning page after page. He started slightly when he came across something: "His investigation has not been completed. It will even be necessary to begin it over again. Next!"

That was all, but it was enormous. Lisa had left radiant. Siberia, perhaps, but not right away. Li was alive, and better yet, his prosecution had bogged down!

Since then, until the telephone call from the Lubianka, every two weeks Lisa had taken her numbered place in the lines waiting in front of Taganka prison. The men in blue behind the window took her twenty-five rubles, but said not a word.

So that afternoon when the anonymous voice on the telephone had asked her to come "immediately" to Lubianka, her heart skipped a beat, but she plucked up her courage. In any case, one had no choice but to obey a summons from the NKVD. She went by metro as far as the Dzerzhinski station. There, at the foot of the People's Commissariat of the Interior, she walked around the building, moving hesitantly along the very sidewalk Li Lisan had taken for the last time one night in February, twenty months earlier. Inside the cavern, she held her breath while the Chekists directed her through well-polished corridors to an office where two men in uniform were waiting for her: a slender man hardly thirty years old, who had looked at her with icy eyes, next to a fat, older man.

"Investigative Commissar Pliuch, Adjunct Investigative Commissar Sinitsyn. Please sit down and write your biography."

They gave her a few sheets of paper, ink, and a pen, and Lisa immediately began the exercise in silence, seated at a table at the side of the room. A routine, the biography. A few minutes later, frowning, Pliuch aggressively looked over Lisa's vital statistics.

"Daughter of a property owner . . . I see. Not surprised you're still with this Li Ming. With the class origins the two of you have, you must get along well! Birds of a feather . . ."

No point in arguing. Lisa caught her breath and replied, "You arrested my husband almost two years ago. He has still not been judged. I am sick of waiting. I want this case to go to court soon."

The tall, thin man had looked her up and down, but the little fat one, who had not said anything yet, stirred on his chair. "Wait a little. You won't have to wait long, I think."

For a fraction of a second, Lisa thought she saw a trace of humanity in his eyes. This man seemed to be transmitting a message to her. Her heart leaped. "When? He's going to be freed? Tell me when!"

She had almost shouted. The man immediately corrected himself, icily interrupting her: "I didn't say that."

As a matter of routine, Pliuch lectured her on vigilance, always greater vigilance, against enemies of the people, traitors, and saboteurs. Then he informed her that the interview was over. Lisa was about to stand up when the other man added, "You can write a few words to your husband. Be brief."

When she picked up the pen and the piece of paper, her heart was beating wildly. What should she write? The pen shaking in her hand, she scribbled the main thing: "I'm continuing my studies. I'm living with my mother. I think about you. I'm waiting for you."

That was almost two weeks ago. The October Revolution was going to celebrate its twenty-second anniversary, and Lisa didn't care, as she lay in her bed this night of November 4. The alarm clock showed that it was past nine o'clock, and she was turning over and over the tangle of lives, telling herself that she had to go to sleep, forget. Suddenly she heard the hoarse sound of the *komunalka*'s doorbell. An unusual hour for visitors.

Without hesitating, Lisa jumped up and cried: "It's him!"

Her mother, stretched out on the bed next to her, had no sooner opened her eyes than her daughter was already at the door.

In the door frame, two men were standing in the shadows. The first stepped forward, and Lisa recognized Sinitsyn, bundled in his furry overcoat and his *chapka*. He pulled forward the man who had been silently standing behind him and said, mockingly, "Here, citizen. Here's your gift from the NKVD for the October celebration!"

It was Li Lisan, blinking, pale, his features drawn, terribly thin. He looked like a traveler who has come from a distant country. Wearing heavy horn-rimmed glasses, he looked intensely at Lisa, with the same look he'd given her when he left the Hotel Lux, 613 nights earlier.

On Tiananmen Square, to the sound of gongs and drums, the undisciplined crowd went on forever, dotted with thousands of red flags flapping in the wind under the cool October sun. The cloudless sky had the blue tone that announced the pale, dry cold of winter. Sitting on the platform of honor, Lisa shivered and said to herself that the view was certainly unbeatable. Far off, at the south end of the square, stood the enormous Front Gate, with its most beautiful profile. Its curved roofs seemed to float in the morning mist, their ocher tiles sparkling. On both sides of the square ran the ramparts, with the crenellations worn away by time, separating the Chinese city from the old, internal Tatar city. Behind the tribune, above Lisa, the Gate of Celestial Peace opened on the Forbidden City. Completely absorbed by the majesty of the place, she almost forgot the solemnity of the moment: on this October 1, 1949, China was relocating its capital. Nanking had fallen, and Beijing, after an eclipse of thirty-eight years, was once again going to dictate the law. An army coming from the northeast, from Manchuria, had finally been victorious.

China was changing its capital because the Communists had won the war. Standing on the rostrum of the Gate of Celestial Peace, Mao Tse-tung and his men were busy making the final preparations before the speech and the victory parade. From below, Lisa tried to see the tall silhouette of Li Lisan among the handful of heroes invited to the baptism of the new republic, alongside the *djouci,* the president. Li was there, all right, his cap on his head, his round glasses on his nose, talking with friends and eating handfuls of pistachios before the ceremony started.

Lisa pinched herself to be sure she wasn't dreaming. She was thirty-five years old and she was witnessing the birth of Communist China before her eyes. So the dreams of that indefatigable dreamer Li Lisan had become realities. She felt intense pride at the idea of having met this man. It was his hour, the hour of the founders and the first cornerstones. Like the captain of a ship in port, Li, the virtuous helmsman, had successfully completed his venture. This Red voyage was tumultuously romantic: she, Lisa, a Russian, was now the wife of a minister in the Chinese government? Moreover, a minister in a historic cabinet, the first of the People's Republic of China? She was ready for anything, even the best, not to mention the honors. When Li had told her the news, on coming back from a meeting with Mao, she tittered for a moment, and then felt dizzy. But her reserves of optimism were inexhaustible. Everything had been moving so fast, and for such long time!

Around her, on the platforms, the few foreign delegations present were chatting in the sun, lost amid at least a thousand Chinese. There were two Frenchmen, the president of the World Federation of Trade Unions, Louis Saillant, accompanied by a leader in the CGT, Leliap. An Italian communist turned around to smile at this dreamy young Russian with bright eyes: "Psst! *Signora! Tovarich!*"

The Italian pulled Lisa away from her dreams; he wanted to talk with her. French served as their Esperanto. Delighted with this windfall, Lisa spoke French with pleasure. Never had she met so many foreigners as during the past few days. The trade union leader at Fiat was curious to know whether her husband up there on the tribune, this Li Lisan, was of Chinese parentage. He had met him along with his delegation. He seemed to him a man who had manners that were, well, almost Western. Different from those of other Chinese officials; more direct, anyway. He thought he discerned foreign blood in him. They agreed that people who have been away from their countries for a long time often change their behavior. Even their gestures change. That was very natural. Lisa observed that Li Lisan was in fact slightly different since he had returned to China. In public, he was more reserved.

"And in private?"

No, he hadn't really changed: attentive, courteous, and direct. The Italian sighed. Chinese restraint confused him. Then, referring to Marco Polo, he pointed to the immensity of Tiananmen Square, raised a hand to his lips, and snapped his fingers as a sign of astonishment: "Rome was a village, compared with this."

Two steps from Lisa, the official Russian delegation was pathetic. To represent the country of Lenin at the Communist baptism of a fourth of the planet, Stalin had sent two proletarian writers, Alexandr Alexandrovich Fadeyev and Konstantin Simonov, authors of the best-sellers *The Young Guard* and *Days and Nights,* about the heroic feats of the Komsomols during the war. They were accompanied by the best dancer in the Bolshoi, Galina Ulianova. The troupe was there, with its accompanists. Officially, the Soviet Union maintained only cultural relations with the Chinese Communist Party. Ambassador Roshchin had left Nanking before the Reds arrived, following Chiang Kai-shek as he fled the continent for Taiwan.

In the Kremlin, the Vojd was negotiating a very sharp turnaround. The advent of a Red Beijing-Moscow axis had not been anticipated so early. In a mad panic, Molotov was writing a communiqué declaring the USSR's recognition of the People's Republic of China. They had almost made a serious mistake. In a cell in Lubianka, Borodin, the former Soviet proconsul of the Northern Expedition in 1926, had been tortured since March 1949 to make him confess that as the ex-head of the *Moscow News,* he had recruited Mao Tse-tung for the CIA. The Vojd was on the edge of war with Tito, who was defying him from Belgrade.

On Mao, just in case, he wanted "materials."

★    ★

ON THE PLATFORMS, PEOPLE WERE MOVING AROUND, LOOKING AT their watches, their eyes turned toward the east. That was where the victorious soldiers were to arrive to parade down the Avenue of Celestial Peace. It would soon be 9:30, and a crackling noise began to come over the dozens of loudspeakers around the immense esplanade. The crowd of three hundred thousand people slowly stopped moving. Soon a nasal voice was heard, seeming to call upon the whole Chinese people, 560 million people devastated by history for the past century. In a reverential silence, the voice resonated to the four corners of the square, the geometrical, cardinal center of the empire. The elderly residents of Beijing listened and frowned. This voice was not that of an orator; it spoke good Mandarin, but with such a heavy provincial accent that the meaning was unclear. One thing was obvious, however: a new mandate had arrived. Lisa and the other foreigners did not understand a single word of it, but they had no doubt that the voice was announcing the entrance of China into communism.

Before long, the voice grew louder, and this time it was as if everyone had understood: an immense clamor arose, followed by a gigantic, cadenced *ola* of slogans and the sounds of gongs and drums in a dance of red flags. Everyone on the tribune was standing, shouting at the top of his lungs, while interpreters translated for the foreigners: President Mao had said that "the Chinese people have stood up on their own feet and would never more be slaves."

In reply, the crowd wished him "ten thousand years of life!"

FINALLY, THE PEOPLE ON THE TRIBUNE SAT DOWN AGAIN, AMID A passionate hubbub. On the benches, there was much sniffling; Chinese women were wiping away tears, furtively exchanging handkerchiefs with their husbands. Before their eyes, the crowd, held back by an honor guard of soldiers with their weapons ready, swayed back and forth, rumbling with rumors. In the front rows, people's eyes were turned toward the east, impatient to see the troops arrive. Behind them, people were shoving, jumping in the air, climbing on their neighbors to get a better view. The Eighth Route Army, the *balou tun,* Mao's imperial legion, was supposed to come first. Laden with victories from the caves of Yan'an to the plains of Manchuria, consisting of the survivors of the Long March, it had descended upon all China, joining up with the armies of the north and the center. The Red Army, the old *hong tun,* the army that took the first steps at Nanchang, had become the People's Liberation Army, *tiefang tun,* the PLA.

When they reached the Yangtze, the soldiers had watered their horses in the great river, and Shanghai had fallen in May. Canton was only a matter of days. China was kneeling down before its conqueror.

Under the rostrum's canopy, Mao Tse-tung was taking refreshments and drinking with his marshals. The parade was glimpsed in the distance when Lisa noticed a great agitation in the first rows along the avenue. Something was coming in front of the troops that aroused people's curiosity. In the middle of the empty pavement, trotting along jauntily, a dog, a Beijing mongrel, one of the thousands of street dogs of uncertain breeding, was walking all alone, his nose and tail in the air, up the Avenue of Celestial Peace. As he went by, the Beijing urchins jeered, while the furious and helpless soldiers looked on. A wave of hilarity swept over the front rows. On the tribunes, people were pointing at the animal; they stood up as the laughter grew louder and louder. At the sight of the triumphant mongrel leading the march, Lisa, standing on the bleachers, was seized in turn with a terrible desire to laugh; in the honor guard, the troopers were giving each other desperate looks: what were the orders?

Steps were taken, people stamped their feet to drive away the accursed hound, who was not about to allow himself to be so quickly deprived of such a windfall: having the avenue all to himself. Plucking up his courage, a lieutenant emerged from the ranks and chased the intruder, who started running, worried by the turn events had taken. The noise redoubled; as the dog passed, some wag yelled, "There's Chiang Kai-shek running away!" The people on the tribunes died laughing while the mongrel took off at top speed, yapping in front of the official tribune and passing underneath the immense portrait of the *djouci* before zigzagging through the crowd and disappearing.

On the balcony overlooking Tiananmen Square, Mao, magnanimous, laughed heartily. The People's Republic was being born in good humor. After all, in Beijing as well, people ate dogs.

★

The troops followed, but their marching was not the kind one saw in military parades in Moscow or elsewhere. Nor were their uniforms, the same jackets of padded, patched cotton the men had been wearing in combat the day before, but clean and ironed. Intrigued, Lisa watched these soldiers advancing in a picturesque approximate order, trying with varying degrees of success to march at the same pace. Thinking of the great victory parade on Red Square in May 1945, Lisa said to herself that she was far away from the processions of the Soviet Red Army, with their martial rigor and geometrical feats. But the sight of all these weathered faces, dried out by the sun and wind of every part of China, demanded Lisa's emotional respect, as well as that of the crowds that applauded vigorously as they passed by: these men marching in a somewhat disorderly way were not used to cities, they had not had time to learn how to goose-step. But they wore their humble garments with all the pride of sons of the people.

Then came the trophies, the tanks taken away from the enemy, little Japanese armored vehicles that moved along with roaring motors and clanking treads, followed by American Dodges, Hotchkisses, and GMCs that had belonged to the Kuomintang's army, pulling artillery pieces or carrying soldiers with solemn or radiant faces.

While the troops filed by, Li had a lump in his throat as he stood there, rather stiffly, the third dignitary to the left of Mao. For the handful of guests on the terrace at the Gate of Celestial Peace, this Saturday was their finest day. They savored the triumph first with a majestic spectacle, while waiting for nightfall and the gigantic fireworks display that was being prepared. Everyone was aware that they were walking on the same tiles that had been trod by the emperors when they showed themselves to the people at the entrance to the Forbidden City to make some solemn announcement. It was as if China had rediscovered a throne that had been vacant for thirty-eight years. The last emperor, Pu Yi, was in Stalin's custody. Captured by Soviet paratroopers in Mukden during the last days of the war, he had been in prison in Khabarovsk for four years, waiting to be handed over to the new masters of the country.

Li looked over at his comrades, who were all a little euphoric, as he was. At his side, Chou En-lai, a thin smile on his lips, also almost had to wipe away a tear when Mao finished his speech. Behind him, alongside Mao, there were the generals, a dozen artisans of the victory who would certainly be made marshals. All or nearly all were veterans of Nanchang and had warmly welcomed Li when he returned from the USSR. Zhu De, the father of the victory, with Lin Biao. The civilians, those from the years of clandestinity, such as Liu Shaoqi, with whom he had shared the miners' hut in Anyuan. And those from his years in France, like Chen Yi, with whom he had taken the boat home from Marseilles after the expulsion from Lyons.

The People's Republic having been declared, at the end of his speech the president's index finger had seemed to indicate the road traveled by pushing a button. A red flag with five yellow stars, one large one and four small ones, was raised to the top of the flagpole that towered over them all.

Everyone under the rostrum's canopy had a debt to the others. The musketeers had often quarreled, sometimes to the point of shedding blood, but victory reunited them. When it was time to distribute the first portfolios in the government of the new China, they had to find names the people knew. They had all agreed: Labor could go only to Li Lisan, in homage to the heroic miners of Anyuan in 1923, a large number of whom had joined in the epic from the outset, and also in homage to the man of May 1925, the gigantic electric shock that had raised up the country. The first minister of labor of the People's Republic. Li knew that peace would require a tremendous amount of work: a country had to be reconstructed and new laws invented.

Chou En-lai had been a real comfort to him on his return in 1946. It was partly thanks to him that Li had been so quickly freed in Moscow. Chou had gone there in August 1939 to be treated for injuries received when he fell from a horse in Yan'an. He had left eight months later, having wrung from Stalin something like an investiture of Mao. Between lectures and interviews on Chinese affairs, he had asked for news of Comrade Li Lisan's case. Invariably, the Soviets told him that they would look into it to find out what was happening. Chou had few illusions regarding the fate of his compatriots and comrades. Stalin's "friendship" came at this price.

Chou had left Moscow in March 1940 without having learned of Li Lisan's discreet liberation four months earlier.

If today was the finest day of their lives for all of them, the one on which Li had finally set foot on Chinese soil was unforgettable for him. One frigid morning at the end of January 1946, a Soviet airplane coming from Vladivostok had unloaded a special passenger in Harbin, Manchuria. Still the most Russian of Chinese cities, Harbin had been occupied by Soviet troops for nine months. When the plane landed on the icy runway of the airport, Li felt his heart beating wildly. A miraculous survivor of the International, he silently wept with joy on coming back to his country. As soon as he had arrived, he took another Red Army Yak to get to Yan'an. There, in Mao's capital, in the country of yellow earth and sandstorms, his peers had been living like troglodytes for ten years. Thanks to a party, an army, and a militia of 4 million members, they ruled over a population of 100 million Chinese. Around this rebellious north, Chiang Kai-shek's armies were on guard and had mounted a blockade. Once Japan had been defeated, the united front against the invader no longer had any raison d'être, and the two camps burnished their weapons, having made up their minds to fight it out.

Yan'an was awaiting Li Lisan with curiosity and affection, as if for the return of a wounded great man—Mao with some concern, Kang Sheng with still more. It had been fifteen years since the "loudmouth" Li Lisan had disappeared into the Soviet Union. All the campaigns in Moscow had not prevented him from being reelected in absentia, a year earlier, to the Central Committee. It was like a message to Stalin: "Give us back Li Lisan." A Party congress had been held in Yan'an in April 1945. An important event; it was the seventh Party congress, but the first since the one held in Moscow in 1928, seventeen years before. It consecrated Mao's supremacy and put down Wang Ming, Stalin's man. Kang Sheng had had time to make himself hated by the whole party. As soon as he arrived from Moscow in 1937, he had remade the political police and Chinese military intelligence on the model he'd learned from his Soviet friends. The Chinese NKVD was called the Department of Social Affairs. From 1941 to 1943, Yan'an had experienced a Red terror, named the rectification movement. In Kang Sheng, Mao had found his Beria. With a rare sense of intrigue, the man had introduced denunciation, torture, and forced confessions. A man of letters, he had given a Chinese touch to Yezhov's methods. Here, in the meetings for public accusation, the victim often stood up, in a traveling players' sort of stage set, his hands behind his back on a platform. Before his eyes had been placed a vial of poison, a bayonet, and a hangman's noose. In front of him, the crowd chanted: "There are three ways to die! Choose one!" or "Confess that you're a counterrevolutionary!"

To be sure of winning Mao's gratitude, Kang Sheng had procured for him a twenty-five-year-old actress in Shanghai's leftist movie industry, Jiang Qing, to serve as his mistress. In 1938, Mao, who was then forty-five, made her his third wife. Flabbergasted, Chou En-lai and the generals didn't like that at all; the starlet had a lurid reputation, and Mao's titular wife, He Zhedjen, was among the heroines of the Long March. One of her two children had died, and the other had been left with peasants. At thirty-eight, exhausted, the first lady had had to bow before her rival and go away for treatment in Moscow. As far as virtue was concerned, the chief's image left much to be desired; in prudish Yan'an, men and women slept in separate dormitories. The new wife's arrival was bitterly debated in the Politburo. It was finally agreed to allow Mao to take a third wife. But she was not to get involved in political affairs or start attending the Politburo's meetings.

Kang Sheng then sealed his alliance with Mao by having Mao's rival, Wang Ming, poisoned with mercury. Wang's accomplice in Moscow, his betrayer in Yan'an, Kang had failed to get his comrade: the nominal head of the Party survived, but suffered a long illness that sidelined him for good. Holed up in a grotto in Yan'an, Wang prayed that the Soviets would bring him back and put him in a hospital in Moscow. From the rectification movement, the Chinese Communists had emerged as Maoists, purged of a few writers and a good fifty thousand members. Most of them were young, educated people who had left the cities in the hope of fighting the Japanese, romantic adolescents attracted by the egalitarian reputation of the place.

The thousands of executions of innocent people had earned Kang Sheng ferocious hatred that erupted in psychodramas at the 1945 Party congress. Mao, who owed Kang a great deal, succeeded in having him re-elected to the Politburo. But a few months later, he had to remove him from "social affairs" as well as from military intelligence. On Li Lisan's return, Kang Sheng, worried, was slinking around Yan'an. The intriguer knew that he was not up to dealing with this ghost, who would certainly testify to his base acts in Moscow. Li had a lot to tell Mao and Chou En-lai about Kang's stay in the Soviet Union, about his mania for drawing up lists of good comrades whom he imagined to be his opponents and making them disappear.

Everyone agreed that Li had been the victim of a lamentable judicial error on the part of the Soviet comrades, whose attitude raised "a certain number of questions" concerning the relations between the "brother parties" that would be settled later. Li prepared reports on the problem. At the moment, something else was more urgent: power came out of the barrel of a gun, and they had to find a new assignment for him.

In February 1946, the Communists and the Nationalists both wanted to resume the civil war. On both sides, there were abundant stockpiles of arms. Their armies had millions of troops, and conflict was imminent. The Americans did everything they could: President Truman sent his chief of staff, the victor in 1945, General George Marshall. The American hero got Mao to board an airplane for the first time in his life and took him to the negotiating table. The negotiations among the opposing Chinese parties were masterpieces of hypocrisy, regularly promising cease-fires and even a democratic China, while at the same time the two sides sharpened their sabers and knives under the table. Separating the Communists and Chiang Kai-shek, there was still the cruel trick played in April 1927 in Shanghai. Everyone knew that blood would never be pardoned. The Americans fell in love with Mao and his ascetic missionaries. Chou En-lai did a marvelous job of leading people by the nose, including Western journalists.

On arriving in Yan'an, Li had the impression that he was picking up his work where he had left off fifteen years earlier. China had its own kind of time. But in this troglodytic universe, in this northern region he knew so poorly, he sensed how the Party had changed. In Yan'an, he no longer met

252 ★ PATRICK LESCOT

anyone but peasants in uniform, hardworking, clever, devoted. The town functioned in accord with the military rules of an entrenched camp, from which orders were sent to all the units in the region. The air was martial, and Li was deeply moved by what he found there. After the air in Moscow, that of the steep hills of yellow earth in Shaanxi seemed perfumed.

His comrades from the early days were waiting for him. He had a long talk with Mao, enjoying using his native dialect. The two men hadn't seen each other for almost twenty years; their youthful quarrels were long past, and neither had any reason to resent the other. Mao had peers, but no longer any rivals. Li was a shade, a ghost. Mao asked about his experiences in the Soviet Union, and about this Stalin who wanted Mao to come to Moscow. Ten years after Li, he had clearly understood what had happened to his predecessor. Mao had demanded and obtained in 1939 the recall of his German adviser, Otto Braun, who had accompanied him on the whole Long March. The Comintern had been dissolved in 1943.

At banquets, the generals teased Li about his repeated deaths. Chen Yi, his old comrade from France, now commanded several armies in central China. In the course of a conversation with Chen, Li learned that the *djouci* had mentioned to an American journalist that in the beginning he had been able to count on only "three and a half friends." The three others had turned out badly, and the half-friend was Li Lisan. With the latter, the president said, his friendship had "never really developed." He claimed that in their student days Li and he had not gotten along in the library of the Changsha normal school. When Edgar Snow reported the anecdote of the three and a half friends in 1936, Li was then a dangerous deviationist, currently being straightened out in Moscow. Ten years later, Li understood that Mao distrusted him. Shrugging his shoulders, he replied that this story of the half-friend made no sense; in Changsha, he was only fifteen years old, and had no relationship with Mao, who was six years older than he.

One evening at table, Chou En-lai, just back from a negotiating session in Nanking, whispered to him that if he wanted to marry, he knew a woman who might be interested in him. A widow past forty. The beautiful Li Yichun, Li's first wife, the wife he'd chosen, the one who had left him for Cai Hesen, his rival and friend in France. Cai had been captured and ex-

ecuted by the Kuomintang in 1931. Li Yichun had remained a Party activist, and her heart was for the taking.

Li smiled, and shaking his head, he told Chou En-lai that at forty-seven
he was still in love with a Russian he'd met back there. She had given him
a child, a daughter, the little Inna, born in Moscow during the war, on August 10, 1943. The mother and daughter were waiting for a visa to join him
in China. That meant a written authorization by the Central Committee of
the Chinese Communist Party.

"What's the mother's name?"

"Lisa."

"Lisha?"

Li understood that in China, Lisa would always be Lisha. It was more
becoming.

He remained only two months among the troglodytes, impatient to return to action. The Party gave him a new assignment. As usual, he was sent
where the situation was the most difficult: Manchuria, alongside Lin Biao.
The young general was preparing to receive the thrust of the Nationalist
armies. The keys to victory were no longer south of the Yangtze, but north
of it, in the shadow of the Soviet big brothers. Li had left Yan'an doubly delighted. Neither Mao, who was not unhappy to see him go away, nor Chou,
who knew him, had raised any objection to Lisa's coming. Soon she would
join him in Harbin, where he would set up his headquarters. For greater security, and in order not to disturb the rank and file of the Party, Li would
not immediately resume his true name. He would go to Manchuria under a
new pseudonym, that of Li Mindjan. With the rank of general.

BACK IN HARBIN, IT SEEMED TO LI THAT HE WAS FINALLY SEEING
the realization of his famous plan for an insurrection in 1930: thanks to Soviet military support and the equipment taken from Japanese troops, the
Chinese Communists now had precious artillery, a few tanks to support
newly outfitted infantry, and the morale of winners.

Li took charge of repatriating Japanese colonists in Manchuria. Sent
home by the tens of thousands and whole boatloads, they were alive, but
their pockets were empty. China announced that there had been as many

victims of Japanese fascism in China as there had been of Hitlerian fascism in the USSR: 20 million dead. In May 1946, Li had watched, dumbfounded and furious with rage, as the Soviet army pillaged Manchuria's heavy and light industry, hauling off anything that could be dismantled, and dynamiting the rest. The war against Japan had not cost Stalin a single man; he had declared war five days before Tokyo capitulated. But he reaped a huge profit: in Manchuria, he made off with enormous booty in the form of war reparations, as the Chinese comrades looked on with astonishment. Moscow also took back two naval bases, Dairen and Port Arthur, which the Japanese had pinched from the czar in 1905.

The deal would have been even better had the Soviet Union been able to get back at no cost the Chinese Eastern Railway, sold to the Japanese ten years earlier at a good price. But Li Lisan was the head of the Chinese delegation to the negotiating sessions on this issue. Things went badly, and all the more quickly since a significant surprise awaited him: he learned that his counterpart in the Soviet delegation, under the name of Kornilov, was none other than a certain Mordvinov. His "slanderer" in the Comintern had served ten years in China before returning to Moscow at the end of the 1930s. He was a hard nut to crack, a veteran of the Red partisans in the Far East during the Russian civil war. In 1942, as a "special agent" in Ankara, he had participated in the failed attempt to assassinate Franz von Papen, the German ambassador to Turkey. Captured and sentenced to twenty years in prison, he had been released two years later.

Their meeting was so stormy that they almost came to blows. Mordvinov complained to Moscow that this Chinaman was sabotaging the negotiations. But China got the railway.

Rather than having him negotiate further with Moscow, Li was sent to negotiate with the Americans. Truces, cease-fires, incidents, and other maneuvers to encircle the two camps were on the agenda. Truman's officials had respect and sometimes pity for these Red warriors, who were far more disciplined and honest than their counterparts in the Kuomintang. In New York, Washington, and the rest of the United States, Stalin was still the hearty "Uncle Joe," thanks to whom the United States had defeated Hitler. Li's discussions with Marshall's men were long, courteous, and useless: in January 1947, Truman's envoy called them off.

China's fate would be settled by arms: on the general staff's maps, Lin Biao conducted the game of *go* with a master's hand. At the age of forty, the general was an expert in maneuvers. He was familiar with Moscow, where he had spent four years in military academies after having gone there for treatment of a wound. He had arrived in Moscow at the height of the terror, after the arrest of Li Lisan in 1938, and left in 1942 without having met him. In Harbin, the two men lived across the street from one another, in comfortable houses requisitioned from White Russians. Sure that he enjoyed Mao's confidence and that of the Soviets, Li Biao, carried away by his successes, treated his entourage in an offhanded manner. He was perpetually late for meetings, and this finally led to Li's giving him a blistering lecture: "Comrade Lin Biao, meetings begin on time! Here, no matter what one's rank, no one has the right to make others wait without some excuse!"

So short that he was nicknamed the Chinese Napoléon, Lin Biao had kept quiet, a pinched look on his face. The loudmouth was back.

It was a Kuomintang newspaper that first unmasked the "Communist negotiator Li Mindjan, alias Li Lisan." In a photo, taken next to a DC-3, the ghost from the 1920s had been recognized, a little older looking, in a PLA uniform, shaking hands with an American general. Li Lisan was back! So he hadn't died in Moscow, as rumor had it. People did the math: this ghost had spent fifteen years, a very long stay, in the Soviet Union.

In the conquered territories, Li took up once again the labor union question, a delicate subject, with at least a million workers whose factories had been hauled away or destroyed by the Soviets.

In the fall of 1948, Lin Biao gave the signal for the final attack. The hell with cutting off cities from the countryside; they were going to move from guerrilla warfare to the war of movement. As in a game of *go*, all the Nationalist defenses would be besieged, sapped from within, betrayed, harassed, and they would collapse one after another. A few fierce battles and many surrenders later, Beijing fell, after Changchun and Mukden, in January 1949.

★

It was a mild autumn day, the parade was ending, and Li said to himself that it would soon be time for dinner. Lisa was waiting for him in the Beijing hotel, at a splendid banquet given in honor of the victory.

In the evening, during the fireworks show, Lisa, her head on Li's shoulder, admired China's pyrotechnical feats. Tiananmen Square was shaking with the explosions, illuminated by the multicolored sprays of light that had been spurting into the night for a good two hours. Inna, now six, and her sister, Alla, two, sat on their parents' knees, awed and shrieking in wonder.

The 1940s seemed so far behind them, that evening! Lisa was a mother, and the two girls seemed to congratulate her on the feat every day: Inna, with her toothy smile in a delicate mixed-race face in which two mischievous eyes shone; Alla, emerging from the chubbiness of infancy, already graceful. The day before Inna was born, Lisa had still been hoeing one of the collective gardens around Moscow where everyone grew potatoes during the war. Alla had been conceived during the terrible winter of 1942–1943, when they had had to sleep in a room in the city where it was about fourteen degrees above zero. By the light of kerosene lamps, the walls glistened with a heavy layer of ice. After two months, they had retreated once again to Lisa's mother's place at Red Gates. There, in the *komunalka,* it was eighteen degrees above zero at night.

Before Inna was born, Lisa had been worried about having a daughter. The reputation of the Chinese in that area was terrible. Li had assured her that a girl would be just as welcome as a boy. Of his progeny in China, he'd had no news for years. When Inna was born, he finally tasted the joys of paternity, even including bathing the infant.

The Great Patriotic War had hardened three generations of Russians. On Tiananmen Square, the sight of the loudspeakers and the crackling voices that emerged from them reminded Lisa of the *tarielka,* the loudspeaker put in every room of the *komunalka* in Moscow, a round, black spot on the wall. The radio set was on the ground floor, in the concierge's room, but all the apartments on the floors above were equipped with speakers connected to it. From the *tarielka* came official music and, sometimes, on big days, the leaders' speeches, before it was shut off at 9:00 P.M. No one escaped it, the sound not being adjustable, and the knobs being in the room of the concierge, who, like every *dvornik,* kept an eye on people.

The war years had begun on the morning of June 22, 1941, a beautiful Sunday. Around 10:00 A.M., Lisa and Li Lisan were getting ready to go on a picnic in the country. The *tarielka* crackled and a tense, unusual voice announced that at noon, Molotov would address the whole nation. The voice repeated, "At noon."

Li Lisan immediately froze, frowning: "We're staying here. We're not going anywhere. Something important is happening. Something *very* important."

What could Molotov have to announce that was so serious? His area was foreign affairs. It couldn't be the death of the Vojd; he was supposed to be in perfect health. Something must have happened in international affairs. Had Hitler invaded England? Where the devil could he be going now, after having taken France? Perhaps the United States had entered the war? Impossible; just the day before, Congress had refused again to allow Roosevelt to get involved in European wars. Fortunately, the homeland of socialism was at peace. Thanks to the farsightedness of the "brilliant Guide of Humanity," the friendship between the German and Soviet peoples was so certain that after the signature of the pact, Voroshilov and Beria had dismantled the defense systems along the border. The war in the West had filled Soviet commentators with joy: the Nazi Reich was destroying bourgeois states one after the other. "Modern war in all its terrifying beauty!" the headline in *Pravda* read. "Heaps of bodies, a pornographic vision in which the jackals are tearing each other apart!" the article went on, next to a telegram of friendly greetings Stalin had sent Hitler.

AT NOON, EVERYONE IN THE *KOMUNALKA* WAS SITTING AROUND THE loudspeakers when Molotov's voice came over them: "Citizens, comrades. Today at dawn, German fascist troops attacked the Soviet Union on several fronts. . . . Odessa has been bombed. Without any declaration, Germany has gone to war against the Soviet Union. . . ."

The stupor was immense everywhere. Eleven hours earlier, a million officers and soldiers had been taken completely by surprise when they were attacked by tanks and planes bearing the Iron Cross.

In the *komunalka,* a leaden silence had ensued: this time, the Vojd, the infallible guide, had made what seemed to be a serious mistake. Everything had changed in a matter of minutes. In the room, Lisa, trembling, went back to her French lessons: the following day, June 23, was the day for the final examination to obtain her diploma at the institute, after five years of studies. She came in first, but her heart was no longer in it. It had been less than a month since Li had found work again after getting out of prison. During the first months of 1940, he had gone around looking for work among his former comrades, but he was turned down again and again, and told each time: "We don't need an opportunist!" He had moved heaven and earth to get the Comintern to review his case; finally, he was sent before a supervisory commission composed of bureaucrats unknown to him. It got rid of him by giving him a "temporary exclusion from the Party for the period of a year." Lisa, who had only her scholarship to live on, saw him come back in a state of shock. Fighting severe depression, Li found a job correcting translations in foreign languages at International Workers' Editions. It was piecework; he earned abut a thousand rubles a month, a windfall that allowed him to gain back a few kilos.

AS SOON AS MOLOTOV'S SPEECH WAS OVER, LI HURRIEDLY WROTE to everyone he could think of, asking to enlist. Without success: war was declared, but not a general mobilization. Only Soviet males born between 1905 and 1917 were allowed to be called up. Like the whole country, Li wondered where the Chief had gone. For eleven days, Stalin remained silent, shut up in a room in his dacha in Kontsevo, somber and downhearted. Sure that his end was near, the Vojd grumbled about the Führer, who had tricked him, or outstripped him, and cursed people who had no "moral standards."

On July 3, shortly after having been put back in the saddle by Molotov, Stalin finally spoke to the nation. Lisa and Li Lisan listened religiously to the expressionless voice interrupted by raspy breathing that was coming out of the *tarielka*. Along with everyone else in Russia, they raised their eyebrows, intrigued, when the Vojd began by addressing his audience as "My brothers and sisters." The word *comrades* had disappeared. "I turn toward you, my friends . . . a grave danger is threatening the country," Stalin went on. At the end of his speech, Stalin did mention Lenin, but along with Pushkin, Tchaikovsky, and Chekhov.

★　　★

WAR CAME TO MOSCOW ON THE NIGHT OF JULY 22. IN THE OPPRES-sive summer heat, the sky was filled with the roar of Stukas and Heinkels. The first incendiary bombs were dropped on the city, under panicky fire from Soviet antiaircraft batteries and accompanied by the howling of air-raid sirens. Muscovites learned to cover their windows at night. The subway, which was more than a hundred yards deep in some places, seemed to have been conceived as an air-raid shelter. The following day, bombs fell in broad daylight, then again at night, almost daily. With thousands of other Muscovites, Lisa and Li Lisan sat huddled together on the benches of the Red Gates subway station, listening to the sounds of the battle above and waiting for the all-clear signal.

UNDER THE ANTIAIRCRAFT BALLOONS, AMONG THE TWO HUNDRED thousand Russian civilians who had been requisitioned, Li Lisan dug trenches and tank traps around the Moscow, participated in fire-fighting exercises, and piled up sandbags. But the military communiqués were no longer fooling anyone: the German armored columns were heading straight for the capital, pushing waves of refugees ahead of them. In early August, Lisa was evacuated to a village on the Volga. By October 16, a group of tanks had reached the outskirts of the city.

Moscow went mad. By the thousands, people rushed to the stations from which trains left for the east, shoving and overwhelming the NKVD's men. The city's air was heavy with the ashes of tons of paper from the archives that had been hastily burned in offices all over town. In the center of the city, soldiers were piling dignitaries' furniture and pictures into trucks, pushing away the frightened crowds that wanted to use the vehicles to escape. Looting of stores turned into riots. The NKVD opened fire. Party officials now had only one watchword: "Every man for himself!" Maps and lists of Party members were carefully shredded or burned. The government hurriedly moved to Kuybyshev, eight hundred miles to the east, accompanied by the diplomatic corps. The next day, an official communiqué announced that "Comrade Stalin will be evacuated tomorrow or later, depending on the circumstances." In the suburbs, at the front lines, soldiers and officers counted their cartridges: three per man, if the Germans showed themselves.

Two weeks later, Li Lisan left a Moscow bristling with barricades and under martial law. Evacuated with the rest of the International Workers' Editions staff, he left in turn for the Volga. By a miracle of the Soviet telephone and telegraph services, at the beginning of November Lisa received in her village a telegram from Li Lisan asking her to join him in Engels, an industrial city further south on the Volga, where he had been assigned. On the river, which was beginning to carry along chunks of winter ice, travel was becoming dangerous. Lisa hitchhiked her way by boat as far as Engels. On November 7, on the bridge of a steamer heavily loaded with groups of refugees heading down the river, she heard the loudspeakers announce that Stalin had not left Moscow, and that he had attended, on this anniversary of the October Revolution, the Red Army's parade. This time the soldiers who filed past looked serious; once they had marched past the Vojd, they headed straight for the front. The battle for Moscow had begun.

On the boat, there was a sort of shiver of relief. After three days of wandering on the river and four months of separation, Lisa rejoined her husband in Engels, living along with twenty foreign Communists in a five-story building with a view over the city and the river. On the other bank of the Volga, Saratov and its armament factories grumbled day and night. Li's building had neither heat nor furniture. Everyone slept on the floor. As new arrivals came in, including four Chinese survivors from Moscow, life gradually took shape, the rooms got beds, and International Workers' Editions went back to work using the materials at hand. Translators began translating what they could, usually war propaganda. Lisa got subsistence rations, a pound of black bread and a watery soup mixed with flour, before she was able to double them by cleaning the grease off the rotary presses set up in the adjoining building. Soon she became a proofreader for the local daily in Engels.

In December, they got news that made them all secretly happy: the Japanese had launched a surprise attack on the United States at Pearl Harbor. The United States was entering the war. It could tip the scales. A month afterward, Lisa and Li Lisan were surprised to see Nadia, Zhang Bao's wife, coming toward them; she had also been evacuated, along with her mother. Because of the war, she had succeeded in getting her job back at International Workers' Editions. Her son, Valery, had left Moscow to go with other children to a vacation camp in the Urals. Nadia resumed her work in the English section of International Workers' Editions; she and her mother moved in with Lisa and Li Lisan. After a few conversations in low voices, Lisa and Li Lisan realized that they mustn't mention Zhang Bao's name in front of her. She still had had no news of him, except that he was in a prison camp somewhere and not allowed to correspond. Li closed his eyes. Would he ever see his old friend again?

At the beginning of 1942, Lisa left, having enrolled in a women's brigade to prepare the harvests in the fields, thirty miles away from Engels. As the brigade traveled there on foot, singing patriotic songs to keep up their spirits, she noticed the strange silence of the hamlets and farms. The countryside was completely deserted: the landowners, 370,000 Germans who lived along the Volga, had been deported in a single week the preceding fall. By families and whole villages, they had left for Siberia and Kazakhstan, leaving behind them wealthy kolkhozy.

Lisa liked working in the fields and preparing food in the evenings with the other women, before going to bed. She made people around her laugh when she discovered the wolves. One night, hearing the howling of a wolf pack in the distance, she listened, intrigued: "What's that noise? A radio, or what?"

In the spring, she went back to Engels, holding her head high with her brigade, proud and exhausted after a thirty-mile walk in the mud, which had been made in one day with the help of many virtuous songs.

This was the time when Chinese, French, Belgians, Germans, Koreans, and Mongols competed to see who would have the best vegetable garden. Who would have the best patch of potatoes, cabbages, or beans? The Chinese gave the others a severe lesson in agronomy. Lisa discovered Li Lisan working the earth, planting his seeds, and turning the soil as if he had done nothing but that all his life, as if it were something innate.

From their apartment building on the hill, they saw the German bombers striking Saratov. They were always high in the sky, subjected to deafening antiaircraft fire whose sound was carried to them over the waters of the Volga.

They never saw the harvest of their vegetable gardens. The order to return to Moscow came in June 1942. The little group got into freight cars, under the suspicious eyes and tight supervision of multiple military patrols.

They all went back to work at International Workers' Editions in Moscow. Lisa was henceforth part of the staff. She began as a translator in the French section, delighted to make use of her training. Around her in the section were French Communists who had arrived in the 1930s, and who were wandering around the USSR at war; Georges Roux, who called himself Rudnikov; Alice Oran, who called herself Alexandra Oranovskaya; Eugénie Kaplan; an old man, Levinson; and a few others.

At the beginning of February 1943, the radio announced that Stalingrad had fallen, and that ninety thousand German prisoners had been taken. The Führer had been stubborn, with his general staff map, and Georgy Zhukov, at the head of the Red Army, had not let the opportunity pass. At International Workers' Editions, the mood veered toward optimism and the vegetable garden competition became even fiercer, in the suburbs this time. Every technique of cultivating potatoes was explored: morning, noon, and night, along with black bread, potatoes allayed their hunger; they were boiled in the samovar, and their skin was carefully preserved, seasoned with a pinch of salt or a bit of butter on special days.

The monotony of the months of war was interrupted by evenings spent with friends, whom Li Lisan and Lisa had learned to choose with care. Liuba Pasneieva, a brilliant graduate of the Institute of Oriental Languages in Moscow, amazed Li Lisan by her competence in Mandarin. She shared the life of a Chinese linguist, Chang Sidju, and was translating a classic of the traditional Chinese novel, *The Gate of the East,* which she longed to put on stage in a Moscow theater. She wanted to know everything about Lu Xun, whom she considered the most important Chinese writer of his generation. Li Lisan told her about the man, whom he had known well in Shanghai in 1929, seven years before his death. He had had several clandestine interviews with him at the time, and used all his influence to get him to found the League of Leftist Writers. Liuba had great ambitions for Soviet sinology and dreamed of having a chair at the university. The two couples shared tea, bread, and potatoes in the course of long evenings, and during the summer they sat in the sun together in their dachas.

Every day, *Pravda* was telling them that the English and the Americans were being slow to join the battle. Bad allies, who had to be asked again and again. It did not say a word about the gigantic supply line that was depositing every week, in the frozen ports of Norilsk and Murmansk, mountains of armaments, materiel, and food sent through the lend-lease program, at the cost of tens of thousands of sailors who went down along with the freighters sunk by German U-boats.

When they awoke on May 9, 1945, around six in the morning, the loudspeakers in the *komunalka* all crackled before a voice, trembling somewhat hysterically, repeated: "Attention! Attention! The war is over, Nazi Germany has surrendered!"

All the doors of the rooms opened at the same time, and then the windows on the street, and all over Moscow people, weeping, cried the same words: *"Vaina zakuentchina!"* ["The war is over!"]

In the streets, however, there was no exuberance. Arm in arm, Lisa and Li Lisan went for a walk with tens of thousands of other Muscovites. The population had come out, but their faces were usually serious. Stalin, the "marshal of victory," had won. But 25 million Russians had died as a result of his blunder, 25 million whose loss was deeply felt.

Almost every day toward the end of June, as they traveled along the train line that took them to their dacha, they met heavy rail convoys of artillery, tanks, and soldiers headed toward Vladivostok and the Far East.

"Stalin is surely going to declare war on Japan, now," Li murmured pensively.

Stalin did so on August 5. The next day, they learned that that morning the Americans had dropped a single bomb on Hiroshima, a bomb loaded with an explosive so powerful that in a blinding flash the city had been wiped off the map. On August 9, it was Nagasaki's turn. The following day, the Empire of the Rising Sun sued for peace.

Two weeks later, the phone rang in the dacha. An impersonal voice asked whether Li Ming was there. Li Lisan took the receiver, and the voice commanded him to come "immediately to the headquarters of the Central Committee of the Communist Party of the USSR" in Staraya Square at the Illyinsky Gates. "Immediately," the voice emphasized.

The Central Committee? It was true that Stalin had dissolved the Communist International. Li had learned of the burial of this dream of Karl Marx's in *Pravda,* on May 22, 1943. In its place, the Central Committee's Department of International Relations dealt with the brother parties.

Very pale, Li kissed Lisa and took the train to Moscow, leaving her in anguish. That evening, he reappeared with a look she had never seen on his face, something that resembled a feverish internal agitation.

In Moscow, a Soviet official had called him comrade and, after having chatted about the weather for a while, asked him point-blank: "Tell me, comrade, would you agree to go back to China?"

Stupefied, Li had cried, "Of course!"

His request to leave was finally going to be reexamined. While waiting for the reply, he could even go to the headquarters of the Communist Party of the USSR as often as he wanted to read the international press. Incidentally, he was informed that Wolfson, his investigator, had not survived his case: he had been executed shortly after Li was freed.

So RUSSIANS WERE AS UNPREDICTABLE FRIENDS AS EVER. LISA HAD shared Li's joy but felt a pang in her heart. The bird was on the branch and was dancing around again before flying off. The young woman knew that with that man, she had married a destiny. In love but frank, Li had repeatedly told her, "Lisa, you must realize that I am first of all in the service of the revolution; I put the party first. . . ."

Starting on September 1, he went every other day to the Central Committee's library, devouring everything he could find on international and Chinese affairs. He was seven years behind, and he had to catch up.

On the evening of December 31, 1945, Lisa was preparing for a New Year's Eve party. They had had a Christmas tree and garlands. Of the three annual holidays—the others being May 1 and October—Christmas was the most private. Li had gone to town to buy some supplies and a gift for

Inna, who was two and a half. The doorbell rang. Lisa opened the door and saw the concierge standing in front of her.

"A telephone call from the Central Committee. Li Ming is supposed to go there immediately."

At eight, Li set down his purchases and hurried off to the holy of holies. Three hours later, at precisely eleven, he opened the door of the room, looking unrecognizable. Lisa had never seen him like this: he was radiant. A mad happiness prevented him from speaking, and his eyes misted over as he looked at her.

"Guess what's happening to me?"

She couldn't guess.

"They've just told me that I was reelected to the Central Committee of the Chinese Communist Party eight months ago."

Lisa, who had good sense, was amazed. "But you aren't even a member of the Party any longer. How can you be on the Central Committee?"

That was how it was. After his temporary exclusion, the war years had wiped the slate clean, without Li having even taken any steps. But back there, in China, people had not forgotten him.

He was free. He could go pick up his passport, his papers, his identity. He could finally leave this accursed country whose earth he had to kiss every day.

Li added: "I have to leave for China in January."

So the time had come. Before little Inna's astonished eyes, Lisa and Li Lisan spent an emotional New Year's Eve. He was wildly happy at the idea of going home, and both were torn apart by the impending separation. They had already sworn never to leave each other again. On the morning of January 1, they promised to do everything they could to get back together again, someday.

On January 15, 1946, Li Lisan got on the Trans-Siberian Railroad at the Yaroslavl station and disappeared in the direction of Vladivostok. Lisa remained on the platform, devastated, holding Inna by the hand.

SIX MONTHS LATER, A TELEPHONE CALL GOT HER OUT OF THE DACHA. She had to go to the Hotel Moskova to meet a famous Chinese general

who had come to Moscow for treatment of wounds received on the battlefield in Manchuria. Lu Chunchuan, accompanied by his wife and an interpreter, presented his compliments to Lisa and gave her news of Li Lisan,
who had arrived safe and sound and was being "very active." He was based
in Harbin. "The Party's Central Committee asked me to tell you that it has
authorized you to join your husband in China," he added.

Lisa almost fainted. For months, she had felt like a widow. The big
move was now near at hand: she was going to have to go to China. She hurried to the Department of International Relations, where she was asked to
fill out dozens of forms. One of the officials soon told her that she must
leave as soon as possible, at the end of September.

Saying good-bye to her mother was painful. She no longer had anyone
but Lisa. Her last son, Lisa's big brother, had died during the war. He had
not survived two years in a work camp for having complained about the
Vojd one night when he was drinking. Lisa, her last daughter, was leaving
her for China. But if all went well, she would have her come to join her
there, later.

On September 22, 1946, the Trans-Siberian took Lisa and Inna toward the
Far East. They were going to see Papa. The trip passed as if in a dream. Lisa
was accompanied by a Chinese student going home, Lin Li, as well as by a
beautiful young theatrical actress, Sung Weishi. Three women and a girl
who surprised people by their destination. Sung Weishi was not yet thirty.
She was going home after studying theater direction with the masters in
Moscow. Cheerful and a passionate lover of Pushkin, she intended, once
she was back in China, to produce plays by Chekhov and Goldoni. She was
the daughter of a Communist martyr, and had been adopted by Chou En-
lai along with other children in the same situation. For this third trip on the
Trans-Siberian, Lisa knew enough to bring sufficient provisions, and pic-
nicked every day in her compartment.

At the end of a week, Inna, three, had learned to be patient as she
watched the countryside sliding past the window. The train had passed the
foothills of the Mongolian plateau and finally reached the station in Chita.
Lisa noticed the large group of Japanese prisoners of war working on the

railbed. Two days later, they climbed into another train leaving for the Chinese border. The three women and the girl got off at the windswept terminus, a station house built of wood in the middle of the dusty steppe, where there was not a soul.

Atpor was not expecting anyone; the place seemed deserted. Lisa and her companions called out all around, looking for someone. Inna, sitting on the suitcases, took it all philosophically. Awakened by the noise, a railroad employee finally came out of a door. He frowned on seeing this trio of women who told him they wanted to cross the border into China. Without letting them finish, he went back to his nap, grumbling, "There aren't any trains here."

Since the war, that had been almost true. What could this Russian woman with her little girl and the two Chinese be doing there? But Lisa persisted, and he asked to see her passport. She didn't have one; she was not one of the privileged Soviet citizens who had such a document. In Moscow, she had been given only a permit to cross the border. The man glanced at it.

"No, no, impossible. The trains don't cross the frontier. There's only the special train here, the one that comes from Harbin. For the two Chinese women, no problem. But you can't go." Lisa showed him the signatures at the bottom of her permit, that of the head of the Department of International Relations and that of General Antonov, commander in chief of the NKVD's border guards.

A second employee finally came out; he had the martial appearance of an officer of the border guards. "Your name?" he asked Lisa.

"Kishkin."

"Good lord! It's you? We've been waiting for you for three days!"

The man was furious. Making the special train come from Harbin was a complicated railroad operation. No one knew any longer to whom this train belonged. In ten years, the Trans-Manchurian Railroad had seen many wars and changed hands several times, among Russians, Japanese, and Chinese. For the time being, the tracks were under twofold command by a Soviet general and a Kuomintang general. In September 1946, the track to Harbin was not at all secure, running through areas where there were highwaymen and fighting between the red and blue armies.

"If you hadn't arrived today, we were going back. The next train comes in a month."

Lisa, who had never left her country, had her first experience with the Soviet customs service. The two officials spent more than two hours inspecting her two suitcases full of clothes. Every seam on each piece of clothing was examined three times.

A train with three cars was waiting for them. It served to carry diplomatic mail and men and supplies for the Soviet consulate in Harbin. Slowly, they traversed a no-man's-land about fifteen miles long as far as Manzhouli, the first town on the Chinese side of the border. Her heart pounding, Lisa eagerly examined the first acres of Li Lisan's native land. She soon saw its inhabitants in the distance, peasants working in their vegetable gardens. This land was inhabited and cultivated, though the land on the other side of the border was deserted.

When the train stopped with a screech of its wheels in the Manzhouli station, Lisa glimpsed through the window, on the platform covered with a large, many-colored crowd, an Orthodox priest walking along, the long hair under his black bonnet blending into an impressive beard, and a large crucifix on his chest. Fascinated, Lisa watched this priest, one such as she had not seen in Russia since she was ten years old. "It's like seeing Chekhov right before my eyes," she murmured. The most incredible thing was that people were crossing themselves and kissing the ecclesiastic's hand as he passed by: they must be White Russians! Russians who had fled communism, who were numerous amid the Chinese crowd in the little border town. Those famous, mysterious compatriots of whom she had never heard anything good.

Lisa got off the train and took a great breath of air. Here she was, on Chinese soil. A squad of soldiers immediately came toward the three young women. Chinese soldiers with rifles on their shoulders, wearing tattered beige tufted jackets, soft caps with red stars, and leggings. A young officer, a boy hardly twenty years old, came up to Lisa. He looked worried. He introduced himself awkwardly, with a timid, embarrassed smile. Silently his men surrounded the travelers and picked up their suitcases, while the officer asked them to follow him.

"Where are they taking us?" Lisa asked Sung Weishi, in a sudden burst of anxiety.

"Don't be afraid. These are men from Lin Biao's Eighth Route Army. It's your husband who has sent them to get us."

The special train to Harbin was waiting for them, magnificent and disquieting. An old, exhausted locomotive, sputtering and wheezing its steam, sat motionless at the platform in front of a few cars bristling with the barrels of machine guns and loaded with sandbags. On the running boards stood armed soldiers.

The three young women and the girl were seated in a separate compartment equipped with comfortable fold-down beds. In front of the door to the compartment stood a sentry, his back to the passengers.

The train started to move and a Russian employee of the Chinese Eastern Railway came into the compartment. He politely told his customers, "Ladies, if you hear the train's machine guns firing, get down on the floor and stay there."

Lisa gulped and asked him what in the world he was talking about. The man explained to the newcomers: "Here, you're in Manchuria. The zones we will be crossing are infested with 'redbeards.' These people are not gentlemen. They're armed bandits, and they attack anything! They're neither Communists nor Nationalists, they're nothing! There are tens of thousands of them, deserters, a veritable army of tramps! They rob, they kill, they rape, they even fight the Reds and the Blues. And it's been going on for more than a decade!"

Li Lisan had told her that China was a country in turmoil. In the Soviet Union, order reigned, in the cities as in the countryside. Here, the war was visible from the train. Soldiers occupied half the compartments. Chinese soldiers of the Eighth Route Army, but also Russian soldiers, a squad of veterans of the White Guard in Harbin. Good machine gunners who, because they had to take the train, were reluctantly cohabiting with these Red Chinese, indifferent and polite.

It took them two days and three nights to get to Harbin. After sunset, the train stopped in a station: there was no question of traveling at night. On the first morning, Lisa and her companions discovered that a miracle had been set down on the compartment's table: eggs, milk, pork, chicken, steamed buns, fruit. Food such as Lisa had never seen on a Soviet table.

She pinched herself while Sung Weishi, as an artist, improvised a sketch on the subject of "the arrival in paradise."

The banquet was provided by the Eighth Route Army. For dessert, an employee brought in a whole pail of cottage cheese, the local specialty. Lisa had never had such a feast.

When they arrived in Harbin, an officer was waiting for them on the platform, but Li Lisan was nowhere in sight. Disappointed and worried, Lisa got into a limousine. On the way in to town, she saw that Harbin was covered with the first snow of October. For a Chinese city, it looked surprisingly Russian, with its Orthodox churches with onion domes, as well as Ukrainian, Polish, and Catholic churches; its stone houses with columns; and its shop signs in Russian, sometimes accompanied by a Chinese inscription.

Lisa was hurt and furious. Here she'd been away from her husband for eight months, she and her daughter had traveled six thousand miles to join him, and he couldn't be bothered to meet them at the station!

"He's in a meeting," the officer had told her.

The car stopped in front of a handsome house in the Russian quarter. As Lisa got out, she saw on the front porch a silhouette of someone who seemed to be waiting for her. Stunned, she recognized Li Lisan, who was looking at her avidly, his eyes sparkling and a discreet smile on his lips. He was wearing an army general's uniform.

She went up the steps and he took her in his arms. The promises had been kept, the achievement was considerable, but the embrace was modest; Li had warned her that in China, people were less effusive than in Moscow. Especially a general in the presence of his men.

The disappointment at the train station was quickly forgiven. Li had arranged a little reception the same day to introduce Lisa to his new entourage. The guests of honor were the neighbors across the street, General Lin Biao and his wife, Ye Chun. She was scarcely taller than he, and also spoke a little Russian, which she had learned in Yan'an. Ye Chun invited Lisa to help her improve her Russian.

That evening, as they were getting ready for bed, Li explained that the uniform was for the Americans' benefit. It was a matter of protocol: he was negotiating war and peace with Marshall's colonels and generals. The Party could do no less than send a general as its representative.

As he spoke, Lisa felt a bit dizzy.


THE HOUSE HAD FIVE HEATED ROOMS, ALL OF THEM FILLED UP. LI Lisan had a personal guard of eight men and a private secretary. Sung

Weishi lived with them. The young actress was cheerful and her presence lightened up the place, which was otherwise a bit austere. Winter had already come, and Lisa quickly adopted Chinese fashions, going with Ye Chun, Lin Biao's wife, to find padded jackets and pants in the markets. Harbin was famous for its cold winters and its ice sculpture contests. The household was family-like and spartan.

Li was working hard, rushing back and forth between meetings at headquarters and three-party meetings with the Americans and the Nationalist generals. The armies were facing each other, and each side was feeling out the other's defenses. Lin Biao, the head of military operations, frequently invited Li and Lisa to dinner at his home. Dinners Lisa didn't much care for. The host, whose health was fragile, was so taciturn that she felt uncomfortable. He seemed to be avoiding looking at her; his eyes, under his extraordinary eyebrows, were riveted on his plate. He spoke only with Li Lisan. Ye Chun turned out to be a hard woman who liked to issue commands. Lisa was shocked by the way she treated the servants. The couple was surrounded by an impressive group of bodyguards.

The evenings spent at their home became even more awkward when Ye Chun discovered that Lin Biao was infatuated with Sung Weishi. He had known the pretty theater actress in Moscow, in 1939. Having left three years later, he was still madly in love with her. Now that she was there, in the house across the street from him, he had been unable to keep his wife from discovering his infatuation, and she cursed her rival.

In November, the beautiful Weishi and her friend Lin Li went off to visit Yan'an, on board an American military plane that flew that route. A month later, Lin Li came back alone.

"Sung Weishi isn't with you?" Lisa asked.

"She stayed in Yan'an. She's furious with you and your husband. She received a telegram signed Li Lisan telling her never to set foot in Harbin again."

Lisa was stunned. When he was told about it, so was Li. He thought for a moment, then suddenly rushed out of the house and across the street to Lin Biao's. Some time later he returned, explaining to Lisa that the mystery had been cleared up. The telegram had been sent by Ye Chun to keep the young actress away from Lin Biao. The problem was that she had signed the cable with his name, Li Lisan. "A very serious mistake," he thundered—one he had no intention of forgetting.

THE WINTER WAS PUNCTUATED BY AIR-RAID ALERTS, SOUNDED WHEN the Kuomintang's reconnaissance planes were flying over the city. Lisa had found something to keep her busy: she was teaching Russian to the officers and cadets of the Chinese Red Army. Young, vigorous men hungry for culture. Some of them already knew the rudiments of Russian, which they had learned in Yan'an. They were all delighted to be introduced to the language of Lenin and the Soviet big brothers, the *guegue*. For Lisa, it was a pleasure to teach. In April, the household moved into a more comfortable house: Lisa was pregnant, and the whole entourage was betting on a son. For his part, Li Lisan relied on genetics. The most famous mixed couple in Harbin was invited to dinners around town. Lisa discovered the art of the banquet alongside a Manchurian bishop, a few worried notables, and many toasts to the moribund united front. On the occasion of the thirtieth anniversary of the October Revolution, she met for the first time a flesh-and-blood capitalist: the former owner of the house, a powerful Jewish industrialist in Harbin, Mr. Lopato. The man seemed normal to her.

Four years after Inna, Alla was born on Chinese soil on October 24, 1947, to the great joy of Li Lisan, who was not at all intimidated by these two daughters. Lisa engaged a nurse, Maria Ionovna. A White Russian past fifty, with whom she could finally talk in their native language, Maria cared nothing about politics, and quickly became part of the family. She had only one defect: as soon as she heard Stalin's name, she began swearing like a madwoman, to the point that Li Lisan had to order her to keep her feelings to herself in public.

One fine morning, a twenty-one-year-old Chinese man appeared at the door. All smiles, with very Russian manners, he fell into Lisa's arms: it was Kolya, Mao Tse-tung's younger son, who had just arrived from Moscow. So happy to see his dear Lisa again; he considered her a sort of mother to him. With her and Li Lisan, in the Hotel Lux, he had gleaned a little affection when he first got to the Soviet capital at the age of nine. Afterward, Kolya had left with his elder brother, Serioja, twelve, for the

Ivanovo orphanage. There, more than two hundred miles northeast of Moscow, in the innermost circle of the Comintern's offspring, they had found themselves rubbing shoulders with the orphans of martyrs and the forgotten children of revolutionary leaders all over the world. Ivanovo was an elite fortress/boarding school carefully supervised by the NKVD. The children also had their nights of terror in the dormitories, when police officers came to take away those whose fathers had fallen into disgrace. The education there was Russian and Soviet; Kolya had forgotten his Chinese, and no longer spoke any language but Pushkin's.

So as soon as he'd arrived in Harbin, he hurried to the home of Lisa and Li Lisan, a couple who could understand him so well. Like a young Soviet, dreamy and somewhat dissolute, he preferred the piano to politics, despite having studied to be an engineer. He had been too young to go to war like his elder brother, who had been drafted into the Soviet army. Here, he had to rediscover his roots and begin to forget his Russian name, Nikolai, and go by his Chinese name, Mao Antsing. But in Lisa's home, he was still Kolya, and he gorged himself on food, as did most new Soviet arrivals. Soon he would rejoin Serioja, who had saved and protected him when, after the public execution of their mother, they'd had to flee Changsha and live on the streets of Shanghai, eating out of garbage cans. Serioja, or Mao Anying, had been trained in a military academy in Moscow; during the war, he had fought in Stalin's tanks and returned to China during the winter of 1944–1945. In Yan'an, he had gotten to know his father. Mao Tse-tung had not seen his elder son since the latter was fifteen.

Lisa was touched by the fate of these two boys. Kolya was a fragile being, alternating between sudden moods of exuberance and moments of depression. He asked Li for news from the front, in order to find out where his father was. Mao had been on the move a lot for the past few months. In March 1947, he had been forced to leave Yan'an, which was being bombed by the Nationalist air force, and begin another march. He was moving closer to Manchuria, pursued by Chiang Kai-shek's troops, who were dangerously lengthening their lines. Kolya was in a hurry to meet this father he didn't know but who was already famous.

Beijing fell in January 1949 amid general indifference elsewhere in the world. In March, Lisa left Harbin for the capital, after spending two years and six months in this town on the outskirts of the country. On the train platform, she ran into Siao Emi, a Chinese Communist poet whom she and Li had known in Moscow in 1935. A childhood friend of Mao's, he was coming from Yan'an and going on to the Soviet Union with a delegation of writers, before attending a peace conference in Stockholm. A handsome man, he spoke fluent Russian. In Moscow, he had married a German photographer of Jewish origin, Eva Sandberg. She had followed him to Yan'an, where she had given him two sons. After five years, during which she was the only Western woman at the base, she had gone back to the Soviet Union with the two children. Siao Emi, who loved her more than anything, was going to Moscow in the hope of finding her again.

"Lisa, you and Li Lisan were really lucky to be able to get together again. It's marvelous . . . ," he added sadly as he left her.

In Beijing, everyone had taken quarters near the leaders of the revolution, on the heights of the Perfumed Hills outside the city, from which the wandering tribe of the Central Committee was directing the last stages of the war while waiting for the new capital to be ready to welcome them.

There, under the umbrella pines of the Perfumed Hills, Lisa had made the acquaintance of Mao Tse-tung. The preceding day, Li had told her, when he returned that evening to their requisitioned house, "Tomorrow, we're going to see President Mao." Lisa was startled. This Mao was still only president of the Party, but he was already something of a *vojd* for China. Li had reassured her: "He's simple man."

In the morning, they went with Inna to the house occupied by the *djouci,* one of those beautiful traditional Chinese homes, all on one floor, surrounded by a wall of gray stone, with a tiny fishpond in the middle of the internal courtyard. Seated on a hard wooden bench, they waited a moment for the president to come in. Mao came out of his bedroom in a tufted military jacket and pants, with neither belt nor weapon, wearing leggings. At fifty-six, his face was getting puffy, his hair fell over his ears, and he had a slight plumpness that his tall stature no longer concealed. He came toward Lisa with his head down and a worried expression on his face. Li introduced them. Mao shook her hand and greeted her with an approving nod of his head. He smiled, showing yellowed teeth, and looking for a moment at this young Russian woman, he exclaimed in a hoarse voice, *"Hao tongdje!"*

Lisa was nervous, and didn't understand that he had called her a "good comrade," but that didn't matter. She seemed to have won his goodwill. Chinese men's taste for foreign women nonetheless intrigued Mao, who asked Lisa to sit down before immediately launching into a discussion with Li Lisan in his preferred dialect, without paying any more attention to her.

The conversation lasted about twenty minutes, and Lisa came away from it with a certain pride. Good comrade! Curious as a salutation, but coming from a Communist leader, it could only be a compliment.

Lisa came back over the following days, invited this time to meet Mao's wife, Jiang Qing. The young woman wanted to learn a little Russian. Wearing a blouse and a skirt, she received Lisa by the fishpond. She was not truly pretty, but she had a very special voice, pleasant and composed, and she had great plans for Chinese film and theater. The former Shanghai actress was a little bored, and at the moment she was interested in Russian culture. She would need to know the language of Chekhov when she went to Moscow, as she surely would someday on an official trip or for her health, which was fragile. The two women agreed to see each other again, with Lisa in the role of teacher.

The fireworks show was over. The last explosions of October 1, 1949, lit up the dark sky over Tiananmen Square. In the bleachers, the crowd was beginning to shake itself, emerging from a dazzled numbness. Li Lisan, Lisa, and their daughters walked back to their house in Dongdan, a neighborhood east of the Forbidden City. In August, the family had moved into the comfortable, German-style house with a pleasant garden, in the very center of Beijing. Some repair work had to be done after the precipitous departure of the former resident, the head of staff of the Kuomintang's air force.

Lisa liked to stroll through this peaceful city that the fighting had spared. Its relaxed crowds and its cheeky common people gave it the feeling of an immense town, despite its seven hundred thousand inhabitants. The spectacle of the streets intrigued Lisa every day; never before had she eaten so many vegetables, brought in from the surrounding countryside every morning by whole cartloads, drawn by horses or mules. Amid the countless trades carried on in the streets, ruddy peasants hurried along, carrying the produce of their gardens on their shoulders and jostled by rickshaw men, who were beginning to give way to their competitors mounted on bicycles. These modes of transportation presented Lisa with a delicate dilemma. For ages, they had been for foreigners the symbol of the downtrodden laborer in this country. Young apprentices or veterans of Beijing's streets, they asked fewer questions and fought for customers. But Lisa couldn't climb into the comfortable seat. Apart from her personal scruples, Soviet morality forbade it. The image of the well-fed Westerner seated in back and pulled along by a Chinese sweating with effort had always been the delight of satirists. Beijing still had no buses, and Lisa got around on foot. The only problem was the dirt in the streets. Covered with rubbish, the city seemed like a gigantic garbage can compared with Moscow. At night, Beijing went to bed early. In the morning you heard cocks crowing, and then the birds in the parks.

Going up Chang'an Avenue, Lisa noticed passersby glancing awkwardly at the scars on the pavement that marked the former sites of the East and West Gates. Majestic replicas of the Front Gate, they had been demolished over the preceding weeks, forever robbing Tiananmen of its original geometry. A colossal and hasty bit of work done to open the way for the triumphal parade. China was sweeping away the past.

# 2 1

Midnight was still far off and the people sitting at the dinner table were laughing wholeheartedly. For New Year's Eve, Lisa and Li Lisan had invited a few friends, all of them Chinese. In the kitchen, Lao Lu was working furiously on little Hunanese dishes, throwing red peppers, fresh vegetables, and pork into his frying pan. At his side, the rows of fresh pot-stickers were waiting, ready to be scalded on a signal from Lisa. The guests were having aperitifs, and the mistress of the house was keeping an eye on things to be sure they went well.

The banquet seemed likely to go on long into the night. Outside, the weather was frigid. The winter was the coldest seen in many years, but bursts of fireworks were exploding all the same in the narrow streets of the *hutong* outside the house. On this February 11, 1957, the Year of the Rabbit began, as usual, with everyone wishing each other happiness and prosperity. At the table, opposite Li Lisan, Chen Yi was waving his chopsticks in the air, impatient to get started. The marshal was in a good mood. Lisa found his squarish head, his low voice, and his inimitable Sichuan accent reassuring. In addition to his healthy looks, Chen Yi shared with Li Lisan the same direct character, though he was two years younger. The two men were delighted to see each other again. Chen Yi had been promoted to the rank of marshal the preceding year, in 1955, at the age of fifty-five. That year, China had appointed ten marshals—men of legend, the men of Nanchang, the Long March, the conquest. With Li Lisan, he liked to talk about the early days, which they had shared with Chou En-lai in France. He had worked as a dishwasher in Paris before going to work at Michelin and Le Creusot. Together, they had been expelled from Lyons and boarded the boat in Marseilles. After thirty years of fierce fighting, Chen Yi was a little bored in his functions as mayor of Shanghai; the past few months, he had spent most of his time in Beijing. A military man to the core, strategy was for him a pastime. Li was his opponent in mysterious, hours-long games of *go*. Inna, who was now thirteen, knew that at those times, when Papa was "playing with buttons," she had to tiptoe around the house. And warn Alla, who liked to jump on her father's knees without warning, proud of her pretty nine-year-old's braids. At the end of the banquet table, the two girls, very excited, were talking in Russian and bursting out laughing: although they spoke Chinese fluently with the *ayi,* their nurse, they understood hardly anything the marshal and their father said, so thick were the latters' provincial accents.

"Like President Mao!" whispered Inna to her sister, with the cunning air of someone who knows what's what. Too bad that his son, Mao Antsing, no longer came to the house. He made a nice big brother, that Kolya, who spoke Russian better than Chinese. The boy adored the two girls, and played with them every week before his music and piano class with Lisa. In front of the servants, they had to call him just Yang. Not even Kolya, his Russian diminutive for Nikolai: security required that no one know where President Mao's son was. Kolya escaped with relief from the Zhongnanhai compound, Mao's austere palace that was adjacent to the Forbidden City. Back in China after more than ten years in the USSR, he and his elder brother had thought they'd found a father. But Mao could lounge for hours in his big wooden bed without giving his children the slightest attention. Too Russian, too Western, these two sons who spoke Chinese so poorly. Their stepmother, Jiang Qing, who was aggressive or indifferent to her entourage, was treating her neurasthenia by watching American movies morning, noon, and night.

At Lisa's house, Kolya found a haven. Tormented and fragile, he liked music, the feeling of a beautiful piano chord, which he shared with Lisa and Inna. The teacher, a Chinese lady, said he had an excellent ear. When his brother died, Kolya sank into a deep sadness: Serioja, Mao Anying, had been killed at the age of twenty-eight by an American bomb, somewhere in North Korea, where he had joined Chinese volunteers in November 1950. Serioja, the elder brother, his lifeline, the one whose hand Kolya had held when they'd wandered the streets of Shanghai after their mother's execution. In Moscow and Harbin, at Lisa and Li Lisan's house, Kolya had felt at home far more than in the Ivanovo orphanage, with other pupils of the worldwide revolution. After the painful winter of 1950, Kolya, who loved Chopin so much, had often come to the house. Inconsolable, lost in his dreams, he had finally disappeared after three years into an endless series of psychiatric institutions.

THE ARRIVAL OF THE POT-STICKERS THREW THE TABLE INTO AN UP-roar, and the clicking of chopsticks that followed did honor to the chef. After ten years in China, Lisa still had trouble pinching her *tiaoze* when she plunged them into the soy sauce. No matter; the herb stuffing was delicious, and Lao Lu was a cook envied in Beijing.

That evening, Lisa's heart was beating in unison with that of China: finally New Year's had come! The spring holiday was here, everyone was gathering with family. After frenetic months of building socialism, with countless campaigns for this or against that, the country was catching its breath. At the Institute of Russian Studies, Lisa was working hard, six days a week. Thousands of students had to be trained in Russian before they went to Moscow to learn all sorts of trades and a single doctrine. Young Chinese hungry for knowledge, hardworking and disciplined students, a real pleasure to teach. There were also Vietnamese, of whom Lisa had become very fond in 1950. She had a class of twenty-two young people, apprentice revolutionaries who had crossed the Chinese frontier through the jungle, at night, defying the French army's surveillance planes. Aged nineteen or twenty, they all spoke French fluently. Lisa therefore undertook to teach them Russian: Ho Chi Minh needed interpreters. Model students, cheerful, relaxed, they insisted on taking off their shoes as soon as they came into the classroom, sitting barefoot at their tables. One fine morning in the winter of 1950–1951, Lisa, flabbergasted, had seen them suddenly become agitated during the class and then run toward the door like children: outside, it was snowing. It was a climatic phenomenon unknown to them, and they immediately started a snowball fight.

"You'll see, in Moscow!" Lisa promised them.

Lisa enjoyed the large stone house that had become her home. At the heart of Dongdan, ten minutes from Tiananmen Square, its eight well-heated rooms, furnished with things she'd bought on her visits to the last antique dealers in Beijing, had easily convinced her of the advantages of a world without *komunalka*.

Life was much calmer since Li was no longer a minister in the government. The guards had been removed; those men ate enormous meals and devoured the household budget.

Li had lost his post, and it was just as well. At least he saw more of his daughters. For four years, the family had not been able to spend more than a few quiet evenings together. Li, absorbed in some proposed law or political difficulty, hardly opened his mouth at dinner. At such times, Lisa and the girls looked at each other out of the corner of their eyes, put their fingers in front of their mouths, and whispered in unison, "Shh, the brain is working." That calmed their desire to laugh and brought the father and husband back to the table.

Until the day in November 1952 when he had come back to the house looking crestfallen. Without a word, he'd gone up to his room and lain down on the bed. Lisa joined him, worried. Li, who never talked about his work at home, finally opened up. He was devastated: Mao had struck, and he had not seen the blow coming.

Li had made another mistake in his political line. He had made a serious error, they said. The minister of labor, the founder of syndicalism, a Party legend, had been ordered to keep his hands off the labor question.

He was even going to be deprived of all his functions as the head of the pan-Chinese Federation of Labor Unions, which he had created.

The blow had come from Mao's private secretary, Chen Boda. A pudgy theoretician, the president's speechwriter, and the inventor of Maoism, he distrusted Li. At the head of the labor unions, he was constructing a machine that could overshadow the Party, one of the "independent kingdoms" Mao feared. In 1951, Li had defended a moderate independence for labor unions. The *Workers' Daily*, which he supervised, had published this or that factory's demands, reported on the increasing number of strikes. Li was immediately accused of "economism," of neglecting the Party's control over the labor unions, the channel of communication. Of caring more about setting up a system of unemployment or retirement insurance than about the Party's interests. The first Communist minister of labor, he want to found laws that would set precedents. Chinese workers remained to be won over. Their condition was not the best, and often worse than what he had seen in Shanghai in 1930. They had hardly participated in the revolution that was conducted in their name by military men and carried out by peasants. In the world of Asian labor unions, Li had long been a celebrity. At the time of reconstruction after forty-five years of civil wars and invasions, the minister had gone slow on the class struggle.

During his first months in office, he had dealt with a general strike of rickshaw men in Beijing. These proletarians were self-employed, and they were worried about the advent of buses. Li had negotiated their gradual incorporation into the new Beijing transportation company. The minister had then inherited the delicate question of the thousands of prostitutes in the capital. Products of the civil war, they were the faded blooms of the "old, corrupt world" who consoled soldiers and government officials in the brothels of Dashala and Tsienmenwai. Their pimps would gladly have worked out a deal with the Communists, as they had with the Kuomintang. They didn't have time. One morning, Dashala and Tsienmenwai were surrounded by the army and the police. The women were put to work in factories and in the fields, while the pimps were sent to prison. They provided a few contingents of counterrevolutionaries and other "black elements" for the firing squads.

The Communists were settling old scores with the underworld. When he entered Shanghai as a victor at the head of his troops, Chen Yi and his military police had dealt with the tongs. The Red April of 1927 was avenged twenty-three years later a hundred times over. The Green Society was decimated, but its leader, Du Yuesheng, fled to Hong Kong. Chen tried without success to moderate the campaign of terror that subsequently struck the elites.

Mao vaunted the "price of blood" and began his reign by "beating the dog." Along with hardened criminals, 2 or 3 million lukewarm, hostile, or merely unlucky Chinese perished in the course of a wave of gigantic public trials. The civil war was over and peace restored, but terror had been driven into people's heads with a bullet in the nape of the neck of enemies of the people.

Mao's distrust of Li Lisan became bottomless after the latter denounced judicial customs in the Soviet Union before the Central Committee. At the end of 1950, the ghost from Moscow had shouted before his peers that back there, fantastic confessions were being extracted by torture. He knew what he was talking about. Li warned them: Chinese legislators should be wary of copying the Russians, especially "in the domain of proofs and methods of judicial inquiry." Moreover, he knew excellent comrades who, according to the latest news, were still in the hands of the Soviet police. Unjustly, and for years. Comrade Ambassador Wang Jiaxiang, in Moscow, would confirm what he said. The matter should be on the agenda of meetings with the Soviet comrades.

Mao and the hundred or so Communist leaders present listened to Li in a leaden silence, attentive and embarrassed. At the time of the "great friendship," Li was accusing Stalin, the world's Guide, of injustice and criminal errors. He was saying it in an irreproachable jargon, which nonetheless sounded true.

Justice was another unaccustomed leitmotif before this prestigious assembly. The only kind of justice these men knew was expedient, political, or military. Chou En-lai promised to put discreetly on the agenda for discussions with their big brothers the question of the Chinese comrades who had disappeared in Russia. As for the creation in China of a legal system worthy of the name, they would see about that later. In the meantime, Li's report would remain secret.

★   ★

LI KEPT HIS TITLE AS MINISTER UNTIL 1954, SITTING WITH THE FIF-
teen other governors of the kingdom around Chou En-lai. The first popular national assembly was elected that year. It voted for the new
constitution. The country was placed under single-party rule; the eight
other parties, moribund, pledged allegiance in exchange for the lives of
their leaders. The preamble to the Basic Law declared firmly that the
friendship with the USSR was indestructible. Immediately afterward, as
part of a ministerial rearrangement, Li was kicked out and replaced by a
humble and transparent servant.

Out of work, he licked his wounds by leaving Beijing with Lisa for a
three-month trip around China. It was a second honeymoon, after Sochi, on
the Black Sea, in 1937. He showed her Nanking, on the Yangtze; Canton, the
republican caldron; and then the non-Chinese peoples, the "national minorities" in Yunnan, and the coconut beaches on the island of Hainan.

Back in Beijing, he refused to be in charge of ideology at the head of
the Party's theoretical weekly, *Red Flag*. He also declined an offer to be in
charge of agriculture for the Central Committee; he knew nothing about
it, didn't conceal that fact, and wouldn't for anything in the world venture
onto Mao's special terrain, the peasants. Mao still wanted to shake up the
countryside, accelerate the march toward collective farms begun a year
earlier. Li finally took over the direction of the Office of Industry, where
Chen Yun, his boss, was trying to reduce chaos to a plan and to draw statistics from it. Li would have to be concerned only with Manchuria, which he
knew so well.

FOR HER PART, LISA WAS NOT UNHAPPY TO GIVE UP THE LIFE OF A
government minister's wife. The endless banquets tired her. Her Chinese
was improving, but she was still the odd person out, the only Westerner
among wives of ministers or dignitaries. Fortunately, hundreds of Russian
technical, military, or diplomatic advisers had arrived in Beijing, whom she
might run into at receptions. Tiruisky, the consul general, had given her a
complete set of dishes for the housewarming party in Dongdan. A courteous and cultivated sinologist, he dreamed only of losing himself in the
Academy of Sciences in Moscow to write dictionaries. Soviet artists were
rushing to discover China, the USSR's "twin jewel" and a good opportunity

to get out of the country. The Kirov ballets from Leningrad had their hour of glory in the theater. Lisa had served as a guide in the stores of Beijing for Dudinskaya and her husband Sergeiev, the stars of the troupe.

Each time, it was an incredible surprise for her compatriots to discover that she was the Russian wife of a Chinese dignitary: "How did the Party organs ever allow such a romance to develop?" For some of them, the answer was patently obvious: "Because Lisa is part of the Party organs, of course!" Soviet agents were the best, it was well known; a Russian wife in a Chinese minister's bed was a great coup. For those who knew her better, too many details didn't fit: "Lisa a Chekist? Come now!" Not even a member of the Party. The daughter of an aristocrat who was ill at ease with political cant and an outstanding teacher of Russian. Something was missing in the picture, probably a matter of character. At the Soviet consulate, officials had pulled long faces when she went there in 1952 to ask for a visa to visit her family in Moscow.

Her five years of intense study of French now served her little. She often heard people talk about France, but she had received its last representatives at her dinner table four years earlier, one night in 1950. Two leaders of the CGT on an official visit, Louis Saillant and Leliap. Lisa had served as interpreter for Li Lisan, who laughed gently about this new encounter with the French proletariat. The minister of labor had a few good stories about his time to tell, about Le Creusot, the French police, and M. Herriot. Saillant told him that the CGT's troops had been roughly handled by the CRS* in 1947. But the party back there was stronger than ever. They drank to a communist France, to the revolution, to the Commune, to labor unions, and to internationalism, before coming to the real question: which of the two cuisines, Chinese or French, was the better?

Since then, Lisa had been picking up bits of news by reading *Izvestia,* which arrived without delay from Moscow. French intellectuals seemed to be more fascinated than ever with Soviet enlightenment. Hadn't the "intellectual's daily" jubilantly reported how Jean-Paul Sartre, on his return

---

*Compagnies Républicaines de Sécurité, a national police agency founded in 1944, charged chiefly with maintaining public order; frequently involved in riot control. —Trans.

from Moscow in 1954, had made Saint-Germain-des-Prés shiver with this booming and definitive statement: "Freedom of criticism is total in the Soviet Union"?


GRADUALLY, LISA HAD LEARNED TO LIKE BEIJING, ITS FALSELY VIL-lagelike atmosphere, its cheekiness, its slowness, and its secrets. In the summer, the family left for Beidahe, Beijing's seaside resort on the Gulf of Bo Hai, a haven of coolness in the summer heat. Mao was fond of the place, and the Central Committee had met there every year, holding paunchy conclaves in the sun that prepared the way for the plenary meetings in the fall. By turns, people stayed for two or three weeks in one of the houses constructed at the time of the concessions, under the umbrella pines on the hills overlooking the sea. The most favored had the finest houses, which had views of the beach. The rest shared houses or hotels, depending on their rank. Li got a simple, honorable house—three rooms back from the sea, alongside that of Chen Yi, and across the street from that of Liu Bocheng. Always calm and outgoing, the one-eyed marshal, a veteran of Nanchang and the Long March, brought his nine children with him and went out alone to look for mushrooms. Chen Yi came every day at the appointed hour for his game of *go* with Li. The girls went to the beach, and Lisa swam in the waves with the wife of Liu Shaoqi, the beautiful Wang Guangmei, before enjoying lying on the sand in the sun.

The wives made fun of their husbands and unanimously agreed that Chou En-lai was the best dancer. Especially for waltzes. A result of his stay in France and Germany, no doubt. Mao was as stiff as could be, leading his partner around as if they were on parade. Zhu De, the marshal, was the funniest; he danced alone in place, tranquilly waddling to one side like a bear, right foot, left foot . . .

The first time, Lisa had almost broken out laughing at the ball in Zhongnanhai. Mao gave a ball every week, at the beginning, and noticed who failed to show up. At the end of a few months, in 1950, Li, who was a terrible dancer, had ceased to grace the dance floor at the pavilion of the Lotus of Spring, to Lisa's great relief. The other wives still went there, amid battalions of young women from the army's best cultural services, who were delighted to dance with the *djouci* and to do what he wanted. The president was fickle; that was well known. In Beidahe, the wives started learning Russian again with Lisa. Zhang Tian, Chen Yi's wife, spoke Russian fluently. Wang Guangmei told them news about Mao, who lived farther on, on his private beach, protected by some fifty bodyguards. When her husband was invited to the president's villa, she accompanied him, and she was the only wife who was tolerated there. The whole place, which it was forbidden to approach, was guarded by a special army unit. But Beidahe, with its mushrooms and seafood, always left Li and Lisa with a delicious taste in their mouths that made them forget Sochi.

As they sat at the banquet table, Lisa and Chen Yi's wife wondered whether there would be room in Beidahe that summer. Li and Chen Yi were talking about the day's editorial in the *People's Daily*. Chen Boda, President Mao's theoretician, was certain that "there is no sign of overpopulation in China." In five years, the country's population had topped 600 million, at the rate of 12 million additional mouths to feed each year. With Mao's grand plan for agriculture, Chen Boda swore that ten years from now they would be able to feed 600 million more Chinese. "One mouth is two arms!" the president declared.

"Two arms, that's one mouth to feed," sighed Chen Yi, who had been following Mao for twenty-five years with a very military rectitude. But so far as administration was concerned, he preferred to know that Chou En-lai was in charge.

The big question of the hour was the Twentieth Party Congress that the Soviet comrades were going to open four days later, on February 14. Nikita Khrushchev wanted détente, and talked about peaceful coexistence with the United States and with capitalism. Competition, without war. They were going to catch up with the United States by the end of the century!

Chen Yi was still moved by the diplomatic success China had won a year earlier at Bandung, Indonesia. He had accompanied Chou there, where the latter had turned the Afro-Asian conference against colonial states, especially the French and British empires. From Algeria to Vietnam, the capitalist metropolises were being surrounded by the third world, just as Chinese cities had been encircled by the Chinese countryside. At the Geneva conference on Vietnam, after the French disaster at Dien Bien Phu, Western diplomats thought that Chen Yi, a military man with whom they could talk, had done very well.

The détente announced by Moscow interested Li intensely. At Stalin's death, he had had to go and do homage before his portrait, as had everyone in Beijing. There were uprisings in East Berlin and Leipzig three months later. Soviet tanks had put them down in a few days, with dozens of dead. But Khrushchev had then made an extraordinary admission to the brother parties: Beria was not a very commendable character, and hadn't been for a long time. Stalin successor began traveling a great deal, unlike the Vojd. He went to Beijing to seek Mao's support. He got it, in exchange for a promise to help the Chinese make an atomic bomb. The Soviets and the Chinese agreed to establish a little more equality among Communists. In Belgrade, Khruschev made excuses to Tito for the insults and bloodshed since 1948. The person responsible for all that was Beria, of course. Not yet Stalin.

In Budapest, Warsaw, and Prague, hope was being reborn, and concern as well. The workers were striking under socialism, the students were agitating, and the police didn't know which way to turn. Red leaders hesitated, panicked, and voted unanimous, solemn resolutions one day, then denounced them the next. In the middle of the uproar, Khrushchev gave the "socialist camp" an arm: The Warsaw Pact was born, and NATO had to just hold on, while Chen Yi and Li Lisan thought it wise for China to keep out of it.

Moscow was bustling about preparing for the Twentieth Party Congress and Chou En-lai was about to depart to represent China at the meeting. In advance, Chen Yi and Li Lisan agreed that the congress's work promised to be exciting. Khrushchev had a reputation as a marathon speaker, having spoken for as much as six hours at a time, but he would be presenting his "new course." No doubt there would be surprises.

The socialist camp's calendar was so well arranged that in September the Chinese Communists continued with their congress, the first since 1945, eleven years earlier. The statutes provided called for a congress to be held every four years, but Mao, like Stalin, hated these useless ceremonies. This time, however, after six years in power, it was necessary to take stock of the situation. In Beijing, people whispered that Mao had expressed the desire to step back and leave the Party, and even the presidency, to Liu

Shaoqi. Helped by the young Deng Xiaoping, and with Chou En-lai as prime minister, Liu Shaoqi, Li's old comrade in Anyuan and Shanghai, seemed to have a brilliant future before him.

In this way, Mao could stand above the fray. Chen Yi felt confident, Li less so: the meandering of the president's thought processes, his ability to surprise people, were a little beyond Li. The millions of portraits of Mao that covered the country made him look like a familiar sphinx, but now no one but a handful of insiders approached the former comrade. Li, who read *Pravda* regularly, noticed that for months it had been emphasizing the virtues of collective leadership of the party, the state, industrial complexes, and kolkhozy.

"The problem is that we don't have enough intellectuals in China," Chen Yi admitted after taking a long drink of hot rice wine. "There are not even 3 million of them, and they're terrorized." The marshal didn't have a lot of respect for men of letters. For him, intellectuals were engineers, technicians, and scientists. Mao had thrown in prison the most famous theater critic, Hu Feng. Since then, the Chinese intellectuals had kept quiet. The president kept an eye on arts and letters. Hu Feng had publicly criticized the "authoritarian and sectarian" policy of the Party, and listed "five daggers" plunged into the brains of writers and artists, who were called upon to work in the genre of proletarian epic. Three months earlier, the Politburo had had to examine *The Dream of the Red Chamber,* a classic novel of the seventeenth century. Mao didn't like the commentary on the novel written by Yu Pingbo, a man of letters who knew nothing about Marx but whose book was a great success. Since then, Chou En-lai had had the devil of a time convincing intellectuals that they were indispensable to socialism.

It was almost midnight. Outside the house, a shadow was approaching hesitantly, making its way through the narrow streets of the *hutong.* His lips stung by the icy cold, the man stopped for a moment and pulled from the pocket of his heavy overcoat a wrinkled piece of paper, which he carefully unfolded. Using his lighter, he read the address written on it and set off again.

In the house in Dongdan, toasts were being drunk one after another at an accelerating pace. Lisa looked at her guests, a cheerful group caught up in a barrage of Chinese wit that Li occasionally translated for her. Chen Yi was promising Li a memorable defeat in the game of *go* that would inevitably follow the feast. Li took up the challenge: a man from Hunan had nothing to learn from a native of Sichuan.

Lao Gao, the butler-chauffeur of the house, timidly entered the room, trying to catch Li's eye. Coming up to him, he whispered a few words in his master's ear.

"What? What did you say?" Li said, stunned.

"There's a man outside who claims that he has just arrived from Moscow and that he knows you. He said to me: 'Tell Li Lisan that Zhang Bao is back.' Should I show him in?"

Li remained speechless for an instant, and then gave a hoarse shout. Without even excusing himself, he stood up and hurried into the garden, heading straight for the gate. On the other side, he saw a frozen figure with a *chapka* on his head and his coat collar turned up. When they were face to face, at first they didn't say a word. The man who was looking at him with shining eyes and a strange smile on his lips seemed ageless. But he wasn't dreaming: it was really Zhang Bao.

"You're alive!" Li couldn't say any more. The two men embraced, their throats tight.

"It took me a while to find the way here, comrade," Zhang finally said, with a small, bittersweet laugh.

"Come in and warm yourself," Li replied, pushing him toward the house.

With his arm around his friend's shoulder, Li brought Zhang into the room, wearing a radiant smile that Lisa had seldom seen on him.

"Zhang Bao! My God!" Had she seen a ghost, she would not have been more jolted. For her, this man had disappeared into the camps long ago,* along with many. others.

Amid the excitement, Chen Yi, waving his chopsticks in the air, was

---

*Zhang Bao had in fact spent nearly eighteen years in captivity, mainly in work camps in the far north of the Soviet Union. —Trans.

trying to identify the newcomer; where could he have come from, this man who looked so moved, who was dressed in the Soviet manner, and whose arrival unleashed such intense feeling?

Li made the introductions: "An old comrade who has finally returned from Moscow. Marshal Chen Yi, perhaps you've heard of him."

Zhang Bao was seated at the marshal's right. At the foot of the table, Inna and Alla, their eyes wide, stared at the man who was making Papa and Mama laugh and cry. When Li raised his glass to toast the newcomer, at first he couldn't get the words out. Zhang was no longer paying any attention to the tears that were rolling down his cheeks. He raised his glass to his country, to the happiness of returning to it after thirty years of wandering through the world, excused himself for intruding upon the party, and drank to friendship.

Chen Yi wanted to know all about his peregrinations. Zhang, his nose in his bowl, quickly relearned the use of chopsticks and the taste of pot-stickers. He was laconic about prison and the camps: "It was hard, very hard. They hit you . . ." The words wouldn't come, and in any case, he wanted to hear only about the present and the future. He wanted to know what was happening throughout the world. The glasses of precious mao-tai, a vodka made from sorghum, diffused in him a delicious warmth. He'd thought he would never experience this precise moment, this quiet happiness of freedom regained.

He hardly heard Chen Yi whisper to him that not only was the country going to find him a job and a place to live, but that they were going to find a way to bring his wife and son from Moscow as soon as possible. Moreover, the New China News Agency needed a competent man to set up its Russian office. It was indispensable for communications with the brother countries. Zhang had the ideal qualifications, and his Russian was perfect. Zhang, who had so longed dreamed of being a journalist, was finally going to be able to go to work.

CHAPTER

# 2 2

The Chinese Party congress had hardly ended before a "counterrevolutionary uprising" took over Budapest and threatened to spread to Hungary's neighbors. Mao congratulated Khrushchev on having once again sent in his tanks. Two months later, a long editorial in the *People's Daily,* which clearly expressed Mao's view, sang the praises of the great Stalin to a vigorous tune. Trumpets sounded and the message was clear: in China, there would be no détente, but rather "permanent revolution."

Toward the end of spring, Mao had arrested en masse intellectuals, engineers, teachers, students, and other rebellious spirits who had expressed doubts about the way things were being done.

The roundup was all the more awful in that two months earlier, these same intellectuals had been called upon to criticize the regime. Throughout the country, and especially in the universities, people had had to assemble at the Party's behest in order to criticize the Party. Not so foolish as to do so, the assemblies had been evasive, saying as little as possible. The Party had urged them on, accusing those who remained silent of having ulterior motives, of not being sincere. There was no longer any question of taking shelter behind phrases such as "No, really, I'm sorry, but I can't see anything to criticize in President Mao's correct line."

When your turn came, you had to get up in front of everyone and find something to criticize. And then do it all over again, but more sincerely this time. Put it all down in black and white, on posters stuck to the wall, in *dazibao* signed with your name. Mao demanded it: "Let a hundred schools of thought contend, let a hundred flowers bloom!" At the institute, Lisa had observed, from as far away as she could, the agitation among students and teachers, a chaotic mixture of daring and infinite prudence. Soon the machine really got going, and criticisms rained down more and more heavily. Three months later, it got so intense that the regime was subjected to a blistering critique, to the applause of the crowd: arrogance, incompetence, and cruelty were denounced as the plagues of the new China. They were hardly distinguishable from those of the old China.

When summer came, Mao, a sore loser, sent half a million intellectuals to camps in Laogai, for twenty years or for life. The new secretary-general, Deng Xiaoping, had undertaken this task, along with Kang Sheng, who was running the show. The hunt for right-wingers had begun. In China, one could make a mistake, but only if the mistake was on the left. On the right, it was tantamount to a crime.

China was embarking upon the Great Leap Forward. Popular communes were Mao's latest discovery. With them, China would move directly to communism: "In May 1958, like the rising sun, there appeared on the vast horizon of East Asia a new form of social organization, the popular commune."

The spirit of the Paris Commune was to blow constantly over every district in China, in the countryside as well as in the city. The peasant cooperatives founded four years earlier were to be combined into one; they would include as many as twenty thousand families, distributed into work brigades. Private property would be completely abolished, right down to the apple trees in the garden, the furniture in one's home, the chickens, and even the family pig. All meals would be taken in canteens. Children would eat together, and be put into dormitories as soon as possible. Everyone would be a soldier, as well. The brigades would form an immense and invincible popular militia. The kind of work one did would be changed at will. Soon, even money would be done away with; everything would be free, and everyone would receive in accord with his needs, no longer in accord with his labor.

At this rate, Mao swore, China would reach the stage of communism before the Soviet Union. Lenin, after all, had allowed Russia to skip the capitalist stage. Mao, in China, would go him one better: he was going to reduce the socialist phase to a minimum. In Moscow, *Pravda* maintained a polite but stubborn silence regarding the Maoist outrages being committed against Party doctrine, praising even more fulsomely the radiant life in the kolkhozy.

IN CHINA, THERE WAS A NEW, IMPRESSIVE MOBILIZATION OF HUMAN energy, directed toward the achievement of the craziest objectives imagined since Stalin. The first popular commune was named Sputnik. In Moscow, Mao said that China could catch up with Great Britain in steel production within fifteen years. That is, it could produce 15 million tons instead of the 300,000 it had begun with. In the meantime, it would suffice to double production every year.

The Soviets, who'd heard all this before, couldn't believe their ears, and soon their eyes. Steel furnaces were built, some of brick, others of adobe, all over China. The construction of small blast furnaces became a national exercise in masonry. The best were dominated by a tall, factory-like chimney, as on the proletarian posters. "Small is beautiful," Mao's aphorism said, but he thought big: from the tiniest village among the rice paddies of Jiangxi to the yellow earth of Gansu, the blast furnace chimneys rose into the sky, smoking totems erected to proletarian rule. The campuses, the research laboratories, the hospitals, the New China agency, every neighborhood street, the infantry regiments, and soon even Mao's palace had its little blast furnace and records to beat.

Below the chimneys, people loaded the furnaces day and night, in brigades, with everything that would burn in order to melt down every bit of iron to be found in China, from cellars to attics. Kettles, saucepans, utensils, and old souvenirs—President Mao wanted record numbers, and he got numbers such as the Soviets had never imagined.

To Soviet visitors, the peasants in the Party explained with unfathomable aplomb how they had increased the harvest by 100, 200, even 300 percent over the year. In China, the economy ran on enthusiasm, Mao insisted. Delegations of Soviet experts listened, fascinated, hardly able to hold back contagious, mad laughter as the Party's peasant explained that if his corn was producing fantastic results that year, it was because President Mao had caressed the ears as he passed by on his visit. Every ear of corn touched by Mao bore a little red ribbon. The experts smiled, a little embarrassed, too: on seeing this naïvete and exemplary submission, everyone remembered that in their own country people said the same sort of thing under Stalin, and even believed it a little, at that time. The Chinese were boastful and ridiculous, but they were holding up a mirror to the Soviets: "Look, we're going to do even better than you."

In the land of Confucius, the family was denounced as reactionary; it was suspended, forbidden. Parents saw their children taken away from them, and meals were somber in the evenings, among adults, in the obligatory collective cafeterias.

Li Lisan was keeping his distance from the inner circle of leaders. At the end of July 1959, he had been called to attend an enlarged conclave with the whole Central Committee, in Lushan, in the green mountains of Jiangxi. Lisa and the girls had remained on the beaches at Beidahe, along with Zhang Bao, Nadia, and their son, Valery, who had just arrived from Moscow for the vacation. Four days later, Li called Lisa.

"Is everything going all right?" Lisa automatically asked. She was used to her husband's laconic responses regarding government affairs, especially on the telephone.

"No, not at all. Something very serious is going on here. An enormous fight. I'll tell you . . ."

He changed the subject, leaving Lisa worried. Li seldom confided in her in this way. Things must in fact be terribly serious for him to open up in this way. When he returned, he told her what had happened. Marshal Peng Dehuai, the minister of defense, a veteran of all the battles, had dared to rise and try to do something unheard of: to convince Mao that he was off course.

Peng questioned whether China could achieve communism "in a single leap." The marshal had been quietly criticizing the president for years—his mania for remaining in bed for days on end, his solitary exercise of power, his habit of getting up at noon, and his sudden whims. The country was heading for a catastrophe. Peng had a sharp tongue, mocking in the corridors the "emperor with three thousand concubines," the girls that lined the walls at the balls in Zhongnanhai before going off with him right in front of everyone.

Peng's attack was frank and direct, but it took everyone by surprise. After a bit of self-criticism, Mao, stung to the quick, had counterattacked, castigating the "military club," these marshals who thought they were peers of the regime. If the Party disavowed him, Mao would not hesitate to resume the civil war. And if the Party was divided, they would "all be swept away by the people," he warned.

Petrified, stupefied, frightened, the Party's leading figures caved in. Those in the army—Zhu De, Chen Yi, and the rest—reluctantly sided with Mao, dragging along with them a distrustful and silent Li Lisan and leaving Peng Dehuai isolated, surrounded by a handful of brave men, a "clique" that Mao constantly ridiculed. Stripped of his functions, put under house arrest, the marshal was dragged publicly through the mud. Lin Biao would succeed him as minister of defense. Mao cared so little about appearances that he handed over to Liu Shaoqi the presidency of the republic. Deng Xiaoping was to deal with the Party, and Chou En-lai with the government. Released from these restraints, the *djouci* could devote himself to his favorite pleasure: inventing the future, surprising his adversaries. In Moscow, Khrushchev said bitterly and mockingly of him: "That guy doesn't carry out God's plans, he thinks God is carrying out his . . ."

ON THE TRIBUNE AT TIANANMEN SQUARE FOR THE OCTOBER 1 PArade in 1959, Lisa, sitting under the portrait of Mao, had immediately noticed that Khrushchev looked furious. The secretary-general of the Soviet Communist Party had rushed up the steps to the tribune, passing in front of her in order to join Mao at the rostrum. Mikhail Andreyevich Suslov, the new head ideologist in Moscow, his hair disheveled and looking still more furious, followed him with the Soviet delegation. Lisa understood that there were serious conflicts between the two countries. The fat was in the fire. Khrushchev was coming from the United States, where his triumphal visit had made Mao fear that the Cold War was over.

The Soviet leader did not want a war between India and China, either. In New Delhi, the parliament was accusing Beijing of having stolen a small area of Indian territory in the Himalayas. Mao had sent the army to close the frontier to Tibetans, who were fleeing the terror. The clashes with the Indian army worried Khrushchev, and he told Comrade Mao this. The conversation had been stormy, and Mao had refused to allow Khrushchev's submarines to put in at China's ports.

"Comrade Mao Tse-tung," Khrushchev had pleaded in a final effort to convince his interlocutor, "the NATO countries aren't hesitating to cooperate! Whereas we, on such a simple question, can't we even come to an agreement?"

"The answer is no," the president repeated to his guest for the third time, "and I don't want to hear anything more about it. We don't want you here. We've already had the British and other foreigners on our territory for years. We will never again allow anyone to use our land for his own purposes."


A YEAR EARLIER, KHRUSHCHEV HAD MADE A SECRET VISIT TO MAO, who had received him in a manner that flabbergasted Stalin's successor. Wearing swimming trunks, stretched out on the bed set up next to his indoor pool, Mao, imperially invited the secretary-general to don trunks. Mao wanted Khrushchev to join him for a swim! That would relax him and do him good.

Khrushchev didn't know how to swim, and he couldn't make up his mind whether to laugh or to launch into one of the fits of anger that had made him famous. He decided to laugh. A buoy was found, and he lowered himself into the water behind Mao, who shared judicious observations on Marxism with him as he paddled along, with interpreters running alongside the pool shouting translations in Russian. Khrushchev half drowned and left Beijing on the edge of a nervous breakdown.

Three weeks later, thousands of Chinese cannons opened a heavy, nonstop artillery barrage on Quemoy and Matsu, two small islands not far off the coast of Fujian that had been fortified by the Kuomintang Nationalists. Mao wanted to pull the American tiger's mustache, so he unleashed a memorable combat alert for the U.S. Navy in the Formosa Strait. Washington, the protector of Taiwan and Chiang Kai-shek, showed its teeth and its aircraft carriers. Mao mentioned to his doctor that he was impatient with the notion that President Eisenhower might drop an atomic bomb on Fujian: "Maybe ten or twenty million people would die. Chiang Kai-shek wants the U.S. to use the bomb against us. Let them do it. We'll see what Khrushchev says then. . . ." Khrushchev and Eisenhower would have to have their peaceful coexistence without Mao.

Six weeks and several million artillery shells later, the great Chinese strategist began an unprecedented kind of cease-fire. Puzzled, military observers learned that China, while waiting for the bomb, would now pound the Nationalist islands only on odd days of the month. Every other day, at a fixed time, with a pause for lunch and the artillerymen's siesta. The reconquest of Taiwan would be pursued at this pace.

ON OCTOBER 1, 1959, RED CHINA WAS CELEBRATING ITS TENTH BIRTH-day, but Stalin's successor had left three days after he had arrived, a record in brevity that resounded like a slammed door and startled Lisa, Nadia, and their husbands.

The summer of 1959 had been a very hot one, and Mao had been given a fright. In Lushan, he had avoided being overthrown, and the army had remained faithful to him. Relieved, he was able to relaunch China's assault on heaven.

Famine had killed 30 million people, and there had not been a single line about it in the newspapers. The country had not seen such hunger for a century, not since the Taiping.* In the villages, people went back to cannibalism, to the detriment of little girls. Families exchanged them, sparing the parents the horror of having to eat their own children. The boys survived, until the whole family disappeared. Others refused to eat human flesh, preferring to die together. From Heilongjiang to Hebei, the old proverb from the times of misfortune had reemerged: "*Yi zi, er shi.*" ["Exchange children, and eat."] During the daytime, the music of brass bands playing the "International" crackled over the loudspeakers, endlessly repeating the line "Arise, ye prisoners of starvation." At night, people started guarding the tombs of their ancestors to defend them against starving people who were prowling about. Communist Party officials unexpectedly descended on people's homes to take their last grains of wheat, homes that had already been emptied of everything that had been burned in the village blast furnaces, even the window frames.

By the millions, peasants converged on the cities. Those around Canton fled to Hong Kong, submerging the Crown colony. Elsewhere, the army opened fire on rioters. In Tibet, the insurrection reached the capital in March 1959. Lhasa was taken with the help of artillery fire, but the Dalai Lama slipped through Mao's fingers, protected by Kham horsemen† until he reached India. In Beijing, hunger arrived insidiously, with the appearance of rationing coupons and something people had never seen before: lines waiting in front of empty stores. The volleyball courts at universities and research institutes were turned into vegetable gardens. The residents of Beijing started raising chickens on balconies and in apartments, although this was forbidden. The city became an immense village, awakened at dawn by the cry of roosters. The government, which was doing away with domestic pets, backed down before fowl: since the people didn't have rice, meat, or vegetables, they would eat eggs. The last dogs that had survived the great canine liquidation ended up on the butcher's display table.

---

*A Chinese religious and political movement that provoked a major popular revolt in 1850 against the Ch'ing dynasty. —Trans.

†Tibetan warriors from eastern Tibet, the spearhead of the resistance to the Chinese Red Army.

At Li Lisan's home, the family fox terrier, Groshka, was not allowed to go out or to bark in the garden, for reasons of security. On a socialist day excursion outside town, Lisa and Nadia saw the trunks of the holm oaks that dotted the countryside. During the winter of 1961–1962, a strange disease decimated them: they had all lost their bark as high up as man could reach. Chinese experts were evasive about the origin of the disease. But everyone in Beijing knew what was in the evening soup in the people's communes.

The old peasants silently cursed the new emperor and the stupid clods that were governing the country, where people were dying of hunger "worse than under the Japanese." Beijing's streets were full of hundreds of thousands of poor wretches who had come there to look for something to eat. The police had to drive them away, to send them back to the countryside, to their tombs. Next, the police forbade the publication of death notices and the wearing of mourning bands, which were too numerous and too conspicuous.

In January 1961, China secretly bought wheat from foreign capitalists for the first time. Glorious self-sufficiency was a thing of the past. But Mao was still more explicit: the communist stage was approaching so quickly that it was now only a matter of a few years. The Soviet Union, still on the starting line, was sure to be beaten.

The new Chinese elite was supplied with food, but Li's servants discreetly suggested to Lisa that vegetables be planted in the garden. Their families were prepared to pay for the produce.

For Li and his friends, the alert was sounded at the beginning of 1962. Summoned by the Central Committee, he learned that grave accusations of espionage had been made against Lisa. Furious, he went to see Chou En-lai. The prime minister found the affair annoying. It was foolish to claim that Lisa was a spy. But Kang Sheng was behind it all, obviously.

The uncontrollable, unavoidable Kang Sheng. Since his return as head of the police, Yezhov's pupil had resumed his favorite exercise: purging. He could finally work on the scale of the whole country. There was no question of picking up one by one those who vituperated, criticized, or grumbled. Kang Sheng applied the quota method: half a percent of right-wingers here, 2.5 percent of counterrevolutionaries there, with a sprinkling of former members of the Kuomintang. The Gong'an, the national police, worked hard and methodically. File cards had been compiled on the whole population for years. In his neighborhood, factory, or office, everyone had written his biography, with his class origin, his attitude during the civil war, that of his parents, his children, cousins, and friends. Altogether, there were 2 or 3 million cards, which had to be filed by hand: the Chinese police amassed, sorted, manipulated them. Kang Sheng wanted percentages of executions and quotas for the camps where people were reeducated through labor.

Laogai needed lots of labor. China still didn't have a system of justice, but it did have a gulag. An empire within the empire, its camps, its farms, its factories, its mines, and its major public works projects wove their web from the rice-growing subprefectures in Hebei to the forests of Heilongjiang. In Xinjiang Uygur's sands, Chinese work camp prisoners were putting the finishing touches, sometimes with their last breaths, on the atomic site that was going to see rise into the air the mushroom cloud of victory, the luminous grail of omnipotence.

From the height of his police machine, Kang Sheng, a close associate of Mao's, watched over the political. In the evening, in one of the thirty-nine rooms in his residence in the Bamboo Garden, he constructed traps, prepared pitfalls, and hatched his assassination plots while smoking the finest Burmese opium and glancing fondly at his calligraphy collection from time to time. Kang sent spies throughout the world, infiltrated the United States, fomented coups d'état in Africa. He even nibbled on the coattails of the European communist parties, where Maoism had had little success. The KGB kept an eye on the ingrate, this talented pupil who was now so critical of the Russians in order to conceal his debt to them. He was the greatest antirevisionist, with his loud and always stinging talk against "social imperialism" and the "new czars."

The few hundred thousand Chinese who had frequented Soviet experts made good prey; their brains had to be straightened out.

Li Lisan knew too much about Kang Sheng's stay in Moscow.

Nicknamed the Rotten Egg, he had notoriously turned his comrades in to the Soviet police before demanding a few hundred executions too many in Yan'an, in 1942. Kang Sheng held grudges: Li's return to China had cost him six years of being on the sidelines before he took over the reins of the police again.

THIS ACCUSATION OF ESPIONAGE GREATLY EMBARRASSED CHOU EN-lai. One day, he suggested to Li: "Maybe a divorce . . . No?"

Li made his greatest outburst in many years. Chou had not seen him that angry since the 1920s.

"Listen to me, En-lai: I know my wife, I know her very well! I'm sure of her. I will never divorce her, you hear? Never! If you don't believe me, it's very simple: I'll turn in my Party card."

The Red mandarin remained silent. His obsequious malleability with regard to Mao and Kang was limitless. But confronted by Li Lisan, he had old memories and a few fears. Turning in one's Party card was worse than an obscenity, it was a sacrilege; the violation of an oath paralleled only by suicide, it was the equivalent of treason.

Li Lisan slamming the door of the Chinese Communist Party? That would give people in Taiwan, in the Kuomintang, a good laugh. People in Moscow as well, probably. Clearly, this comrade's inflexibility would destroy him.

Chou En-lai tried to calm him down, but Li left in a state of extreme agitation. Never had he uttered more serious words: "I'll turn in my Party card." How many times had he said to Lisa, "You must know that I put the Party first, and you second"?

This was too much. Sidelined for ten years, that was one thing. The long humiliation before the 1956 Party congress had seemed to reassure Mao. Li had reappeared before the supreme authority of the Party for the first time since the Moscow congress in 1928. In fifteen years of absence, he had missed only one congress, the one in 1945, the last one. Those who expected to see if the loudmouth would attack Mao were disappointed: he was a phantom of his legend. Li showed everyone that he had no intention of starting a war between leaders. In Moscow, Stalin's verdicts were being revised. In Beijing, Mao retained the Vojd's judgment on Li: the Party wanted the former leader to kowtow before the new emperor. History was written by Chen Boda, and Lilisanism still raised "certain questions" that the congress had to discuss. Li, who wanted peace, got off with a self-criticism even longer and more sincere than the ones he'd made in Moscow.

In the audience, comrade journalist Zhang Bao listened as a connoisseur. Li was still the champion of that delicate oratorical art. He was in fine form, even more than when he was facing Wang Ming in Moscow. He had added to his official repentance the missing touch of Maoism, freely acknowledging that he had gravely neglected the inestimable role of peasants in the proletarian revolution. He traced the story from the 1920s up to his latest sin, his "economistic deviation" as minister of labor. He called himself a petit bourgeois and recognized that the Party was right all along the line. The victory had only one father, Mao Tse-tung, and Li Lisan was a living catalog of the errors to be avoided: from left-wing to right-wing, he had now covered the whole spectrum.

The self-criticism was so vast and so profound that it seemed to close the subject definitively. The veteran bowed his way out, carrying his cross to the end. The congress liked it, and reelected him to the Central Committee for the honor of the thing, ahead of Wang Ming, who, coming in far behind, was avoiding China in Moscow.

On reading the *People's Daily,* old comrades and former miners in Anyuan thought Li had gone a little overboard. He was, after all, the only one of the two true leaders who had preceded Mao who was still alive.

CHOU EN-LAI HAD DARED TO PULL LI OUT OF HIS OBSCURITY IN the Northern Office to tell him *kliveta,* police tall tales starring Lisa as a Soviet spy! Chou En-lai, the old comrade from his days in France, was letting him down. Li had thundered, and Chou had been afraid, but the investigation dragged on for ten months. Ten hushed, hypocritical months, during which Lisa, without being outwardly concerned, sometimes woke up in the middle of a nightmare about the last nights in the Hotel Lux. That lasted until one morning she awoke and told Li with a smile that she had dreamed she was climbing a mountain enveloped in mist, and then came out at the summit to find brilliant sunlight.

Li remained silent, and smiled as he took her in his arms. It was a curious dream, even if it was the harbinger of such good news: her case had just been dismissed for lack of evidence. Lisa was not a revisionist spy.

Li was called in for another interview with Chou En-lai and came back shattered. The prime minister had offered him a compromise: "Lisa can stay, on condition that she become a Chinese citizen and renounce her Soviet citizenship." This was a personal commitment on Chou's part, and he promised to put his own signature on this extraordinary legal document. The Westerner would become Chinese, and this sleight of hand would save face for the government. Lisa, who was attached to Russia, took her time: "I need time to think about it."

She thought about it for months. Li respected her concern, assured her that he understood, that he would support her no matter what she decided. But when Nadia decided to return to the Soviet Union, leaving Zhang Bao behind, Lisa felt the pressure on her increase. She could go back to Russia at any time. One evening, Li confided in Inna, during a conversation in her room. His eldest daughter was twenty, and she loved to converse with her father.

"I have to talk with you, Inna. For stupid reasons, the Central Committee wants me to divorce your mother. But if she changes nationality, if she becomes a Chinese citizen, we'll be able to remain together. I can't, I don't want to divorce her. I love her, and we have been together for such a long time. When I was in prison, she supported me, she waited for me, she didn't betray me. I can't divorce her, especially not for vile reasons. Besides, if I did it, it would throw suspicion on her. That's even worse. So I won't divorce her.

"But I'm asking you to help me. If we can convince her to become a Chinese citizen, we'll stay together. That's the only solution. I know it's hard for her, that she loves her country . . ."

Inna had learned by accident that her father had been in prison under Stalin. In Moscow, in 1956, during a family visit with Lisa, she had overheard a conversation in the next room. Lisa and her mother were talking about the Yezhov years.

"My Lord, I remember when they threw Li Lisan in prison . . . ," Lisa sighed.

Papa in prison? The family secret was out of the bag. At thirteen, Inna saw her world crumble around her. Prison was for thieves, murderers, and enemies of the people. Back in Beijing, she wanted to know all about it. Li had explained at length that "many errors" had been made in this way, under Stalin. But errors that were always corrected in the end. . . .

"In Moscow, people also say crimes."

"No, we should call them *errors*. Stalin committed errors, Inna, not crimes."

Li was inflexible. All he needed was for his daughters to go about saying that Stalin was a criminal. Mao's sensitivity on that subject was notorious.

Since then, Inna, who had both passports, had chosen China. She hadn't liked Moscow when she returned there in 1959, and came back after a year. In Beijing, she was getting ready to enter the Institute of Foreign Languages, where she was planning to study Russian and Spanish.

Convinced by her father, she had a long talk with her mother. Lisa told her openly that she feared above all that she would never be able to go back to see her family in Moscow.

But she would become a Chinese citizen. Li's relief would be immense. After he was released from prison, they'd sworn never to leave each other again. She had joined him at the other end of the earth. She would say yes, and she accepted this destiny: becoming Chinese. She would even do it in the gardens of the Summer Palace, where they liked to take lovers' walks on Sundays.

After all, citizenship was just a matter of pieces of paper. At the age of fifty, she had taken up residence for life in this country. To hell with national borders! What would be would be. Probably she would not be the only one, the only Westerner to do so: Eva might also agree to become a Chinese citizen.

Eva Sandberg, one of the last three Soviet women in China, was facing the same dilemma as Lisa. She had become Eva Siao since her marriage in Moscow to Emi Siao, the poet and childhood friend of Mao's, and she had to choose between her country and her husband. Born in Germany, a photographer and Jewish, Eva had a Soviet passport. After having photographed China from every angle with her Leica, she was now filming it for Eastern European news agencies and magazines. Recently, her travels were being counted against her. Her husband, tired of singing Mao's praises, was sinking into the silence of poets.

Lisa and Eva defended Grania, the third remaining Soviet woman, who had the most serious problem. Grania's Chinese husband had suddenly repudiated her. Before the court, the man, a terrified liar, had accused her of revisionism, of having "taken the capitalist path." That kind of offense called for an exemplary divorce, which he obtained without custody of their child. At the trial, the three women had stood together. Lisa and Eva had testified in favor of Grania, while Li Lisan, indignant, wrote her defense plea and testified to her morality. Grania cared nothing about politics, and came from a simple and little-educated part of Russia. She lost some of her legendary sense of humor, wounded to the core by this hateful and servile betrayal. Alone in Beijing, she was raising her child without any citizenship, and with only Lisa and Eva for support. Her husband, Chang Zhenhao, was guilty of many things that he had to hope Kang Sheng and Mao would pardon. During the Long March, he had been on the opponents' general staff, along with Zhang Guotao. It was he who had denounced Lisa as a Soviet spy. From then on, he was to denounce many more.

Once she was a Chinese citizen, Lisa hoped she would no longer be harassed about her citizenship. Love knew no borders; her daughters were there, and wanted to have parties at the house. Inna was wearing short skirts and putting her hair in a bun that made her boyfriends' heads turn. They were all diplomats' sons, or Cuban, East German, Czechoslovakian, or Romanian students. From them, Alla, at seventeen, was learning to dance rock and roll and the cha-cha. Whether it amounted to a restoration of capitalism or not, their parents' ideological war was running out of steam to the sound of phonograph records hidden at the bottom of suitcases brought back from Havana or Berlin.

People pointed at Inna and Alla because of the way they dressed, which was openly Western. Li had to listen to remarks about them. The family was mocked as an "ultrademocratic" one in which the girls threw their arms around their father in public and didn't hold their tongues at table. Chen Yi delighted in the grace of their enthusiasm, but Kang Sheng detested their manners, to the point of telling Li one day: "You ought to keep an eye on those daughters of yours. They aren't Chinese in any way, and they dress like Western bourgeois girls. Short skirts, much shorter even than in Moscow. And they'd better be careful, always hanging out with their revisionist pals. . . ."

Li sent the Rotten Egg packing, but at the dinner table that evening he talked to Inna about the importance of moderation in the way she dressed, triggering an immediate outcry. Okay, so everything was political, but men knew nothing about fashions. Besides, the Sun Yat-sen jacket Li wore every day didn't look as good on him as Western suits, even Soviet ones: a tie was more chic and less dreary. They drove a hard bargain, and finally agreed on reasonably moderate dress at the institute. At home or when the girls were out on the town, they could dress as they liked.

That was the way Li was; he couldn't refuse his women anything. In exchange, he was the law at home. But Inna and Alla were beautiful, and as passionate about Cuba as he was. They would have their parties, and to hell with the malcontents. Their parents would go for a walk in the gardens of the Summer Palace.

# 23

The August heat was so dry and so intense that it seemed to have reduced the city to silence. Sitting under the tree in the garden, Lisa and Li Lisan were looking for the coolness of the slightest breath of air. It was late morning. High in the sky, the sun was heating Beijing to over a hundred degrees. Stretched out not far away, Groshka, the fox terrier, was panting noisily; his tongue hung out of his mouth as he watched his masters out of the corner of his eye.

The couple talked little and in low voices. For weeks, everyone in the household had been economical in his movements and words, as if slowly and silently waiting for something.

Suddenly, Groshka perked up his ears and tilted his head to the side. Then he jumped up and went to sniff the entry gate, looking concerned.

At the same time, Lisa and Li heard the first echoes of a dull clamor mounting in the distance.

"Another one," Li said darkly.

A demonstration, a riot. It was the end of August 1966, and Beijing, for the first time under the new regime, was prey to anarchy. An orgy of violence such as the capital had never seen. Commando units of university and high school students wearing red armbands were fanning out through the city, brandishing the "Little Red Book," a collection of Mao's sayings. It was open season on anything old. The mere sight of elderly people triggered the anger of the young Red Guards. Beaten and left for dead on the sidewalks, old people were staying home. Holding lists in their hands, the commandos of young revolutionaries burst into houses and apartments, which they sacked amid cries, slogans, and furor. Books, furniture, knick-knacks, and souvenirs were smashed or burned. Girls and women who wore braids or long hair were assailed in the streets, denounced for their bourgeois tendencies, slapped at the slightest protest, and released after the avenging scissors had shortened their hair or cut it off entirely. Elegant or absentminded women who had put on a dress or skirt in the morning and hadn't turned back when they saw the Red Guards coming were insulted and humiliated, left weeping and clutching the tattered remains of their clothes, which had been savagely cut to pieces: proletarian blue or khaki pants were now the only acceptable attire.

Never had Beijing's garbage cans held so many patent leather shoes with high heels, surreptitiously thrown into them at night along with their owners' lipsticks: only cotton espadrilles proved that one was really on the side of the people and not on that of its sworn enemies. In the universities, revisionists and revolutionaries were fighting everywhere. No one gave in: the revisionist, the one who took the capitalist path, was the other one, the one on the other side. Since June, there had been a few dead and wounded in the two camps.

After long months of silence spent in the provinces, President Mao was back in the capital. People had thought him ill; the whole world learned that at the age of seventy-three he'd swum ten miles down the middle of the Yangtze, followed by five thousand compatriots. That was in July, and the weather was splendid, but above the photo of the president on its front page, the *People's Daily* ran a curious headline: LET'S ALL ADVANCE THROUGH THE VIOLENT STORM BY FOLLOWING PRESIDENT MAO!

On August 18, before an audience of a million young delirious Red

Guards, Mao mounted the rostrum in Tiananmen Square, something he usually did, like Stalin, only twice a year, on May 1 and October 1. The mere appearance of the Beacon of Humanity, the Beloved Rising Sun of the Peoples of the World, the Great Helmsman, was in itself a signal that the situation was serious. For a million adolescents, the summer of 1966 remained unforgettable: not only had they seen Mao with their own eyes, but he had magnanimously given Chinese youth a revolution. Since then, revolution had been not only permitted, but obligatory.

Lisa and Li Lisan were talking in low voices, wondering if Inna would come to see them this weekend. She had been a resident student at the institute for two years now. She had just returned from eight months in the countryside with her classmates. In 1963, Mao had launched the "movement for socialist education" around peasants, in order to construct the new proletarian man. Intellectuals had to go see the base in order to be inspired by the masses. Inna had come back from this virtuous vacation upset by the sordid poverty of the rural people after the cataclysm of the Great Leap Forward.

At twenty-two, like all her friends, Inna was mad about President Mao, but she had great difficulty convincing her Red Guard comrades at the institute that her hair was naturally curly and not curled with an iron.

"Are you Chinese or a foreigner?"

"Chinese, of course!"

"Then what are these ridiculous Western clothes? You have bourgeois manners, comrade!"

Inna had come home one evening to put the problem before her mother: she had to have some proletarian pants, right away. It was a question of fashion, again, but this time not one of elegance. At the institute, girls were competing to see who had the most stylish uniform, the best cut from the best fabric. Inna warned Alla and Lisa that they had better do the same. The three women went to see a seamstress in the neighborhood, an old Japanese woman who had remained in Beijing, and she made to measure impeccable ordinary Chinese jackets and pants for them.

Li was waiting for Inna to come back so he could share the latest news with his eldest daughter. Since June, he had been completely cut off from his channels of communication, forbidden access to his work, under house arrest. On his return from a visit to a factory in Tientsin, a comrade had given him a document informing him that he was forbidden to set foot in the Northern Office, which the Central Committee had charged with industrializing the country. No reason was given; the order came from the *zhongyang,* the Center.

Li didn't need an explanation. He understood that it was all starting over again, and would always be starting over again.

HOWEVER, NO ONE HAD SEEN THE STORM COMING. THERE HAD been Mao's articles on literary matters, but his hatred for men of letters was not a new fancy. Above all, the president had to some extent been crying in the desert for the past six years. The Party listened to him politely, but since Lushan and the great famine of the three bad years, the Great Leap had not moved forward. Everyone was busy repairing the damage. The people's communes were now occupied only with administration, and the work brigades consisted chiefly of reunited families.

Before seven thousand Party officials summoned to Beijing in 1962, Mao had had to take a self-critical tone, the first time he had ever been heard to do that. He grudgingly admitted that he knew nothing about economics, but only in order to once again warn against the danger of "the restoration of capitalism" that was lurking everywhere, according to him. Only Chou En-lai and Lin Biao had stood up to defend him. Sent back to his studies with a chorus of praise, Mao, vexed, had left the running of the country to Liu Shaoqi and Deng Xiaoping. A rebellious current had taken advantage of the breach, and voices had even been heard demanding that Peng Dehuai be rehabilitated. In Lushan, the marshal had been brave. He said the right thing before everyone else. Liu Shaoqi didn't dare to go so far as to ask for a pardon.

China consoled itself by laughing up its sleeve at the latest opera: *The Destitution of Hai Rui* represented, in classical style, a courageous and forthright sixteenth-century mandarin who had defied the emperor. Its author, Wu Han, a talented essayist and historian, had already attracted attention three years earlier with a premonitory *Hai Rui Reprimands the Emperor,* published in the *People's Daily* a few weeks before Lushan. Li Lisan had also enjoyed Deng Tuo's columns in the official press. With innuendoes and limpid allusions, they commented ironically and acerbically on the president's whims, while Chou En-lai and Liu Shaoqi swore once again to the intellectuals that the country wanted them.

China had found its Stakhanov, and he wore the uniform of the People's Liberation Army. An ordinary soldier, Lei Feng had been promoted to the rank of a "national model" by Mao. His life was a repertory of proletarian devotion. An orphan—his father had been killed by the Kuomintang's torturers and his mother had died of hunger during a famine—the illustrious trooper had first been a model employee in the administration, and then a model tractor driver in the people's communes, and named eighteen times a model worker in the Anshan steel mill before donning a military uniform. As a soldier, Lei Feng distinguished himself by the indefatigable zeal with which he propagated the thought of President Mao and served the people. At night, he repaired his sleeping comrades' torn clothing or waxed their shoes. During the day, he fought floods on the Yangtze with his bare hands, harvested, or helped an elderly person cross the street, before going on to unmask spies from Taiwan. His only leisure was reading the "Little Red Book," which he always carried with him. According to the legend, Lei Feng died in the line of duty at the age of twenty-two when, on an unlucky day, a telegraph pole fell on his head. An ordinary death, worthy of these everyday heroes who were called upon to pick up where the demigods of the Long March left off.

From babies to adults, China was summoned to attend sessions to study Lei Feng, President Mao's spiritual son. The country was submerged with millions of articles, pamphlets, and comic strips narrating in detail the countless episodes of his life, while on street corners loudspeakers whined the conventional speeches, punctuated by strident appeals: "*Sueci Lei Feng mofan!*" ["Let us study the example of Lei Feng!"] In meetings, people yawned as they wondered where the devil this fellow had found the time to do all that. But the new man finally had an ideal: to be the little screw, the *siao ding,* without which the great machine could not run.

Soldiers, under the aegis of the new minister of defense, Lin Biao, were becoming more Maoist by the day, unlike their leaders, who had been offended by the ignominy heaped on Peng Dehuai. Of the ten marshals of the empire, Lin Biao, short, sickly, and retiring, was the least popular. But he had become unbeatable for glorifying the president's genius, as the inventor of "Marxism-Leninism for our time." China had exploded its first nuclear bomb in 1964, in a desert in Turkmenistan. Lin Biao immediately described Mao's thought as "the spiritual atomic bomb."

From his retreat, Mao showed an increasingly urgent concern about youth. As he traveled through the provinces in his special train, he surrounded himself with a large court of young women. On occasion, young men in his guard also shared his bed. His debauchery was notorious among the regime's insiders. In youth, Mao loved the "blank page" that he stubbornly sought in China in order to pour his dreams onto it, to put his seal on that soft wax.

In the universities, the sons of Party officials were champing at the bit. Young people's revolutionary enthusiasm was as old as the world. These young people had heard about nothing but epics and were burning to have one of their own.

The peasants, the workers, the intellectuals, and even the Party itself were resisting Mao's fancies. To recover the power he felt slipping away from him, he decided to subject the country to a pincers maneuver, catching it between its youth and its army. At the risk of destroying it, once again.

The first shot had been fired from Shanghai. Obliquely, in a newspaper article violently attacking *The Destitution of Hai Rui,* the opera by Wu Han, who also happened to be the adjunct mayor of Beijing. Li Lisan had paid little attention to this scathing article. In November 1965, it was old news. Three weeks later, the *Army Daily* had sounded the same note, and Wu Han was now in for it. The Politburo was forced to reexamine Mao's literary quarrels. Peng Zhen, a prominent dignitary, had tried to calm the situation. That was a mistake; on May 16, 1966, a national circular made a solemn call for purification: "All representatives of the bourgeoisie who have been infiltrated into the Party, the government, the army, or any sector of the cultural domain constitute a group of counterrevolutionary revisionists" and must be cleaned out. Mao warned: "There are individuals like Khrushchev who are sleeping alongside us."

Khrushchev had been overthrown two years earlier by Leonid Brezhnev, but Mao didn't care. In order to save socialism from itself, another revolution within the revolution was necessary. He had said it over and over: the transition from socialism to communism was not a smooth one. Violence was necessary. "There is no construction without destruction!" The revolution would be cultural, for this time they were going to root out the weeds of bourgeois revisionist ideas.

In private, the president reveled in this, repeatedly saying, *"Wo xihuan tianxia da luan."* ["I love great chaos on earth."]

On May 25, a female philosophy teacher at the University of Beijing, Nie Yuanzi, picked up the ball and launched the Cultural Revolution on the campus, calling for the overthrow of "reactionary gangs" and the rector of the university. At Mao's command, her long *dazibao* was read over the radio. The conflagration had been lit.

In the wake of these events, the mayor of Beijing, Peng Zhen, was thrown out of office. Li Lisan followed this episode with anxiety: his direct superior at the Northern Office, Li Suefeng, succeeded Peng. Like all the regime's top officials, he was lost in conjectures. What was Mao up to now? The situation was still more serious than it had been at Lushan. It was whispered that Lin Biao, the great apostle of people's war, had sent troops faithful to Mao to surround Beijing, where there were already quite a few troops. Kang Sheng was playing the role of an intellectual and parading around triumphantly. To everyone's stupefaction, Mao's wife, Jiang Qing, emerged from obscurity. After twenty-five years of silence, the former starlet from Shanghai left her private projection room in order pose before meetings of soldiers, old men in uniform, whom she tried to persuade of the urgency of reforming the Beijing Opera. Jiang Qing wanted revolutionary ballets glorifying the People's Liberation Army. She couldn't say enough bad things about the arch-reactionary parody of *Hai Rui*. Thanks to her, the army's cultural department grew much larger, under the collusive eye of Lin Biao. Never had a marshal had so many artists in uniform.

At the beginning of June, Li found a new threat every day as he read the *People's Daily*. The paper was now in the hands of Mao's secretary-philosopher, Chen Boda. Its journalists had been fired and replaced with others from the

*Army Daily*. On June 1, the headline called for "getting rid of all the monsters and evil geniuses." "Hundreds and hundreds of millions" of Chinese had to bring specialists, scientists, authorities, and other "mentors" to heel.

The following day, it was necessary to "change men's hearts." Each person concealed within himself "two internal armies," the bourgeois and the proletarian: the former had to be done away with. On June 3, every Chinese was called upon to choose: "Are you revolutionary proletarians or royalist bourgeois?" The next day, the *People's Daily* vituperated against the foreign bourgeois slogan "Liberty, equality, fraternity." President Mao's thought was the "telescope and microscope" of the world. Thanks to it, more was known about these monsters and demons to be destroyed: they were "apparently loyal, but secretly traitors, smiling tigers and demons with human faces, brandishing the red flag the better to fight against it. . . ."

Henceforth, the paper announced, "a person's attitude toward President Mao's thought, whether he accepts it or resists it, supports it or opposes it, loves it or hates it, is the dividing line."

The salvo attained its maximum intensity on June 8, when the imperious demand resounded: "We are the critics of the old world. Let the seven hundred million Chinese rise up and destroy it!"

THE UNIVERSITIES FEVERISHLY CARRIED OUT AN INTERNAL TRIAGE, classing everyone, whether student or professor, into "red species" and "black species." The unfortunates relegated to the latter category were forbidden to read President Mao's books and driven out of the dormitories. Liu Shaoqi and Deng Xiaoping sent "work teams" to the campuses, toughs who were supposed to ride the Maoist tiger before putting down juvenile enthusiasm with a good purge. Until late into the night, students denounced each other, made each other confess and perform self-criticisms in a climate of police hysteria.

One weekend, Inna escaped and came home to tell all this to her father. Li had just been put under house arrest, and thought sending in the teams was a mistake. Inna had already come back horrified by the sacking of apartments: "Methods worthy of fascist hoodlums!" Alla, just back from one of these school expeditions, remained silent, as if petrified by what she had seen. Li told Inna she was right, but she was sure that all this had nothing to do with President Mao's thought.

Li observed Mao's strategy but could not really understand it. On the chessboard, the former teacher in Changsha was obviously pushing all his pawns into battle, in a gigantic, headlong rush forward. The question was how far he would go, and if this adolescent spark was going to set the whole country on fire. In mid-July, the work teams, Liu Shaoqi's and Deng Xiaoping's *gongtsuo dui,* were dissolved and withdrawn from the campuses. The Red Guards had won the right to found revolutionary organizations, which immediately flourished in exchange for their complete devotion to the president. The students, who were enjoying the free-for-all and the new freedom, enrolled en masse in Red Flag and other rebel regiments. Inna chose the first group because its extremism was less xenophobic than the others'.

It was the time of processions behind a giant photo of the living god. People hurried to join them at the urging of the neighborhood committees and at the behest of students. Lisa, curious, went into town on foot. She was astonished by the crowds that flowed through the capital from morning until evening, hundreds and even thousands of people shouting their fervor to the sound of gongs and cymbals. Along the procession, the megaphones of "social agitators" spat hatred in regular verses repeated by the demonstrators. The spectacle seemed to her to resemble in strange ways an Orthodox procession. All that was missing was the incense, so much pomp surrounded the icon carried by the faithful.

Like almost all the participants, Lisa did not understand what in the world was going on. In mid-June, she joined Li in his idleness. She was Chinese, but still a foreigner, and the institute had sent her home; this was no longer a time to be teaching Russian. Lisa tiptoed away, a little sad. She got her last image of the Chinese teaching staff from the bus that was taking her to work. Caught in a traffic jam in front of the Institute of National Minorities, she had seen something unusual: on the lawn, venerable, elderly professors were lined up on all fours, pulling up weeds as their students mocked them. From their necks hung signs on which she read NIGUI SHISHEN ("horned demons").

Another day, it was a procession of trucks surrounded by demonstrators. Lying in the truck beds were hundreds of statues of Buddha that had been taken from their temples and were to end up being smashed with avenging sledgehammers. Beijing's last three churches, now frequented only by a few stubborn old women, were closed. Elsewhere, in Muslim areas, among the Hui and the Uighurs, young Chinese transformed the mosques into pigsties, forcing old people to take care of their animals in them. The hurricane had reached Tibet, where temples were falling by the thousands under the blows of pickaxes.

Lisa had rediscovered fear, the same fear she'd felt in Moscow on the day she met her first *dai maozi* in the street. At the head of a new procession, an unfortunate person wearing a tall dunce cap and a sign around his neck was walking along, shoved and harassed by a highly excited crowd that promised him a terrible fate. He might have been a teacher, an engineer, or a retired person; the megaphones shouted, *Da dao!*—down with this and down with that, condemning such varied things that Lisa couldn't follow them. But the police, tense, accompanied the processions and observed the devastation without ever attempting to calm people.

At night, groups of old women and children armed with sticks patrolled as a militia to protect themselves from mysterious demons. It wasn't known quite where they were hiding, but under the circumstances, it was wiser to keep an eye out, and strangers were stared at without friendliness.

*Dazibao* had flourished at the institute, and Ania Zhaosun, the head of the department of linguistics and an old Chinese friend of Lisa's, came to see her in Dongdan. On posters, Lisa's students were attacking her bourgeois lifestyle.

"You know, Lisa, I think it's preferable that we not see each other any more," she said as she left, ashamed and afraid.


THE CHINESE COMMUNIST PARTY'S CENTRAL COMMITTEE MET IN August without inviting Li to attend. Pale with rage and silent, he found out about the meeting by reading the *People's Daily*. Liu Shaoqi, the regime's number two man, had been demoted to the eighth level of the hierarchy. Deng Xiaoping followed him in his fall. On August 5, Mao laid down his cards: "Attack the general staff!"

Everything was clear now. Cultural or not, this revolution was really a revolution. Mao was breaking to pieces what he had built at such cost.

Like Stalin before him, he was going to strike at the heart of the Party. The heart was on the right, and Mao vaunted the "proletarian left." The plenary session called for "not fearing disorder"; only "physical coercion" was declared out of bounds. All Party officials were to attend compulsory sessions to study the president's thought. On that day, Li understood: "We're all in for it," he told Lisa as he folded up his newspaper.

Lisa's optimism was rock solid, and the ordeal in Moscow had hardened it, but the ordeal in Beijing seemed difficult to assess.

As soon as the Central Committee's meeting was over, posters appeared in the Northern Office attacking Li Lisan. Lao Gao, Li's faithful chauffeur, reported the content to him. Nothing too serious: a long *dazibao*, "Down with Li Lisan's bourgeois lifestyle!," denounced him as a "slave of the foreigner."

In Li Lisan's home, people didn't sit at table like Chinese. His daughters had been seen wearing dresses and jewelry. Li had a domestic staff. A chauffeur, a cook, a concierge, a servant. And so? What were those flunkies waiting for? Why didn't they revolt? It didn't matter that they had been assigned these tasks by the Central Committee.

Although they were Communists, neither Lao Gao, nor Lao Lu, nor Lao Wang wanted to hear any criticism of their master, any more than did the *ayi,* Siao Hu.

Lisa and the girls laughed incredulously when they heard the accusation made on one of the posters: "In Li Lisan's home, they despise the Chinese people!" The proof given was that "when a Chinese guest spends the night there, they change the sheets, before and after. In that house, they won't sleep in the same sheets as a Chinese!"

The three women laughed again when Alla deduced from this that they were like Russian bourgeois women during the October Revolution. Inna reprimanded her mother when Lisa added somberly, in a low voice: "Or rather, as in 1937 . . ."

"Mama! Don't talk like that!"


THE "SOCIAL AGITATORS" HAD FORGOTTEN THE CAR. LAO GAO, THE minister of labor's chauffeur, had first been given a Buick taken from the Kuomintang. He missed it when a powerful Russian ZIM, less luxurious than the Politburo's ZIS, replaced it. Li was inflexible regarding its use: it was not to be taken to do errands; the girls would go to school in rickshaws, and Lisa would go to the institute by bus. It was a matter of morality: state money was not to be used for little privileges. By instinct, in the spring Li had exchanged the ZIM for a Victory, the Soviet Pobieda, the basic car for Communist officials who ranked just above those who rode bicycles. Lao Gao thought his status was constantly sinking, but he agreed with his boss: with the Pobieda, they would pass almost unnoticed, and could even be mistaken for the police.

For the first time, to Lisa's great dismay, they had to make up their minds to hang a portrait of Mao on the wall. A simple precaution, but Li Lisan and Lisa no longer saw any other solution. They really seemed to be the only people left in China who didn't have one. A home without a portrait of the *djouci* was clearly one in which people refused to follow President Mao's line. At any time, Red Guards could knock at the door. Above the mirror in the living room, they even hung one of the Great Helmsman's slogans. Lisa took no pleasure in the new decorations, and had no illusions, either: "If they do come, that won't change anything at all."

Rumors were running through the city, Groshka couldn't keep still at the gate, and all at once the clamor was at the entrance to their street. A tumult that grew louder at every step, the thousands of steps that were coming closer as furious slogans were chanted. Lisa and Li Lisan went pale in their garden.

"They're coming for us, this time," Lisa had time to say in an expressionless voice, as Li quickly stood up.

The crowd was not coming for them, but for the people across the street. The handful of small apartment buildings that stood there in a quiet garden sheltered the finest physicians in China. Doctors who had practiced at the Rockefeller Hospital before 1949; surgeons and highly qualified professors of medicine. Courteous neighbors, many of whom had come back to China from abroad, sure that they could help in reconstructing the country.

"Down with the nest of bourgeois experts!" the Red Guards chanted as they pushed through the gate, followed by a young human tide, breath-less and overexcited. Lisa and Li Lisan watched the scene through the gaps in their gate. Howling, the Red Guards disappeared into the apartments on the upper floors. The sound of breaking glass ensued; windows were smashed, and an astonishing flood of objects—furniture, books, vases, and knickknacks—flew out of them. Banners and vengeful signs appeared on the balconies, accompanied by the sounds of megaphones and speeches. The Red Guards occupied the place for several hours, beating and tor-menting the doctors and their terrified families.

The savage violence of this operation stupefied Lisa. The only images that came to her mind were those of Nazi mobs chasing Jews in Germany, which she had seen in Moscow in photos from the 1930s.

They had to keep Groshka quiet; he was ready to attack in order to defend the threatened family territory. Going back into the house, Li said to himself that they were going to have to do something about the dog. He was becoming dangerous. Tolerated in the neighborhood for the past fif-teen years, Groshka had escaped the famine. But recently Lisa had received anonymous telephone calls asking strange questions: "You have a little dog in the house, don't you?"

"What?"

"You give him a little milk, right?"

"Yes," she mumbled.

"He sleeps on a mattress?"

"Yes, he does . . ."

Childish voices, kids not yet twelve, with a mocking tone that made a chill run down your back. Li Lisan knew what was going on: "They're learning to make a file. . . . The final crime of the Li Lisan household, no doubt. . . ."

They had to save Groshka. Lao Gao would put him in the car and take him to a peasant family he knew, near the airport. A reliable family that did not eat dogs. The hardest part would be telling Alla afterward. Since she was an infant, Groshka had been far more than a teddy bear for her.

There was the dog, and there were the memoirs. It was time to burn all the notebooks filled with countless memories that Li had begun to write down over the past few years.

CHAPTER

# 2 4

How many of them were there? Ten, fifteen, twenty thousand? In any case, a multitude that filled a football field. A crowd in khaki uniforms, dotted with the thousands of little red stars shining on the front of their caps, and reddened still more by their armbands and the scarlet flags that were waving vigorously above them. The crowd vibrated nervously in cadence, raising their fists when the signal was given, swinging their forearms back and forth, urged on by the sound of gongs and cymbals. A crowd of thousands of frowning brows, of mouths shouting furious or factitious indignation, a thundering chorus whose clamor was seconded by the nasal roaring of the loudspeakers set on the stage or hung at the top of the goalposts at the Beijing Normal School.

On the platform, Li Lisan had been standing up to the crowd for two hours, and no longer heard anything, his tall figure stooped, his hands clasped behind his back, his Sun Yat-sen jacket tattered and torn, his collar open, the skin of his neck irritated by the cord around it that held the sign that hung over his chest, bearing a handful of ideograms scribbled in black ink: LI LISAN, COUNTERREVOLUTIONARY REVISIONIST.

On this day, June 18, 1967, exhausted, he refused to listen any longer, wobbling in place, silently begging his legs to continue to hold him up. The young prosecutors had been taking turns since the beginning of the session, walking up and down the stage with the microphone in their hands, screeching their indictments of the turpitudes of the "old counterrevolutionary Li Lisan," whose activities on behalf of his masters in Moscow had finally been unmasked. Calling upon the crowd as their witnesses, they sometimes approached him so closely that he closed his eyes to shut out their cries.

Since February, and the beginning of the current struggle, Li Lisan had not confessed, and he was making his case worse. At every new session, each *pidao hui,* he replied with a hoarse, stubborn no to the accusations of espionage, sabotage, and conspiracy.

The Red Guards were scarcely twenty years old, and their anger was turning into rage against this elder who was nearly sixty-eight, but refused to bow to them.

"Confess that you have always followed a black line, that you have always fought President Mao Tse-tung!"

No, he couldn't say that. A hundred times over he had told them that he was willing to recognize all his errors in the 1920s, and even those of the time when he was minister of labor. That he had already done so countless times and would do it again, if they wished. But to make him an enemy of the regime, no, certainly not. As in Moscow, it was the regime that was declaring war on him, for reasons just as obscure.

"Confess that you have always followed a line that was anti-Party, anti-Marxist, and anti–President Mao Tse-tung!"

"No, I can't say that."

"Confess that you are a revisionist spy!"

"Never."

"You see, comrades, how this old counterrevolutionary lies and persists! That's the proof that he's the worst of the black kind who reject the righteous anger of the masses!"

"I stick to the facts."

Then the crowd started repeating *Da dao Li Lisan!*—a phrase that was coming over the loudspeakers and punctuated a long list of slogans that were to be chanted in unison. On the platform, just anger struck. The Red Guards took hold of Li, pulled his arms, his hair, bent down his head. The session of *tsuo feiti* could begin. Li Lisan adopted the airplane position for an hour, two hours, his joints and muscles in intense pain, his shins beaten mercilessly at the slightest sign of weakness.

During this time, they brought in another person, who occupied his place at the front of the stage.

When the signal was given, it would be time to go for the quarry. How many people had died under the blows and bullets? Five hundred thousand, a million already? On Tiananmen Square, the past summer, a triumphant high school girl had shown the crowd of Red Guards her hands, dripping with the blood of her assassinated teacher.

But the quarry would be attacked only when the signal was given. Li Lisan "struggled against" in public was a carefully organized spectacle. People went to it only by *danwei,* by whole work groups, in processions or in trucks. Invitations were distributed by Kang Sheng, Lin Biao, Mao's wife, and her friends on the Cultural Revolution Committee, China's new headquarters. Everyone knew that Li Lisan was an old story that had returned to the stage, the ancient epic of the 1920s, somewhat faint in the memories of the young. A story of the time before Mao was Mao, the time of Li Lisan and the first tentative steps, the childhood of the Party. The Red Guards feverishly prepared themselves for the spectacle by rereading their *Precis of the History of the Party,* the faithful Chen Boda's manual. In the name of the "struggle between the two lines," the secretary-philosopher, at the height of his glory, was drawing up lists of people to be struck down. In the *danwei,* in study sessions on the workday, the masters of ceremonies took up once again the old conflicts between Li Lisan and Mao. Since there were very few of them, many were invented.

For a long time, everyone in China had known by heart who was Mao's childhood "half-friend," the one of the three and a half friends who had disappointed the president, the one with whom his friendship had never developed. The study of Li Lisan's line provided grounds for students' flights of fancy regarding his scorn for the president's perceptiveness and the peasant masses. Worse yet, he had oppressed and repressed President Mao in his youth. Everywhere and always, Li Lisan's gravest sin had always been "subjectivism," that "petit bourgeois malady."

On the successive stages where they continued to attack him, Li Lisan never had anything to add to his self-criticisms, the ones he'd made in Moscow and in Beijing, in 1956, before the Party congress. The cup he'd drunk to the dregs was now empty and dry. He had only this stubborn movement of his head, accompanied by a *bu* ("no") shouted in a hoarse and stoic voice, a voice so firm that the veterans of the Gong'an, the police, in the audience shook their heads and grumbled that "that one is going to have a bad end." The others seldom made such a fuss.

The Red Guards had been handing him back and forth for nearly five months, from one *pidao hui* to another, like a film that one comes out of with the desire to see it again. Kang Sheng had brought together no less than sixty-seven organizations into a "committee for coordinating and deepening the struggle against Li Lisan." They came from Manchuria, Tientsin, and elsewhere to receive the directives of the new Center and especially to bring in material. The criticism needed anecdotes, whether small or large, picked out of memories of Li Lisan as he visited a factory or a local prefect. With the material collected, stories were constructed that infinitely multiplied the criticism. Li Lisan, dismantled piece by piece since his early youth, seemed to end up as scraps to be thrown to the crowd.

The only thing that was lacking was confessions. Li was almost sixty-eight, and they had to take a few precautions. His health had declined rapidly as soon as the sessions of public harassment began.

THEY HAD BEGUN ON FEBRUARY 1, 1967, WITH A PHONE CALL AT seven o'clock in the morning. Li had hung up after a brief conversation. Putting down the receiver, he turned to Lisa and calmly told her, "That's it. They're coming. They're coming to get me for a struggle session."

At eight, a squadron of Red Guards from the Northern Office showed up, middle-aged men. Li was put into a gray Pobieda belonging to the national police that was waiting for him. He was not put under arrest, and came home in the evening. Lisa saw him return staggering, exhausted, and silently go upstairs to lie down on the bed. Lisa spent long hours sitting at his side, trying to buck him up, listening to him turn the puzzle over and over from every angle, simply being with him.

What did they want from him now? Old stories from Manchuria had resurfaced twenty years afterward. In 1947, Li had opposed Lin Biao on a matter of military tactics, along with Peng Zhen. The *Army Daily* was now violently hostile to Li Lisan: Marshal Lin Biao, the sickly and taciturn opium addict, held bitter grudges. And his wife, Ye Chun, who was deeply involved in politics along with Mao's wife, had not forgotten a certain telegram cabled to Yan'an from Harbin, and what it had cost her to have usurped the name of Li Lisan.

IN JANUARY 1967, SHANGHAI HAD PROCLAIMED WITH GUNSHOTS its commune, the most recent avatar of the "glorious Paris Commune." During this time, at the Northern Office, the Red Guards were excommunicating each other. The ones who were taking down Li Lisan fell in their turn before people who were more extreme than they. There was no question of admitting that Li Lisan was a dead tiger! Being rebellious and opposing other Red Guards who were considered soft was the latest fashion. As a result, the revolution within the revolution continued to find new enemies, and the army, called upon from all sides, smashed them in province after province. The police in the streets were keeping a low profile. The Maoist chessboard was turning into a kaleidoscope, but the president and his wife were refereeing the melee. At the Northern Office, the matter was simple and the orders clear: "Fire at Li Lisan!"

They came back every two or three days. The Pobieda would take him away for another session at the Institute of Transportation, the Normal School, the Northern Office, or some work unit or other gathered together for the occasion.

In May *tchaotia,* house searches, began. Lisa came home one evening on the bus and found the house with all the lights on and the windows open. In the courtyard, people were bustling around a parked van. Inside, there was an indescribable chaos, while a team of Red Guards, consisting of both boys and girls, was going through each room. When they saw the girls' dolls, gifts sent from abroad, the revolutionaries sniggered: "Did you have toys like that when you were a kid?"

Lisa was wandering through the shambles when a female Red Guard, furious, shoved a pair of stockings under her nose.

"Are you the one who wears these?"

"Yes."

"Bourgeoise!"

Lisa didn't reply. The photo albums were taken away in the van. In the bedroom, Li Lisan had not even gotten up. Lying on the bed, he had simply asked when the racket abated, "Is it over?"

"It's over," Lisa answered.

"What did they take away?"

"My nylons, the dolls, the knickknacks . . ."

His eyes on the ceiling, he smiled without saying anything.

They next came back in June. An older, rougher team, typographical workers at the Northern Office.

"How much do you make?" one of them asked Lisa cheekily.

"Two hundred and forty yuans."

"Tsss! Look at that! She doesn't do anything and she makes a salary like that! Fifty yuans more than a factory worker!

Lisa got angry, something no one had ever seen before.

"What do you mean, I don't do anything! I teach hundreds of students at the institute!"

"Bullshit! Liar! Three or four hours a day . . ."

The quarrel was interrupted by the arrival of the leader, who was searching the kitchen. Triumphantly, the man held up the family food processor, bought in Moscow.

"Look! I've found the secret radio! That's how she communicates with Moscow! It's a transmitter-receiver!"

Lao Lu, the cook, had nonetheless sworn that he was the only person who used the device, that you could put carrots, potatoes, anything you wanted in it, but no transistors. The man refused to listen and the blender, confiscated, was taken away for examination.

The team left after having scribbled vengeful slogans on the walls of the living room: "Break the dogs' backs! Boil the two revisionist spies in oil!"

Lisa objected that they were on state property, that they would probably have to leave it, but someone else would come to live here, and this damage would therefore have to be paid for by the collectivity.

"Anyway, you're not going to hang around here for long!" the leader retorted mockingly as he went out the door.

THIS TIME, THEY WERE PUT UNDER HOUSE ARREST, AND FORBIDden to cross the street or receive visits. During the winter, Li Lisan had been able to go into town, wrapped up in his military overcoat, his *chapka* pulled down over his head and the white antipollution mask over his nose, so that he would not be recognized. Followed at a distance by Lao Gao, his chauffeur and bodyguard, he went to find the *dazibao,* the ones that talked about him and others, stuck up by the thousands on the walls of the city.

When he returned, he joked with the irony and bitterness of his youth: "As for the clandestinity, it reminds me of Shanghai in the late twenties . . ."

Pensively, he tried to put together the puzzle of this revolution that was clouding the issue and concealed a coup d'état. The chairman of the People's Republic had disappeared. Kidnapped, secretly held in a jail, Liu Shaoqi was paying in his turn for his stubbornness in trying to govern China without Mao. His wife, the beautiful Wang Guangmei, had been exhibited before the crowds, made up and dressed as a whore. China's first lady thus paid for the elegance of an outfit—a long, black sheath dress and a pearl necklace—worn one evening at a reception for the president of Indonesia. Mao's wife hadn't liked it, and she was having executed or sent to the prison camps in Laogai anyone who knew about her short career in her twenties in Shanghai's film studios.

Teams of young Red Guards were soon taking turns staying in the house. Four or five of them forbade anyone to go out or come in. They were students of eighteen or twenty, aggressive and arrogant, whose mission was to reeducate Li Lisan and Lisa. Every day, the latter had to read the "Little Red Book" for an hour in front of these adolescents, repeating with them the quotations from Chairman Mao and absorbing their immense importance. Li Lisan, stretched out on the bed, allowed them to interview him about his life, his choices, and his love affairs. The students wrote page after page of notes, in exchange for which he had to read the president's works and comment on them with the students, which he did without difficulty, though also without interest.

Afterward, the parade became incessant. People came from all over to question Li Lisan, to "investigate," by *danwei* or by campus, the past of the Communist Party. But it was impossible to get a word out of him against Liu Shaoqi, public enemy number one: "I cannot invent things. I stick to the facts." Li didn't vary an inch, and he was therefore in the camp of the defenders of the "black line."

His only consolation came one day in the form of a visit from a man who had arrived from Anyuan. He had traveled fifteen hundred miles to make the acquaintance of the man about whom the miners still talked so much. A middle-aged schoolteacher, the man spent two hours talking with Li. He brought him the news that down there, the miners were still proud of him, and that the old men were perpetuating his memory.

Inna came in one evening boiling with enthusiasm for the revolution given to young people of her age. Alla, who was part of a team with her cousin Mao-Mao, had joined the movement. The discussion with their father had been difficult, and the disagreement painful. In meetings of the Red Guards, the girls had managed to get Li classified in the category of Communist Party officials who were salvageable because they were not right-wingers. Their father's errors were left-wing errors, that went without saying.

When the girls tried to convince him that his difficulties came from the fact that his self-criticisms were probably not sufficiently radical, Li exploded. His daughters had never seen him in such a state. He, who almost never raised his voice among the family, who always welcomed hugs when they came home from school, had shut everyone up by slamming the door in a "clearly reactionary" way.

Before being put under house arrest, Lisa had been able to go one last time to the institute, and thus to take a furtive look at this Cultural Revolution. She came across a struggle session against Chen Yi. Several thousand furious students were booing the minister of foreign affairs. His fidelity to Mao had been of no help to him. The marshal was not, however, on the platform; he had managed to escape Kang Sheng's henchmen and was hiding somewhere in the provinces.

Curious, Lisa noticed two foreign students, a European couple dressed as Red Guards in khaki uniforms, caps, and belts. On the platform, they were shouting against Chen Yi accusations even harsher and more fanatical than those of their Chinese colleagues. Prudently, Lisa asked people around her who they were.

"Belgian Maoists. The Perrots, or Perri, I'm not sure," a woman student whispered back. There were others like them on campus—Americans, French, British, and Australians.

China no longer had diplomats or a minister of foreign affairs, but in Bolivia, Ernesto "Che" Guevara, Lin Biao's manual of popular guerrilla warfare in his hand, was wandering through the jungle in search of unlikely peasant uprisings. Never had Beijing seen so many leaders of African states pass through. The ambassadors had been recalled and replaced by Red Guards assigned to convert foreign barbarians to presidential thought. In the heart of Western Europe, at the Sorbonne, on campuses in California and from Berlin to Harlem, Maoism was making noticeable inroads on the most capable minds. In Thailand and the Philippines, Mao was sending students into guerrilla warfare, convinced that "power comes out of the barrel of a gun." In Cambodia, the Khmer Rouge guerrillas chose Mao over Brezhnev, arousing the ire of Prince Sihanouk, who threatened to break with Beijing. In Burma, the heads of Chinese Maoists were being cut off with sabers in the streets of Rangoon, alongside those of Chinese shopkeepers rounded up to serve as examples.

In Indonesia, two years earlier, half a million Chinese had been lynched by mobs or massacred by the army, as a result of poor calculation on Kang Sheng's part. His attempt at a Communist putsch in an Islamic country had gone bad.

"You know, lisa, i may be one of the victims of this revolution," Li confided to his wife one evening in June when the *pidao hui* session had been more severe than the earlier ones.

Lisa closed her eyes and said to herself that all this couldn't be true.

Something in the torment was worse than in Moscow in 1937: the fluidity of this terror, its overt casualness, its absence of form and administration. She said to Li, "I can't help thinking that if all this were happening in the Soviet Union, we would long ago have been arrested and sent before a tribunal. . . ." Li looked at her intensely over his glasses before winking at her with complicity.

The hardest thing to accept was not Mao's attitude, but that of Chou En-lai. Was that what a comrade was? The prime minister spoke in unison with the *djouci,* brandishing the "Little Red Book" behind his back with the same mechanical fervor as Lin Biao, Kang Sheng, and the rest of them. Li Lisan had written Chou several letters over the past few weeks, one of which asked for the authorization to be hospitalized. Chou had not deigned to reply, anymore than had Mao, who had also been asked.

Chou had his protégés in the army, who protected him in return. Chen Yi was one of them. But not the other comrades from France. The Red Mandarin's nightmare was something else: not letting Mao get too close to the atomic buttons. In public, the president made fun of the Russian and American paper tigers. He promised the former an explanation: he was fighting the latter for Vietnam, China's ancient vassal. He had sworn to Ho Chi Minh that "the seven hundred million Chinese are the Vietnamese people's most powerful support, and the vast extent of their territory provides it with a secure retreat."

MAO WAS DELIGHTED, HUMMING *"WO XIHUAN TIANXIA DA LUAN."* ("I love great chaos on earth.") All the lukewarm people were biting the dust. At seventy-three, Mao had ended up taking a liking to the giant ceremonies held in Tiananmen Square, before millions of Red Guards who had come from all over the country to admire the living god. Mao showed himself as a smiling sphinx surrounded by the current masters who stood behind him, waving in rhythm the cute little red bible.

The book, with a deep red plastic cover bearing a yellow star, had broken all world publishing records. Stirred up, the country's rotary presses were no longer printing anything but billions of copies of Mao's *Works, Thoughts,* and *Quotations,* in every language imaginable, in giant or minuscule formats, on bible paper or recycled paper.

At the end of three hours, Li Lisan had been taken away, carried off by his guards, his feet dragging on the floor of the stage. He knew it: this time, he would not go home. That Sunday morning, when they'd come in their Pobieda to get him, they'd told Lisa, when Li was already in the car: "Pack some underwear and toothpaste."

She felt at once all the weight of the leaden years in Moscow descending upon her shoulders. "History is repeating itself," she murmured as she wept, quickly folding up a few things without forgetting the little blue bottle of sleeping pills. Since he had been in prison, Li no longer slept without them. Three pills a day to be sure to sleep at night. There were not more than four or five in the bottle; the week's dose had been used up. Too bad.

"Tell me where you're taking him," she begged.

"Don't worry about it. Where we're taking him, he'll be far more at peace than he is here."

# 25

Facing the platform, Lisa closed her eyes for a moment. Her hands behind her back, the sign—"revisionist Soviet spy"—attached to her neck, she was going to have to climb the steps and go on stage in her turn. Thrown to the mob, she had already held out three hours the first time, alongside Li Lisan. Three hours of standing at attention, head bowed, before the gibes, before the curious faces sweating with hatred, of a crowd assembled in the great lecture hall of the Northern Office.

Her turn had come, and Lisa held out. Of course, there had been blows on the shins every time she tried to change position to relieve her legs. Her vision was going blurry with fatigue. And above all, there was the torrent of memories that flowed behind the eyes fixed on the floor. That Chinese citizenship that Chou En-lai had signed, guaranteed, which was not worth the paper it was written on. Or, rather, which gave her the right to this punishment.

*A Soviet spy.* It was child's play to show them that the accusation was absurd. But Lisa knew the radical bad faith of those words, and the endless list of grievances against her, barked by the masters of ceremony, left her dazed, incredulous. There was mention of a fox terrier, dolls, a blender, a television set, laundered sheets, and other obvious signs of bourgeois corruption, of the decadence so characteristic of revisionists.

For a spy of international stature, the file seemed pretty thin, Lisa said to herself as she listened to the litany. She was there only to impress the gallery, it seemed. People hurried to see the "couple of spies, Li Lisan and Lisa." The main attraction was Li Lisan, a few steps away from her, but she was nonetheless the only white woman in China shown to the mob. From time to time, Lisa, her head hanging, stole a quick glance at the audience, recognizing here and there former students of hers who'd been summoned to see their professor in a new light.

There were six people lined up in front of the crowd this time. People she didn't know, except for her husband. Li Lisan stood nearby, separated from her by a secretary from the Northern Office who had been put on the hot seat along with two other employees for having refused to join the pack.

After three hours, the session was closed, but Li had been ill. He asked for a doctor and was taken to the hospital in Dongdan, behind the Beijing Hotel. There, a clinician pretended to examine him, and another came up to Lisa and told her in a low voice that every day he saw twenty to thirty people come in, people who'd just come out of a struggle session.

"We don't have the right to hospitalize them without express authorization from the Cultural Revolution Committee. Sorry, but without that, we can't do anything."

Li left as he had come in. That evening, in bed, he looked at Lisa and found the strength to smile: "You've moved up in the hierarchy, did you see that this morning? They've put you with the party secretaries, on the stage."

A simple joke, but it cheered Lisa. If he still had a little sense of humor, perhaps they would make it through the storm. . . .

On June 18, Li had been taken away, with his underwear and toothpaste. Two days later, they came in a car to get Lisa at the house, around noon, with a written order signed by Chen Boda. Panicked, Siao Hu, the faithful *ayi,* had pulled her out of her nightmares: "Lisa, wake up! The Red Guards have come to take you away."

In the room in the Northern Office, they had hung the same sign around her neck before pushing her toward the stairs. From the platform, Lisa looked down on the audience, which was small in comparison with the first time. There were a hundred or so people, and they were calmer. This was not a struggle session, but rather a public interrogation. Lisa was the only one on the stage, and they talked about fox terriers and blenders again. An acerbic or crude comment was occasionally shouted from the audience. Didn't the disarming candor of this Russian woman conceal a secret insolence, a supreme cleverness?

Lisa was responding in a loud, clear voice, in her fluent Chinese, when a door opened and he came in. Supported by two Red Guards, Li Lisan was roughly pushed onto the stage. Lisa saw him coming toward her, staggering, unrecognizable. His long, thin body appeared fleshless. He seemed to have aged a thousand years in two days. He had to have been beaten, to put him in this state. Their eyes met, and Lisa saw in them a spark, a little flame that was dancing in the depths of his eyes and telling her to hold on. She said to herself that never had she loved the man so much.

Then he turned toward his tormentors and asked them for a chair. "Excuse me, I can't stay standing up. Allow me to sit down. . . ."

A leaden silence fell over the hall. Lisa felt she would faint, but to her surprise, after a brief consultation, a Red Guard brought a chair. Li sat down, and the questioning session resumed: "Tell us what you told your sister-in-law when she came to visit you in Beijing in 1957. What did you say about the policy of the Chinese Communist Party?"

Lisa wondered what good it would do to tell them about her conversations with Sonia, the widow of her brother, Vladimir. Her three months' visit to Beijing, ten years earlier, had left her with good memories, that's all. They'd talked about their families, Russia, compared standards of living. Sonia had plenty of courage and good humor, but her intellectual baggage consisted of three years in elementary school. Arguments about doctrine were not her strong point.

"What materials did you give her?"

"Materials?"

"Yes, materials: information about China . . ."

Li Lisan, next to her, whispered on his chair, sweeping aside questions with dry, concise answers.

The session went on like that for two long hours. Finally, they were signaled to get down. Li Lisan, leaning on Lisa's arm, slowly moved forward, his hand gripping his wife's. In an adjacent room, two chairs were waiting for them. Lisa collapsed on one, and Li drank a glass of boiled water.

They remained sitting in silence, huddled together, for about ten minutes, alone in the room. Li whispered, "Will you be all right?"

He took her hand before the door opened and a voice cried, "All right, get up! Follow us!"

They walked toward the exit, where a car was waiting for them. Plainclothes policenen opened the door for them before taking their places in the front seat. The man next to the driver turned around and barked, "No talking. Not a word!" The car started off, followed by another.

Sitting in the backseat, the couple held hands in silence. It would soon be six o'clock, and the light had the softness of summer evenings. Slowly, the car went down the almost deserted street, passing under the walls of Zhongnanhai, Mao's palace. An inner voice told Lisa that this time she was going to prison. She pressed Li's hand, and he pressed hers. She felt a still more terrible presentiment coming, but the car was already braking to stop at the side of the road, near the bridge in Beidahe's park. The man in front got out and opened the door.

"Get out, now," he told Lisa.

A dull panic came over her and she turned around. Li was eating her up with his eyes, his head resting on the seat back. Their eyes closed, they pressed each other's hands again, and then Lisa got out.

On the sidewalk, the policeman pointed to the second car parked behind them. It was waiting for her, with its motor running and four men on board. She bent over to say good-bye to the man she had always loved.

"*Dosvedania!*" she whispered, leaning in at the window.

"*Dosvedania,*" Li replied in an expressionless voice, with a feeble gesture of his hand, enveloping her with his eyes for one last time.

The silence of the prison was infinite, and it had been going on for eight years. Soon it would be three thousand days, three thousand nights during which Lisa had not heard much of anything except the faint rustle of her black cotton uniform or the hushed sound of her espadrilles on the cement floor of the cell. Even the guard in the corridor made no more noise than a shadow when he put his eye to the slit in the door every two or three minutes.

The eye. The sole metronome of a time that had disappeared, a dark eye, surmounted by a thick black eyebrow, which appeared for a few seconds in the small slit, which was open day and night.

Eight years without anyone but herself to talk to. The walls in Tsinsheng prison were so thick that neighbors didn't exist.

Would there be a walk today, tomorrow, soon? The last

one was at least two weeks ago. The guards never told you in advance when the next one would be. The surprise was all the better for it. Lisa drew on an unexpected energy during those forty minutes of walking around the minuscule little courtyard surrounded by high walls, hardly larger than her cell. Above her, blue or gray, the square of sky glimpsed before the door slammed shut behind her always seemed to be smiling. But even the sky was forbidden in Tsinsheng: immediately, you had to lower your eyes, put your hands behind your back, and walk back and forth for forty minutes. Sentries pacing the catwalks above the courtyard barked if they saw someone lift his nose.

What did it matter? When she was walking, everything was good. On the ground, when spring came, there was sometimes a scrawny flower or a bit of grass that had come up between the disjointed slabs of cement, a slender glimpse of a parallel vegetable life that persisted. Lisa caressed them with her eyes before dreaming about them in her cell, as if they were a whiff of hope. The guards probably knew that, and methodically pulled out everything that grew in the courtyards. One winter, a glint on the ground aroused her marveling curiosity: just a bit of ice, a few drops of frozen water, but they evoked a whole world she had lost, even its memory.

Walking, everything was good, starting with the sound of the footsteps in the corridor that broke the sepulchral silence, the clattering of the key in the enormous lock of the first, wooden door of the cell, and then in the second, wire-mesh door six inches behind it. Faces, finally, then words—two words: "Walk! Go!"

In the corridor, there was a row of doors leading to ten other silent cells. In eight years, Lisa had been moved four times, ending up on the third story of one of Tsinsheng's eight five-story buildings, arranged in the shape of a star. At first, she had thought she discerned human voices in the corridor. Then, by a few brief whispers that came to her ears from the corridor, she'd concluded that she was in the women's wing. Never had she seen the face of even one of the other women detained here. Whether she was going to the shower, once a week, or for a walk, two or three times a month, the other doors never opened behind her until she had turned the corner in the corridor. But the corridor had windows, and behind one of them there was a tree. Every time she passed it, the mere sight of it overwhelmed her, especially in the fall, when its foliage was on fire.

Life had been going on like this, minuscule and silent, ever since June 22, 1967. The universe was no longer more than twelve paces long and five paces wide. Lisa had traveled hundreds, thousands of miles by going back and forth between the cot, a fold-down partition, the latrine can in the corner, well within view of the slit in the door and the guard, and the sink beneath the little window with frosted glass. Neither table, nor chair, nor stool, and it was forbidden to lie on the bed during the daytime. One was allowed to sit on the bed, but it was so hard that Lisa preferred to walk.

She walked up and down for hours, taking small steps, and concealing behind these gymnastics her countless daily mental exercises, her tricks for killing time, the slow, powerful, meticulous time of prison.

The guard's eye appeared in the slit like the second hand on a clock: the prison's hour and minute hands began to move at six in the morning. A bronze bell tolled in the distance; time to wake up and wash her face. At seven, the slight creaking of the meal cart resounded in the corridor; a knock on the door before it was opened, and Lisa got down on all fours in front of the trapdoor through which an anonymous hand held out the bowl of rice soup, coming again at noon and at six in the evening, just as furtively.

Eight years of eating exactly the same thing: rice soup at breakfast, rice soup at noon with a few pieces of salted vegetables and a *mantou,* a little steamed bun made of cornmeal, then a glass of hot, boiled water. For dinner, another cornmeal bun, the *wowutu,* which contained a few bits of onion. Never any meat or fat; only boiled cabbage from time to time. A tenacious, permanent hunger led every prisoner to go immediately down on his knees in front of the door at the signal, before gulping down the bowl of soup and chewing up every crumb of bread.

Nights in Tsinsheng were electric. From the first evening, Lisa had no longer known darkness. A single forty-watt bulb burned all night, pitilessly. The first night, she tried to escape it by putting a sock over her eyes. From the slit in the door, the guard had immediately barked the rule. Next, the guard had awakened her with a blow on the door, to order her to turn over, this time: it was forbidden to sleep facing the wall, with your arms under the covers, or to hide your face with your hands. From the slit, he must be able at all times to see Lisa in her sleep, to be able to tell whether she was alive or dead.

"*Fanshen!*" ("Turn over!") The order had often been shouted during the following nights, awakening the forgetful Lisa lost in her dreams. Under the lightbulb, sleep had finally won out over exhaustion and habit. Here days had disappeared, and there were no more nights.

TSINSHENG WAS A PRISON FROM WHICH NO ONE ESCAPED. SOME thirty miles north of Beijing, the special prison, built by Soviets at the end of a mountain valley, enclosed its captives in complete isolation behind a double wall fifteen meters high, with rows of electrified barbed wire, watchtowers, searchlights, and sentries that made any idea of escape futile. How many times had Lisa smiled inwardly on thinking of the *Count of Monte Cristo,* of the Château d'If of her childhood, from which one could escape with a little trickery and daring?

In Tsinsheng, Lisa had lost even her name. The first night, the woman guard who had brought her in curtly recited the rules. As she left, she turned around and added: "One more thing. Here, starting now, you no longer have a name. You are number seventy-seven. That's all, Seventy-seven."

Three weeks afterward, the interrogations began. Lisa was called before fifteen men, led by their investigative commissar, a policeman by the name of Luo. Lisa assumed they were judges and thought she was before a military tribunal.

"Tell us everything. Tell us all about your relations with Krymov!" Krymov? Yes, she knew him. A Chinese man who had married a Soviet woman in Moscow in the 1930s. His original name was Guo Shaotun. A friend of Li Lisan's, he had also been arrested under Stalin, a month earlier. Like Zhang Bao, he had spent eighteen years in the Gulag. His wife had also been sent to the camps. Both had survived, but when he was freed in 1956, Krymov had remained in Moscow and taken Soviet citizenship. He was working back there as a professor of economics in an institute. Invited by Chou En-lai, he had come to visit Beijing in 1957. Lisa and Li

Lisan had had him to dinner several times, along with Zhang Bao, to whom Krymov had much to tell.

Yes, she knew Krymov, and had nothing to hide. She told them what she knew.

"What are you trying to tell us? Tall stories! What we want, here, is the truth! Your espionage activities, that's what interests us!"

Krymov, they had decided, was a master spy or maybe a liaison agent, they weren't quite sure, with whom Lisa and Li Lisan had always maintained culpable relations. Then they took turns insulting Lisa, shouting accusations she didn't understand, and she was reduced to mumbling exhausting denials as she stood before them, for hours.

The worst came in February 1968. Three weeks in a row, she was interrogated at night, until four or five in the morning, before staggering back to her cell to collapse on her bed. An hour later, the prison's bell and a bang on the door got her out of bed. If the guard found her sitting on the bed during the daytime, he jerked her out of her somnolence: *"Tsilai ba!"* ["Get up!"]

In the evening, about nine o'clock, they came to get her for another session: "What about the television? Admit that Krymov gave it to you as payment for your services. . . ."

In the spring of 1973, Lisa was overcome by dizziness and nausea. In the infirmary, a nascent ulcer was diagnosed. A more detailed examination was to be made in Beijing, in a civilian hospital.

Lisa was put in a police van. Her hands were handcuffed behind her back, and then her hair was tied up in a piece of cloth that looked like a rag. A policeman put on her nose a strange pair of glasses that immediately blinded her. Glasses like those used by welders, with lenses so dark that she wondered what she must look like in such a getup. One thing was certain: the policemen wanted to hide this foreigner, and when they reached the hospital, she was guided to the doctor like a blind person.

She came out in the same way, unrecognizable amid the men who were holding her up, assured that she did not have an ulcer, but only serious problems of malnutrition.

★    ★

THE FOLLOWING YEAR, THE DOOR TO HER CELL OPENED ONE MORN-
ing to admit a woman of about forty, wearing the green uniform of the police. She was a doctor, who inquired about 77's health and talked to her
gently when Lisa told her how unbearable solitude was becoming for her.

"Your children, think about your children, that will help you."

A thousand times she had asked, begged Investigative Commissar Luo
to give her news of Inna and Alla. Each time, he limited himself to saying
"Don't worry, everything is going fine for them."

The doctor came back almost every day for a brief conversation, with
the door open so that the guard could keep an eye on things. Her words
were simple, and her eyes betrayed something that looked like kindness.

Even the tone of the guards and sentries became gentler—as if, on
the outside, the Chinese had become weary of invective and bellowing. In
the fall of 1974, a female guard, one of the toughest in the early years, had
whispered behind her as she accompanied her to the showers: "You must
ask for a meeting with your children. It's permitted, now. Shhh . . ."

On the morning of May 18, 1975, the door opened and 77 got up, thinking the doctor had come for a visit. A guard came in and told her, "Come
quickly! Your children are waiting downstairs, in the visitors' room."

Her heart thumping, Lisa hurried down unknown corridors, crossed
a courtyard, and pushed open a door. Behind it, Inna was waiting for her
with Alla and a man, a Chinese. Inna was thirty-two and had a husband;
Alla was twenty-eight and seemed exhausted. Lisa came up to them, real-
izing by the way her daughters looked at her how much she must have
changed during those eight years when she had never seen a mirror. So
much so that her daughters hesitated for a moment when their mother
appeared in her *bianfu,* her black prison pajamas, with her snow-white
hair and her blue eyes that were so distant, so lost. The shock was so great
that no one cried. Lisa ended up touching her daughters, as if to be sure
they were really there, before she sat down on one of the chairs put at

their disposal. Words in Russian, her mother language, no longer came to her, or came only with difficulty, and no one was sure where to begin. But three hours later, next to an enormous basket filled with fresh fruit and delicacies, Lisa and Inna were still murmuring to each other, while Alla was dreaming and looking at her mother, wearing a thin smile on her lips, and a somewhat absent air.

Before long, Lisa asked, "And Li Lisan, Papa?"

Looking embarrassed, Inna pretended she didn't know anything, and turned away her eyes. Alla remained silent.

Lisa felt intense pain, but did not insist, and changed the subject. Inna had just entered the Institute of Foreign Languages to teach Russian and perhaps Spanish there. She had worked in the fields after her parents were arrested, as had Alla. The two girls had been judged "salvageable." Alla was still working hard in the countryside, near Tientsin, and was pining for her sister, for Beijing, for all the rest.

Lisa had been told without believing it that more than seventy people had been thrown in prison for having met Li Lisan and herself. The chairman of the republic, Liu Shaoqi, was left without medical treatment and died in jail in 1969. Chen Yi, broken, had soon followed him. All their friends were in prison, and the two most faithful, Grania and Eva, were surely in Tsinsheng. Grania had lost her mind and didn't even recognize her son Victor when he was finally able to visit her. Eva's husband, Emi Siao, the poet and Mao's childhood friend, was also in prison. The beautiful Sung Weishi, who had accompanied Lisa in the train from Moscow to Harbin, had never produced Chekhov in Beijing. Although she was Chou En-lai's "adopted daughter," she had died in prison: Mao's wife didn't like her theater, and Lin Biao's wife remembered her husband's love affair. Lisa's friend Fifi had also gone mad, as had a good Russian interpreter, O'Yang Fei, who had often visited her home. Zhang Bao had been in prison for a few years. He was alive, people said, and back in Beijing. For the rest of them, there was no prospect of a trial, a judge, or, of course, an attorney.

Inna's husband, whom she had met on the campus, did not speak Russian and seemed worried stiff inside these walls. Inna told Lisa that she had a two-year-old son, Pavlik. On leaving her, her daughters affectionately told Lisa that with her white hair, she would make a beautiful grandmother when she got out.

That evening, in her cell, intoxicated by this whiff of freedom, by having seen again the flesh of her flesh, Lisa said to herself that Tsinsheng was a very strange place: when she first entered it, it had been almost a relief, so frightened had she been by the Chinese crowds to whom she had been thrown. Now that hope seemed to be coming back, now that she was able fondly to imagine an end to all that, she was almost afraid of leaving: outside, without Li Lisan?

Inna and Alla went back to Beijing and Tientsin. On the way, the two sisters silently wondered how they would reveal their double secret to their mother, when Investigative Commissar Luo finally authorized them to do so. First, that their father was dead; second, that they had spent two years in Tsinsheng, in cells 83 and 89, two tiny rooms four yards by two, just a short distance from their mother.

Red Guards or not, the two sisters had been arrested the day after Lisa had been imprisoned, on June 23, 1967, and thrown for three months into Gongdelian prison, an old fortress with thick walls built in Beijing by a northern warlord. In October, they had been transferred to Tsinsheng. There, in their black, patched clothes, they had also been constantly watched by the guards, even during their weekly showers; interrogated by Luo and his team; deprived of sleep; and subjected to "massive attacks" by wild questioners and insults. The worst threat was that they would be handed over to the revolutionary people in the street if they didn't testify against their father.

Seven hundred eighty-six days after she was arrested, Inna was summoned by Commissar Luo and told that on reflection, the party had magnanimously decided that the two sisters were "reeducable." Under the "surveillance of the masses," Inna and Alla were going to be able to correct their grave errors, which were due chiefly to their deplorable class origins, by planting rice near Tientsin.

Inna was about to leave when Commissar Luo, with a contrite look, signaled that she should sit down again. "There's something else you must know," he said. "Your father, Li Lisan, died two years ago. He was an antagonistic contradiction, whereas you are a contradiction among the people. I can't tell you any more. Your mother is here, in the prison. You're not to mention that to anyone, ever, as long as you have not been authorized to do so. The only person whom you can tell is your younger sister. Alla is next door, waiting for you. She is not in very good health."

The two sisters climbed into a gray Pobieda with Luo, who took them back to Beijing. On the way, Inna, absorbed in mourning, had not felt like marveling at having recovered her freedom. Despite the anguish of the days to come, Alla also seemed to be floating in a reality that they would have to relearn, including feelings.

At the Northern Office, before leaving for the rice paddies in Hanguo, Inna had to force herself to tell her secret to Alla. Her little sister was slowly recovering from the nightmare, and spoke little, enjoying, dreamily and alone, the sun, smells, and noises. Her eyes closed; she was walling off her pain. Then she left with Inna to labor to make China's rice grow, while they waited for peace.


FOUR DAYS AFTER HAVING SEEN HER DAUGHTERS AGAIN, LISA LEFT her cell. On May 22, 1975, the door swung open. Seventy-seven folded her blanket, and in the room reserved for interrogations, a young woman in uniform politely asked her how she felt.

"Today, you are getting out of prison."

Lisa hesitated before asking, "And where am I to go?"

"To Yucheng, in the province of Shanxi."

"In prison?"

"No, in exile. There you will spend your old age."

At the front desk, her handbag was returned, her only possession when she came in. It still contained her watch, a pen, a little underwear, and a pair of sandals. Lisa had finally taken off her *bianfu* and put on a dress. A black Volga with little curtains took her to the Beijing station, a plainclothes policewoman sitting on each side of her in the backseat. Her first thought had been that she was going to see Li Lisan again. The officials had been almost friendly to her. In the train taking her to Yucheng, she traveled in a first-class compartment along with her escorts. A fourth man joined them, a former colleague of Lisa's at the institute.

"I've been assigned to accompany you," he said simply.

He spoke Russian, and during the eighteen-hour train ride, they had time to hint at news regarding their colleagues—those who were still alive and those who had died. When Lisa dared to mention Li Lisan, her colleague told her he knew nothing, whereas the other man, a policeman, pricked up his ears and said, "Wait, we'll tell you later."

In the lavatories on the train, Lisa had gone pale when she suddenly saw her face in the mirror. When she was arrested, she was fifty-three, in the prime of life. At sixty-one, she undeniably looked like a promising grandmother.

Day by day, in a slow thaw, Lisa had recovered her senses in Yucheng, in a little house surrounded by a garden that stood on the edge of the large rural town of sixty thousand inhabitants. For a long time, the three rooms—all on one floor, with a bed, a bench, and a little kitchen— seemed to her unreal. She was not allowed to go out of the garden without permission, and no one was to know the identity of this white woman exiled in the depths of Shanxi. But the courtyard and its apple trees in bloom were a constant miracle. The bed was a real bed, night was finally dark, and the whole sky had been given back to her.

During a visit in January 1976, Inna plucked up her courage. Chou En-lai had just died of cancer, the New Year was coming up in February, and Lisa's unbearable doubt couldn't go on any longer.

"Mama, I have to tell you something sad. Papa died, a long time ago. He died on June 22, 1967, in Beijing. They say he couldn't take it, and committed suicide with sleeping pills."

Lisa closed her eyes and didn't hide her tears. To the end, she had retained a tiny, minuscule bit of hope. They had dared to do it. Li Lisan was dead; he had died the day after they last saw each other. As if the immense career of the man who had taken her away forever with a kiss along the banks of the Moscow River in the summer of 1935 had been cut short as soon as he'd learned that Lisa had been arrested.

A moment later, she blew her nose and frowned, murmuring as if to herself: "Li Lisan, commit suicide? With sleeping pills?"

In December 1978, Lisa was authorized to leave her exile in Shanxi. She immediately returned to Beijing, where she took up residence in a room at the Institute of Foreign Languages while waiting to resume teaching Russian.

Her mourning was difficult. With her daughters, she decided that it was time to bang her fist politely on the table. That she had not been notified of her husband's death was one thing. But she wanted to know how he died. Li Lisan, commit suicide? That wasn't like him. Lisa recalled what he had said one day in the spring of 1967, when he was expecting to be arrested: "If some day they tell you I've committed suicide, don't believe them."

The three women began a determined siege of the Chinese bureaucracy. In Sidan, even in the newspapers, people were demanding "reversals of verdicts." Tens of millions of Chinese, dragged through the mud and thrown into prison camps over for the past twenty years, were trying to get rid of the terrible labels "right-wingers" and "counterrevolutionaries," those labels that stuck to the skin for as many as three generations, as strongly as one's class origins at birth.

At the top, the new Communist leaders also had to cleanse themselves of former Maoist accusations. Deng Xiaoping, the "little Chinese Khrushchev" who had been shamed by Mao, had also experienced reeducation in the countryside.

Going from office to office, Lisa and her daughters picked up confused and embarrassed explanations. Li Lisan was supposed to have died the day after they last saw each other by taking the sleeping pills in the little blue bottle, the one Lisa had put in his bag on the day he was arrested, Sunday, June 18, 1967. Lisa had seen him for the last time on Tuesday, June 20, on the platform and in the car, for their final *dosvedania*.

Afterward, they said, he had been taken to prison. A strange, anony-mous prison, an unoccupied apartment belonging to a *ganbu,* a party offi-cial in Ministry Number 2, the Ertibu, called Basic Constructions. There, at number 65 Sanlihe Street, in the heart of the capital, near Fuxingmen, two men guarded him day and night. The first, Wang Yaosian, was a chief of police in Tientsin, one of Kang Sheng's men, mature and experienced, a government official at the number fifteen rank in the national hierarchy. The second man obeyed him implicity: Zhang Tie was a young Red Guard, a student at the University of Hebei who had come up to Beijing, where the Cultural Revolution Committee had assigned him to police work. The two men spent four nights with their prisoner, whose health visibly declined as the struggle sessions went on. On the morning of Friday, June 22, the head of a rebel Red Guard organization appeared at the head of a small gang. They wanted Li Lisan for the afternoon. Still another struggle meeting. They were fighting over him. His guards even explained to him that if he was not in a normal prison but rather hidden in this apartment, that was because another band of Red Guards that had come from Tientsin wanted to take him home as a trophy.

"I'm afraid my health does not allow me to follow you this afternoon. Couldn't we do this later?" Li Lisan was supposed to have replied.

The Red Guards talked it over. They were going to ask the upper ech-elon. They quickly returned: out of the question. Li Lisan would have his struggle meeting in a few hours.

Li sat down at his table and wrote a few pages, as he had been doing ever since he was arrested. Toward noon, Wang Yaosian and Zhang Tie opened the door to signal that his lunch was waiting for him.

"Just a moment, I'm finishing writing something. . . ."

A few minutes later, they said, they found the white-haired old revo-lutionary with his head on the table, unconscious, a cigarette burning in the ashtray next to him, alongside the empty blue bottle.

His two guards were then supposed to have immediately taken him to the hospital, where he was declared dead on arrival.

At the Northern Office, they said Li Lisan had committed suicide to atone for his crimes. As for the sleeping pills, according to their account it was Lisa who had secretly given them to him in the car, the last time they'd seen each other. And that was just what a spy would do, since the KGB had certainly ordered her to eliminate the head of Soviet intelligence in China. Others claimed that Wang Yaosian and Zhang Tie had come to see them after Li's arrest to ask for these pills, without which he was unable to sleep.

His body was then supposed to have been taken to a crematorium, and his ashes were scattered in an unknown place east of Beijing, in the countryside.

LISA LISTENED WITH EXTREME ATTENTION TO THE OFFICIAL ACCOUNTS of her husband's death. Two things bothered her, and nullified these stories. At the crematorium, she discovered that, strangely, Li Lisan's body had been registered under his Moscow nom de guerre, Li Ming, in the eternal anonymity of the person without family. Above all, the autopsy report referred to a man one meter sixty-eight centimeters in height. Li Lisan seemed to have shrunk by a good eight centimeters.

Finally, this story of sleeping pills didn't hold water. The blue bottle, which she could still see in her mind as if she had held it in her hand yesterday, contained not more than four or five capsules. Chinese tranquilizers, so weak that you had to take three a day to produce the desired effect in the evening. A friend who was a doctor confirmed their suspicions: it was impossible to commit suicide with those drugs. Even if, on the nights of the eighteenth, nineteenth, twentieth, and twenty-first, Li had gone to sleep without taking his last pills. And even if one supposed that Wang Yaosian, an experienced policeman, had failed to confiscate them.

SO THE OFFICIAL VERSION OF LI LISAN'S DEATH WAS A FINAL LIE. HE may well have died at his writing table, struck down by a heart attack. But if so, why the devil didn't they say so? Why would they cook up this story of a "suicide" that stuck a final traitor's mask on him? Had Li Lisan been executed by his so-called comrades? Shot down shamefully, like people in Moscow prisons? Who were the last Red Guards to have seen him alive?

One man in China knew, and still knows, if he is alive: Zhang Tie, the student from the University of Hebei, who has disappeared. His boss, Wang Yaosian, can no longer testify. Transferred to Datong, in Shanxi, he was killed sometime later by a colleague, under mysterious circumstances, "in the course of a brawl."


ON MARCH 20, 1980, LISA AND HER DAUGHTERS RECEIVED AN apology from the government. The trees in Sun Yat-sen Park, near the Forbidden City, were still leafless, but in the government building, people thronged to the "reversal of verdict" ceremony. The new masters of China were all there, behind Deng Xiaoping. Beaten, humiliated, and downtrodden by Mao, they had a revenge to take and a debt to pay for all the years when they had let him do as he pleased. Verdicts issued in the past were being overturned right and left, but there was to be no more revolution! The country had had enough, and its leaders were busy calculating: for the benefit of history, they decided that from the 1920s until his death, Mao had been right "seventy percent of the time."

At present, they were going to shelve the other "thirty percent." Mao had committed "errors," granted. He had made a serious mistake regarding Li Lisan.

His comrades all bowed three times before an empty urn, in final farewell to the phantom of the Chinese revolution. In the ranks, a delegation of old miners from Anyuan had insisted on being there.

One by one, they all somberly shook the hands of Lisa and her daughters, while the empty urn was taken to the martyr's cemetery.

SAINTRAILLES-PARIS, FEBRUARY 1996–AUGUST 1999

# CHRONOLOGY

**1899**  Birth, on November 18, of Li Longzhi, called Li Lisan, in Liling, Hunan province. A hundred miles away, Mao is six years old. China is having trouble recovering from the greatest insurrection in history, the Taiping Rebellion (1850–1864), which caused between 30 and 50 million deaths.

**1911**  Fall of the last Manchu dynasty, the Ch'ing (Qing in pinyin spelling), which began in 1644, and Sun Yat-sen's proclamation of an ephemeral republic, prey to the warlords. Pu Yi, the last emperor, is five years old.

**1914**  Birth of Elisabeth Kishkin, the youngest daughter of a family of the "enlightened" Russian rural minor aristocracy, in the province of Saratov (Volga). Her father commits suicide during the civil war. To escape the famine, Elisabeth flees to Moscow with her mother, Praskovia.

**1917**  Fall of Czar Nicholas II in Petrograd, in February; in November, the Communists, under Lenin's leadership, seize power. Civil war immediately ravages the country.

**1919**  First student demonstration in Beijing, in May, to protest the Treaty of Versailles, which officially accepts Japanese control over China, as well as that of the great powers, especially Britain and France.

The first Chinese student-workers leave for France. They will provide the first generations of Chinese Communists. Li Lisan is among them. He works at Le Creusot factory and two years later is expelled from France, along with more than a hundred others, after participating in a protest occupation of government offices in Lyons.

**1922**  Li Lisan leads the first victorious strike by Chinese miners, in Anyuan, near his native city.

**1925**  In Shanghai, British police open fire in May on Chinese demonstrators, killing thirteen. Li Lisan launches a gigantic wave of protest that spreads to the whole country.

**1926**  In July, opening of the Northern Expedition—the beginning of the republicans' reconquest of China, which had fallen under the control of the warlords. Its leader, Chiang Kai-shek, is the successor of Sun Yat-sen, the founder of the republic, who died a year earlier. Chiang has the support of Moscow, which is training his army and has sent Borodin to China as Soviet proconsul.

**1927**   In January, the British government gives up its sovereignty over the Hankow concession after popular demonstrations against it. In April, Chiang Kai-shek crushes the Communists in Shanghai; this puts an end to their alliance with the Nationalists. Civil war follows and continues until 1949.

In August, before the walls of Nanchang, Li Lisan, Chou En-lai, and other Communist leaders, without Mao, found the Red Army, the ancestor of the current People's Liberation Army (PLA).

In December, in Moscow, Stalin easily wins out over his rival Trotsky, while in China the pseudo-commune of Canton, controlled by Moscow, is repressed (five thousand deaths). Li Lisan is sent to reconstruct the Communist organization.

**1928**   Li Lisan's first trip to Moscow, where the Chinese Communists are holding a meeting. He comes back as the de facto leader of an entirely clandestine party. The Communist International (Comintern) calls for "class war," predicts the "imminent" collapse of capitalism, and ignores the rise of fascism.

**1930**   Li Lisan launches a vast counteroffensive combining urban insurrections with attacks on cities by the Red Army. The campaign is a general failure. Stalin calls Li Lisan to Moscow, decapitates the Chinese Communist Party, and names his protégé Wang Ming as its new head. In the Soviet Union, the peasantry is devastated by famine, deportations, and executions.

**1932**   Zhang Bao, having been secretly spirited out of the United States, begins training in Moscow, where he meets Li Lisan.

**1934**   On December 1, the number two man in the Soviet regime, Sergei Kirov, is mysteriously assassinated in Leningrad (formerly Petrograd). Stalin launches a gigantic mass terror campaign that is to continue, with varying degrees of intensity, until his death in 1953. The Gulag has begun.

**1935**   The last meeting of the Communist International takes place. A prominent role is given to the antifascist popular fronts. In Moscow, Li Lisan emerges from his purgatory and reestablishes contact with the men of Mao's Long March. Since January, Mao has been the leader of the Chinese Communists.

Li Lisan begins, with Zhang Bao, the crypto-Cominternian periodical *Save the Homeland,* which becomes the *Time of National Salvation.* The imminent danger in China is from Japan, and the periodical, distributed throughout the world, preaches national unity against Tokyo.

Li Lisan meets Elisabeth Kishkin, a young Soviet Komsomol who is working as an editor and taking evening courses to prepare herself for entering the university.

**1937**   In July, Japan invades China. Chiang Kai-shek and the Communists suspend their own conflict in order to make a united front against the invasion.

**1938**   In February, Li Lisan and Zhang Bao are arrested by the NKVD, along with thousands of others. The Comintern is destroyed. Li Lisan is tortured and interrogated for two years before finally being released toward the end of 1939. Zhang Bao is sent to the Gulag, where he remains until December 1955.

**1939**   In August, the Russo-German Nonaggression Pact is signed. Hitler attacks Poland immediately afterward, marking the beginning of the Second World War.

**1946**   Li Lisan returns to China after fifteen years in the Soviet Union. Despite his difficulties, he has been reelected to the Chinese Communist Party's Central Committee, of which he was no longer even a member. He has spent the war in the USSR with Lisa, with whom he has had a daughter, Inna, born in Moscow in 1943. They rejoin him in Harbin, Manchuria, where he is working with the Communist general staff. The Cold War begins. Chiang Kai-shek and the Communists resume hostilities; American mediation fails.

Alla, Li Lisan's and Lisa's second daughter, is born in Harbin in 1947.

**1949**   On October 1, the People's Republic of China is founded. On the platform, Li Lisan is the third on Mao's left. Chiang Kai-shek takes refuge on Taiwan. Li Lisan is named minister of labor in Mao's first cabinet, a post from which he is rapidly dismissed following differences of opinion that emerge in December 1951. In a secret report, he warns the Chinese leadership about Soviet police and judicial practices—his warning is not heard—and intervenes on behalf of the Chinese who have disappeared into the Gulag.

**1953**   Stalin dies. Khrushchev succeeds him, and liquidates Beria with the help of the army.

**1956**   Loosening up and insurrections in Eastern Europe against Soviet occupation and Communist reforms. The Budapest uprising is brutally repressed. In Beijing, the Communists hold a meeting and try to erode Mao's power. Li Lisan has to carry out a general self-criticism.

Zhang Bao, freed from the Gulag in December 1955, rejoins Li Lisan in Beijing in 1957.

**1958**   Mao launches the Great Leap Forward, which is supposed to enable China to catch up in record time to the Soviet Union and the capitalist countries. The result: by 1962, 30 million people die from hunger, no doubt the worst famine China has ever known. Mao is sidelined by his comrades. Li Lisan, who has been expelled from the core leadership, is working on the country's industrialization at the Northern Office. Lisa is teaching Russian at the Institute of Foreign Languages.

**1966**   Mao instigates the Cultural Revolution. Li Lisan and Lisa are put under house arrest, then subjected to pitiless "struggle sessions" and exhibited in public. Arrested in June 1967, Li dies a few days later on June 22; officially, he has "committed suicide." He is the most important figure in the Chinese revolution to have died thus far. Two years later, Liu Shaoqi, the former chairman of the People's Republic, dies in prison, for lack of medical care.

Lisa is sent to Tsinsheng prison, where she remains in solitary confinement for eight years before spending almost four years in exile in Shanxi province.

Zhang Bao is imprisoned and sent for "reeducation" in a May 7 school, a prison camp in (eastern) Jiangxi, which he leaves in 1973.

**1976**  Mao Tse-tung dies on September 9. His wife, Jiang Qing, is arrested by soldiers a month later, along with the rest of the Gang of Four, the extremists of Maoism.

**1980**  Official rehabilitation, postmortem, of Li Lisan by Deng Xiaoping, also a "veteran of France." China is "opening up."

**1999**  In Beijing, at the age of eighty-five, Lisa is writing her memoirs and watching over her descendants.

# BIBLIOGRAPHY

I ask novelists and essayists to forgive me: the following selection does not take into account fictional works, and is limited to direct testimony and other documents on which I have drawn. The list is not, of course, exhaustive.

On China and the 1920s and 1930s, the following works have been particularly useful:

*The Tragedy of the Chinese Revolution*, by Harold Isaacs, the nonfictional version of André Malraux's novel *La Condition humaine* [*Man's Fate*] on the subject. Harold Isaacs was there in person. 2nd ed. rev., Stanford, Calif.: Stanford University Press, 1967.

*The Rise of the Communist Party, 1928–1938*. The memoirs of Chiang Kuo-t'ao, the only systematic work by one of the founding fathers of Chinese Communism, who became a "renegade." Lawrence, Kansas: University Press of Kansas, 2 vols., 1972.

*L'Envol du communisme en Chine*. The memoirs of Peng Shuzhi, another witness of the earliest period. Paris: Gallimard, 1983.

*Memoirs of a Chinese Revolutionary*, by Wang Fan-hsi. New York: Columbia University Press, 1991.

*Histoire du Parti communiste chinois*, by General Jacques Guillermaz. A life's work. Paris: Payot, 1975.

*Red Star over China*, by Edgar Snow. A biased work, but the only one from the period. 1937; repr., New York: Grove Press, 1973.

*China Correspondent*, by Agnes Smedley. Still more biased, as instructive about the author as about China. London: Pandora, 1943.

*Memoirs*, by Marshal Peng Dehuai. Beijing, 1981.

*Memories*, by Marshal Nie Rongzhen. Beijing, 1984.

*Mao's Betrayal*, by Wang Ming. Moscow, 1975.

*Dans le jardin des aventuriers*, by Joseph Shieh with Marie Holzman. Paris: Seuil, 1995.

*The Vladimorov Diaries: Yenan, China, 1942–1945,* by Peter Vladimorov. New York: Doubleday, 1975.

As for academic studies, here are a few that may be consulted:

*Grèves et politiques à Shanghai, 1927–1932,* by Alain Roux. Paris: EHSS, 1995.

*L'Âge d'or de la bourgeoisie chinoise, 1911–1937,* by Marie-Claude Bergère. Paris: Flammarion, 1986.

*La Chine: Dictionnaire biographique du mouvement ouvrier international,* ed. Lucien Bianco and Yves Chevrier. Paris: Presses de la Fondation nationale des sciences politiques, 1985.

*Les Dirigeants de la Chine révolutionnaire, 1850–1972,* by Chun-Tu Hsueh. Paris: Calmann-Lévy, 1971.

*Chinese Communism and the Rise of Mao,* by Benjamin I. Schwartz. Cambridge, Mass.: Harvard University Press, 1951.

*A Documentary History of Chinese Communism,* by Conrad Brandt, Benjamin I. Schwartz, and John K. Fairbank. Cambridge, Mass.: Harvard University Press, 1967.

*Shanghai on Strike: The Politics of Chinese Labor,* by Elizabeth J. Parry. Stanford, Calif.: Stanford University Press, 1993.

*Engendering the Chinese Revolution: Radical Women, Communist Politics, and Mass Movements in the 1920s,* by Christina Kelley Gilmartin. Berkeley: University of California Press, 1995.

*From Friend to Comrade: The Founding of the Chinese Communist Party, 1920–1927,* by Hans J. Van de Ven. Berkeley: University of California Press, 1991.

*The Chinese Communist Movement: A Report of the United States War Department, July 1945.* Stanford, Calif.: Stanford University Press, 1968.

*The Shanghai Green Gang: Politics and Organized Crime, 1919–1937,* by Brian G. Martin. Berkeley: University of California Press, 1996.

*Chiang Kai-shek's Secret Past: The Memoirs of his Second Wife, Ch'en Chieuh-ju.* Boulder, Colo.: Westview Press, 1993.

*Chine, l'archipel oublié,* by J. L. Domenach. Paris: Fayard, 1992.

*Précis d'histoire du Parti communiste chinois,* by Hu Sheng. A very official history. Beijing: Éditions en langues étrangères, 1994.

In another register, and because he spent his childhood in China at the time of the warlords, see the work of Lucien Bodard, especially *Monsieur le Consul*

(Paris: Grasset, 1973), *La Vallée des roses* (Paris: Grasset, 1977), and *Les Grandes Murailles* (Paris: Grasset, 1987).

On the Comintern:

*Sans patrie ni frontière,* by Jan Valtin. Paris: Actes Sud, Babel, 1997.

*L'Œil de Moscou,* by Jules Humbert-Droz. Paris: Fayard, 1964.

*The Case of Richard Sorge,* by F. W. Deakin and G. R. Storry. London: Chatto and Windus, 1996.

*Shanghai Conspiracy: The Sorge Spy Ring, Moscow, Shanghai, Tokyo, San Francisco, New York,* by Charles A. Willoughby. Boston: Western Islands, 1965.

*Hôtel Lux: Les partis frères au service de l'Internationale communiste,* by Arkadi Vaksberg. Paris: Fayard, 1993.

*Histoire de l'Internationale communiste,* by Pierre Broué. Paris: Fayard, 1997.

*Histoire intérieure du Parti communiste,* by Philippe Robrieux. Paris: Fayard, 1980.

*Jacques Doriot, du communisme au fascisme,* by Jean-Paul Brunet. Paris: Balland, 1986.

On the Soviet Union:

*I Chose Freedom: The Personal and Political Life of a Soviet Official,* by Victor A. Kravchenko. New York: Scribner's, 1946.

*Au pays du NEP et de la Tchéka,* by Boris Cederholm. Paris: Taillandier, 1928.

*The Gulag Archipelago, 1918–1956: An Experiment in Literary Investigation,* by Alexander Solzshenitsyn. New York: Harper and Row, 1974.

*Récits de Kolyma,* by Varlam Chalamov. Paris: Maspero, 1980.

*Essais sur le monde du crime,* by Varlam Chalamov. Paris: Gallimard, 1993.

*Déportée en Sibérie,* by Margarete Buber-Neumann. Paris: Seuil, 1949.

*7,000 jours en Sibérie,* by Karlo Stajner. Paris: Gallimard, 1983.

*L'Aujourd'hui blessé,* a collection of reports by women of the Gulag. Paris: Verdier, 1997.

*Le Manuel du Goulag,* by Jacques Rossi. Paris: Le Cherche-Midi, 1997.

*Fragments de vie,* by Jacques Rossi. Paris: Elikia, 1995.

*The Confession,* by Artur London. Trans. A. Hamilton. New York: Morrow, 1970.

*Orient,* by Édouard Herriot. Paris: Hachette, 1934.

*Russie, 1837—1937, les trésors retrouvés de la "Revue des Deux Mondes."* Paris: Maisonneuve and Larose/Éditions des Deux Mondes, 1997.

*Des monts célèstes aux sables rouges,* by Ella Maillart. Paris: Payot, 1990.

*Moscow.* 2 vols. Moscow. Mysl, 1986.

*Les Saisons de Moscou, 1933—1941,* by Lila Lounguina. Paris: Plon, 1990.

*L'URSS en 1930,* by Boris Suvarin. Paris: Ivréa, 1997.

*Mémoires d'un révolutionnaire, 1901—1941,* by Victor Serge. Paris: Seuil, 1951.

*Histoire véridique de Moshé, ouvrier juif et communiste au temps de Staline,* by Moshé Zalcman. Paris: Encres, 1977.

*Les Derniers Jours,* by Anton Kolendic. Paris: Fayard, 1982.

Other relevant studies and essays are too numerous to cite all of them here. I limit myself to mentioning first of all two books by Robert Conquest, *The Great Terror: A Reassessment* (New York: Oxford University Press, 1990), and *The Harvest of Sorrow: Soviet Collectivization and the Terror-Famine* (New York: Oxford University Press, 1986), and the works of Annie Kriegel and her team, including *Le Livre noir du communisme: Crimes, terreurs et répression* (Paris: Laffont, 1997). Also indispensable are the pioneering studies by David Rousset, *The Other Kingdom,* trans. R. Guthrie (New York: Fertig, 1982), and by Paul Barton, *L'Institution concentrationnaire en Russie, 1930—1957* (Paris: Plon, 1959).

Also very useful are *Au pays des soviets, le voyage français en Union Soviétique, 1917—1939* (Paris: Archives, 1979), *Moscou, 1918—1941* (Paris: Autrement, 1993), and *Ozerlag, 1937—1964* (Paris: Autrement, 1991).

Finally, we may mention *Anthologie de la littérature soviétique* (Paris: Gallimard, 1935) and *La Parole resuscitée: Dans les archives littéraires du KGB,* by Vitali Chetalinsky (Paris: Laffont, 1993).

On Mao Tse-tung's China, one may consult the works of Simon Leys, an excellent collection of which appeared in 1993 (Paris: Laffont, 1993).

For personal reports, we may cite:

*Prisoner of Mao,* by Bao Ruo-wang and R. Chelminski. Harmondsworth, U.K.: Penguin, 1973.

*Re-Encounters in China: Notes of a Journey in a Time Capsule,* by Harold Isaacs. Armonk, NY: M. E. Sharpe, 1985.

*La Vie privée du président Mao,* by Dr. Li Zhisui. Paris: Plon, 1994.

*Une Vie pour la Chine: mémoires du général Jacques Guillermaz, 1937—1989,* by Jacques Guillermaz. Paris: Laffont, 1989.

*Chinois, si vous saviez . . . Li Yizyhi: à propos de la démocratie et de la légalité sous le socialisme.* Paris: Bourgois, 1976.

*Un Vol de nid d'hirondelles ne fait pas le printemps de Pékin.* Paris: Bourgois, 1980.

*Le Printemps de Pékin, novembre 1976–mars 1980,* by Victor Sidane. Paris: Archives, 1980.

*The Revenge of Heaven: The Journal of a Young Chinese,* by Ken Ling, with M. London and Ta-ling Lee. New York: Putnam, 1972.

*Six Récits de l'école des cadres,* by Jiang Yang. Paris: Bourgois, 1983.

*Le Préfet Yin, et autres histoires de la révolution culturelle,* by Chen Jo-hsi. Paris: Denoël, 1979.

*Les Années rouges,* by Hua Linshan. Paris: Seuil, 1987.

*Vie et mort à Shanghai,* by Nien Cheng. Paris: Albin Michel, 1987.

*Cygnes sauvages,* by Jung Chang. Paris: Plon, 1992.

*Le Cauchemar des mandarins rouges,* by Liu Binyan. Paris: Gallimard, 1989.

We mention also the remarkable work of Jasper Becker on the great Chinese famine under Mao, the first of its kind: *Hungry Ghosts: Mao's Secret Famine* (New York: Free Press, 1996).

Regarding biographies:

On Stalin, they are not so numerous that one cannot read all of them. We will therefore mention, for the record, Boris Suvarin's heroic *Stalin: A Critical Survey of Bolshevism,* trans. C. L. R. James (New York: Arno Press, 1972), a masterwork written in 1935. At that time, André Malraux refused Suvarin his seal of approval, adding, "I believe you are right, Suvarin, but I will be on your side when you are the strongest."

Han Su-yin's biography of Chou En-lai, *Eldest Son: Zhou Enlai and the Making of Modern China* (London: Jonathan Cape, 1994), belongs to the category of hagiography.

Kang Sheng has been the object of a first attempt at a biography by R. Faligot and R. Kauffer, *Kang Sheng et les services secrets chinois* (Paris: Laffont, 1987), which deserves to be republished in a revised and corrected edition. We may also mention *The Claws of the Dragon: Kang Sheng, the Evil Genius behind Mao and his Legacy of Terror in People's China,* by John Byron and Robert Pack (New York: Simon and Schuster, 1992).

# ACKNOWLEDGMENTS

I would like to thank M. Roderick MacFarquhar for having made the archives of Harvard's Fairbank Foundation available to me; Mme Tamara Petchkova for her valuable testimony in Saint Petersburg regarding the theater in the Gulag; and historians, librarians, and journalists in Nashville and Moscow. Thanks also to Hélène Châtelain for having sent me in advance of publication precious translations of the testimonies of women in the Gulag. Finally, let me salute Mme Jeanne Caussé, of the *Revue des Deux Mondes,* thanks to whom this book was published.

# INDEX